You Can Excel with Caddell

Sign up & take a FREE diagnostic SAT with advanced assessment at CaddellPrep.com/join

We're here to help you succeed

Reach your goals with the help of a personal tutor or prep class & get into your dream college

See our special SAT prep offer for purchasers of this book: caddellprep.com/sboffer

BEFORE	AFTER
1020 on PSAT & Full of Doubt	**1430 on SAT & Relieved**
Anxious about future	Accepted to dream college

Results are not typical or guaranteed

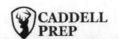

Table of Contents

Introduction	1
Lesson 1	7
• 1.1 Common Math Tricks	9
• 1.2 Combining Like Terms & Solving Equations	21
• 1.3 System of Equations	43
Lesson 2	59
• 2.1 Ratios & Proportions	61
• 2.2 Data & Probability	74
Lesson 3	111
• 3.1 Evaluating Functions	113
• 3.2 Linear Functions	125
• 3.3 Quadratic Functions	135
Lesson 4	163
• 4.1 No Solution & Infinite Solutions	165
• 4.2 Percent	175
• 4.3 Exponential Growth & Decay	188
• 4.4 Exponents	197
• 4.5 Imaginary Numbers	210
Lesson 5	223
• 5.1 Circles	225
• 5.2 Angles, Polygons, & 3-D Shapes	239
• 5.3 Trigonometry	283
• 5.4 Simplifying Rational Expressions	292
Lesson 6	303
• 6.1 Equating Coefficients	305
• 6.2 Dividing Polynomials	309
• 6.3 Transforming Functions	316
• 6.4 Solving for a Variable in Terms of Another	327
• 6.5 Absolute Value	339

Math Practice Test 1   349

Math Practice Test 2   389

Additional Practice   431
- Common Math Tricks: Practice 1 & 2   433
- Combining Like Terms & Solving Equations: Practice 1 & 2   445
- System of Equations: Practice 1 & 2   456
- Ratios & Proportions: Practice 1 & 2   474
- Data & Probability: Practice 1 & 2   484
- Evaluating Functions: Practice 1 & 2   510
- Linear Functions: Practice 1 & 2   526
- Quadratic Functions: Practice 1 & 2   547
- No Solution & Infinite Solutions: Practice 1 & 2   584
- Percent: Practice 1 & 2   597
- Exponential Growth & Decay: Practice 1 & 2   606
- Exponents: Practice 1 & 2   617
- Imaginary Numbers: Practice 1 & 2   627
- Circles: Practice 1 & 2   638
- Angles, Polygons, & 3-D Shapes: Practice 1 & 2   659
- Trigonometry: Practice 1 & 2   698
- Simplifying Rational Expressions: Practice 1 & 2   709
- Equating Coefficients: Practice 1 & 2   722
- Dividing Polynomials: Practice 1 & 2   729
- Transforming Functions: Practice 1 & 2   737
- Solving for a Variable in Terms of Another: Practice 1 & 2   744
- Absolute Value: Practice 1 & 2   758

Introduction

Need to improve 200 points?

We love working with students who are serious about their SAT scores - that means you!

Special Tutoring & Test Prep Offer for You

 caddellprep.com/sboffer

Introduction

How to Use This Book

First Step

The first step that we always recommend to students is to take a diagnostic test.

You can take a free diagnostic SAT by signing up for a free account on caddellprep.com. You'll find the link for the diagnostic SAT on the "My Profile" page.

Scan to create a free account on CaddellPrep.com

Next Step

Your next step after taking the practice test depends on how you did on the diagnostic test, how much time you have, and what your goal is.

If you have a very limited amount of time to study (less than 30 hours of available study time), you should focus your attention on topics that have the most room to improve. You can see which topics have the most room to improve from your online assessment. Don't skip lesson 1.1 Common Math Tricks, though.

If you have more than a month to study or can dedicate at least 30 hours to studying, you should go through all of the lessons, the two math practice tests, and the necessary additional practice. You will learn some tricks that can help you save time for topics you may already be good at and learn how to solve questions you struggle with.

Layout of This Book

Math Lessons & Homework

This book is organized into six math lessons, which are further broken down into 21 different topics.

The lessons are organized based on which topics show up most often but are also in order according to what you need to learn to answer questions in the next chapter.

The first three lessons cover the heart of the math questions on the SAT.

Most lessons will include an example with a walk-through demonstrating how to solve the problem and then a practice problem for you to attempt.

NOTE: Some of the practice problems are open-ended. They are not necessarily meant to resemble student-response questions. Instead, they are there for you to fully practice your math skills without answer choices available. You may end up with a negative answer or another type of answer that cannot be entered on the student response portion of the SAT. It's okay. The purpose of those questions is just to practice your math.

After each chapter, there is "Homework". This is what you should practice a day or two after completing a lesson to refresh your mind and help you remember how to answer the questions.

Practice Tests

There are two math practice tests. Each test has a no-calculator section and a calculator section, just like the real SAT.

Enter your results online to get your scaled score and assessment.

Additional Practice

Based on your practice tests, you can identify what areas you need to focus on more. Use the additional practice in the book to hone your skills on specific topics.

All of the additional practice problems are part of chapter 9. There is additional practice for each lesson. For best results improving your score, the additional practice shouldn't be attempted until you have completed the corresponding lesson.

Introduction

What to Expect on the Math Tests & Math Tips

1. Multiple choice math questions increase in difficulty from the beginning of a section to end. The difficulty restarts for the student-response questions.
2. Always put an answer (even for student-response questions). If you don't know the answer, put a reasonable answer or 1.
3. All figures are drawn to scale, unless otherwise noted. This means angles and lengths are drawn to scale.
4. You can't bubble in a negative answer in student-response questions.
5. Don't round your answer unless you are asked to.
6. Don't start with a zero when writing your answer.

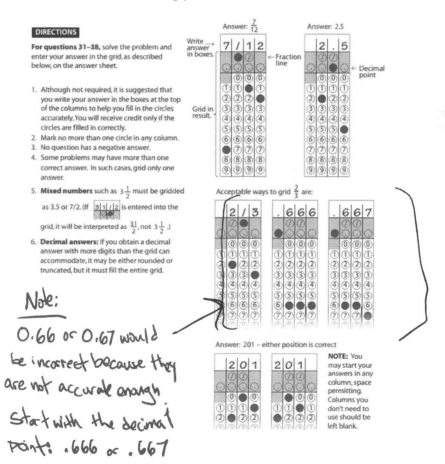

Note:
0.66 or 0.67 would be incorrect because they are not accurate enough. Start with the decimal point: .666 or .667

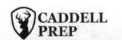

Lesson 1

Want to break a 1400?

We love working with students who are serious about their SAT scores - that means you!

Special Tutoring & Test Prep Offer for You

 caddellprep.com/sboffer

1.1 Common Math Tricks

Adding and Subtracting Equations

Example

If $3x + 2y = 30$ and $2x + 3y = 5$, what is the value of $x + y$?

$$3x + 2y = 30$$
$$2x + 3y = 5$$
$$5x + 5y = 35 \Rightarrow \frac{5x+5y}{5} = \frac{35}{5}$$
$$x + y = \boxed{7}$$

Practice 1

If $5x + 3y = 8$ and $4x + 4y = 6$, what is the value of $x - y$?

Using Factors

Example

What is the average of x and y, if $x^2 - y^2 = 54$ and $x - y = 9$?

$Avg = \frac{x+y}{2}$ need $x+y$ and given $x-y$, both are factors of $x^2 - y^2$

$x^2 - y^2 = 54$
$(x+y)(x-y) = 54$
$(x+y)(9) = 54$
$x+y = 6$

Avg: $\frac{x+y}{2} = \frac{6}{2} = \boxed{3}$

Example

What is the value of $(a + b)^2$ if $a^2 + b^2 = 7$ and $ab = 5$?

$(a+b)^2 = (a+b)(a+b) = a^2 + ab + ab + b^2 = a^2 + 2ab + b^2$

$= a^2 + b^2 + 2ab$
$= 7 + 2(5) = \boxed{17}$

Practice 2

$x^2 + 2xy + y^2 = 81$, what is one possible value of $x + y$ if $x + y$ is a positive integer?

1.1 Common Math Tricks

Practice 3

If $x + y = 6$ and $x^2 - y^2 = 8$, what is the value of $x - y$?

Using the Answer Choices

Example

The length of a rectangle is 5 more than its width. If the area of the rectangle is 66 sq in, what is the length, in inches, of the rectangle?

A. 5
B. 6
C. 8
D. 11 ✓

Handwritten work:
A) $l=5$ $w=0$ $A=0$
C) $l=8$ $w=3$ $A=24$
D) $l=11$ $w=6$ $A=66$ ✓

Practice 4

LeSean is six years older than his sister Tonya. If LeSean will be twice as old as Tonya in three years, how old is LeSean now?

    A. 16
    B. 12
    C. 10
    D. 9

Picking Numbers

If you are asked to simplify a difficult expression, pick numbers for the variables and evaluate the expression. Then, plug the variables into the answer choices and see which answer choice has the same value.

- Avoid picking 0, 1 and 2 as values for the variables
- Try to keep the numbers small, so start with 3 for one variable, 4 for the next and so on

1.1 Common Math Tricks

Example

Which of the following is equivalent to $\dfrac{3t}{4x-1} - \dfrac{t+1}{2}$, if $x \neq 0$?

A. $\dfrac{5xt-1}{8x-2}$

Ⓑ. $\dfrac{-4xt+7t+4x-1}{2(4x-1)}$

C. $\dfrac{2(2xt+1)}{4x-1}$

D. $\dfrac{-4xt+5t}{2}$

Handwritten work:
$t=3$, $x=4$

$\dfrac{3(3)}{4(4)-1} - \dfrac{3+1}{2} = \dfrac{9}{15} - \dfrac{4}{2} = \dfrac{18}{30} - \dfrac{60}{30} = \dfrac{-42}{30}$

A. $\dfrac{5(4)(3)-1}{8(4)-2} = \dfrac{59}{30}$

B. $\dfrac{-4(4)(3)+7(3)+4(4)-1}{2(4(4)-1)} = \dfrac{-42}{30}$ ✓

Practice 5

Which of the following is equivalent to $\dfrac{wv-tuv}{uv^2}$, if $u \neq 0, v \neq 0$?

A. $\dfrac{w-tu}{uv}$

B. $\dfrac{w-tu}{v^2}$

C. $\dfrac{w-tu}{v}$

D. $w - tu$

Estimating Lengths

On the SAT, all figures are drawn to scale unless there is a note stating that the figure is not drawn to scale.

This means we can estimate lengths of sides and line segments..

To estimate lengths, use the lengths that are labeled to create your own ruler. Use the edge of a piece of paper. Start at the corner of the paper and mark where the lengths are.

Example of Estimating Lengths

In the figure below, estimate the length of side AB.

1.1 Common Math Tricks

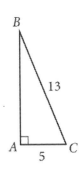

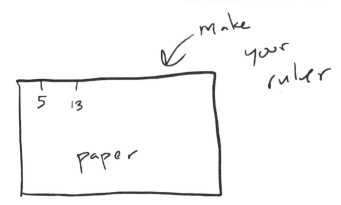

Actual answer is 12.

Practice 6

In the figure below, the length of side AD is 4. The length of side BC is 15. Estimate the length of side DE.

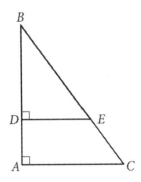

Estimating Angles

We can also estimate angles.

Start with a 90 degree angle.

Estimate angles smaller than 90 degrees be comparing it to a right angle.

1.1 Common Math Tricks

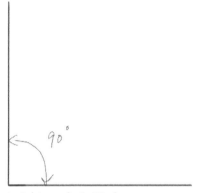
A right angle is 90 degrees.

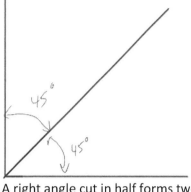
A right angle cut in half forms two 45 degree angles.

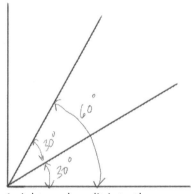
A right angle split into three, creates three 30 degree angles, which can also be used to estimate a 60 degree angle.

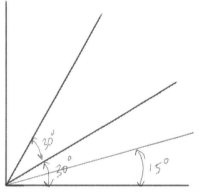
A 30 degree angle can be split in half to create 15 degree angles.

To estimate angles larger than 90 degrees, draw a 90 degree angle and estimate the remaining portion.

Let's estimate the measure of the angle below.

1.1 Common Math Tricks

Draw a 90 degree angle.

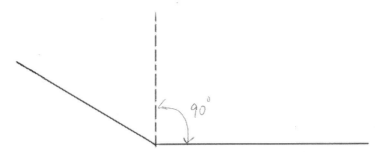

Now, we have to estimate the remaining portion of the angle. To estimate it, I will add another line so we can estimate based on a right angle.

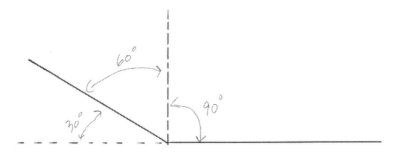

Based on my estimated angles, the total measure of the angle is 150 degrees.

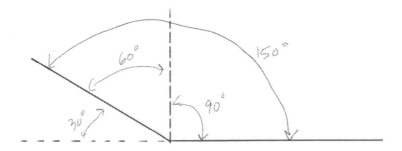

1.1 Common Math Tricks

Example

In the diagram below, estimate the value of x.

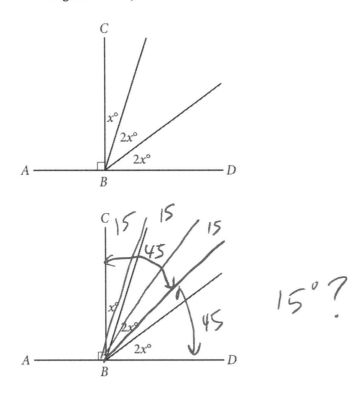

Actual answer is 18.

Practice 7

In the diagram below, estimate the measure of angle B.

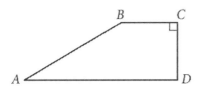

Common Math Tricks Homework

Homework 1

What is the value of $x - y$, if $x^2 - y^2 = 8$ and $x + y = 2$?

Homework 2

What is the value of xy, if $x^2 + y^2 = 12$ and $(x + y)^2 = 18$?

Homework 3

What is the average of x and y, if $x^2 - y^2 = 20$, and $x - y = 4$?

Homework 4

If Sam is thirteen years older than Rick, and in 8 years, Sam will be double Rick's age. How old is Rick now?

    A. 4
    B. 5
    C. 13
    D. 21

Homework 5

$$\frac{t-5}{t+1} - \frac{8}{t-1}$$

Which of the following is equivalent to expression above?

    A. $\frac{-7t-6}{t^2-1}$
    B. $\frac{-7t-13}{t^2-1}$
    C. $\frac{t^2-14t-3}{t^2-1}$
    D. $\frac{t-13}{2t-1}$

Homework 6

In the diagram below, estimate the measure of angle QMR.

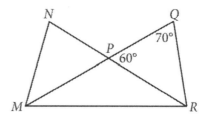

1.1 Answers to Practice Problems (Common Math Tricks)

Practice 1: 2

If $5x + 3y = 8$ and $4x + 4y = 6$, what is the value of $x - y$?

$$5x + 3y = 8$$
$$-(4x + 4y = 6)$$
$$x - y = 2$$

Practice 2: 9

$x^2 + 2xy + y^2 = 81$, what is one possible value of $x + y$ if $x + y$ is a positive integer?

$$x^2 + 2xy + y^2 = 81$$
$$(x+y)^2 = 81$$
$$\sqrt{(x+y)^2} = \sqrt{81}$$
$$x + y = 9$$

Practice 3: 4/3 or 1.33

If $x + y = 6$ and $x^2 - y^2 = 8$, what is the value of $x - y$?

$$x^2 - y^2 = 8$$
$$(x+y)(x-y) = 8$$
$$6(x-y) = 8$$
$$x - y = 8/6 = 4/3$$

Practice 4: D

LeSean is six years older than his sister Tonya. If LeSean will be twice as old as Tonya in three years, how old is LeSean now?

A. 16
B. 12
C. 10
D. 9

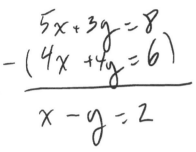

A. L = 16   T = 10   not
    +3 ↓ 19   +3 ↓ 13   double

D. L = 9   T = 3   double ✓
    +3 ↓ 12   +3 ↓ 6

Practice 5: A

Which of the following is equivalent to $\dfrac{wv - tuv}{uv^2}$, if $u \neq 0, v \neq 0$?

A. $\dfrac{w - tu}{uv}$

B. $\dfrac{w - tu}{v^2}$

C. $\dfrac{w - tu}{v}$

D. $w - t$

pick $u = 3$, $v = 4$
$w = 5$, $t = 6$

$$\frac{wv - tuv}{uv^2}$$

$$\frac{(5)(4) - (6)(3)(4)}{(3)(4)^2}$$

$$\frac{20 - 72}{48} = \frac{-52}{48} = \frac{-13}{12}$$

1.1 Common Math Tricks

4. $\dfrac{w-tu}{uv} = \dfrac{5-(6)(3)}{(3)(4)}$

$= \dfrac{-13}{12}$ ✓

Practice 6: 8

The actual length is 8

Practice 7: 150

The actual measure of the angle is 150

Homework 1: 4

What is the value of $x - y$, if $x^2 - y^2 = 8$ and $x + y = 2$?

$x^2 - y^2 = 8$

$(x+y)(x-y) = 8$

$\dfrac{2(x-y)}{2} = \dfrac{8}{2}$

$x - y = 4$

Homework 2: 3

What is the value of xy, if $x^2 + y^2 = 12$ and $(x + y)^2 = 18$?

$(x+y)^2 = 18$

$(x+y)(x+y) = 18$

$x^2 + xy + xy + y^2 = 18$

$x^2 + y^2 + 2xy = 18$

$12 + 2xy = 18$

$-12 \quad\quad -12$

$\dfrac{2xy}{2} = \dfrac{6}{2}$

$xy = 3$

Homework 3: 2.5 or 5/2

What is the average of x and y, if $x^2 - y^2 = 20$, and $x - y = 4$?

Avg of $x + y = \dfrac{x+y}{2}$, so we need $x+y$

$x^2 - y^2 = 20$

$(x+y)(x-y) = 20$

$\dfrac{(x+y) \cdot 4}{4} = \dfrac{20}{4}$

$x+y = 5$

$$Avg = \frac{x+y}{2} = \frac{5}{2} = \boxed{2.5}$$

Homework 4: 5

If Sam is thirteen years older than Rick, and in 8 years, Sam will be double Rick's age. How old is Rick now?

A. 4
B. 5
C. 13
D. 21

TRY ANS. CHOICES

RICK = 5
SAM = 5 + 13 = 18

In 8 years,
Rick = 13
Sam = 26 ✓ DOUBLE

Homework 5: C

$$\frac{t-5}{t+1} - \frac{8}{t-1}$$

Which of the following is equivalent to expression above?

E. $\frac{-7t-6}{t^2-1}$
F. $\frac{-7t-13}{t^2-1}$
G. $\frac{t^2-14t-3}{t^2-1}$
H. $\frac{t-13}{2t-1}$

pick t=3

$$\frac{t-5}{t+1} - \frac{8}{t-1} = \frac{3-5}{3+1} - \frac{8}{3-1}$$

$$\frac{-2}{4} - \frac{8}{2}$$ get common denominators

$$\frac{-2}{4} - \frac{16}{4} = \frac{-18}{4} = \frac{-9}{2}$$

now, check ans. choices

C. $\frac{t^2-14t-3}{t^2-1}$

$$\frac{3^2-14(3)-3}{3^2-1}$$

$$\frac{9-42-3}{9-1} = \frac{-36}{8} = \frac{-9}{2}$$ ✓

Homework 6: 30

The actual measurement is 30.

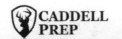

1.2 Combining Like Terms & Solving Equations

Combining Like Terms

Like terms have the same combination of variables and exponents but may have different coefficients.

When combining like terms, simply add the coefficients together.

$$4x^2 + 6x^2$$

In the example above, the coefficients are 4 and 6. We simply add them together to get

$$10x^2$$

More examples:

$$9x^3y^2 + 2x^3y^2 = 11x^3y^2$$
$$-12a^3b^2c^6 + a^3b^2c^6 = -11a^3b^2c^6$$

We only add coefficients together of like terms. In the example below, there are many terms and not all of them are like terms.

$$12x - 4y + 3x^2 - 20y + 3xy - 4x + 2xy$$

We can combine $12x$ and $-4x$ to get $8x$.

Notice that I treated the minus sign in front of $4x$ as a negative sign. Make sure to take the signs in front of the numbers along with the terms when combining like terms.

We can combine $-4y$ and $-20y$ to get $-24y$

We can also combine $3xy$ and $2xy$ to get $5xy$

That's all of the like terms, so we end up with

$$8x + 5xy + 3x^2 - 24y$$

Practice 1

Simplify

$2(x^2 + 3x - 5) + 2x - 3$

Adding & Subtracting Expressions

When questions ask us to add and subtract expressions, we are really being asked to combine like terms.

Example

What is the sum of $x^2 - 2x + 7$ and $2x^2 - 3x - 4$?

To solve this let's add them together.

$$(x^2 - 2x + 7) + (2x^2 - 3x - 4)$$

Distribute the plus sign $(+1)$ to each of the terms in the second expression. When you do that, all of the terms remain the same and we can drop the parentheses.

$$x^2 - 2x + 7 + 2x^2 - 3x - 4$$

Now, just combine like terms to get

$$3x^2 - 5x + 3$$

Example

$$(4x^2 - 5x + 2) - (2x^2 + x - 3)$$

Distribute the minus sign (-1) to each of the terms in the second expression. When you do that, all of the terms get negated and we can drop the parentheses.

$$4x^2 - 5x + 2 - 2x^2 - x + 3$$

Now, just combine like terms to get

$$2x^2 - 6x + 5$$

Practice 2

What is the sum of $3x^2 - 4x + 8$ and $-5x^2 - 5 + 2x$?

1.2 Combining Like Terms & Solving Equations

SUPER TIP
If one expression is being subtracted from another, make sure to distribute the minus sign and negate the terms inside the parenthesis.

Practice 3

$$(-5x^2 + 2x - 8) - (3x^2 - x + 5)$$

If the expression above is rewritten in the form $ax^2 + bx + c$, where a, b, and c are constants, what is the value of b?

1.2 Combining Like Terms & Solving Equations

Distribute or Divide to Solve Equations

If there is a number outside a set of parentheses, you can choose to distribute it or divide it.

Solve by distributing first	Solve by dividing first
$3(x - 4) = 15$	$3(x - 4) = 15$
$3(x-4) = 15$ $3x - 12 = 15$ $+12 \quad +12$ $\dfrac{3x}{3} = \dfrac{27}{3}$ $x = 9$	$\dfrac{3(x-4)}{3} = \dfrac{15}{3}$ $x - 4 = 5$ $+4 \quad +4$ $x = 9$

Practice 4

Solve for x in the equation below.

$5(2x - 6) = -60$

Struggle with basic algebra?

If you need help with solving basic equations, sign up for a free account on CaddellPrep.com

Then go to https://caddellprep.com/learn-math/pre-algebra/

To review lessons and try practice problems solving one-step and multi-step equations

1.2 Combining Like Terms & Solving Equations

If you are going to divide, instead of disturbing, the expression has to be by itself first. For example, in the example below on the right, we will move the 5 to the right side of the equation first.

Solve by distributing first	Solve by adding 5 and then dividing
$4(x + 8) - 5 = 43$	$4(x + 8) - 5 = 43$
$4(x+8) - 5 = 43$ $4x + 32 - 5 = 43$ $4x + 27 = 43$ $ -27\ -27$ $\dfrac{4x}{4} = \dfrac{16}{4}$ $x = 4$	$4(x+8) - 5 = 43$ $ +5\ +5$ $\dfrac{4(x+8)}{4} = \dfrac{48}{4}$ $x + 8 = 12$ $ -8\ -8$ $x = 4$

Practice 5

Solve for x in the equation below.

$-2(x - 6) + 4 = 20$

1.2 Combining Like Terms & Solving Equations

Multiply by the Reciprocal to Divide by a Fraction

$\frac{3}{4}x = 45$	$\frac{7}{8}x + 31 = 45$
$\left(\frac{4}{3}\right)\frac{3}{4}x = 45\left(\frac{4}{3}\right)$	$\frac{7}{8}x + 31 = 45$
$x = \frac{45}{1}\left(\frac{4}{3}\right)$	$-31 -31$
	$\frac{7}{8}x = 14$
$x = 60$	$\frac{8}{7} \cdot \frac{7}{8}x = 14 \cdot \frac{8}{7}$
	$x = 16$

Practice 6

Solve for x in the equation below.

$$\frac{3}{4}(x - 24) = 6$$

1.2 Combining Like Terms & Solving Equations

Be Mindful of Your Steps

The two examples below are very similar. However, if you distribute the $\frac{4}{5}$ in the set of parentheses the numbers work out well since $\frac{4}{5}$ of 20 is an integer. If you distribute $\frac{4}{5}$ in the set of parentheses in the equation below on the left, you will not get such an easy number to work with. In this case, it is better to multiple by the reciprocal first.

$$\frac{4}{5}(x-20) = 24 \qquad \frac{4}{5}(x-19) = 24$$

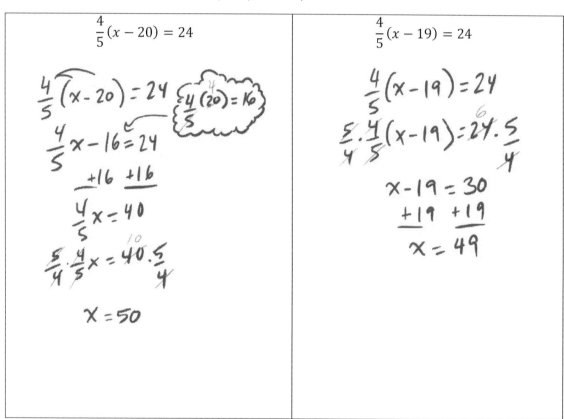

Practice 7

Solve for x in the equation below.

$$\frac{2}{3}(2x + 14) = 16$$

1.2 Combining Like Terms & Solving Equations

Multiply by Least Common Denominator to Eliminate Fractions

$$\frac{2}{3}x - \frac{4}{5} = \frac{1}{6}$$

$\frac{2}{3}x - \frac{4}{5} = \frac{1}{6}$

LCD = 30

$(30)\frac{2x}{3} - (30)\frac{4}{5} = \frac{1}{6}(30)$

$20x - 24 = 5$
$ +24 +24$

$\frac{20x}{20} = \frac{29}{20}$

$x = 29/20$

$$\frac{5}{8}x + 4 = \frac{5}{3}x$$

$\frac{5}{8}x + 4 = \frac{5}{3}x$

LCD = 24

$(24)\frac{5}{8}x + (24)4 = \frac{5}{3}x(24)$

$15x + 96 = 40x$
$-15x -15x$

$\frac{96}{25} = \frac{25x}{25}$

$\frac{96}{25} = x$

Practice 8

If $\frac{1}{4}x + \frac{1}{6}y = 4$ what is the value of $6x + 4y$?

Cross Multiply When a Fraction Equals a Fraction

Example

Solve for x in the equation below.

$$\frac{2x-7}{4} = \frac{2x-1}{12}$$

$$\frac{2x-7}{4} = \frac{2x-1}{12}$$

$12(2x-7) = 4(2x-1)$

$24x - 84 = 8x - 4$

$-8x -8x$

$16x - 84 = -4$

$+84 +84$

$16x = 80$

$\frac{16x}{16} = \frac{80}{16}$

$x = \frac{80}{16}$

$x = 5$

Practice 9

Solve for x in the equation below.

$$\frac{2x+10}{6} = \frac{-x+7}{15}$$

Practice 10

In the equation below, what is the value of t?

$$\frac{6(t+3)-9}{6} = \frac{15-(9-t)}{9}$$

A) $\frac{-15}{16}$

B) $\frac{15}{16}$

C) $\frac{-15}{17}$

D) $\frac{17}{16}$

Solving First Degree Inequalities

The rules for solving first degree inequalities with one variable are the same for solving first degree equations with one variable, except if you multiply or divide by a negative number you must flip the inequality sign.

$-3x + 8 \leq 50$	$2(x + 12) < -6$
$-3x + 8 \leq 50$ $\quad -8 \quad -8$ $-3x \leq 42$ $\frac{-3x}{-3} \leq \frac{42}{-3}$ divide by a negative #, so flip inequality $x \geq -14$	$2(x+12) < -6$ $2x + 24 < -6$ $\quad -24 \quad -24$ $2x < -30$ $\frac{2x}{2} < \frac{-30}{2}$ divide by a positive #, so DON'T flip the inequality $x < -15$

1.2 Combining Like Terms & Solving Equations

Practice 11

Solve for x.

$5 - 2x > 13$

Solving First Degree Compound Inequalities

Solving compound inequalities is similar to solving regular inequalities. When solving an equation or inequality, a basic rule is that whatever you do to one side of the equation, you do to the other.

In a compound inequality, whatever you do to one part of the inequality, you do to the other two.

When solving, just focus on getting the x-term by itself.

$-6 < 2x - 8 \leq 8$	$-\dfrac{4}{5} < -\dfrac{2}{5}x + 12 < 8$
$-6 < \boxed{(2x-8)} \leq 8$ Focus on isolating x $\begin{array}{r} -6 < 2x - 8 \leq 8 \\ +8 +8 +8 \\ \hline 2 < 2x \leq 16 \end{array}$ $\dfrac{2}{2} < \dfrac{2x}{2} \leq \dfrac{16}{2}$ $1 < x \leq 8$	$-\dfrac{4}{5} < -\dfrac{2}{5}x + 12 < 8$ We can use our trick & multiply each term by the LCD, 5. $(5)\dfrac{-4}{5} < (5)\dfrac{-2}{5}x + (5)12 < (5)8$ $-4 < -2x + 60 < 40$ $\phantom{-4 <} -60 -60 -60$ $\overline{-64 < -2x < -20}$ $\dfrac{}{-2} \dfrac{}{-2} \dfrac{}{-2}$ Flip the inequality $32 > x > 10$ $10 < x < 32$

1.2 Combining Like Terms & Solving Equations

Practice 12

If x is an even integer, what is one possible solution to the inequality $5 < 3x + 2 < 12$?

Practice 13

If $-4 < -5t + 10 < -\frac{3}{2}$, what is one possible integer value of $10t - 20$?

Solving Equations that Include Radical Expressions

To solve an equation with a radical term, try to get the radical term alone first. When it is alone, square both sides of the equation.

Example

Solve for x in the equation $\sqrt{x} + 2 = 7$.

$$\sqrt{x} + 2 = 7$$
$$-2 \quad -2$$
$$\sqrt{x} = 5$$
$$\sqrt{x}^2 = 5^2$$
$$x = 25$$

The above problem was pretty straight-forward. Sometimes, we run into a questions that will require squaring a binomial.

1.2 Combining Like Terms & Solving Equations

Example

Solve for x in the equation $\sqrt{x-5} - x = -11$.

$\sqrt{x-5} - x = -11$

Get the radical by itself.

$\sqrt{x-5} - x = -11$
$\phantom{\sqrt{x-5}} +x +x$
$\sqrt{x-5} = x - 11$

$\sqrt{x-5}^2 = (x-11)^2$
$x - 5 = (x-11)(x-11)$
$x - 5 = x^2 - 11x - 11x + 121$
$x - 5 = x^2 - 22x + 121$
$-x + 5 -x + 5$
$0 = x^2 - 23x + 126$

Note: You almost never have to do this!
★ Tip on next page

$0 = x^2 - 23x + 126$
$0 = (x-14)(x-9)$

$x - 14 = 0 \qquad x - 9 = 0$
$x = 14 \qquad x = 9$

We must check the answers

$\sqrt{x-5} - x = -11 \qquad \sqrt{x-5} - x = -11$
$\sqrt{14-5} - 14 = -11 \qquad \sqrt{9-5} - 9 = -11$
$\sqrt{9} - 14 = -11 \qquad \sqrt{4} - 9 = -11$
$3 - 14 = -11 \qquad 2 - 9 = -11$
$-11 = -11 \qquad -7 = -11$
$\checkmark \qquad \qquad \times$

$x = 14$

1.2 Combining Like Terms & Solving Equations

> **SUPER TIP**
> If we solve for x in an equation with a radical expression, we have to check our answers anyway, so we should just check the answer choices on multiple choice questions. Don't waste time solving for the answers to check.

Example

What is the solution to the following equation $\sqrt{x+3} = x - 3$?

A) $\{1\}$
B) $\{1, 6\}$
C) $\{6\}$
D) $\{0\}$

$\sqrt{x+3} = x-3$

A) $\{1\}$ Try the answers
B) $\{1,6\}$ $\sqrt{(1)+3} = (1)-3$
C) $\{6\}$ $\sqrt{4} = -2$
D) $\{0\}$ No, so A & B are wrong.

$\sqrt{(6)+3} = (6)-3$
$\sqrt{9} = 3$
$3 = 3$ ✓

Practice 14

What is the solution to the following equation $\sqrt{x+8} = x - 4$?

A) $\{8\}$
B) $\{1, 8\}$
C) $\{-4\}$
D) $\{-4, 1, 8\}$

1.2 Combining Like Terms & Solving Equations Homework

Homework 1

Simplify

$-2(3x - y) + 4x - 5$

Homework 2

What is the sum of $2xy + 3x - 8$ and $2x^2 - 5xy + 7$?

Homework 3

$(3x^2 + 8x + 4) - 2(4x^2 + 3x - 7)$

If the expression above is rewritten in the form $ax^2 + bx + c$, where a, b, and c are constants, what is the value of b?

Homework 4

$4(2x - 7) = -52$

Homework 5

$-3(5 - 3x) = -18$

Homework 6

$\frac{2}{9}(x - 7) = -2$

Homework 7

$\frac{1}{3}x + \frac{2}{5}y = 4$, what is the value of $5x + 6y$?

Homework 8

$\frac{3x + 6}{8} = \frac{6x + 9}{14}$

Homework 9

$-5 \leq -2x + 7 \leq 12$. If x is an integer value, what is the greatest possible value of x?

1.2 Combining Like Terms & Solving Equations

Homework 10

$\sqrt{2x - 9} = 7$, what is the value of x?

- A) {29}
- B) {-20}
- C) {4.5}
- D) {29, -20}

Homework 11

$\sqrt{20 - 2x} = 6 - x$

- A) {2}
- B) {8}
- C) {2, 8}
- D) {0, 2, 8}

1.2 Answers to Practice Problems (Solving Equations)

Practice 1: $2x^2 + 8x - 13$

Simplify $2(x^2 + 3x - 5) + 2x - 3$

$$2(x^2 + 3x - 5) + 2x - 3$$
$$2x^2 + 6x - 10 + 2x - 3$$
$$2x^2 + 8x - 13$$

Practice 2: $-2x^2 - 2x + 3$

What is the sum of $3x^2 - 4x + 8$ and $-5x^2 - 5 + 2x$?

sum is the answer to an addition problem

$$(3x^2 - 4x + 8) + (-5x^2 - 5 + 2x)$$
$$3x^2 - 4x + 8 - 5x^2 - 5 + 2x$$
$$-2x^2 - 2x + 3$$

Practice 3: 3

$(-5x^2 + 2x - 8) - (3x^2 - x + 5)$

If the expression above is rewritten in the form $ax^2 + bx + c$, where a, b, and c are constants, what is the value of b?

$$(-5x^2 + 2x - 8) - (3x^2 - x + 5)$$
$$-5x^2 + 2x - 8 - 3x^2 + x - 5$$
$$-8x^2 + 3x - 13$$
$$ax^2 + bx + c$$

$$\boxed{3}$$

Practice 4: -3

$$\frac{5(2x-6)}{5} = \frac{-60}{5}$$
$$2x - 6 = -12$$
$$+6 +6$$
$$\frac{2x}{2} = \frac{-6}{2}$$
$$x = -3$$

1.2 Combining Like Terms & Solving Equations

Practice 5: -2

$$-2(x-6)+4=20$$
$$-2x+12+4=20$$
$$-2x+16=20$$
$$\underline{\quad -16 \quad -16}$$
$$\frac{-2x}{-2}=\frac{4}{-2}$$
$$x=-2$$

Practice 6: 32

$$\frac{3}{4}(x-24)=6$$

$$\frac{3}{4}(x-24)=6 \quad \text{OR} \quad \frac{3}{4}(x-24)=6$$
$$\frac{3}{4}x-18=6 \qquad \frac{4}{3}\cdot\frac{3}{4}(x-24)=6\cdot\frac{4}{3}$$
$$\underline{+18 +18}$$
$$\frac{3}{4}x=24 \qquad\qquad x-24=8$$
$$\frac{4}{3}\cdot\frac{3}{4}x=24\cdot\frac{4}{3} \quad +24 \ +24$$
$$x=32 \qquad\qquad\qquad x=32$$

Practice 7: 5

$$\frac{2}{3}(2x+14)=16$$
$$\frac{3}{2}\cdot\frac{2}{3}(2x+14)=16\cdot\frac{3}{2}$$
$$2x+14=24$$
$$\underline{-14 \ -14}$$
$$\frac{2x}{2}=\frac{10}{2}$$
$$x=5$$

Practice 8: 96

$$\frac{1}{4}x+\frac{1}{6}y=4 \qquad 6x+4y=?$$

$$LCD=12$$
$$(12)\frac{1}{4}x+(12)\frac{1}{6}y=4(12)$$
$$3x+2y=48$$
$$2(3x+2y=48)$$
$$6x+4y=96$$
$$96$$

Practice 9: -3

$$\frac{2x+10}{6}=\frac{-x+7}{15}$$

$$6(-x+7)=15(2x+10)$$
$$-6x+42=30x+150$$
$$\underline{+6x \qquad +6x}$$
$$42=36x+150$$
$$\underline{-150 \qquad -150}$$
$$-108=36x$$
$$\overline{36}\quad\overline{36}$$
$$-3=x$$

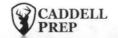

1.2 Combining Like Terms & Solving Equations

Practice 10: A

$$\frac{6(t+3)-9}{6} = \frac{15-(9-t)}{9}$$

$$\frac{6t+18-9}{6} = \frac{15-9+t}{9}$$

$$\frac{6t+9}{6} = \frac{6+t}{9}$$

$$9(6t+9) = 6(6+t)$$
$$54t+81 = 36+6t$$
$$-6t \qquad -6t$$
$$48t+81 = 36$$
$$-81 \quad -81$$

$$\frac{48t}{48} = \frac{-45}{48}$$

$$t = \frac{-45}{48}$$

$$t = \frac{-15}{16}$$

Practice 11: $x < -4$

$$5 - 2x > 13$$
$$-5 \qquad -5$$
$$\frac{-2x}{-2} > \frac{8}{-2}$$
$$x < -4$$

Practice 12: 2

$$5 < 3x + 2 < 12$$
$$-2 \quad -2 \quad -2$$
$$3 < 3x < 10$$

$$\frac{3}{3} < \frac{3x}{3} < \frac{10}{3}$$

$$1 < x < 3\frac{1}{3}$$

x must be an even integer,
so $x = 2$

Practice 13: 4, 5, 6, or 7

$$-4 < -5t + 10 < -\frac{3}{2}$$

$10t - 20 = ?$
If we multiply the inequality by -2, we can solve for $10t - 20$ without solving for t.

$$(-2)(-4) < (-2)-5t + (-2)10 < (-2)-\frac{3}{2}$$

multiply by a negative #, so flip inequality

$$8 > 10t - 20 > 3$$

1.2 Combining Like Terms & Solving Equations

$3 < 10t - 20 < 8$

The answer must be an integer, so possible answers are

$4, 5, 6,$ or 7

Practice 14: A

$\sqrt{x+8} = x-4$

A) $\{8\}$
B) $\{1,8\}$
C) $\{-4\}$
D) $\{-4, 1, 8\}$

TRY ANS.

$\sqrt{8+8} = 8-4$
$\sqrt{16} = 4$
$4 = 4$ ✓

$\sqrt{1+8} = 1-4$
$\sqrt{9} = -3$
$3 \neq -3$ ✗

Homework 1: $-2x + 2y - 5$

$-2(3x-y) + 4x - 5$

$-6x + 2y + 4x - 5$

$\boxed{-6x} + 2y \boxed{+4x} - 5$

$-2x + 2y - 5$

Homework 2: $2x^2 - 3xy + 3x - 1$

$(2xy + 3x - 8) + (2x^2 - 5xy + 7)$

$2xy + 3x - 8 + 2x^2 - 5xy + 7$

$\boxed{2xy} + \boxed{3x} - \boxed{8} + \boxed{2x^2} - \boxed{5xy} + \boxed{7}$

$2x^2 - 3xy + 3x - 1$

Homework 3: 2

$(3x^2 + 8x + 4) - 2(4x^2 + 3x - 7)$

$(3x^2 + 8x + 4) - 2(4x^2 + 3x - 7)$

$3x^2 + 8x + 4 - 8x^2 - 6x + 14$

$\boxed{3x^2} + \boxed{8x} + \boxed{4} - \boxed{8x^2} - \boxed{6x} + \boxed{14}$

$-5x^2 + 2x + 22$

1.2 Combining Like Terms & Solving Equations

Homework 4: -3

$4(2x-7) = -52$

$8x - 28 = -52$

$+28 +28$

$8x = -24$

$\overline{8} \overline{8}$

$x = \boxed{-3}$

Homework 5: -1/3

$-3(5-3x) = 18$

$-15 + 9x = 18$

$+15 +15$

$9x = -3$

$x = \boxed{-1/3}$

Homework 6: -2

$\left(\dfrac{9}{2}\right)\dfrac{2}{9}(x-7) = -2\left(\dfrac{9}{2}\right)$

$x - 7 = -9$

$+7 +7$

$x = \boxed{-2}$

Homework 7: 60

$15\left(\dfrac{1}{3}x + \dfrac{2}{5}y = 4\right)$

$5x + 6y = \boxed{60}$

Homework 8: 2

$\dfrac{3x+6}{8} = \dfrac{6x+9}{14}$

$14(3x+6) = 8(6x+9)$

$42x + 84 = 48x + 72$

$12 = 6x$

$\boxed{2} = x$

1.2 Combining Like Terms & Solving Equations

Homework 9: 6

$$-5 \leq -2x+7 \leq 12$$
$$ -7 -7 -7$$
$$-12 \leq -2x \leq 5$$
$$\overline{-2} \overline{-2} \overline{-2}$$
$$6 \geq x \geq -2.5$$

$\boxed{6}$

Homework 10: A

$\sqrt{2x-9} = 7$

TRY ANS.

$\sqrt{2(29)-9} = 7$

$\sqrt{49} = 7$ ✓

$\sqrt{2(-20)-9} = 7$

$\sqrt{-49} = 7$ ✗

Homework 11: A

TRY ANS.

$\sqrt{20-2x} = 6-x$

$\sqrt{20-2(2)} = 6-2$

$\sqrt{16} = 4$ ✓

$\sqrt{20-2(8)} = 6-8$

$\sqrt{4} = -2$ ✗

2 works, 8 doesn't

1.3 System of Equations

In order to solve for a variable, you need at least one equation. If there are two variables, you need at least two equations to solve for each variable. The set of is known as a system of equations.

Two of the methods we will examine are substitution and elimination.

Substitution

One method of solving for a system of equations is substitution.

In order to use substitution, one equation has to be solved for a variable. In other words, the equation should be $y = $ something or $x = $ something.

Then you can substitute the expressions one variable equals into the other equation.

Example

$y = 4x + 1$

$3x - y = -3$

Solve for x and y in the system of equations above.

Since the top equation is already solved for y, we can substitute $4x + 1$ in for y in the other equation.

$$y = \boxed{4x + 1}$$
$$3x - y = -3$$

Make sure to use parenthesis when you substitute.

$$3x - (4x + 1) = -3$$

1.3 System of Equations

In this case, we have to distribute the negative to each term in the parentheses.

$$3x - 4x - 1 = -3$$

Next combine like terms and solve for x.

$$-x - 1 = -3$$
$$+1 \quad +1$$
$$-x = -2$$
$$\overline{-1} \quad \overline{-1}$$
$$x = 2$$

Now that we have solved for x, we can solve for y by substituting 2 in for x in either of the equations.

$$y = 4x + 1$$
$$y = 4(2) + 1$$
$$y = 8 + 1$$
$$y = 9$$

Therefore, $x = 2$ and $y = 9$.

1.3 System of Equations

Practice 1

$$\begin{cases} y = 2x + 7 \\ 6x + 5y = 3 \end{cases}$$

- A. (-3,2)
- B. (-2,3)
- C. (2,-3)
- D. (3,-2)

Practice 2

$$\begin{cases} 4x - 8y = -4 \\ y = -4x - 22 \end{cases}$$

- A. (5,2)
- B. (-5,-2)
- C. (2,5)
- D. (-2,-5)

1.3 System of Equations

Elimination

Another method to solve a system of equations is by using elimination.

In order for elimination to work, both equations have to be aligned properly.

For example, the equations $2x + 3y = 12$ and $4x - 6y = 8$ are aligned properly.

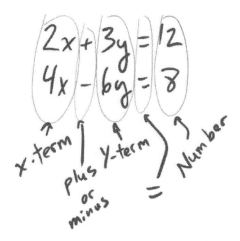

The x-terms, y-terms, plus or minus, equal signs, and numbers all line up properly.

In order for elimination to work, one of the variables should cancel out when the equations are added together.

Example

Solve for x and y in the system of equation below.

$3x + 2y = 8$

$4x - 2y = 6$

In the system above, if we add the equations together, the y-terms will cancel out.

$$3x + 2y = 8$$
$$4x - 2y = 6$$
$$\overline{}$$
$$7x = 14$$

1.3 System of Equations

Now, we can solve for x.

$$\frac{7x}{7} = \frac{14}{7}$$

$$x = 2$$

Since we know $x = 2$, we can substitute the value into either of the equations and solve for y.

$$3x + 2y = 8$$
$$3(2) + 2y = 8$$
$$6 + 2y = 8$$
$$-6 \qquad -6$$
$$\frac{2y}{2} = \frac{2}{2}$$
$$y = 1$$

Therefore, $x = 2$ and $y = 1$.

1.3 System of Equations

Example

Let's look at the example from the beginning of this section again.

$$2x + 3y = 12$$
$$4x - 6y = 8$$

If we add the two equations above together, neither of the variable would cancel out when we add them together.

We could multiply the top equation by 2, so the top equation will have a $6y$ and the bottom equation will have a $-6y$. Then when we add them together the y-terms will cancel out.

$$2(2x + 3y = 12)$$
$$4x - 6y = 8$$

Distributing the 2 gives us the following.

$$4x + 6y = 24$$
$$4x - 6y = 8$$

Add the equations together

$$4x + 6y = 24$$
$$4x - 6y = 8$$
$$\overline{}$$
$$8x = 32$$

1.3 System of Equations

Solve for x.

$$\frac{8x}{8} = \frac{32}{8}$$

$$x = 4$$

We can substitute 4 in for x in either of the equations and solve for y.

$$2x + 3y = 12$$
$$2(4) + 3y = 12$$
$$8 + 3y = 12$$
$$-8 \qquad -8$$
$$\frac{3y}{3} = \frac{4}{3}$$
$$y = \frac{4}{3}$$

Therefore, $x = 4 \text{ and } y = \frac{4}{3}$

1.3 System of Equations

Practice 3

$$\begin{cases} 3x + 6y = 18 \\ -3x - 5y = -19 \end{cases}$$

A. (1,-8)
B. (8,-1)
C. (-8,1)
D. (-1,8)

Practice 4

$$\begin{cases} 2x - 4y = -8 \\ 3x + y = 9 \end{cases}$$

A. (4, 0)
B. (2, 3)
C. (-1,-12)
D. (3, -2)

1.3 Systems of Equations Homework

Homework 1

$$\begin{cases} 3x - y = -7 \\ -6x + 2y = 14 \end{cases}$$

   A. (-2, 1)
   B. (-3,-2)
   C. (-1,-4)
   D. (0,7)

Homework 2

$$\begin{cases} 6x - 5y = 26 \\ -7x + 5y = -27 \end{cases}$$

   A. (1,-4)
   B. (-4,1)
   C. (4,-1)
   D. (-1,4)

Homework 3

$$\begin{cases} y = -3x + 5 \\ 2x + y = -4 \end{cases}$$

   A. (-2,-1)
   B. (-1,-2)
   C. (0,5)
   D. (-3,2)

Homework 4

$$\begin{cases} y = 4x + 5 \\ 2x + 2y = 10 \end{cases}$$

   A. (-1,1)
   B. (-3,-2)
   C. (-2,-3)
   D. (1,9)

1.3 Answers to Practice Problems (System of Equations)

Practice 1: B

$$\begin{cases} y = 2x + 7 \\ 6x + 5y = 3 \end{cases}$$

$6x + 5(2x+7) = 3$
$6x + 10x + 35 = 3$
$16x + 35 = 3$
$16x = -32$
$x = -2$

Practice 2: B

$$\begin{cases} 4x - 8y = -4 \\ y = -4x - 22 \end{cases}$$

$4x - 8(-4x - 22) = -4$
$4x + 32x + 176 = -4$
$36x + 176 = -4$
$36x = -180$
$x = -5$

Practice 3: B

$$\begin{cases} 3x + 6y = 18 \\ -3x - 5y = -19 \end{cases}$$

$y = -1$

Practice 4: B

$$\begin{cases} 2x - 4y = -8 \\ 3x + y = 9 \end{cases}$$

$2x - 4y = -8$
$4(3x + y) = 9$

A. (4, 0)
B. (2, 3)
C. (-1, -12)
D. (3, -2)

$12x + 4y = 36$

$14x = 28$
$x = 2$

1.3 System of Equations

Homework 1: C

$$\begin{cases} 3x - y = -7 \\ -6x + 3y = 18 \end{cases}$$

A. (-2, 1)
B. (-3, -2)
C. (-1, 4)
D. (0, 7)

$2(3x - y = -7)$
$-6x + 3y = 18$

$6x - 2y = -14$
$-6x + 3y = 18$
_____
$y = 4$

Homework 2: A

$$\begin{cases} 6x - 5y = 26 \\ -7x + 5y = -27 \end{cases}$$

A. (1, -4)
B. (-4, 1)
C. (4, -1)
D. (-1, 4)

$6x - 5y = 26$
$-7x + 5y = -27$
_____
$-x = -1$

$x = 1$

Homework 3: B

$$\begin{cases} y = -3x - 5 \\ 2x + y = -4 \end{cases}$$

A. (-2, -1)
B. (-1, -2)
C. (0, 5)
D. (-3, 2)

$2x + (-3x - 5) = -4$

$-x - 5 = -4$

$-x = 1$

$x = -1$

Homework 4: C

$$\begin{cases} y = 4x + 5 \\ 2x + 2y = -10 \end{cases}$$

A. (-1, 1)
B. (-3, -2)
C. (-2, -3)
D. (1, 9)

$2x + 2(4x + 5) = -10$

$2x + 8x + 10 = -10$

1.3 System of Equations

$$2x + 8x + 10 = -10$$
$$10x + 10 = -10$$
$$ -10 \quad -10$$
$$10x = -20$$
$$\frac{10x}{10} = \frac{-20}{10}$$
$$x = -2$$

Lesson 2

Need to improve 200 points?

We love working with students who are serious about their SAT scores - that means you!

Special Tutoring & Test Prep Offer for You

 caddellprep.com/sboffer

2.1 Ratios & Proportions

Rates/Ratios/Proportions

An example of a rate is 25 miles/hr, which means the object will move 25 miles for every hour that passes.

An example of a ratio is 2 eggs:3 ounces of flour, which means the recipe calls for 2 eggs for every 3 ounces of flour used.

A statement that 2 rates or ratios are equal is a proportion.

$$\frac{2\ eggs}{3\ oz.\ flour} = \frac{8\ eggs}{12\ oz.\ flour}$$

Check by cross multiplying.

$$\frac{2}{3} = \frac{8}{12}$$

$$24 = 24$$

Since we get the same number on both sides of the equation, we know that the two ratios are equal and the proportion is correct.

2.1 Ratios & Proportions

Setting Up a Proportion

When setting up a proportion, always write down how you will set it up

$$\frac{pages}{minute}$$

Then insert the values.

$$\frac{pages}{minute} \quad \frac{13}{4} = \frac{x}{22}$$

Use cross multiplication to solve for a missing value in a proportion

$$\frac{13}{4} = \frac{x}{22}$$

$$286 = 4x$$

$$\frac{286}{4} = \frac{4x}{4}$$

$$71.5 = x$$

Practice 1
The ratio of boys to girls in a class is 3: 2. How many boys are there if there are 12 girls?

2.1 Ratios & Proportions

Problems with Ratios and a Total

To solve for values when a ratio and a total is given, multiple each number in the ratio by *x* and then create an equation in which they all add up to the total. Then solve for *x*, and use that value of *x* to determine the other values.

Example:
The ratio of boys to girls in a class is 2:3. If there are 25 students, how many boys are there?

$$\text{Boys} + \text{Girls} = 25$$
$$2x + 3x = 25$$
$$5x = 25$$
$$\frac{5x}{5} = \frac{25}{5}$$
$$x = 5$$

Now, we can find the number of boys

$$\text{Boys} = 2x = 2(5) = \boxed{10}$$

2.1 Ratios & Proportions

Practice 2

A recipe for cake calls for 2.5 cups of flour to be mixed with 2 cups of sugar. The two ingredients should be mixed first before other ingredients are added. If the total mixture of flour and sugar should be 18 cups, how many cups of sugar should be used?

Use Matching Units in the Proportion

Make sure to correct the units if they are different, before setting up the proportion.

Example

Tammy can read 10 pages in 4 minutes. How many pages can she read in 2 hours?

$$\frac{\text{pages}}{\text{min}} \quad \frac{10}{4} = \frac{x}{2} \quad \leftarrow \text{Not the correct units}$$

$$2 \text{ hours} = 120 \text{ minutes}$$

$$\frac{10}{4} = \frac{x}{120} \quad \leftarrow \text{Now, it has the correct units}$$

$$1200 = 4x$$

2.1 Ratios & Proportions

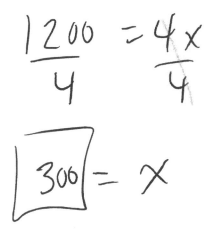

Practice 3

Michelle works in a shirt printing company. If she can print 40 shirts per hour and works 6 hours each day, how many shirts can she print if she works three days?

Ratios Involving Formulas

When given a formula, we can determine how one value will be affected by altering other values.

For example,

The weight of an object, F_g, is found by multiplying the mass of an object, m, by gravity, g.

$$F_g = mg$$

If the mass, m, is doubled, the weight, F_g, will be doubled.

Just like when we solve equations, whatever we do to one side of the equation, we have to do to the other side of the equation.

2.1 Ratios & Proportions

>  **SUPER TIP**
> To see how doubling the value of an input variable in a formula will impact the result, insert a 2 for the variable and 1s for the other variables. Then, compare it to what the value would have been if all 1s were used.

For example, to see how double the mass would affect the weight:

$$F_g = mg \qquad\qquad F_g = mg$$
$$= (1)(1) \qquad\qquad = (2)(1)$$
$$= 1 \qquad\qquad\qquad = 2$$

$\text{times 2} \longrightarrow \text{Double}$

We end up with 2, which is twice as big as 1, so it means the new weight will be twice as big (doubled).

This is very useful for more complicated formulas, including ones with variables that are raised to an exponent.

Example

The formula to calculate kinetic energy is $K = \frac{1}{2}mv^2$. How will K be affected if we double v?

$$K = \frac{1}{2}mv^2 \qquad\qquad K = \frac{1}{2}mv^2$$
$$= \frac{1}{2}(1)(1)^2 \qquad\qquad = \frac{1}{2}(1)(2)^2$$
$$= \frac{1}{2} \qquad\qquad\qquad = \frac{1}{2}(4)$$

2.1 Ratios & Proportions

2 is four times as big as $\frac{1}{2}$, so doubling v quadruples K.

Practice 4

$$F_g = \frac{Gm_1m_2}{r^2}$$

The formula above is used to calculate the gravitational attraction between two masses. What will happen to the value of F_g if m_1 is tripled and r is tripled?

A) F_g will be tripled.
B) F_g will be nine times as large as its original value.
C) F_g will remain the same.
D) F_g will be one-third of its original value

2.1 Ratios & Proportions

Proportions in Shapes

Similar figures and shapes have proportionate side lengths.

A useful way to write down how we are setting up a proportion regarding geometric shapes is:

$$\frac{\text{Large}}{\text{Small}}$$

SUPER TIP
When dealing with proportionate shapes, make sure that you're dealing with corresponding lengths. It is common for a question to ask for the length of a segment and not a full side.

Example

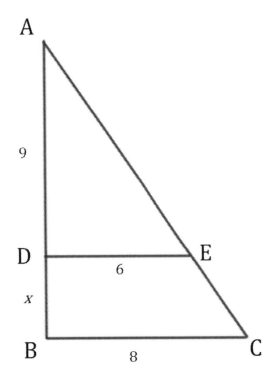

What is the value of x in the figure above?

2.1 Ratios & Proportions

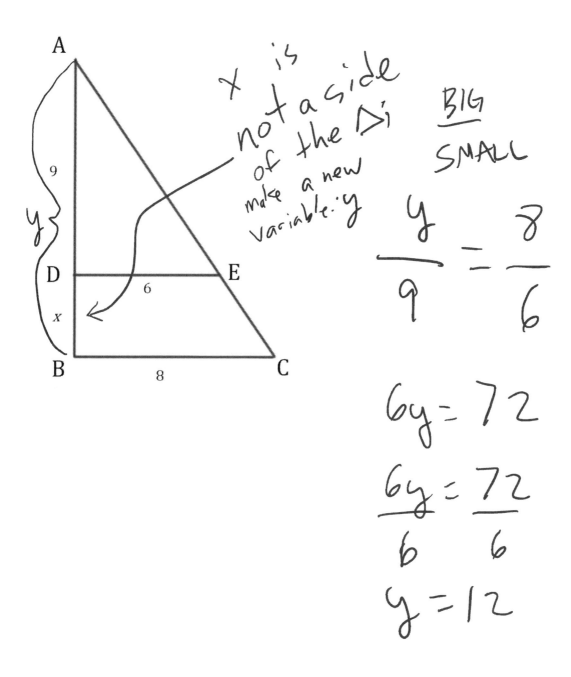

x is not a side of the △; make a new variable: y

$$\frac{BIG}{SMALL}$$

$$\frac{y}{9} = \frac{8}{6}$$

$$6y = 72$$

$$\frac{6y}{6} = \frac{72}{6}$$

$$y = 12$$

2.1 Ratios & Proportions

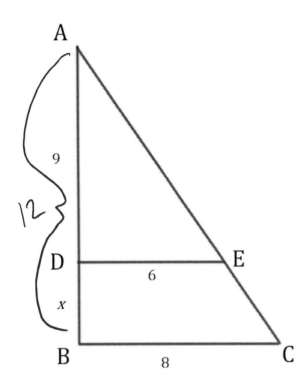

$x + 9 = 12$

$-9 \quad -9$

$x = \boxed{3}$

Practice 5

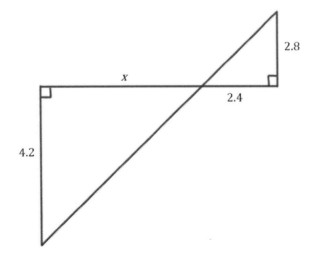

What is the value of x in the figure above?

2.1 Ratios & Proportions

2.1 Ratios & Proportions Homework

Homework 1

The ratio of chocolate chip cookies to oatmeal cookies in a display case is 7:2. If there are 56 chocolate chip cookies, how many oatmeal cookies are there?

Homework 2

To prepare concrete it is advised to use 600 pounds of cement, 1450 pounds of sand, 1600 pounds of stone and 260 pounds of water. If it is estimated that a project will require 46,920 pounds of concrete. How many pounds of water will be needed?

Homework 3

Noriko can type 50 words per minute. How many words can she type in 3 hours?

Homework 4

The formula $P = \frac{Fd}{t}$ is used to calculate power, P. If t is doubled and F is halved, how will that affect P?

A) P will be doubled.
B) P will be halved.
C) P will be quartered.
D) P will be quadrupled.

Homework 5

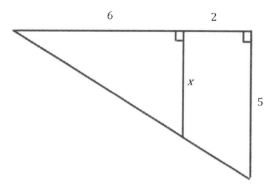

What is the value of x in the figure above?

2.1 Answers to Practice Problems (Ratios & Proportions)

Practice 1: 18

Boys : Girls
3 : 2

Girls = 12

$$\frac{B}{G} \quad \frac{3}{2} = \frac{x}{12}$$

$$36 = 2x$$

$$\frac{36}{2} = \frac{2x}{2}$$

$$18 = x$$

Practice 2: 8

Flour : S
2.5 : 2

18 total

Flour + Sugar = 18

$$2.5x + 2x = 18$$

$$4.5x = 18$$

$$\frac{4.5x}{4.5} = \frac{18}{4.5}$$

$$x = 4$$

Sugar = $2x$
= $2(4)$
= 8 cups

2.1 Ratios & Proportions

Practice 3: 720

40 shirts/hr
6 hrs/day
3 days

$\dfrac{sh}{h}$ $\dfrac{40}{1} = \dfrac{x}{?}$

Need total hours

$3 \text{ days} \times \dfrac{6 \text{ hrs}}{\text{day}} = 18 \text{ hrs.}$

$\dfrac{40}{1} = \dfrac{x}{18}$

$720 = x$

Practice 4: D

Original:

$F = \dfrac{Gm_1 m_2}{r^2}$

$F = \dfrac{(1)(1)(1)}{(1)^2}$

$F = 1$

New:

$F = \dfrac{Gm_1 m_2}{r^2}$

triple m_1
triple r

$F = \dfrac{(1)(3)(1)}{(3)^2}$

2.1 Ratios & Proportions

$$F = \frac{3}{9} = \frac{1}{3}$$

$$3.6 = x$$

Homework 1: 16

Compare

CH : OAT
7 : 2

$$1 \to \frac{1}{3}$$

$$CH = 56$$
$$OAT = ?$$

$\frac{1}{3}$ of original

$$\frac{CH}{OAT} \quad \frac{7}{2} = \frac{56}{x}$$

Practice 5: 3.6

$$7x = 112$$

$$\frac{BIG}{SMALL} \quad \frac{4.2}{2.8} = \frac{x}{2.4}$$

$$\frac{7x}{7} = \frac{112}{7}$$

$$x = 16$$

$$10.08 = 2.8x$$
$$\frac{10.08}{2.8} = \frac{2.8x}{2.8}$$

2.1 Ratios & Proportions

Homework 2: 3,120

Cement = 600
Sand = 1450
Stone = 1600
Water = 260

$$\begin{array}{r} 600 \\ 1450 \\ 1600 \\ 260 \\ \hline 3910 \end{array}$$

∑ all materials to make concrete

$$\frac{water}{concrete}$$

$$\frac{260}{3910} \diagdown \diagup \frac{x}{46920}$$

$$12{,}199{,}200 = 3910x$$

$$\frac{12{,}199{,}200}{3910} = \frac{3910x}{3910}$$

$$\boxed{3120} = x$$

Homework 3: 9,000

50 words/min

words in 3 hrs = ?

#3 hrs = 180 min

$$\frac{w}{min} \quad \frac{50}{1} \diagdown \frac{x}{180}$$

$$9{,}000 = x$$

2.1 Ratios & Proportions

Homework 4: C

Original:

$$P = \frac{Fd}{t} = \frac{(1)(1)}{(1)} = 1$$

New:

$$P = \frac{Fd}{t}$$

double t
halve F

$P = ?$

$$P = \frac{Fd}{t}$$

$$P = \frac{\left(\frac{1}{2}\right)(1)}{2}$$

$$P = 1/4$$

P is 1/4 of the original

2.1 Ratios & Proportions

Homework 5: 3.75

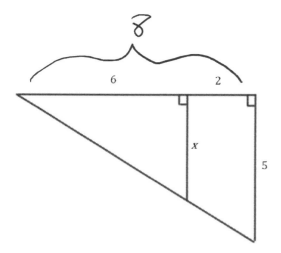

$$\frac{BIG}{SMALL} \quad \frac{8}{6} = \frac{5}{x}$$

$$8x = 30$$

$$\frac{8x}{8} = \frac{30}{8}$$

$$x = 3.75$$

Data & Probability

Surveys

It is common to see a question on the SAT that asks why a survey conducted is unreliable. Most of the times it is unreliable because of a possible bias related to who was surveyed, where they were surveyed, when they were surveyed, or how they were surveyed.

When choosing the group of people to be surveyed, the group should be a random sample of the entire population to be surveyed. For example, a survey to determine a town's favorite pizzeria should randomly survey people from the town.

Most of the time, the answer won't be because of the sample size.

Here are some examples of creating a bias based on who was surveyed:

1. A survey of the favorite class of students at a high school would not be reliable if only students from the freshmen class were surveyed or if any of the grades were excluded from the survey.
2. A survey of car enthusiasts to find out which car is the most popular would not be reliable if the survey was sent to a mailing list of people who earned a certain type of sports car.

Here are some examples of creating a bias based on location:

1. A survey of adults to determine the average number of children per household would not be reliable if the survey was done at a location where there are likely children because most of the adults there will have children. For example, at a playground the adults there are likely there with children, so it is less likely to survey an adult with no children.
2. A survey of people's favorite activity would not be reliable if it was held at a place related to one of those activities. For example, at a movie theater the people are likely to choose going to the movies or at a bookstore the people are more likely to choose something related to reading.
3. A survey of whether people prefer watching sports in person or at home would not have reliable results if the survey was done outside a stadium before a game. The people there may be going to the game to watch it in person. Plus, it excludes the people who are home and waiting for the game to start.

2.2 Data & Probability

Here are some examples of creating a bias based on when they were surveyed:

1. A survey of the most popular occupation in a town would not be reliable if people were randomly survey inside a supermarket on a weekday during the workday because people with professions that require them to work during normal work hours would be excluded from the survey.
2. A survey done to determine the opinion of the population of a town will likely not be reliable if done at a time when the majority of the population is expected to be sleeping.

An example of how a bias could be created is:

A survey that requires people to use a specific type of phone or through a specific social media application because it will exclude people who don't have the specific type of phone of the specific application.

However, if the purpose is to survey owners of a specific phone, then it should be required that they use that type of phone to participate.

SUPER TIP
If a question asks why a reasonable conclusion is not likely, it won't be because of the size of the group surveyed or because people were allowed to opt out of answering

Practice 1

For her class project, Chloe wanted to determine the percent of students who thought the school should spend part of its budget on renovating the sports field. One Saturday, she interviewed every fourth student who entered the stands to watch the high school's football team. If someone didn't want to participate, she simply allowed them to not participate. When she was done, she had interviewed 40 students and 5 students refused to participate. Which of the following factors makes it least likely that a reliable conclusion can be drawn about the preferences of all of the students of Chloe's school?

A) The sample size
B) The number of people who refused to participate
C) Where the survey was given
D) The fact that Chloe interviewed every fourth student instead of every student who entered

2.2 Data & Probability

Scatterplots

Correlation

When a relationship appears to exist among data points appear it is said that there is correlation.

For example, as time increases, the cost of college increases. Since they both go up, it is said that there is positive correlation.

Below is an example of a positive correlation between x and y.

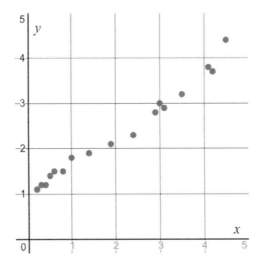

Another example would be as time increases the population of a specific species decreases. Since one value increases while the other decreases, it is said that there is a negative correlation.

2.2 Data & Probability

Below is an example of a negative correlation between x and y.

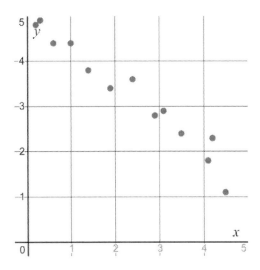

The more apparent that there is a relationship, the stronger the correlation is said to be.

Below are two examples of a negative correlation between x and y. However, the graph on the right shows a stronger correlation than the graph on the left.

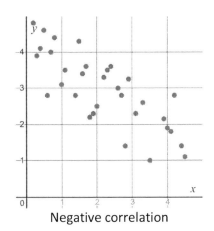
Negative correlation

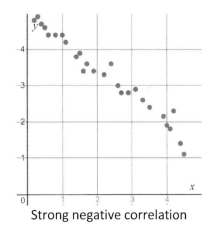
Strong negative correlation

2.2 Data & Probability

Trendlines

Trendlines (lines of best fit) can be applied to scatterplots that show correlation.

For example, a trendline has been added to the scatterplot below.

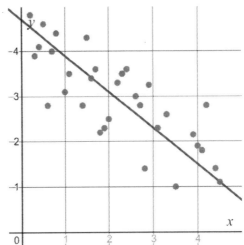

The line of best fit is modeled by $f(x) = -\frac{4}{5}x + 4.7$

Obviously, each point on the scatterplot is not on the line of best fit. However, it does show the trend of the data and can be used to make estimations.

Based on the line of best fit, we can estimate the y-value when x is 4 by substituting 4 into the function $f(x) == \frac{4}{5}x + 4.7$.

$$y = -\frac{4}{5}x + 4.8$$
$$y = -\frac{4}{5}(4) + 4.8$$
$$y = 1.6$$

If we look at the graph, we can see that when x is 4, y is approximately 1.9, not 1.6. It's important to remember that we use the line of best, or a trendline, to estimate values.

Practice 2

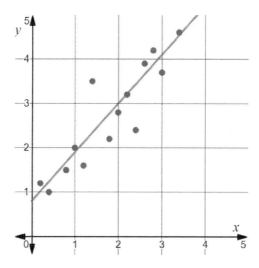

The scatterplot above shows the average frequency of homes, y, for each home value in millions of dollars, x. The frequency of homes, $f(x)$, can be estimated with the function $f(x) = 1.1x + 0.8$. Based on the information in the graph above, what is the estimated frequency of homes with a value of $3 million?

A) 2
B) 3.8
C) 4.1
D) 2,000,000

Mean, Median, Mode, & Range

Mean (Average)

$$Mean = \frac{Sum\ of\ Items}{Number\ of\ Items}$$

For example, let's find the mean of: 80, 90, 90, 95, 95

$$Mean = \frac{80 + 90 + 90 + 95 + 95}{5} = 90$$

Many times, on the SAT it is important to be able to find the sum of the items in order to solve the problem.

$$Sum\ of\ Items = (Average) * (Number\ of\ Items)$$

Example

Mike's average for 5 math tests is 90. His teacher is going to drop his lowest test, a 70. What will his average be for the remaining four tests?

It is important to realize that we do not need to know what the other four test grades are. We only need to know what they add up to.

First let's find his total including all 5 tests

$$Sum\ of\ Items = (Average) * (Number\ of\ Items)$$
$$Sum\ of\ Items = (90) * (5)$$
$$Sum\ of\ Items = 450$$

Now to find his new total, after dropping the 70, we simply have to subtract 70.
$$New\ Sum\ of\ Items = 450 - 70$$
$$New\ Sum\ of\ Items = 380$$

To find his new average we use the Arithmetic Mean (average) formula

$$\text{Arithmetic Mean} = \frac{\text{Sum of Items}}{\text{Number of Items}}$$

$$\text{Arithmetic Mean} = \frac{380}{4}$$

$$\text{Arithmetic Mean} = 95$$

Practice 3

Jose's average after 5 tests is 75. If his grades for the first 4 tests are 90, 80, 62 and 71, what was his grade for his 5th test?

Practice 4

Mark and Sandra collected seashells from the beach. They each collected four seashells. The mean of the masses of the rocks that Sandra collected is 1 gram more than the mean of the masses of seashells that Mark collected. What is the value of x?

	Masses (grams)			
Mark	12.4	10.2	12.0	14.2
Sandra	13.0	10.6	11.7	x

Median, Mode, & Range

Median: The middle number in a set of numbers when arranged in order numerically.
Mode: The number that appears most often. It is possibly to have more than one mode.
Range: The difference between the largest number and the smallest number.

2.2 Data & Probability

Example

Mary had the following bowling scores: 125, 215, 136, 195, and 202. How much greater is the mean score than the median?

$$125, 215, 136, 195, 202$$

To find the median, put the scores in order:

$$125, 136, \boxed{195}, 202, 215$$

median = 195

$$\text{mean} = \frac{125+136+195+202+215}{5}$$

$$= \frac{873}{5} = \boxed{174.6}$$

$$195 - 174.6 = \boxed{20.4}$$

Mean, Median, Mode and Range of Data from a Table

Mean from a Table

Tests Scores	# of students
100	1
90	3
80	5
70	0
60	1
50	0

To find the mean from a table, total all of the rows and then divide by the total frequency of values.

We can find the total of the values by multiplying each value by the frequency then adding.

2.2 Data & Probability

In the table above, there is one 100, three 90s, five 80s, etc. Instead of adding them individually, we can find the total of each row.

Tests Scores	# of students	
100	× 1	100
90	× 3	270
80	× 5	400
70	× 0	0
60	× 1	60
50	× 0	0

Then we can add up those totals to get 830, and we can find the total number of values by adding up the frequency.

Tests Scores	# of students	
100	× 1	100
90	× 3	270
80	× 5	400
70	× 0	0
60	× 1	60
50	× 0	0
	10	830

Finally, we can find the mean (average)

$$\frac{830}{10} = 83$$

Practice 5

Tests Scores	# of students
100	3
90	7
80	4
70	6

What is the mean test score in the table above?

Median from a Table

To find the median, we don't want to write out all of the values. Instead, we want to determine which term will be the middle term from the table.

To find which term will be the median, use the following formula

$$Median\ Term = \frac{n+1}{2}$$

Where *n* is the number of terms. Note: If there is an even number of terms, we will get an answer that ends in ".5". This means the median is the average of the numbers in the places before and after.

Example

If there are 13 numbers, which one will be the median?

$$\frac{13+1}{2} = \frac{14}{2} = 7$$

7th term

2.2 Data & Probability

Example

If there are 14 terms, which one will be the median?

$$\frac{14+1}{2} = \frac{15}{2} = 7.5$$

Avg of the 7th & 8th terms

Example

Tests Scores	# of students
100	15
90	30
80	50
70	10
60	5
50	20

Based on the data in the table above, what is the median test score?

First let's find out how many terms there are, then what term the median is.

Tests Scores	# of students
100	15
90	30
80	50
70	10
60	5
50	20

130 terms

$$\frac{130+1}{2} = 65.5$$

Avg of 65th & 66th terms

Now, we have to find the 65th and 66th terms. Let's start counting from the top.

Tests Scores	# of students
100	15
90	30
80	50
70	10
60	5
50	20

15
45
95 ← 80 is the 46th through 95th term, so it is also the 65th and 66th

Let's also count from the bottom to be certain.

Tests Scores	# of students
100	15
90	30
80	50
70	10
60	5
50	20

85 ←
35
25
20

80 is the 36th through 85th, so it is the 65th and 66th

The median in 80, because the average of 80 and 80 is 80.

Practice 6

Tests Scores	# of students
100	3
90	5
80	2
70	9

What is the median test score in the table above?

Mode from a Table

Tests Scores	# of students
100	1
90	3
80	5
70	0
60	1
50	0

Mode is the easiest to find from a table, but still trips up some students.

The value with the greatest frequency is the mode, so in this case 80 is the mode because 5 students scored an 80 (the frequency is 5).

Some student might get tripped up and pick 0 or 1 because they appear the most, twice.

However, we have to realize that the second column represents frequencies.

Really, this is the data in the table:
100, 90, 90, 90, 80, 80, 80, 80, 80, 60

Now, it is clearer that the mode is 80.

Practice 7

Tests Scores	# of students
100	3
90	7
80	4
70	6

What is the mode test score in the table above?

Range from a Table

Tests Scores	# of students
100	1
90	3
80	5
70	0
60	1
50	0

Finding the range from a table is fairly straight forward, simply find the difference between the highest value and the lowest.

Be certain to subtract values and not frequencies.

Also, make sure the value exists in the data set. For example, if we look at the table above, it looks like 50 is the lowest value, so the range would be $100 - 50 = 50$. However, there are no 50s (the frequency is 0), so the lowest test score is actually 60.

The range is $100 - 60 = 40$.

Practice 8

The table below shows the number of houses that sold for different price values in the town of North Fakeness last month. How much greater was the mode sale price than the median sale price?

Sale Price ($)	Frequency
350,000	6
400,000	3
450,000	7
500,000	8
550,000	12

Drawing Appropriate Conclusions

One of the most important things to remember about drawing conclusions from a survey is that we can only infer what it <u>likely</u> true about the entire population of <u>that group</u>.

For example, if a survey of 50 8th graders from a school in New York City reveals that 40% of the students surveyed like football more than baseball, we can infer that it is likely that 40% of the entire 8th grade class in that school likes football more than baseball. However, it would be in correct to apply that information to the entire school since only 8th graders were surveyed, and it would be wrong to apply that information to all 8th graders in New York City because only 8th graders from one school were surveyed.

Practice 9

In a small town there are two types of owls, A-owls and B-owls. A-owls have a slightly bigger beak but a smaller wingspan. To study the owl population of the small town, a researcher randomly caught 50 owls, studied them quickly, and then released them back into the wild. 35 out of the 50 owls were A-owls. Based on the random sample, which of the following conclusions can appropriately be made?
  A) If there are 5,000 owls in the small town, then 3,500 of them will likely be A-owls.
  B) If there are 5,000 owls in the small town, then 3,500 of them will likely be B-owls.
  C) There are more A-owls that B-owls in the USA.
  D) Bird with bigger beaks are more likely to be caught by a researcher than birds with smaller beaks.

Filling in Tables

Sometimes data will be presented in a table. In those tables one column and/or one row may represent totals.

The values should add up correctly and give the right totals.

For example, let's look at the following table

	Saw the Movie	Didn't See the Movie	Total
Men	58	192	250
Women	238	12	250
Total	296	204	500

	Saw the Movie	Didn't See the Movie	Total
Men	58	192	250
Women	238	12	250
Total	296	204	500

The total number of people who saw the movie (296) equals the sum of number of men who saw it (58) and the number of women who saw it (238).

The total number of people who didn't see the movie (204) equals the sum of number of men who didn't see it (192) and the number of women who didn't see it (12).

The total number of people (500) is the sum of the total number of men (250) and the total number of women (250).

	Saw the Movie	Didn't See the Movie	Total
Men	58	192	250
Women	238	12	250
Total	296	204	500

The total number of men (250) equals the sum of the number of men who saw the movie (58) and the number of men who didn't see the movie (192).

The total number of women (250) equals the sum of the number of women who saw the movie (238) and the number of women who didn't see the movie (204).

The total number of people (500) equals the sum of the number people who saw the movie (296) and the sum of the number of people who didn't see the movie (204).

Since we can add up the values, we can solve for missing values.

Practice 10

	Male	Female	Total
Arabian	45		94
Clydesdale		72	
Total			216

The table above shows the type of and gender of the horses at specific farm in North Carolina. Based on the data in the table above, how many horses are male Clydesdales?

Probability

Probability is the likeliness of something occurring.

For example, if you roll a die, there is a $1/6$ chance of it landing on 3.

$$Probabilty = \frac{\# \; of \; favorable \; outcomes}{total \; possible \; outcomes}$$

For rolling a 3, there is only one 3 on a die, so the number of favorable outcomes is 1. There are 6 possible outcomes, so the number of total possible outcomes is 6. Therefore, the probability is $1/6$.

Probability can be expressed as a fraction, a decimal or a percent.

$$\frac{1}{6} = 0.167 = 16.7\%$$

SUPER TIP
Many times on the SAT, probability questions will be based on a table of data. It is very important to read the question carefully to identify the total possible outcomes (out of which group we are finding the probability of something occurring).

Example

Television Programs Watched Each Week

	None	1 to 3	4 or more	Total
Group A	5	38	57	100
Group B	7	45	48	100
Total	12	83	105	200

For a science project, a student interviewed 200 people. Group A consisted of 100 adults and Group B consisted of 100 high school students.

Part 1
If a person is chosen at random from Group A, what is the probability that the person watches 4 or more television programs each week?

2.2 Data & Probability

Television Programs Watched Each Week

	None	1 to 3	4 or more	Total
Group A	5	38	(57)	(100)
Group B	7	45	48	100
Total	12	83	105	200

Group A & watches 4 or more → 57

Total of Group A → 100

$$\boxed{\dfrac{57}{100}}$$

Part 2

If a person is chosen at random from those who watch at least 1 television program per week, what is the probability that the person belonged to Group B?

Television Programs Watched Each Week

	None	1 to 3	4 or more	Total
Group A	5	38	57	100
Group B	7	45	48	100
Total	12	83	105	200

Watch at least 1 television program per week & Group B: 93

Watch at least 1 television program per week: 188

$$\boxed{\dfrac{93}{188}}$$

Part 3
If a person who participated in the science project is chosen at random, what is the probability that the person was from Group A and watched 1 to 3 television programs per week?

Television Programs Watched Each Week

	None	1 to 3	4 or more	Total
Group A	5	38	57	100
Group B	7	45	48	100
Total	12	83	105	200

Group A & watched 1 to 3 television programs

participated

$$\frac{38}{200} = \boxed{\frac{19}{100}}$$

Practice 11

	6th Graders	7th Graders	8th Graders	Total
School A	345	395	326	1,066
School B	410	445	432	1,287
Total	755	840	758	2,353

The table above shows the number of 6th, 7th, and 8th graders at two different middle schools.

Part 1
If a student from School A is chosen at random, what is the probability that the student will be a 6th grader?

Part 2
If a 7th or 8th grader is chosen at random from either of the two schools, what is the probability that the student will be from School B?

2.2 Data & Probability

Standard Deviation

In many cases, values tend to be centrally located.

For example, the test grades of a class might be as follows:

Test Grade	Frequency
70	2
75	3
80	5
85	12
90	7
95	2
100	1

The average test grade in the class is 84.5. From the table, we can see that most of the test grades are close to 84.5.

A dot plot of the data would give us the following:

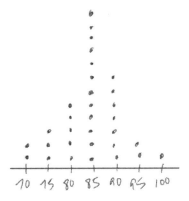

If follows a bell shape.

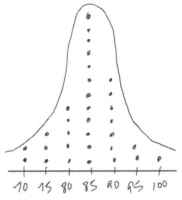

2.2 Data & Probability

When data is normally distributed, we can use standard deviation to make estimates about the data. Two concepts that come up on the SAT are: about 68% of the values are estimated to be within one standard deviation of the mean and about 95% of the values are estimated to be within two standard deviation of the mean.

For example, if the mean chemistry final exam score for a school is 78 and the standard deviation is 6, we can estimate that 65% of the students scored between 72 (6 less than the mean) and 84 (6 greater than the mean). 95% of the values will be within two standard deviations (12) of the mean, so we can estimate that 95% of the students scored between 66 (12 less than the mean) and 90 (12 more than the mean).

Below is a diagram to help show the concept visually.

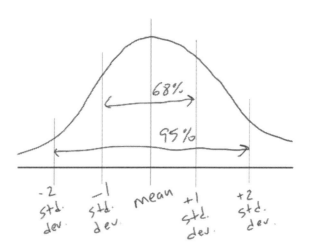

2.2 Data & Probability

SUPER TIP
The closer the values are to the mean, the smaller the standard deviation.

For example, below are the grades for two classes. Both classes have 23 students, a low score of 75, and a high score of 100. However, they have different standard deviations.

Class A		Class B	
Test Score	Frequency	Test Score	Frequency
75	1	75	5
80	3	80	4
85	5	85	2
90	8	90	5
95	4	95	3
100	2	100	4

Most of the scores in Class A are between 85 and 95. But the scores in Class B are spread throughout the range. As a result, the standard deviation of Class A's scores is smaller than the standard deviation of Class B's scores.

Practice 12

The weights of 100 volunteers who took part in a health study were recorded. The mean weight was 185 pounds, and the standard deviation was 8 pounds. Which of the following ranges or weights would it be reasonable to assume that 64 of the volunteers' weights, w, fall within?

A) $181 < w < 189$
B) $177 < w < 185$
C) $185 < w < 193$
D) $177 < w < 193$

2.2 Data & Probability

Average Increase/Decrease

To find the average increase or decrease of a value over time, we just have to focus on the initial and final values.

Let's look at this graph that shows the price of an item over time.

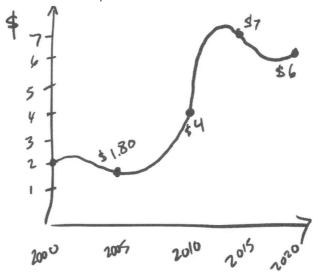

The price changed at different rates at different times. In fact, at times the price was increasing and at other times it was decreasing.

 SUPER TIP
We can find the average increase/decrease by finding the average rate of change by using the slope formula. In most cases, the value changes with time, so the values will be treated as y-values and the times will be treated as x-value.

We can find the average increase or decrease by finding the slope of the line drawn from start to finish.

2.2 Data & Probability

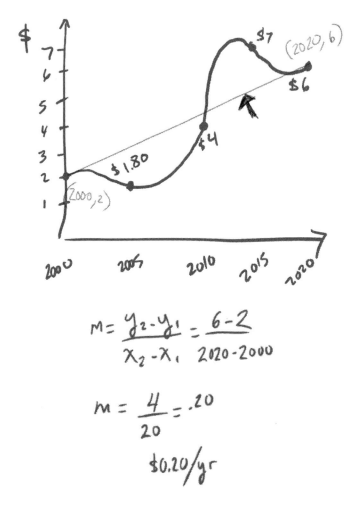

$$m = \frac{y_2 - y_1}{x_2 - x_1} = \frac{6-2}{2020-2000}$$

$$m = \frac{4}{20} = .20$$

$0.20/yr$

The average increase is $0.20/year.

We can find the average change from a table also.

2.2 Data & Probability

Example

Year	Average Home Price ($)
1970	180,000
1980	195,000
1990	220,000
2000	250,000
2010	205,000
2020	230,000

The table above shows the average home prices in Makebelieveville. What is the average annual increase in average home prices from 1980 to 2010?

In 1980, Avg $195,000
In 2010, Avg $205,000

$$\frac{205,000 - 195,000}{2010 - 1980}$$

$$\frac{10,000}{30}$$

$333.33/yr

Practice 13

A plant is grown in a laboratory to test the effectiveness of a new plant food. Each day, the height of the plant is recorded. The data is shown in the table below. What is the average daily increase of the plant's height, in inches per day?

Day	1	2	3	4	5	6	7
Height (in.)	2.40	2.45	2.49	2.52	2.58	2.64	2.74

Practice 14

Two plants were grown in a different laboratory to test the effectiveness of different combinations of light, water and plant food. Each day the heights of the plants were recorded. The data from two of the plants under different condition are shown below. Which of the following statements are true?

Plant A

Day	Height
1	3.25
2	3.28
3	3.32
4	3.45
5	3.51

Plant B

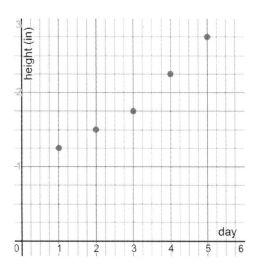

A) Plan A grew 0.76 inches per day faster than Plan B
B) Plant B grew 0.44 inches per day faster than Plant A
C) Plant B grew 0.31 inches per day faster than Plant A.
D) Plant A and Plant B grew at the same rate

Homework

Homework 1

In order to determine if a new weight-loss pill is successful in causing weight-loss, a research study was conducted. From a large population of people who wanted to lose weight, 500 participants were selected at random. Half of the participants were randomly assigned to receive the new weight-loss pill, and the other half did not receive the pill. The resulting data showed that participants who received the pill lost more weight than the participants who didn't. Based on the design and results of the study, which of the following is an appropriate conclusion?

A) The new weight-loss pill is better than all other weight-loss treatments.
B) The new weight-loss pill will work for anyone who takes it.
C) The new weight-loss poll is likely to help people who use it lose weight.
D) The new weight-loss poll will cause a substantial amount of weight-loss.

Homework 2

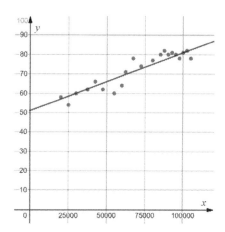

A survey was conducted that asked people to rate their happiness on a scale of 0 to 100. The average ratings for each salary amount, y, was computed and plotted along with the salary, x. The line of best fit is also shown and has the equation $y = \frac{3}{10,000}x + 51,000$. Which of the following best explains how the number $\frac{3}{10,000}$ in the equation relates to the scatterplot?

A) The lowest happiness rating is about $\frac{3}{10,000}$.
B) It can be estimated that the happiness rating increases by 3 for every additional $10,000 in salary.
C) The happiness rating for someone with no income would be estimated to be $\frac{3}{10,000}$.
D) Only 3 out of every 10,000 people were surveyed.

2.2 Data & Probability

Practice questions Homework 3, 4 and 5 refer to the following information.

	Engineering	Liberal Arts	Medical	Law	Business	Total
High School A	252	43	176	102	74	647
High School B	58	75	295	202	54	684
High School C	8	54	2	7	24	95
High School D	24	653	72	35	430	1,214
Total	342	825	545	346	582	2,640

The table above shows the preferred fields of study of high school juniors from four different high schools.

Homework 3

Based on the table, if a student who prefers the medical field is chosen at random, which of the following is closest to the probability that the student is from High School B?

A) 0.111
B) 0.206
C) 0.431
D) 0.541

Homework 4

Based on the table, if a student is chosen at random from High School B or High School C, which of the following is closest to the probability that the student prefers liberal arts?

A) 0.156
B) 0.166
C) 0.313
D) 0.490

Homework 5

Based on the table, if a student is chosen at random, which of the following is closest to the probability that the student is from High School B and prefers engineering or is from High School D and prefers law?

A) 0.035
B) 0.049
C) 0.135
D) 0.719

2.2 Answers to Practice Problems (Data & Probability)

Practice 1: C

Where the survey was given. Since Chloe interviewed students who attended a football game, they are more likely to support renovating the sports field than the overall student population. The sample size is fine. People are expected to not participate, and she can't control it. For a survey, it isn't necessary to survey everyone.

Practice 2: C

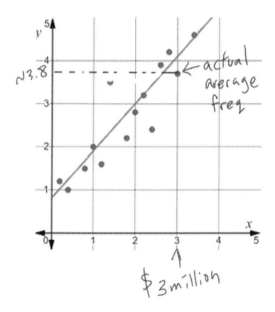

Practice 3: 72

Sum of 5 tests is 75

Sum = (Avg)(#)

Sum = (75)(5)

Sum = 375 ← all 5 tests

We can find the sum of the first 4

90 + 80 + 62 + 71 = 303 ← first 4

375 − 303 = [72] ← 5th

2.2 Data & Probability

Practice 4: 17.5 or 35/2

Calculate the mean (avg.) mass of Mark's seashells

$$\frac{12.4 + 10.2 + 12.0 + 14.2}{4} = \frac{48.8}{4}$$

$$= 12.2$$

Mean of Sandra's is 1 more than Mark's, so

Sandra's mean = 13.2

$$Sum = (Avg)(\#)$$
$$Sum = (13.2)(4)$$
$$Sum = 52.8$$

Sandra's add up to 52.8

3 of them (13, 10.6, 11.7) add up to 35.3

Missing seashell mass:

$$52.8 - 35.3 = \boxed{17.5}$$

Practice 5: 83.5

Tests Scores	# of students	
100	3	300
90	7	630
80	4	320
70	6	420
	20	1670

$$\frac{1670}{20} = 83.5$$

Practice 6: 80

Tests Scores	# of students
100	3
90	5
80	2
70	9
	19

$$\frac{n+1}{2} = \frac{19+1}{2} = 10$$

10th term is the median

Tests Scores	# of students	
100	3	3
90	5	8
80	2	10
70	9	19

80 is the 9th & 10th term, so 80 is the median

Practice 7: 90

Mode is the one that appears most often. There are seven 90s, so 90 is the mode.

Practice 8: 50,000

Sale Price ($)	Frequency
350,000	6
400,000	3
450,000	7
500,000	8
550,000	12

Total: 36

$\frac{36+1}{2} = \frac{37}{2} = 1$

Median is aver. 18th + 19th te

Let's count up from the bottom.

Sale Price ($)	Frequency
350,000	6
400,000	3
450,000	7
500,000	8
550,000	12

500,000 is the 1 through 20th ten it is the 18th & 19th

The median is 500,000.

The mode is the one that appears the most, the most frequent number. 550,000 has a frequency of 12 which is the most, so 550,000 is the mode.

The mode is 50,000 more than the median.

Practice 9: A

Based on the sample, if there are 5,000 owls total, we can estimate the number of A-owls and B-owls.

Set up a proportion to find the # of A-owls if there are 5,000 owls.

$\frac{\text{A-owl}}{\text{Total}} \quad \frac{35}{50} = \frac{x}{5000}$

$175000 = 50x$

$\frac{175000}{50} = \frac{50x}{50}$

$3,500 = x$

3,500 A-owls
1,500 B-owls

We can estimate that if there are 5,000 owls, then 3,500 will likely be A-owls. Choice C may appear to be correct because we estimate there to be more A-owls than B-owls. However, there are two things that make it wrong. Choice C definitively says that there are more, which we don't know for sure. Also, choice C states that there are more A-owls than B-owls in the USA, but we only have enough data to make an assumption about the one town.

2.2 Data & Probability

Practice 10: 50

Based on the table, we can find the total number of Clydesdales since we know there are 216 total horses and 94 Arabian horses.

	Male	Female	Total
Arabian	45		94
Clydesdale		72	+122
Total			216

There must be 122 Clydesdales.

Since there are 122 total Clydesdales and 72 of them are female, we can find the number of male Clydesdales.

	Male	Female	Total
Arabian	45		94
Clydesdale	50 +	72 =	122
Total			216

There are 50 male Clydesdales.

Practice: 11

Part 1: 345/1,066

	6th Graders	7th Graders	8th Graders	Total
School A	345	395	326	1,066
School B	410	445	432	1,287
Total	755	840	758	2,353

School A & 6th grade

out of

$$\frac{345}{1,066}$$

Part 2: 877/1,598

	6th Graders	7th Graders	8th Graders	Total
School A	345	395	326	1,066
School B	410	445	432	1,287
Total	755	840	758	2,353

7th & 8th from School B
445 + 432 = 877

7th or 8th grader
840 + 758 = 1598

$$\frac{877}{1598}$$

2.2 Data & Probability

Practice 12: D

64% of the data should fall within one standard deviation of the mean. There are 100 volunteers, so 64% would be 100 volunteers.

The mean is 185 and the standard deviation is 8, so the range would be from 177 (8 less than 185) to 192 (8 more than 185).

Practice 13: 0.57

Day 1: 2.40 in.

Day 7: 2.74 in.

$$\frac{\text{change in height}}{\text{change in time}}$$

$$\frac{2.74 - 2.40}{7 - 1}$$

$$\frac{0.34}{6}$$

0.57 in/day

Practice 14: C

$$\frac{\text{Change in height}}{\text{Change in days}}$$

Plant A
$$\frac{3.51 - 3.25}{5 - 1}$$
$$\frac{0.26}{4}$$
0.065 in/day

Plant B
$$\frac{2.75 - 1.25}{5 - 1}$$
$$\frac{1.5}{4}$$
0.375 in/day

0.375 - 0.065
0.31 in/day

Plant B grew 0.31 in/day faster than Plant A

Homework 1: C

It is likely to help because the participants who used it lost more weight than the participants who didn't. We can't jump to the conclusion in choice A that it's better than other treatments because we aren't given any information about other treatments. We can't choose B because it states that it will work for anyone who takes it, but that's too strong of a statement to make. There can be exceptions. We can't choose choice D because we don't know how much weight-loss it will cause.

Homework 2: B

In the equation $y = \frac{3}{10,000}x + 51,000$, the number $\frac{3}{10,000}$ represents the slope of the trend line. Slope tells us the average rate of change of y over x. In this case y is the average happiness rating and x is the salary.

2.2 Data & Probability

Homework 3: D

Chosen out of: prefers medical (545)
HS B students who prefer Med.: 295

	Engineering	Liberal Arts	Medical	Law	Business	Total
High School A	252	43	176	102	74	647
High School B	58	75	295	202	54	684
High School C	8	54	2	7	24	95
High School D	24	653	72	35	430	1,214
Total	342	825	545	346	582	2,640

$$\frac{295}{545} = \boxed{0.541}$$

Homework 4: B

Student from HS B or HS C chosen at random.
out of HS B + HS C
684 + 95 = 779

	Engineering	Liberal Arts	Medical	Law	Business	Total
High School A	252	43	176	102	74	647
High School B	58	75	295	202	54	684
High School C	8	54	2	7	24	95
High School D	24	653	72	35	430	1,214
Total	342	825	545	346	582	2,640

HS B or HS C that prefers
Liberal Arts: 75 + 54 = 129

$$\frac{129}{779} = \boxed{0.166}$$

Homework 5: A

Out of all students: 2640

	Engineering	Liberal Arts	Medical	Law	Business	Total
High School A	252	43	176	102	74	647
High School B	58	75	295	202	54	684
High School C	8	54	2	7	24	95
High School D	24	653	72	35	430	1,214
Total	342	825	545	346	582	2,640

HS B + Engineering: 58
HS D + Law: 35

HS B + Eng or HS D + Law
58 + 35
93

$$\frac{93}{2640} = \boxed{0.035}$$

Free Goodwill

People who help others (with zero expectation) experience <u>higher levels of fulfillment, live longer, and make more money</u>.

I'd like to create the opportunity to deliver this value to you during your studying experience.

If you have found this book valuable so far, please take a brief moment right now to leave an honest review of the book and its contents. It will cost you $0, take less than 60 seconds, and earn you some free goodwill.

Your review will help other students reach their goals, just like this book is helping you reach yours.

To easily review this book, scan here:

Lesson 3

Want to break a 1400?

We love working with students who are serious about their SAT scores - that means you!

Special Tutoring & Test Prep Offer for You

 caddellprep.com/sboffer

3.1 Evaluating Functions

Basic Functions

Let's start by looking at the equation of a line, $y = mx + b$.

We can find points on the line by substituting in values for x and evaluating it to find the associated values of y.

For example, if we have the equation $y = 2x + 1$ we can substitute in some values for x and find the associated y-values.

When $x = 3$, we would have $y = 2(3) + 1 = 7$. The value of the function would be 7 when x is 3.

We can find many different values for y by substituting different values for x. Here is a table showing different x-values and different y-values (function values).

x	$2x + 1$	y
0	$2(0) + 1$	1
1	$2(1) + 1$	3
2	$2(2) + 1$	5
3	$2(3) + 1$	7
4	$2(4) + 1$	9

We can plot those points on a graph

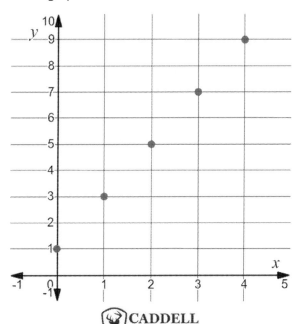

3.1 Evaluating Functions

There are more values to the function than just the ones we evaluated. Every x-value can be evaluated for this function. Here are some more:

x	$2x+1$	y
2.1	2(2.1) + 1	5.2
2.2	2(2.2) + 1	5.4
2.3	2(2.3) + 1	5.6
2.4	2(2.4) + 1	5.8
2.5	2(2.5) + 1	6.0
2.6	2(2.6) + 1	6.2

Let's include those points on the graph also.

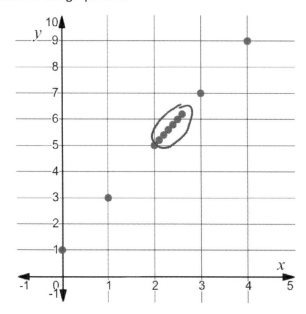

As you can see, the function is taking shape. We can see a straight line forming. Here is the graph of the function $y = 2x + 1$ along with the plotted points. If all of the points were graphed for when x equals 2.00001, 2.00002, etc. and even smaller values of x, we would end up with a continuous function.

3.1 Evaluating Functions

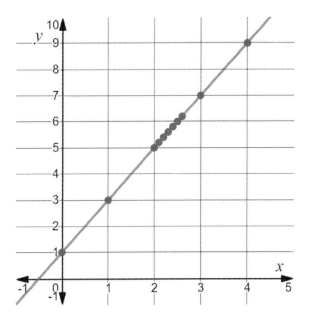

Practice 1

Evaluate the function $y = x^2 - 3$ at the points stated in the table below.

x	$x^2 - 3$	y
0		
1		
2		

Plot the points on the graph below

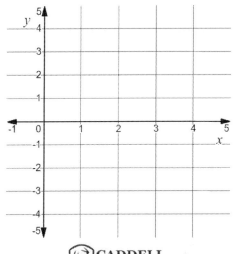

3.1 Evaluating Functions

$f(x)$, $g(x)$, and $h(x)$

We looked at the simple function $y = 2x - 1$. It can be written as $f(x) = 2x - 1$, $g(x) = 2x - 1$, $h(x) = 2x - 1$, $p(x) = 2x - 1$, $q(x) = 2x - 1$, etc.

Don't be confused when you see the notation $f(x)$, it is similar to y.

$f(x)$ is the notation used to refer to the function when it is in terms of x.

However, if we want to show the value of a function at a specific x-value, we would substitute the value in for x.

For example

$$f(x) = -2x - 5$$
$$f(3) = -2(3) - 5$$
$$f(3) = -11$$

Let's look at a table

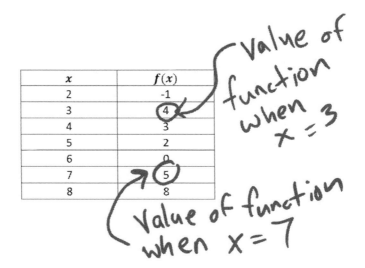

If we want to find out what $f(3)$ or what the value of the function is when $x = 3$, we would look at the value of $f(x)$ when the x-value is 3. In this case $f(3) = 4$.

If we want to find out what $f(7)$ or what the value of the function is when $x = 7$, we would look at the value of $f(x)$ when the x-value is 7. In this case $f(7) = 5$.

3.1 Evaluating Functions

Practice 2

x	$f(x)$
1	5
2	-2
3	1
4	2
5	11
6	4
7	-4

Based on the table above,

a) what is the value of the function when $x = 4$?
b) What is $f(1)$?
c) If $f(a) = 1$, what is a?

Evaluating a Function from a Graph

A graph of a function, $f(x)$, will likely have the vertical axis labeled $f(x)$ instead of y. The horizontal axis will be labeled x.

A graph of $s(t)$ will likely have the vertical axis labeled $s(t)$ instead of y and the horizontal axis labeled t instead of x.

Here is an example.

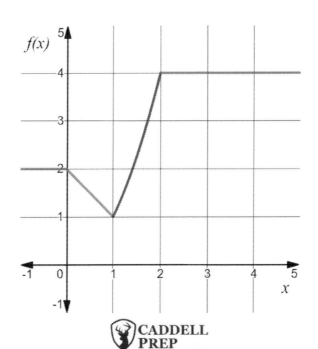

3.1 Evaluating Functions

We can see that the value of the graph changes at different spots on the graph.

The value of $f(x)$ is 2 when x is -1.

$f(2) = 4$, $f(2.2) = 4$, $f(3) = 4$ and $f(4) = 4$. In fact, the value of the function is 4 when x is equal to or greater than 2 and less than or equal to 5.

Example

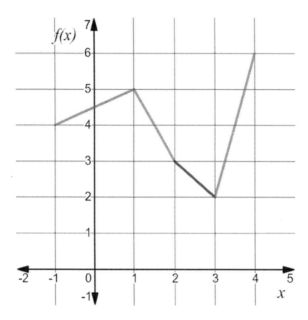

Based on the graph above, what is

 a) $f(2)$?
 b) The value of the function when x is 3?
 c) The value of x when $f(x)$ is 5?

3.1 Evaluating Functions

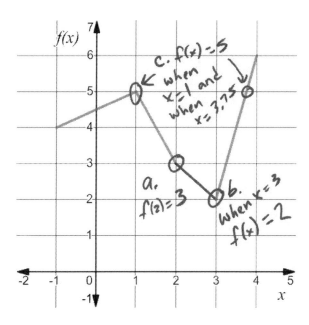

a. $f(2) = 3$
b. when $x = 3$ $f(x) = 2$
c. $f(x) = 5$ when $x = 1$ and when $x = 3.75$

Practice 3

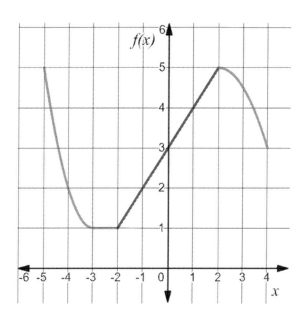

Based on the graph above

a) $f(-2.5) =?$
b) $f(1) =?$
c) How many times does $f(x) = 4$?
d) If $f(a) = f(-1)$, what is the value of a, $a \neq -1$?

3.1 Evaluating Functions Homework

Homework 1

$f(x) = 2x - 5$

x	$g(x)$
0	-2
1	3
2	1
3	-3
4	6

Based on the information above, what is $f(2) - g(3)$?

Homework 2

$h(x) = x^2 - 4$

x	$p(x)$
0	4
1	3
2	2
3	-3
4	-2

Based on the information above, if $p(a) = 4$, what is $h(a)$?

Homework 3

$f(t) = 2t^2 - 5t$ and $g(t) = 4t - 1$. What is $f(g(1))$?

3.1 Answers to Practice Problems (Evaluating Functions)

Practice 1

Evaluate the function $y = x^2 - 3$ at the points stated in the table below.

x	$x^2 - 3$	y
0	$(0)^2 - 3$	-3
1	$(1)^2 - 3$	-2
2	$(2)^2 - 3$	1

Plot the points on the graph below

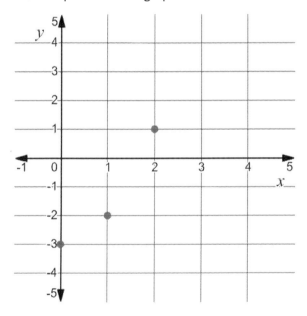

Practice 2

x	$f(x)$
1	5
2	-2
3	1
4	2
5	11
6	4
7	-4

Based on the table above,

a) what is the value of the function when $x = 4$?

2. In the table above, look at the left column to identify when $x = 4$. When $x = 4$, the value of the function is 2.

b) what is $f(1)$?

5. $f(1)$ is the value of $f(x)$ when x is 1. In the table above, look at the left column to identify when $x = 1$. When $x = 1$, the value of the function is 5.

c) if $f(a) = 1$, what is a?

3. $f(a) = 1$ means the value of the function $f(x)$ is 1 at an x-value of a. Based on the table, $f(x)$ is 1 only when x is 3, so a must equal 3.

Practice 3

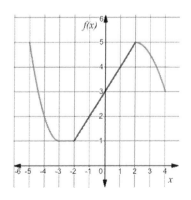

Based on the graph above

3.1 Evaluating Functions

a) $f(-2.5) = 1$

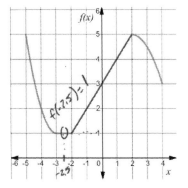

b) $f(1) = 4$

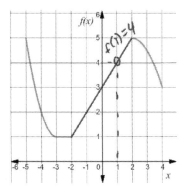

c) How many times does $f(x) = 4$? 3

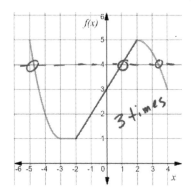

3 times

d) If $f(a) = f(-1)$, what is the value of a, $a \neq -1$? -4

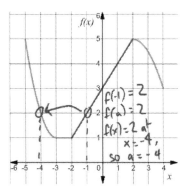

$f(-1) = 2$
$f(a) = 2$
$f(x) = 2$ at $x = -4$,
so $a = -4$

3.1 Evaluating Functions

Homework 1

$f(x) = 2x - 5$
$f(2) = 2(2) - 5$
$f(2) = 4 - 5$
$f(2) = -1$

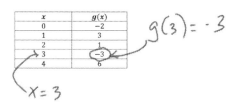

$g(3) = -3$
$x = 3$

$f(2) - g(3)$
$-1 - -3$
$\boxed{2}$

Homework 2

$p(a) = 4$
$a = ?$

$p(x) = 4$ when $x = 0$

$p(0) = 4$
so $a = 0$

Now, we can find $h(a)$, which is $h(0)$
$h(x) = x^2 - 4$
$h(0) = 0^2 - 4 = \boxed{-4}$

Homework 3

$f(g(1))$

need to solve $g(1)$ first

$g(t) = 4t - 1$
$g(1) = 4(1) - 1$
$g(1) = 3$

Now, we can find $f(g(1))$,

$f(g(1)) = f(3)$

3.1 Evaluating Functions

$f(t) = 2t^2 - 5t$

$f(3) = 2(3)^2 - 5(3)$

$f(3) = 2(9) - 15$

$f(3) = 18 - 15$

$f(3) = \boxed{3}$

3.2 Linear functions

Equation of a Line

The equation of a line is typically written in slope-intercept form, $y = mx + b$.

It is called slope-intercept form because you can easily identify the slope and y-intercept.

$$y = mx + b$$

where m is the slope and b is the y-intercept

Example

In the equation $y = 2x + 3$, the slope is 2 and the y-intercept is 3.

A slope of 2 really means the slope is $\frac{2}{1}$. As you move from left to right, the line goes up 2 and right 1.

A y-intercept of 3 means the slope intersects the y-axis at 3. This is a good starting point when graphing.

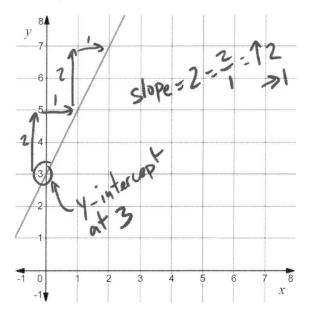

3.2 Linear Functions

Example

In the equation $y = -\frac{3}{2}x + 1$, the slope is $-\frac{3}{2}$ and the y-intercept is 1.

A slope of $-\frac{3}{2}$ means as you move from left to right, the line goes down 3 and right 2.

A y-intercept of 1 means the slope intersects the y-axis at 1. This is a good starting point when graphing.

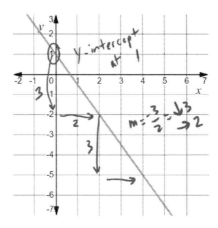

Practice 1

Sketch $y = \frac{1}{3}x - 1$

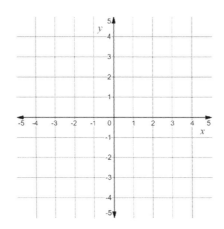

3.2 Linear Functions

Practice 2

Sketch $y = -3x + 4$

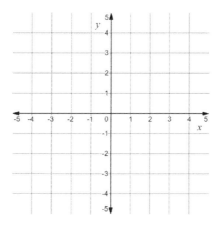

Parallel and Perpendicular Lines

Lines that are parallel have the same slope.

For example, if the equation of one line is $y = 3x - 9$, a line parallel to it could have the equation

$y = 3x + 742$. As long as the lines have the same slope and different y-intercepts, they're parallel.

Lines that are perpendicular, have slopes that are the negative reciprocal of each other.

For example, if the slope of one line is $\frac{2}{5}$, then the slope of a line perpendicular to it will be $-\frac{5}{2}$.

Practice 3

Write the equation of a line that is parallel to the line with the equation $y = \frac{3}{2}x + 7$ and passes through the point $(4,5)$.

3.2 Linear Functions

Linear Functions

Linear functions can be written in a form similar to the equation of a line, $y = mx + b$.

Linear functions are functions that increase or decrease at a constant rate, such as the amount of money paid for a gym membership. The membership may require an initial payment to join, followed by a monthly payment. The total amount of money paid increases at a constant rate since each month the total increases by the set monthly payment.

For example, it may cost $30 to join a gym plus $15 each month. After one month of membership you may have paid $45 ($30 to join and $15 monthly payment). The next month you'll pay another $15, so the total paid will then be $60. The following month will be another $15, so the total paid will then be $75. Each month the total increases by $15. Let's graph it.

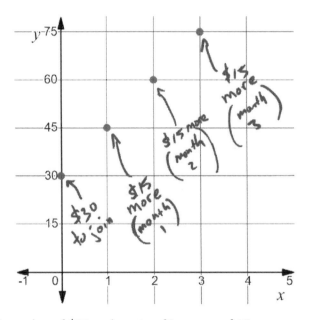

Since we have a starting value of $30 and a rate of increase of 15, we can use the $y = 15x + 30$ to represent the function. Below is a graph including the function and points.

3.2 Linear Functions

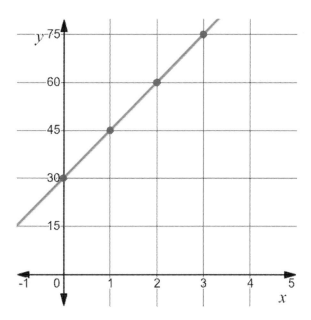

The key point is the if something increases at a constant rate, it can be modeled using the equation of a line as a linear function. The rate of change will be the slope and then initial value is typically the y-intercept.

Note about the variables.

Keep in mind that the variables used in a linear function do not have to be x and y. The variables can be any letter.

In the previous example, the total cost may be represented by C and each month by m. The function would be written as $C = 15m + 30$. In this case m is the variable for number of months and 30 is the slope.

The function is sometimes also written as $C(m)$ instead of just C. $C(m)$ is simply just a way of stating that the cost C is dependent on the months, m. In other words, C is a function of m.

Example

A company's monthly expense is $20,000 each month for rent and other fixed costs. The products that the company creates cost $120 to produce. Write a function that represents the total cost C in terms of the number of products produced, p.

3.2 Linear Functions

In this case, the cost increases at a constant rate. It increases by $120 for each product produced, so the slope is $120. Even if no products are produced, there is a cost of $20,000, so that is the starting value or y-intercept.

$$C = 120p + 20{,}000$$

Practice 4

Marcus is saving money to buy a car when he turns 18. He currently has $350 saved. Each month he saves $225 from the money he earns at his internship. Write a function that represents the total amount of money Marcus will have saved, $S(t)$, after t months.

Practice 5

Tyreek is started writing a novel a year ago. He already has written 83 pages but then stopped for a few months. He has decided to start writing again and dedicate himself to a consistent schedule. He will write the same number of pages every morning from now on. According to the new schedule, his novel will be a total of 107 pages long after four days of writing. Write a function that represents the total number of pages written, T, after d days since starting again.

Practice 6

To make the secret filling inside her famous pastries, Chef Lily uses honey. She uses a lot of honey each week, so she decided to buy a large barrel that hold 6,400 ounces. She used 5% of the honey in the barrel after one day. She uses the same amount of honey each day. Which function can represent the amount of honey left in the barrel, $h(d)$, after d days?

    A) $h(d) = 6{,}400(0.05)^d$
    B) $h(d) = 6{,}400(0.95)^d$
    C) $h(d) = 6{,}400 - 0.05d$
    D) $h(d) = 6{,}400 - 320d$

3.2 Linear Functions Homework

Homework 1

Write the equation of the line that is perpendicular to $y = 2x - 4$ and passes through the point $(6, -2)$.

Homework 2

The number of orders at a pizzeria each day can be estimated by the formula $y = 9.2h + 4$, where y is the total number of orders and h is the number of hours the pizzeria has been open. Which of the following best explains the number 9.2 in the equation.

- A) The pizzeria starts the day with 9.2 orders
- B) Each order is $9.20
- C) The pizzeria makes, on average, 9.2 pizzas per hour.
- D) The pizzeria has, on average, 9.2 orders per hour.

Homework 3

Sebastian bought a box of single-serve coffee capsules. If Sebastian uses 2 capsules per day and the box came with 92 capsules, write a function, $C(d)$, that represents the number of remaining capsules after d days.

3.2 Linear Functions

3.2 Answers to Practice Problems (Linear Functions)

Practice 1

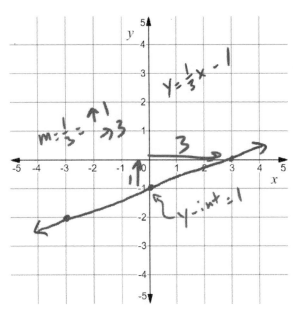

Practice 3: $y = \frac{3}{2}x - 1$

Parallel to $y = \frac{3}{2}x + 7$,

So slope $= \frac{3}{2}$

Equation will be:

$y = mx + b$

$y = \frac{3}{2}x + b$

we need to solve for b.

The line passes through $(4, 5)$, so substitute the values in, and solve for b.

$y = \frac{3}{2}x + b$

$5 = \frac{3}{2}(4) + b$

Practice 2

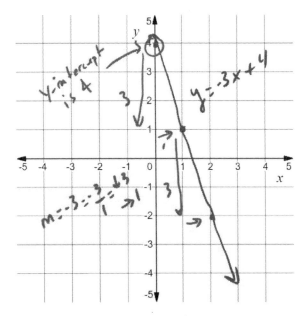

3.2 Linear Functions

$$5 = 6 + b$$
$$-6 \quad -6$$
$$-1 = b$$

Now, we have
$$y = \frac{3}{2}x - 1$$

Practice 4: $S(t) = 225t + 350$

Marcus is saving $225 each month, so the rate (slope) is $225/month. He already has $350, so that is the initial value (y-intercept).

Following the format $y = mx + b$, the function will be $S(t) = 225t + 350$.

Practice 5: $T = 6d + 83$

Tyreek will write the same number of pages each day, so this is a linear function.

He already wrote 83 pages, so the initial value (y-intercept) is 83.

We aren't directly given the rate, but we are told that after four days, the total will be 107 pages. That means he will write $107 - 83 = 24$ pages over four days, which is 6 pages per day. Therefore, the slope is 6.

We can now write the line function following the format $y = mx + b$. The function will be $T = 6d + 83$.

Practice 6: D

Chef Lily had a barrel of honey with 6,400 ounces of honey. After one day she used 5% of the honey. We can find how much honey she used by finding 5% of 6,400.

$$6{,}400 \times 0.05 = 320$$

She used 320 ounces of honey, so the amount of honey will decrease by 320 ounces each day.

She started with 6,400 ounces of honey, so that's the initial value (y-intercept).

Following the format $y = mx + b$. The function will be $h(d) = -320d + 6{,}400$ or rewritten as $h(d) = 6{,}400 - 320d$.

Homework 1: $y = -\frac{1}{2}x + 1$

$$y = 2x - 4$$
$$\text{slope} = 2 = \frac{2}{1}$$

perpendicular line would have a slope of $\frac{-1}{2}$

$$y = mx + b$$
$$y = -\frac{1}{2}x + b$$

We need to solve for b

3.2 Linear Functions

Passes through $(6, -2)$, so substitute the point in and solve for b.

$y = -\frac{1}{2}x + b$

$-2 = -\frac{1}{2}(6) + b$

$-2 = -3 + b$

$\underline{+3 \quad +3}$

$1 = b$

$y = -\frac{1}{2}x + 1$

Homework 3: $C(d) = -2d + 92$

Initial value: 92

rate of change: $\frac{-2 \text{ capsules}}{1 \text{ day}}$

$y = mx + b$

$y = -2x + 92$

$C(d) = -2d + 92$

Homework 2: D

9.2 is the slope in this equation, which is the rate of change, so choice A is out. Slope is change in y per change in x. In this case y is the number of orders, and x is really h, which is hours. Therefore, the slope is in the units orders per hour. Choice D is the answer.

3.3 Quadratic Functions

What is a Quadratic Function?

Quadratic functions have the basic format of

$$f(x) = ax^2 + bx + c$$

where a, b and c are constants.

It isn't necessary to have a bx term or a c term, but it must have an ax^2 term.

Example of quadratics are $f(x) = x^2 + 3x - 5$, $f(x) = 2x^2$, $f(x) = -3x^2 - 5$, and $f(x) = x^2 - 5$.

Graph of a Quadratic Function (Parabola)

A graph of a quadratic function is a parabola (U-shaped).

The vertex is the point on the graph where the parabola changes from decreasing to increasing or from increasing to decreasing.

Parabolas are symmetric over the axis- of-symmetry, which passes through the vertex.

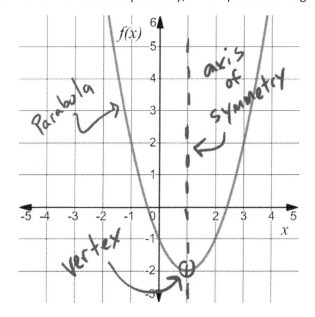

3.3 Quadratic Functions

Zeros (Roots) of a Function

The zeros, sometimes referred to as roots, of a function are the x-values that make the function (y-value) equal to zero.

We can easily identify the zeros of a function from its graph. The graph below is zero (intersects the x-axis) at -1 and 3.

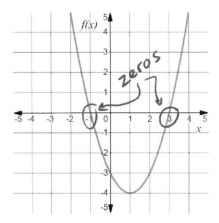

We can also find the zeros algebraically.

Practice 1

What are the zeros of the function $f(x)$ graphed below?

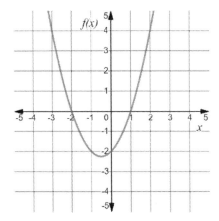

3.3 Quadratic Functions

Solve for the Zeros by Factoring

To solve for the zeros of a function, set the function equal to zero and then solve.

Example

What are the zeros of the function $f(x) = x^2 - 7x + 6$?

$$f(x) = x^2 - 7x + 6$$
$$\text{set it equal to } 0$$
$$x^2 - 7x + 6 = 0$$
$$\text{Factor}$$
$$(x \quad)(x \quad) = 0$$

the terms must multiply to $+6$ and add up to -7

Because the terms have to multiply to equal positive 6, the two terms must be the same sign (both positive or both negative). Since they have to add up to negative 7, they should both be negative.

$$x^2 - 7x + 6 = 0$$
$$(x - \quad)(x - \quad) = 0$$

$-6 \times -1 = 6$ and $-6 + -1 = -7$, so we should use -6 and -1.

3.3 Quadratic Functions

$$x^2 - 7x + 6 = 0$$
$$(x - \quad)(x - \quad) = 0$$
$$(x-6)(x-1) = 0$$

Now that we have the factors, we should set each one of the factors equal to zero and solve for x.

$$(x-6)(x-1) = 0$$

$$\begin{array}{ll} x - 6 = 0 & x - 1 = 0 \\ +6 \;\; +6 & +1 \;\; +1 \\ x = 6 & x = 1 \end{array}$$

The zeros are 6 and 1.

Let's look at a graph of $f(x) - 7x + 6$ to see how it relates to the graph.

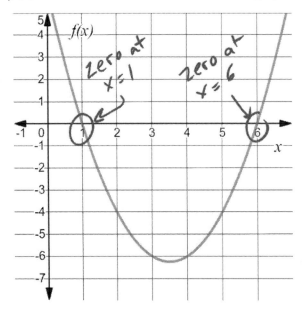

zero at $x = 1$
zero at $x = 6$

3.3 Quadratic Functions

Practice 2

What are the zeros of the function $g(x) = x^2 - 2x - 15$?

Practice 3

What are the roots of the function $h(x) = x^2 + x - 12$?

Practice 4

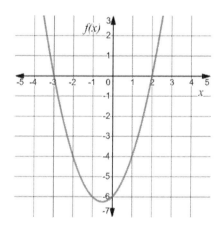

Which of the following could be the function $f(x)$ graphed above?

A) $f(x) = (x - 2)(x + 3)$
B) $f(x) = (x + 2)(x - 3)$
C) $f(x) = x^2 + 10x - 6$
D) $f(x) = x^2 - 3x + 2$

3.3 Quadratic Functions

Solve for the Zeros Using the Quadratic Formula

You can always find the zeros of a quadratic function by using the quadratic formula.

$$x = \frac{-b \pm \sqrt{b^2 - 4ac}}{2a}$$

If you can't figure out the factors or if it isn't factorable, use the quadratic formula.

Make sure to use parenthesis when you substitute the values in.

Let's look at the same function, we looked at earlier $f(x) = x^2 - 7x + 6$.

Example

What are the zeros of the function $f(x) = x^2 - 7x + 6$?

$$x^2 - 7x + 6 = 0$$

$$a = 1 \quad b = -7 \quad c = 6$$

$$\frac{-b \pm \sqrt{b^2 - 4ac}}{2a}$$

$$\frac{-(-7) \pm \sqrt{(-7)^2 - 4(1)(6)}}{2(1)}$$

After we identify the a, b, and c and substitute it in the formula, we can evaluate it.

3.3 Quadratic Functions

$$\frac{-(-7) \pm \sqrt{(-7)^2 - 4(1)(6)}}{2(1)}$$

$$\frac{7 \pm \sqrt{49 - 24}}{2}$$

$$\frac{7 \pm \sqrt{25}}{2}$$

$$\frac{7 \pm 5}{2}$$

The $\pm$ in the formula means that we have to evaluate the expression twice. Once with the $+$ and once with the $-$.

$$\frac{7 \pm 5}{2}$$

$$\frac{7+5}{2} = \frac{12}{2} = \boxed{6}$$

$$\frac{7-5}{2} = \frac{2}{2} = \boxed{1}$$

The zeros are 6 and 1.

Of course, there are times when we may end up with a radical in the answer.

Example

What are the roots of the function $f(x) = x^2 + 2x - 5$

3.3 Quadratic Functions

$$x^2 + 2x - 5 = 0$$

$a = 1 \quad b = 2 \quad c = -5$

$$\frac{-b \pm \sqrt{b^2 - 4ac}}{2a}$$

$$\frac{-(2) \pm \sqrt{(2)^2 - 4(1)(-5)}}{2(1)}$$

$$\frac{-2 \pm \sqrt{4 + 20}}{2}$$

$$\frac{-2 \pm \sqrt{24}}{2}$$

24 is not a perfect square, so the square root of 24 will be an irrational number.

We can still simplify it though.

$$\frac{-2 \pm \sqrt{24}}{2}$$

simplify $\sqrt{24}$

$\sqrt{24}$
$\sqrt{4 \cdot 6}$
$2\sqrt{6}$

$$\frac{-2 \pm 2\sqrt{6}}{2}$$

Reduce

$$\frac{-1 \pm 1\sqrt{6}}{1} = -1 \pm \sqrt{6}$$

Final Answers

$-1 + \sqrt{6}$ & $-1 - \sqrt{6}$

3.3 Quadratic Functions

Practice 5

Use the quadratic formula to find the zeros of the function $f(x) = x^2 - 2x - 1$.

One Zero & No Zeros

The graph of a quadratic function has a U shape, so it's possible that it will only touch the x-axis once or even not at all, resulting in one zero or no zeros.

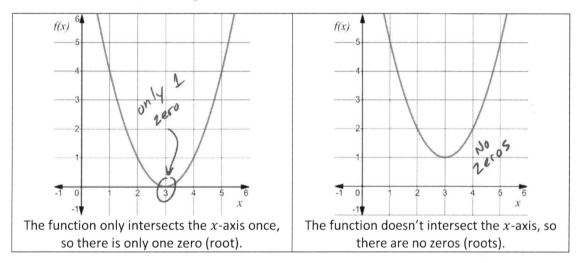

| The function only intersects the x-axis once, so there is only one zero (root). | The function doesn't intersect the x-axis, so there are no zeros (roots). |

Example of One Zero

The function $f(x) = x^2 - 6x + 9$ only has one zero. We can see by factoring or using the quadratic formula.

From factoring:

3.3 Quadratic Functions

$$x^2 - 6x + 9$$
$$(x-3)(x-3)$$

$x - 3 = 0 \quad\quad x - 3 = 0$
$+3 \ +3 \quad\quad +3 \ +3$
$x = 3 \quad\quad\quad x = 3$

repeated root
$x = 3$
(only 1 zero)

From the quadratic formula:

$$x^2 - 6x + 9$$

$$\frac{-b \pm \sqrt{b^2 - 4ac}}{2a}$$

$$\frac{-(-6) \pm \sqrt{(-6)^2 - 4(1)(9)}}{2(1)}$$

$$\frac{6 \pm \sqrt{36 - 36}}{2}$$

$$\frac{6 \pm 0}{2}$$

$$\frac{6+0}{2} = \boxed{3} \quad\quad \frac{6-0}{2} = \boxed{3}$$

Again, we have a repeated solution of 3. There is only one zero, $x = 3$.

3.3 Quadratic Functions

Example of No Zeros

The function $f(x) = x^2 - 6x + 10$ doesn't have a zero. We can't factor it, so let's look at it by using the quadratic formula.

$$x^2 - 6x + 10$$
$$\frac{-b \pm \sqrt{b^2 - 4ac}}{2a}$$
$$\frac{-(-6) \pm \sqrt{(-6)^2 - 4(1)(10)}}{2(1)}$$
$$\frac{6 \pm \sqrt{36 - 40}}{2}$$
$$\frac{6 \pm \sqrt{-4}}{2} \leftarrow \text{square root of negative \# is not real}$$

We end up with the square root of a negative, which is not real, so there are no real roots.

Finding the Number of Zeros

Sometimes on the SAT, a question will ask for the number of roots or a similar question.

The following questions are all asking the same thing:

a) To find the number of real solutions to $x^2 + 3x + 4 = 0$
b) To find the number of zeros the function $f(x) = x^2 + 3x + 4$ has
c) To find number of roots of the function $f(x) = x^2 + 3x + 4$ has

In each of the above questions, we would find the zeros using a graph, factoring, or the quadratic formula.

3.3 Quadratic Functions

Sum & Product of the Roots

To find the sum or product of the roots of a quadratic function, you could solve for the roots and then add them together to find the sum or multiply them to find the product.

The problem is that if the roots are irrational, such as $3 + \sqrt{5}$ and $3 - \sqrt{5}$, it could be a little difficult to find the sum or product.

Instead, we can use two formulas to find the sum or product of the roots immediately.

If the function is in the form $f(x) = ax^2 + bx + c$, we can use the following formulas:

$$\text{sum of roots} = \frac{-b}{a}$$

$$\text{product of roots} = \frac{c}{a}$$

Example

What are the sum and product of the roots of the function $g(x) = 2x^2 + 3x - 8$?

$$2x^2 + 3x - 8$$

$$\text{Sum} = \frac{-b}{a} = -\frac{3}{2}$$

$$\text{prod.} = \frac{c}{a} = \frac{-8}{2} = -4$$

Practice 6

What are the sum and product of the roots of the function $f(x) = x^2 + 2x - 9$?

Practice 7

What are the sum and product of the roots of the function $f(x) = 3x^2 + 12$?

3.3 Quadratic Functions

Forms of the Quadratic Function

Here are three ways of writing the same function:

$$f(x) = x^2 + 2x - 8$$
$$f(x) = (x + 4)(x - 2)$$
$$f(x) = (x + 1)^2 - 9$$

The top form is just a standard form. From $f(x) = x^2 + 2x - 8$, we can identify the y-intercept, -8.

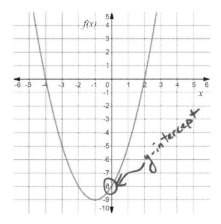

The second form, $f(x) = (x + 4)(x - 2)$ lets us readily identify the zeros (roots) of the function, which are -4 and 2. Since it is a factored form of the function, we would set each factor to zero and solve for x in each.

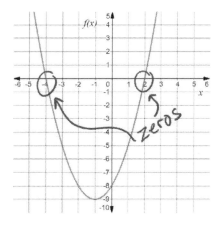

The third form of the function, $f(x) = (x + 1)^2 - 9$, lets us readily identify the vertex and axis of symmetry. This function shows the function x^2 being translated left 1 unit and down 9 units,

3.3 Quadratic Functions

which would put the vertex at $(-1, -9)$. The axis of symmetry also passes through the vertex, so the axis of symmetry is $x = -1$.

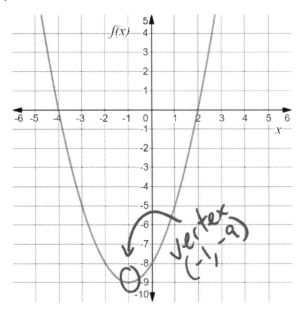

Example

Which of the following formats of the function $f(x) = x^2 + 2x - 3$ can be used to quickly identify the vertex?

A) $(x - 1)^2 + 4$
B) $(x + 3)(x - 1)$
C) $(x + 2)(x + 1)$
D) $(x + 1)^2 - 4$

A. $(x-1)^2 + 4$
B. $(x+3)(x-1)$ ✗ ⎫ NOT IN
C. $(x+2)(x+1)$ ✗ ⎬ VERTEX FORM
D. $(x+1)^2 - 4$

We can eliminate choices B and C because the answers are not written in vertex form. They are written in a way that we can identify the zeros, but not the vertex.

3.3 Quadratic Functions

We should multiply A and D out to see if we get the same functions as the one given.

$$(x-1)^2 + 4$$
$$(x-1)(x-1) + 4$$
$$x^2 - x - x + 1 + 4$$
$$x^2 - 2x + 5 \quad ✗$$

Choice A doesn't work out, so we should try choice D.

$$(x+1)^2 - 4$$
$$(x+1)(x+1) - 4$$
$$x^2 + x + x + 1 - 4$$
$$x^2 + 2x - 3 \quad ✓$$

Choice D is the answer.

Tricks for Finding the Vertex

Trick #1

If the function is written in standard form, $y = ax^2 + bx + c$, we can quickly identify the axis of symmetry of a quadratic function with the following formula:

$$x = \frac{-b}{2a}$$

You might recognize this. It's the first part of the quadratic formula, $x = \frac{-b \pm \sqrt{b^2 - 4ac}}{2a}$.

The axis of symmetry passes through the vertex, so the x-coordinate of the vertex is the same as the axis of symmetry.

3.3 Quadratic Functions

Example

Write the vertex form of the function $y = x^2 + 6x - 5$.

$$x = \frac{-b}{2a}$$

$$x = \frac{-(6)}{2(1)}$$

$$x = -3$$

This means the x-coordinate of the axis of symmetry is -3. We can substitute -3 in for x in the function to find the y-coordinate of the vertex.

$$y = x^2 + 6x - 5$$

$$y = (-3)^2 + 6(-3) - 5$$

$$y = 9 - 18 - 5$$

$$y = -14$$

The vertex form of the equation is $y = (x + 3)^2 - 14$.

Practice 8

Write the function $f(x) = x^2 - 8x + 12$ in vertex form.

Trick #2

If the function is written in a form that allows us to immediately find the zeros, then the second trick we can use is that the vertex and axis of symmetry exist exactly in the middle of the two zeros. You can find the axis of symmetry (x-coordinate of the vertex) by taking the average of the two numbers.

3.3 Quadratic Functions

For example, if a function is $f(x) = x^2 + 2x - 3$, then the zeros of a function are -3 and 1. We can find the axis of symmetry and the x-coordinate of the vertex by taking the average of the two numbers.

$$Average\ of\ the\ zeros = \frac{-3+1}{2} = \frac{-2}{1} = -1$$

The vertex is located at $x = -1$ and the axis of symmetry is $x = -1$.

Since we know the x-coordinate of the axis of symmetry, we can substitute it into the functions to find the y-coordinate.

$$f(x) = x^2 + 2x - 3$$
$$f(-1) = (-1)^2 + 2(-1) - 3$$
$$f(-1) = 1 - 2 - 3$$
$$f(-1) = -4$$

The vertex is $(-1, -4)$.

Below is a diagram to illustrate the concept.

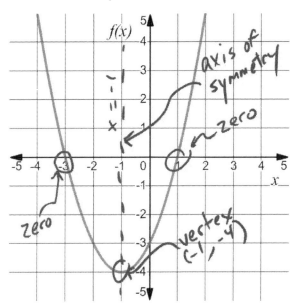

Since the vertex is $(-1, -4)$ and coefficient in front of x^2 is 1, then vertex form of the function is $f(x) = (x + 1)^2 - 4$.

3.3 Quadratic Functions

SUPER TIP

If you are asked to identify equivalent ways to write a function on section 4, you can use your calculator to graph all of the functions. The functions that have the same exact graphs are equivalent functions.

Practice 9

Write the function $f(x) = (x + 1)(x + 5)$ in vertex form.

Projectile Motion

A question that appears on the SAT has to do with using a quadratic function to represent the height of a projectile with respect to time.

Let's look at an example

The height of a projectile fired off a cliff can be determined using the function $h(t) = -16t^2 + 128t + 768$, for $0 \leq t \leq 12$. From what height was the projectile fired?

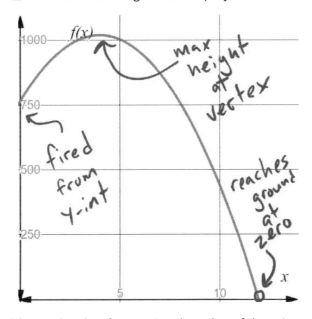

The projectile was fired from a height of 768 units, the value of the y-intercept.

3.3 Quadratic Functions Homework

Homework 1

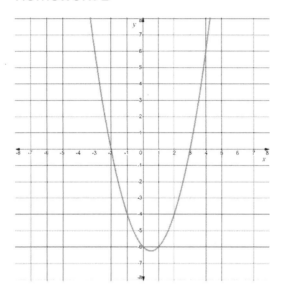

Given the graph of $f(x)$ above. Which of the following could be $f(x)$?

A) $f(x) = (x+3)(x-2)$
B) $f(x) = (x-6)(x+1)$
C) $f(x) = (x-3)(x+2)$
D) $f(x) = (x-6)(x-1)$

Homework 2

$x^2 + 5x + 7 = -7$

If $x > 0$, what is the value of $x + 3$?

Homework 3

What is the product of the roots of the $f(x) = x^2 - 5x + 7$?

Homework 4

$y = x^2 - 5x + 4$

$y = x - 5$

What is the x-value to the solution of the system of equations above?

Homework 5

Which of the equations below can be used to readily identify the zeros of the function $f(x) = x^2 + 3x - 4$?

A) $f(x) = (x+4)(x-1)$
B) $f(x) = (x-3)(x-1)$
C) $f(x) = \left(x + \frac{3}{2}\right)^2 - \frac{25}{4}$
D) $f(x) = x(x+3) - 4$

Homework 6

Which of the following functions can be used to readily identify the minimum value of the function $f(x) = x^2 - 10x + 16$?

A) $f(x) = (x-8)(x-2)$
B) $f(x) = (x+5)^2 + 16$
C) $f(x) = (x-5)^2 - 9$
D) $f(x) = x(x-10) + 16$

3.3 Answers to Practice Problems (Quadratic Functions)

Practice 1

From the graph, the zeros are at -2 and 1.

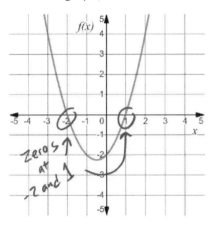

Practice 2: 3, 5

$x^2 - 2x - 15$

$(x \quad)(x \quad)$

Numbers must add up to -2 and multiply to -15

$(x-5)(x+3)$

$x - 5 = 0 \qquad x - 3 = 0$
$+5 \ +5 \qquad +3 \ +3$
$x = 5 \qquad x = 3$

Practice 3: -4, 3

$x^2 + x - 12$

$(x \quad)(x \quad)$

#s must add to 1 and multiply to -12

$(x+4)(x-3)$

$x + 4 = 0 \qquad x - 3 = 0$
$-4 \ -4 \qquad +3 \ +3$
$x = -4 \qquad x = 3$

Practice 4: A

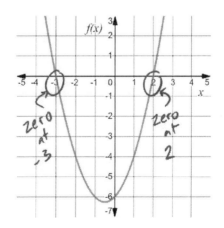

Since the zeros of the function are -3 and 2. The factors are $(x+3)$ and $(x-2)$. The function could simply be $f(x) = (x-2)(x+3)$.

3.3 Quadratic Functions

Practice 5: $1 + \sqrt{2}$ and $1 - \sqrt{2}$

$f(x) = x^2 - 2x - 1$

$a = 1 \quad b = -2 \quad c = -1$

$x = \dfrac{-b \pm \sqrt{b^2 - 4ac}}{2a}$

$x = \dfrac{-(-2) \pm \sqrt{(-2)^2 - 4(1)(-1)}}{2(1)}$

$x = \dfrac{2 \pm \sqrt{8}}{2}$

This can be reduced further.

$\dfrac{2 \pm \sqrt{8}}{2}$

$\sqrt{8} \to \sqrt{4\sqrt{2}} \to 2\sqrt{2}$

$\dfrac{2 \pm 2\sqrt{2}}{2}$

$\dfrac{2 \pm 2\sqrt{2}}{2}$

$1 \pm \sqrt{2}$

$1 + \sqrt{2}, \ 1 - \sqrt{2}$

Practice 6: sum = -2, prod. = -9

What are the sum and product of the roots of the function $f(x) = x^2 + 2x - 9$?

$x^2 + 2x - 9$

$\text{Sum} = \dfrac{-b}{a} = \dfrac{-2}{1} = -2$

$\text{prod.} = \dfrac{c}{a} = \dfrac{-9}{1} = -9$

Practice 7: sum = 0, prod. = 4

What are the sum and product of the roots of the function $f(x) = 3x^2 + 12$?

3.3 Quadratic Functions

$3x^2 + 12$
is the same as
$3x^2 + 0x + 12$

$\text{sum} = \dfrac{-b}{a} = \dfrac{-0}{3} = 0$

$\text{prod} = \dfrac{c}{a} = \dfrac{12}{3} = 4$

Practice 8: $y = (x-4)^2 - 4$

$x^2 - 8x + 12$

axis of symmetry

$x = \dfrac{-b}{2a} = \dfrac{-(-8)}{2(1)} = 4$

x-coordinate of vertex is 4.

$y = x^2 - 8x + 12$
$y = (4)^2 - 8(4) + 12$
$y = 16 - 32 + 12$
$y = -4$

vertex: $(4, -4)$

Vertex form:
$(x-a)^2 + b$ where the vertex is (a, b)

$(x-4)^2 + 4$

Practice 9: $f(x) = (x+3)^2 - 4$

$f(x) = (x+1)(x+5)$,
So zeros are: -1 and -5

The x-coordinate of the vertex is in the middle of (average of) the zeros.

$$\frac{-1+-5}{2} = -3$$

Vertex: $(-3, ?)$

Find the y-coordinate of the vertex by substituting -3 in for x in the function.

$y = (x+1)(x+5)$
$y = (-3+1)(-3+5)$
$y = -4$
Vertex: $(-3, -4)$

vertex form: $(x-a)^2 + b$ where vertex is (a, b)

$(x+3)^2 - 4$

Homework 1: C

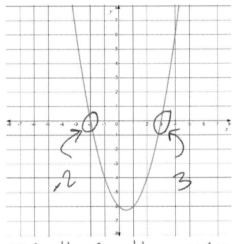

If the function passes through -2 and 3, then factors are $(x+2)$ and $(x-3)$.

3.3 Quadratic Functions

Homework 2: 5

$x^2 + 5x - 7 = 7$

Get one side equal to 0, then factor.

$x^2 + 5x - 7 = 7$
$ -7 -7$
$x^2 + 5x - 14 = 0$

$(x+7)(x-2) = 0$

$x + 7 = 0 \quad\quad x - 2 = 0$
$ -7 -7 \quad\quad +2 +2$
$x = -7 \quad\quad x = 2$

The question states x must be greater than 0, so $x = 2$.

$x + 3 = ?$
$2 + 3 = \boxed{5}$

Homework 3: 7

To solve for the roots, set the function equal to 0 and solve.

$x^2 - 5x + 7 = 0$

Can't be factored. However, we can easily find the product of the roots.

$\text{prod.} = \dfrac{c}{a}$

$\text{prod} = \dfrac{7}{1} = \boxed{7}$

3.3 Quadratic Functions

Homework 4: 3

Set the functions equal to each other and solve for x

$$x^2 - 5x + 4 = x - 5$$

Get one side equal to 0, then factor.

$$x^2 - 5x + 4 = x - 5$$
$$ -x + 5 -x + 5$$
$$x^2 - 6x + 9 = 0$$
$$(x-3)(x-3) = 0$$
$$x - 3 = 0$$
$$x = \boxed{3}$$

Homework 5: A

$$f(x) = x^2 + 3x - 4$$

We can readily find the zeros if the function is factored. Only choices A & B are factored, so C & D are wrong.

Either factor the function and find the answer or multiply out choices A & B to see which one gives us $x^2 + 3x - 4$.

A.
$$(x+4)(x-1)$$
$$x^2 - x + 4x - 4$$
$$x^2 + 3x - 4 \checkmark$$

B.
$$(x-3)(x-1)$$
$$x^2 - x - 3x + 3$$
$$x^2 - 4x + 3 \; ✗$$

Homework 6: C

$$f(x) = x^2 - 10x + 16$$

minimum occurs at vertex, so put the function in vertex form.

3.3 Quadratic Functions

x-coordinate of vertex can be found with

$$x = -\frac{b}{2a}$$

$$x = \frac{-(-10)}{2(1)}$$

$$x = \frac{10}{2} = 5$$

Vertex form is
$$f(x) = (x-a)^2 + b$$
if the vertex is (a, b).

Our vertex is $(5, ?)$, so it will be

$$(x-5)^2 + ?$$

The answer must be C.

However, I'll continue to demonstrate how to get the missing value.

$x = 5$, so substitute 5 in for x in the original function to solve for y.

$$x^2 - 10x + 16$$
$$5^2 - 10(5) + 16$$
$$-9$$

Vertex is $(5, -9)$

Vertex form is

$$(x-5)^2 - 9$$

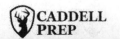

Lesson 4

Need to improve 200 points?

We love working with students who are serious about their SAT scores - that means you!

Special Tutoring & Test Prep Offer for You

 caddellprep.com/sboffer

4.1 No Solution & Infinite Solutions

No Solution

If you think of the two equations as functions, they would be two functions that never intersect.

If they are both linear equations, they will have the same slope but different y-intercepts.

For example, if we had the system of equations $y = x^2 + 4$ and $y = 2x - 3$, we could graph them and see that they never intersect.

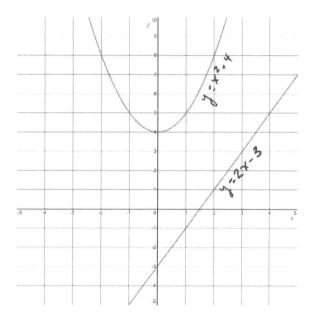

Here is an example of two linear equation that never intersect.

$y = \dfrac{2}{3}x + 1$

$3y = 2x - 6$

It isn't easy to immediately notice, but both equations have the same slope. Solve for y in the second equation.

4.1 No Solution & Infinite Solutions

$$\frac{3y}{3} = \frac{2x}{3} - \frac{6}{3}$$

$$y = \frac{2}{3}x - 2$$

slope = 2/3

Both lines have a slope of $\frac{2}{3}$. Here is a graph of the two lines.

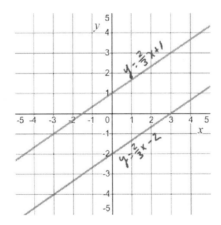

Practice 1

In the system of linear equations below, a is a constant. If the system has no solution, what is the value of a?

$$\frac{1}{5}x - \frac{1}{10}y = 10$$

$$ax - 2y = 15$$

- A) 4
- B) 2
- C) 3
- D) 1

4.1 No Solution & Infinite Solutions

SUPER TIP
If the question asks for the number of real solutions, you may have to use the quadratic formula to see if the solutions are imaginary (not real). Also, if the greatest exponent is 2, it is only possible to have 2, 1 or 0 solutions.

Example

How many solutions are there to the equation $2x^2 - 4x = 9x + 1$?

- A) 3
- B) 2
- C) 1
- D) 0

In this case, you can immediately eliminate choice A, because there can't be 3 solutions if the greatest exponent is 2.

Since the greatest exponent is 2, we should get one side of the equation equal to zero then see if we can factor. If we can't factor, use the quadratic formula.

$$2x^2 - 4x = 9x + 1$$
$$ -9x \quad -9x$$
$$2x^2 - 13x = 1$$
$$ -1 \quad -1$$
$$2x^2 - 13x - 1 = 0$$

use the quadratic formula

$$a = 2, \; b = -13, \; c = -1$$

$$\frac{-b \pm \sqrt{b^2 - 4ac}}{2a}$$

4.1 No Solution & Infinite Solutions

$$\frac{-(-13) \pm \sqrt{(-13)^2 - 4(2)(-1)}}{2(2)}$$

$$\frac{13 \pm \sqrt{169 + 4}}{4}$$

$$\frac{13 \pm \sqrt{173}}{4}$$

We can stop here. We don't have to find the exact solutions, just the number of real solutions.

There are two real solutions, they are:

$$\frac{13 + \sqrt{174}}{4} \text{ and } \frac{13 - \sqrt{174}}{4}$$

The answer is B) 2.

Infinite Solutions

If you think of the two equations as functions, they would be graphed on top of each other.

If they are both linear equations, they will have the same slope and y-intercept.

For example, the following system of equations has infinite solutions.

$3y - 12x = 9$

$5y = 20x + 15$

4.1 No Solution & Infinite Solutions

solve for y in both equations

$3y - 12x = 9$ $5y = 20x + 15$

$\underline{+12x \quad +12x}$ $\dfrac{5y}{5} = \dfrac{20x}{5} + \dfrac{15}{5}$

$3y = 12x + 9$

$\dfrac{3y}{3} = \dfrac{12x}{3} + \dfrac{9}{3}$ $y = 4x + 3$

$y = 4x + 3$

Same equation, so infinite solutions

There will be infinite solutions, if they two equations are multiples of each other.

For example, the following equations are multiples of each other and the system has infinite solutions.

$2x - y = 12$

$6x - 3y = 36$

$2x - y = 12$ $6x - 3y = 36$

$\dfrac{6x}{3} - \dfrac{3y}{3} = \dfrac{36}{3}$

Same equation, so infinite solutions

$\rightarrow 2x - y = 12$

4.1 No Solution & Infinite Solutions

Practice 2

In the following system of equations, a is a constant. What is the value of a if the system of equations has infinite solutions?

$ax + 2y = 10$

$3y - 6x = -15$

- A) -2
- B) -1
- C) 3
- D) 6

4.1 No Solution & Infinite Solutions Homework

Homework 1

The system of equations $4x + 8y = 12$ and $ax + 6y = 9$ has an infinite number of solutions. What is the value of a?

Homework 2

The system of equations $6x + 9y = 14$ and $ay + bx = -3$ have no solutions. What must $\frac{b}{a}$ equal?

A) $\frac{3}{2}$
B) $\frac{2}{3}$
C) $\frac{7}{3}$
D) $\frac{3}{7}$

4.1 No Solution & Infinite Solutions

Answers to Practice Problems (No Solution & Infinite Solutions)

Practice 1: A

Solve for y in both

$$\frac{1}{5}x - \frac{1}{10}y = 10$$

Least Common Denominator = 10

$$10\left(\frac{1}{5}x - \frac{1}{10}y = 10\right)$$

$$2x - y = 100$$

$$\underline{-2x \qquad -2x}$$

$$-y = -2x + 100$$

$$y = 2x - 100$$

$$ax - 2y = 15$$

$$\underline{-ax \qquad -ax}$$

$$-2y = -ax + 15$$

$$\frac{-2y}{-2} = \frac{-ax}{-2} + \frac{15}{-2}$$

$$y = \frac{a}{2}x - 7.5$$

No solution → Same Slope

$$y = 2x - 10 \qquad y = \frac{a}{2}x - 7.5$$

$$2 = \frac{a}{2}$$

$$(2)\,2 = \frac{a(2)}{2}$$

$$4 = a$$

Practice 2: -4

Solve for y in both equations

$$ax + 2y = 10 \qquad 3y - 6x = 15$$

$$\underline{-ax \qquad -ax} \qquad \underline{+6x \quad +6x}$$

$$2y = -ax + 10 \qquad 3y = 6x + 15$$

$$\frac{2y}{2} = \frac{-ax}{2} + \frac{10}{2} \qquad \frac{3y}{3} = \frac{6x}{3} + \frac{15}{3}$$

$$y = \frac{-a}{2}x + 5 \qquad y = 2x + 5$$

4.1 No Solution & Infinite Solutions

Infinite Solutions:
Same slope & same y-int.
These both have a y-int of 5.
The slopes should also equal.

$$\frac{-a}{2} = 2$$

$$\frac{-a}{2}(-2) = 2(-2)$$

$$a = -4$$

$$\frac{8y}{8} = \frac{-4x}{8} + \frac{12}{8}$$

$$y = -\frac{1}{2}x + \frac{3}{2}$$

$$ax + 6y = 9$$
$$-ax \qquad\qquad -ax$$

$$6y = -ax + 9$$

$$\frac{6y}{6} = \frac{-ax}{6} + \frac{9}{6}$$

$$y = \frac{-a}{6}x + \frac{3}{2}$$

Homework 1: 3

Infinite number of solutions means the lines are the same.
Solve for y in both.

$$4x + 8y = 12$$
$$-4x \qquad\qquad -4x$$

$$8y = -4x + 12$$

4.1 No Solution & Infinite Solutions

They both have a y-int of $-3/2$. Their slopes must match up also.

$$-\frac{1}{2} = -\frac{a}{6}$$

$$(-6)-\frac{1}{2} = -\frac{a}{6}(-6)$$

$$\boxed{3} = a$$

The slopes must equal, so

$$\frac{-2}{3} = -\frac{b}{a}$$

We have to find $\frac{b}{a}$, so multiply both sides by -1

$$(-1)\left(\frac{-2}{3}\right) = \left(\frac{-b}{a}\right)(-1)$$

$$\boxed{\frac{2}{3}} = \frac{b}{a}$$

Homework 2: B

No solution → parallel lines (same slope)
Solve for y in both equations

$$6x + 9y = 14 \qquad ay + bx = -3$$
$$-6x \qquad -6x \qquad -bx \quad -bx$$

$$9y = -6x + 14 \qquad ay = -bx - 3$$

$$\frac{9y}{9} = \frac{-6x}{9} + \frac{14}{9} \qquad \frac{ay}{a} = \frac{-bx}{a} - \frac{3}{a}$$

$$y = \frac{-2}{3}x + \frac{14}{9} \qquad y = -\frac{b}{a}x - \frac{3}{a}$$

4.2 Percent

Fractions to Percentages

A percent represents the number you would expect out of 100.

If you are only correct 1 out of every 2 questions, then you would be correct 50 out of 100 times, or 50% of the time.

To change a fraction to a percent, you can create an equivalent fraction with a denominator of 100. The numerator is the percent.

$$\frac{3}{4} = \frac{75}{100} = 75\%$$

$$\frac{1}{10} = \frac{10}{100} = 10\%$$

$$\frac{2}{5} = \frac{40}{100} = 40\%$$

Practice 1

Convert the following fraction to a percent.

$$\frac{3}{20} =$$

Decimals to Percentages

To change a decimal to a percent, use the fact that 0.38 means 38 hundredths = $\frac{38}{100}$ = 38%, or simply move the decimal 2 places right.

$$0.45 = 45\%, \; 0.05 = 5\%, \; 0.4 = 0.40 = 40\%$$

4.2 Percent

Practice 2
Convert the following decimals to percentages.

$$0.7 =$$

$$0.043 =$$

$$0.58 =$$

$$1.25 =$$

Percent Formula

$$\frac{Percent}{100} = \frac{Part\ (is)}{Whole\ (of)}$$

Or we can find the percent of a number using the following equation:

$$Part = Percent\ (as\ a\ decimal) * Whole$$

For example. If we have the question "What is 30% of 60?" we can solve the questions using either method.

$$\frac{Percent}{100} = \frac{Part\ (is)}{Whole\ (of)} \quad\quad \text{or} \quad\quad Part = Percent\ (as\ a\ decimal) * Whole$$

$$\frac{30}{100} = \frac{x}{60} \quad\quad\quad\quad\quad\quad\quad\quad\quad\quad x = 0.30 * 60$$

$$1800 = 100x \quad\quad\quad\quad\quad\quad\quad\quad\quad\quad x = 18$$
$$18 = x$$

Practice 3
What is 20% of 15?

4.2 Percent

Practice 4

7 is what percent of 28?

Practice 5

8 is 5% of what?

Tax, Mark-up, and Discount (Increase and Decrease)

Increase by a Percent

Tax and mark-up increase the cost of a purchase.

For example, if a pair of shoes is $80 and there is 8% tax, we would have to add the tax on to the total cost.

Price: $80
Tax: 8%

$$\begin{array}{r} \$80 \\ \times\ .08 \\ \hline 6.40 \leftarrow tax \end{array}$$

$$\begin{array}{r} \$80.00 \\ +\ 6.40 \\ \hline \$86.40 \leftarrow total \end{array}$$

4.2 Percent

Another way to look at it is that 100% of the price of the shoes is $80.
If it increases by 8% because of tax, the cost is now 108% of $80.

Price: $80

Tax: 8% → 108%

108% = 1.08

$$\begin{array}{r} 1.08 \\ \times\ 80 \\ \hline 86.40 \end{array}$$ $86.40

The same concept applies to all increases.

If something increases by 40%, it will be 140% of what it previously was.

If something increases by 7.5%, it will be 107.5% of what it previously was.

If something increases by 100%, it will be 200% of what it previously was.

Practice 6
If the cost of a dress is $130, what will the total cost be after 7% tax? (Try to find the answer in one step)

Decrease by a Percent

Discount decreases the cost of a purchase.

For example, if a pair of shoes is $80 and there is 30% discount, we would have to subtract the discount from the total cost.

Price: $80
Discount: 30%

$$\begin{array}{r} 80 \\ \times\ .3 \\ \hline 24.0 \end{array} \leftarrow \text{Discount}$$

$$\begin{array}{r} 80 \\ -\ 24 \\ \hline 56 \end{array} \leftarrow \text{Sale Price}$$

Another way to look at it is that 100% of the price of the shoes is $80.
If it decreases by 30% because of tax, the cost is now 70% of $80.

Price: $80
Discount: 30% → 70%

70% = .7

$$\begin{array}{r} 80 \\ \times\ .7 \\ \hline 56.0 \end{array} \qquad \boxed{\$56}$$

The same concept applies to all decreases.

If something decreases by 40%, it will be 60% of what it previously was.

If something decreases by 7.5%, it will be 92.5% of what it previously was.

If something decreases by 24%, it will be 76% of what it previously was.

Practice 7

If the cost of a tablet is $840, what will the total cost be after 25% discount? (Try to find the answer in one step)

Equations that Incorporate Percents

On the SAT, you may be asked to identify equations that can be used to solve for a variable. In other words, sometimes you don't have to solve for a missing value, you just need to choose the equations that can be used to solve for the missing value.

First, let's review some expressions.

If a book costs x and there is 5% tax, the total cost would be $1.05x$ because we have to increase the cost by 5%.

If a book costs x and there is 15% discount, the total cost would be $.85x$ because we have to decrease the cost by 15%, which would leave us with 85% of the cost.

If a book costs x, but there is a 15% discount and 5% tax, the total cost would be $1.05(.85x)$.

Practice 8

James purchases movie tickets that cost $12.95 each plus tax. The tax is equal to 9%, and James spends an additional untaxed amount of $7.00 for snacks. Which of the following represents James' total charge in dollars, for x movie tickets?

A) $(12.95 + 0.09x) + 7$

B) $1.09(12.95 + 7)x$

C) $1.09(12.95x) + 7$

D) $1.09(12.95x + 7)$

Percent Change

The formula for percent change, whether increase or decrease, can be found with a simple equation.

$$percent\ change = \frac{change}{original} \times 100\%$$

For example, if a stock increased from $80 to $100, the change is $20 and the original value was $80. Let's use the formula to find the percent change.

$$percent\ change = \frac{change}{original} \times 100\%$$

$$percent\ change = \frac{20}{80} \times 100\% = 25\%$$

IF the stock decreased from $100 to $80, the change is still $20, but this time the original value is $100. Let's use the formula to find the percent change in this scenario.

$$percent\ change = \frac{change}{original} \times 100\%$$

$$percent\ change = \frac{20}{100} \times 100\% = 20\%$$

4.2 Percent

Practice 9

The data in the table shows the number of people in each profession for a fake town for the years 2009 and 2019. Which profession had the greatest percent increase from 2009 to 2019?

	2009	2019
Doctor	580	640
Lawyer	375	410
Engineer	605	590
Hockey Player	2	4

4.2 Percent Homework

Homework 1

A pair of shoes were originally p dollars. If they increased in value by 20%, what is the new value of the shoes in terms of p?

- A) $p + 0.2$
- B) $0.2p$
- C) $1.2p$
- D) $1 + .02p$

Homework 2

In a school of 500 students, 30 students were absent. 12 of the absent students had an excused absence. What percent of the absent students did not have an excused absence?

- A) 2.4%
- B) 4%
- C) 40%
- D) 60%

Homework 3

After a 30% increase, the price of stock reached $20.80. What was the price of the stock before the 30% increase?

- A) $27.04
- B) $20.50
- C) $16.00
- D) $14.56

Homework 4

The enrollment of students at the local community college decreased from 5,400 to 4,900. What is the approximate percent change in the enrollment?

- A) 5.0%
- B) 9.3%
- C) 10.2%
- D) 90.7%

4.2 Answers to Practice Problems (Percent)

Practice 1: 15%

$$\frac{3}{20} = \frac{15}{100} = 15\%$$

Practice 2

$0.7 = 0.70 = 70\%$

$0.043 = 0.043 = 4.3\%$

$0.58 = 0.58 = 58\%$

$1.25 = 1.25 = 125\%$

Practice 3: 3

20% of 15

20% × 15

20% = 0.2

$$\begin{array}{r} 15 \\ \times\ .2 \\ \hline 3.0 \end{array}$$

Practice 4: 25

7 is what percent of 28?

$$\frac{\%}{100} = \frac{Part}{Whole}$$

$$\frac{x}{100} = \frac{7}{28}$$

$$28x = 700$$

$$\frac{28x}{28} = \frac{700}{28}$$

$$x = 25$$

Practice 5: 160

8 is 5% of what?

$$\frac{\%}{100} = \frac{Part}{Whole}$$

$$\frac{5}{100} = \frac{8}{x}$$

$$5x = 800$$

$$\frac{5x}{5} = \frac{800}{5}$$

$$x = 160$$

4.2 Percent

Practice 6: 139.10

Price: $130
Tax: 7%

7%↑ = 107%

$$\begin{array}{r} 130 \\ \times 1.07 \\ \hline 910 \\ 000 \\ 130 \\ \hline 139.10 \end{array}$$

$\boxed{\$139.10}$

Practice 7: 630

Price: $840
Discount: 25%

25%↓ = 75%

$$\begin{array}{r} 840 \\ \times .75 \\ \hline 4200 \\ 5880 \\ \hline 630.00 \end{array}$$

$\boxed{\$630}$

Practice 8: C

x movie tickets for $12.95 each
$7 for snacks (untaxed)
9% tax

Cost of movie tickets: 12.95x

Cost of movie tickets with tax: 1.09(12.95x)

Plus, $7 for snacks:
1.09(12.95x) + 7

Practice 9: Hockey Player

Doctor 580 → 640
$\frac{60}{580} \times 100\% = 10.3\%$

Lawyer 375 → 410
$\frac{35}{375} \times 100\% = 9.3\%$

Engineer 605 → 590
decreased

Hockey Player 2 → 4
$\frac{2}{2} \times 100\% = 100\%$

$\boxed{\text{Hockey Player}}$

4.2 Percent

Homework 1: C

20% increase is 120% of original

$$\boxed{1.2p}$$

Homework 2: D

What percent of the absent students did not have an excused absence?

30 absent & 12 excused
therefore, 18 not excused

$$\frac{\%}{100} = \frac{P}{W}$$

$$\frac{x}{100} = \frac{18}{30} \quad \leftarrow \text{not excused} \\ \leftarrow \text{out of absent}$$

$$30x = 1800$$

$$x = \boxed{60\%}$$

Homework 3: D

30% increase = 130%

$$1.3p = \text{new}$$
↑
original

$$1.3p = \text{new}$$
$$1.3p = 20.80$$
$$p = \boxed{16}$$

OR TRY ANSWERS

A) $27.04 → too high
B) $20.50
C) $16.00
D) $14.56

B. $20.50(1.3) = 26.65$ ✗

C. $16(1.3) = 20.80$ ✓

D. $14.56(1.3) = 18.93$ ✗

Homework 4: B

$$\text{percent change} = \frac{\text{change}}{\text{original}} \times 100\%$$

5,400 → 4,900

change = 500
original = 5,400

$$\frac{500}{5400} \times 100\%$$

9.259 %

$$\boxed{9.3\%}$$

4.3 Exponential Growth & Decay

To have a strong understanding of exponential growth and decay, you need knowledge of percentages first.

If you haven't gone through the chapter on percent, I suggest you go back and review that chapter first.

Exponential Growth

Exponential growth is typically caused by growth that is based on a percentage or ratio.

To better understand the difference, compare exponential growth to linear growth.

Suppose you deposited $100 in the bank and received $10 every year from the bank for keeping your money there. The amount of money in your account would increase linear because it would increase at a constant rate: $10/year.

The amount of money in the account could be represented by the function $f(t) = 10t + 100$

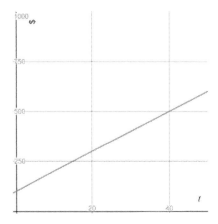

Suppose you deposited $100 in a different bank and received 5% interest each year. The first year you would only receive $5 because 5% of $100 is $5. However, the next year you would receive $5.25 because you would get 5% of $105. The following year, you would receive 5% of $110.25, which is $5.51. The amount of money you receive each year is bigger than the previous year's amount. This is exponential growth.

More precisely, since it is growing by 5%, each year will be 105% of the previous year, so each year will be a multiple of 1.05 of the previous year.

4.3 Exponential Growth & Decay

The amount of money in the account could be represented by the function $g(t) = 100(1.05)^t$

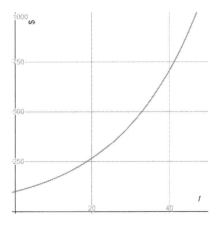

Here is a comparison of the two. As you can see from the graph, exponential growth results in a graph that is curved upward.

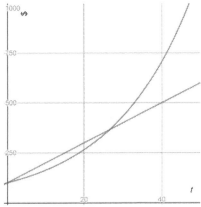

The function $g(t) = 100(1.05)^t$ is based on an initial value of $100 that increases by 5% each year. It is based on the general formula:

$$A = A_0(1 + r)^t$$

where A is the value, A_0 is the initial value (in this case $100), r is the rate (in this case .05 for 5%), and t is time (in this case in years)

Since we add the rate to one, we end up with growth.

4.3 Exponential Growth & Decay

Practice 1

This practice question has two parts.

Semande opened a savings account with $10,000. The savings account earns 3% annual interest. If Semande doesn't make any deposits or withdrawals, the value of his account could be found using the formula $V = 10,000(k)^t$.

Part 1

If t represents years, what number should be used for k?

Part 2

What would be the value of Semande's account in 10 years? Round to the nearest dollar.

Exponential Decay

Like exponential growth, exponential decay is typically based on a percentage or ratio. However, since it is decaying (decreasing) the ratio is less than one.

Let's look at an example. Suppose the population of an organism was initially 10,000 and the population decreases by 5% each year. The first year, the population would decrease by 5% of 10,000, which is 500. The population next year would start at 9,500 and would decrease by 5% again that year, so it would decrease by 475. Each year, the population decreases by 5%.

More precisely, since it is decreasing by 5%, each year will be 95% of the previous year, so each year will be a multiple of 0.95 of the previous year.

The population of the organisms could be represented by the function $P(t) = 10,000(0.95)^t$

Here is a graph of $P(t)$.

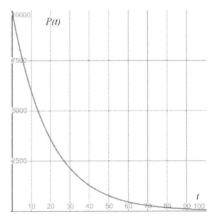

The function $P(t) = 10{,}000(0.95)^t$ is based on an initial value of 10,000 that decreases by 5% each year. It is based on the general formula:

$$A = A_0(1 - r)^t$$

where A is the value, A_0 is the initial value (in this case 10,000), r is the rate (in this case .05 for 5%), and t is time (in this case in years)

Since we subtract the rate from one, we end up with decay.

Practice 2

The population of ducks at a particular park have been decreasing each year. A researcher found that the population decreases by 7% each year. If the population of the ducks 2 years ago was 2,400, what will the population of the ducks be in 5 years?

4.3 Exponential Growth & Decay

SUPER TIP
Sometimes it easier to do the math by hand, such as when a value doubles, halves, or triples.

Example

Since 2000, the population of deer in a town has doubled. If the population in 2003 was 9,920, what was the deer population in the town in 2001?

Population doubled each year, so to find the population of the previous year we just halve the number.

2003: 9,920
2002: 4,960
2001: **2,480**

4.3 Growth & Decay Homework

Homework 1

An investment is projected in increase by 6% each year. If a $10,000 investment is made, how much will it be worth in 5 years? (Round your answer to the nearest dollar)

Homework 2

A company has spent $24,000 on equipment. The accountant predicts that the equipment will decrease in value by 18% each year for the next 10 years. How much will the equipment be worth in 4 years? (Round your answer to the nearest dollar)

Homework 3

The number of subscribers to a local newspaper has halved each year for the past 4 years. If there are currently 120,000 subscribers, how many subscribers did the newspaper have two years ago?

4.3 Exponential Growth & Decay

Answers to Practice Problems (Exponential Growth & Decay)

Practice 1

Part 1: 1.03

Increase of 3% → 103%

103% = $\boxed{1.03}$

OR

$A = A_0 (1+r)^t$

$A = A_0 (1+.03)^t$

$A = A_0 (1.03)^t$

↳ $\boxed{1.03}$

$V = 10,000(1.03)^t$

$t = 10$

$V = 10,000(1.03)^{10}$

$V = 13,439.163$

$\boxed{\$13,439}$

Part 2: 13,439

4.3 Exponential Growth & Decay

Practice 2: 1,444

2 years ago: 2,400 ducks
decrease by 7% → 93%

$$P = 2,400(.93)^t$$

2,400 was 2 years ago
To find P 5 years from now, we need to use $t = 7$

$$P = 2,400(.93)^7$$
$$P = \boxed{1,444}$$

6% increase = 1.06

$$10,000(1.06)^5$$
$$13,382.256$$
$$\boxed{\$13,382}$$

Homework 1: $13,382

4.3 Exponential Growth & Decay

Homework 2: $10,851

18% decrease → 82%

$$24{,}000(.82)^4$$

$$10{,}850.922$$

$$\boxed{\$10{,}851}$$

Homework 3: 480,000

Subscribers halved each year, so the previous year would be double.

This year: 120,000

Previous year: 240,000

2 years ago: $\boxed{480{,}000}$

4.4 Exponents

Multiplying Terms with Exponents

When you multiply terms that have the same base, you add exponents.

$$x^2 \times x^5 = x^7$$

Here is a more complicated one

$$x^2 y^3 z \times xy^5 z^4$$

If there is no exponent written, there is an exponent of 1.

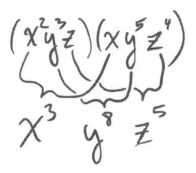

Practice 1

Simplify $(a^3 b^2 c^5)(a^2 c^4)$

Dividing Terms with Exponents

When you divide terms that have the same base, you subtract exponents.

$$\frac{x^8}{x^3} = x^5$$

Here is a more complicated one

$$\frac{x^5 y^3 z^4}{x^2 y^3 z}$$

4.4 Exponents

The y^3 terms in the numerator and denominator cancel out.

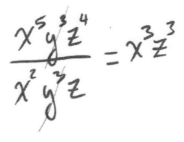

Practice 2

Simplify the expression below.

$$\frac{a^5 b^7 c^3}{a^3 b c^2}$$

Raising an Expression with Exponents to Another Power

When you raise an expression with exponents to another power, you multiply the exponents.

Example

Simplify the expression below.

$(a^3 b^2 c^8)^3$

$$(a^3 b^2 c^8)^3$$

multiply each exponent by 3

$$a^9 b^6 c^{24}$$

4.4 Exponents

Example

Simplify the expression below.

$(3a^4b^7)^2$

$(3a^4b^7)^2$

Raise everything to the second power.
3 gets squared.
Multiply the exponents by 2.

$9a^8b^{14}$

Practice 3

Simplify the expression below.

$(3x^2y^5z)^4$

Exponent of Zero

Any number raised to zero is 1.

$$x^0 = 1$$

Also

$$\left(\frac{x^2y^3 - 32}{4x^5 - 3z^2}\right)^0 = 1$$

4.4 Exponents

There are a lot of terms, but the entire expression is raised to 0, so it is equal to 1.

Be careful.

$$xy^0 = x(1) = x$$

In this example, only the y is raised to 0, so y^0 becomes 1. The x remains x.

Practice 4

Simplify the expression below.

$$\left(\frac{x^4 y^2 z^{12}}{4x^{15} y^2 - 5x}\right)^0$$

4.4 Exponents

Negative Exponents

Think of a negative exponent as a sign that the term is in the wrong spot. If it is in the numerator, move it to the denominator and make the exponent positive. If it is in the denominator, move it to the numerator and make it negative.

For example

$$\frac{x^2 y^3}{a^{-4} b^2}$$

In the example above, the exponent for the a is negative, so move it to the numerator.

$$\frac{a^4 x^2 y^3}{b^2}$$

Here is another example

$$\frac{2x^{-4} y^2}{z^3}$$

Only the x has a negative exponent, so only the x should move to the denominator with its exponent. Do not move the coefficient, 2. Moving the 2 along with the x is a common mistake.

We would end up with

$$\frac{2y^2}{x^4 z^3}$$

Example

Write the following with only positive exponents

$$\frac{5x^3 y^{-4} z^{-2}}{-2a^5 b^{-3}}$$

4.4 Exponents

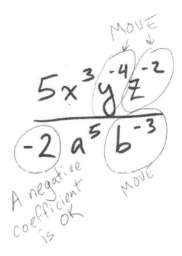

We end up with

$$\frac{5x^3 b^3}{-2a^5 y^4 z^2}$$

Practice 5

Simplify so there are no negative exponents.

$$\frac{-3x^4 y^{-2}}{x^2 y^3}$$

Fractions as Exponents

A fraction in the exponent represents a root, such as a square root or cubed root.

$$x^{\frac{1}{2}} = \sqrt{x}$$

$$x^{\frac{1}{3}} = \sqrt[3]{x}$$

$$x^{\frac{1}{4}} = \sqrt[4]{x}$$

The denominator of the exponent represents the root.

4.4 Exponents

It is possible for the numerator to be a number other than 1. Treat the numerator like a regular exponent.

$$x^{\frac{4}{3}} = \sqrt[3]{x^4}$$

The 4 in the numerator means to the 4th power. The 3 in the denominator means cubed root.

Example

Rewrite $x^{\frac{5}{2}}$ with an integer power and root.

$x^{\frac{5}{2}}$ → 5th power
→ square root

$\sqrt{x^5}$

Practice 6

Rewrite the following as an expression without a fraction in the exponent.

$y^{\frac{4}{7}}$

Questions on the SAT will combine many of the rules together in a question.

Practice 7

Simplify the expression below.

$$\left(\frac{3x^2 y^{-3} z^4}{x^{-3} y^2 z}\right)^2$$

4.4 Exponents

Sometimes, the exponent questions will incorporate other skills too.

Practice 8

$$\frac{2^{3x}}{2^{3y}}$$

What is the value of the expression above if $x - y = 3$?

4.4 Exponents Homework

Homework 1

$$\frac{y^{-3}\sqrt{x}}{x^{-2}\sqrt[3]{y}}$$

Which of the following is equivalent to the expression above?

A) $\frac{2x}{3y}$
B) $\frac{x}{y}$
C) $\frac{x^2\sqrt{x}}{y^3\sqrt[3]{y}}$
D) x^2y^3

Homework 2

$$\left(\frac{x^a}{x^b}\right)^2$$

If the expression above equals 1, what does $a - b$ equal?

Homework 3

$$\frac{2^{x^2}}{2^{y^2}}$$

If $x + y = 2$ and $x - y = 3$, what is the value of the expression above?

4.4 Answers to Practice Problems (Exponents)

Practice 1: $a^5 b^2 c^9$

Simplify $(a^3 b^2 c^5)(a^2 c^4)$

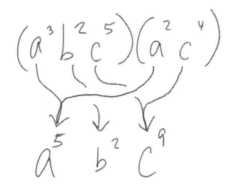

$a^5 \quad b^2 \quad c^9$

Practice 2: $a^2 b^6 c$

$$\frac{a^5 b^7 c^3}{a^3 b \cdot c^2}$$

Subtract exponents

$a^{5-3} \quad b^{7-1} \quad c^{3-2}$

$\boxed{a^2 b^6 c}$

Practice 3: $81 x^8 y^{20} z^4$

$(3x^2 y^5 z)^4$

$(3x^2 y^5 z)^4$

Raise each term to the 4th

$3^4 = 3 \cdot 3 \cdot 3 \cdot 3 = 81$

$(x^2)^4 = x^8$

$(y^5)^4 = y^{20}$

$(z)^4 = z^4$

$\boxed{81 x^8 y^{20} z^4}$

Practice 4: 1

The entire expression is raised to 0, so it becomes 1.

Practice 5: $-\dfrac{3x^6}{y^5}$

$\dfrac{-3 x^4 y^{-2}}{x^{-2} y^3}$

4.4 Exponents

$$\frac{-3x^4 x^2}{y^3 y^2}$$

Practice 7: $\dfrac{9x^{10}z^6}{y^{10}}$

$$\left(\dfrac{3x^2 y^{-3} z^4}{x^{-3} y^2 z}\right)^2$$

$\dfrac{-3 \;\widehat{x^4 \; x^2}\;}{\;\widehat{y^3 \; y^2}\;}$ add exponents / add exponents

Square each term.

$$\dfrac{9 x^4 y^{-6} z^8}{x^{-6} y^4 z^2}$$

$$\boxed{\dfrac{-3x^6}{y^5}}$$

$$\dfrac{9 x^4 \;\widehat{y^{-6}}\; \widehat{z^8}}{\;\widehat{x^{-6}}\; y^4 z^2}$$

Practice 6: $\sqrt[7]{y^4}$

$y^{4/7}$ power / root

$\sqrt[7]{y^4}$

$$\dfrac{9 x^4 x^6 z^8}{y^4 y^6 z^2}$$

$$\dfrac{9 x^{10} z^8}{y^{10} z^2}$$

4.4 Exponents

$$\frac{9x^{10}z^8}{y^{10}z^2}$$ Can be reduced $8-2=6$

$$\frac{9x^{10}z^6}{y^{10}}$$

Practice 8: 512

$x-y=3$

$$\frac{2^{3x}}{2^{3y}}$$ ← Dividing, so subtract exponents

2^{3x-3y}

$2^{3(x-y)}$

$2^{3(3)}$

2^9

$\boxed{512}$

Homework 1: C

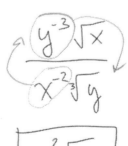

$$\frac{x^2\sqrt{x}}{y^3\sqrt[3]{y}}$$

4.4 Exponents

Homework 2: 0

$\left(\dfrac{x^a}{x^b}\right)^2 = 1$, $a-b = ?$

$\left(\dfrac{x^a}{x^b}\right)^2 = 1$

$\dfrac{x^{2a}}{x^{2b}} = 1$

$x^{2a-2b} = 1$

$x^{\overset{0\ (x^0=1)}{\boxed{2a-2b}}} = 1$

$2a - 2b = 0$

$\dfrac{2a}{2} - \dfrac{2b}{2} = \dfrac{0}{2}$

$a - b = \boxed{0}$

Homework 3: 64

$x + y = 2$, $x - y = 3$

$\dfrac{2^{x^2}}{2^{y^2}}$ ← dividing, so subtract exponents

☆ $x^2 - y^2 = (x-y)(x+y)$

$x^2 - y^2 = (3)(2)$

$x^2 - y^2 = 6$

$2^{x^2 - y^2}$

$2^{x^2 - y^2} = 2^6 = \boxed{64}$

4.5 Imaginary Numbers

Imaginary number, i

$\sqrt{-1}$ does not result in a real number. There is no real number that when multiplied by itself will result in -1.

$\sqrt{-1}$ is imaginary. We represent this imaginary number with the letter i.

$$\sqrt{-1} = i$$

Combining Like Terms with i

When combining like terms, treat i as if it's a variable.

For example, 3 and $3i$ are not like terms but $12i$ and $-3i$ are, just like 3 and $3x$ are not like terms, but $12x$ and $-3x$ are.

When combining like terms, just add the coefficients.

A simplified expression is typically in $a + bi$ form, where the number is written first followed by the i-term.

Example

Simplify $3 + 2i - 8i + 7$.

Here we will combine like terms by adding the like terms together. 3 and 7 are like terms, so we can add them together to get 10. $2i$ and $-8i$ are like terms, so we can add them together to get $-6i$.

We end up with $3 - 6i$, which is in $a + bi$ form. In this case, a is 3 and b is -6.

Example

Simplify $4xi + 12i - 6xi + 4$.

Here we will combine like terms by adding the like terms together. $4xi$ and $-6xi$ are like terms, so we can add them together to get $-2xi$.

Those are the only like terms, so we end up with $-2xi + 12i + 4$. Notice that we cannot write this $a + bi$ form since there is an x-term.

4.5 Imaginary Numbers

Example

Simplify $(9i - 7) + (-2i - 3)$.

To simplify, we should first get distribute to get rid of the parenthesis.

There is nothing written in front of $(9i - 7)$, so we can simply drop the parenthesis.

In front of $(-2i - 3)$ is a plus sign. If we distribute positive 1 to the terms, they will stay the same. We can drop this set of parentheses also.

We end up with $9i - 7 - 2i - 3$.

Combine the $9i$ and $-2i$ by adding them to get $7i$.

Combine the -7 and -3 by adding them to get -10.

The final answer is $7i - 10$.

Example

Simplify $(9i - 7) - (-2i - 3)$.

To simplify, we should first get distribute to get rid of the parenthesis.

There is nothing written in front of $(9i - 7)$, so we can simply drop the parenthesis.

In front of $(-2i - 3)$ is a minus sign. If we distribute negative 1 to the terms, they will get negated, resulting in $2i + 3$.

We end up with $9i - 7 + 2i + 3$.

Combine the $9i$ and $2i$ by adding them to get $11i$.

Combine the -7 and 3 by adding them to get -4.

The final answer is $11i - 4$.

4.5 Imaginary Numbers

Practice 1

Simplify $2i + 4 - 3i - 12$.

Practice 2

Find the sum of $3 + 2i$ and $-7 + 6i$.

Practice 3

Find the difference of $6 + 2i$ and $9 - 3i$.

Multiplying and Simplifying Expression with i

Since $\sqrt{-1} = i$, then $i^2 = -1$.

When we multiply terms or expressions that have i, we may end up with terms that have i^2. It's important to remember that i^2 is imply -1.

Example

Simplify $(2 - 5i)(3 + 2i)$.

To simplify this, we will have to distribute twice (FOIL).

$$2 \times 3 = 6$$
$$2 \times 2i = 4i$$
$$-5i \times 3 = -15i$$
$$-5i \times 2i = -10i^2$$

4.5 Imaginary Numbers

So, we would end up with

$$6 + 4i - 15i - 10i^2$$

We an combine the like terms, $4i$ and $15i$, to get

$$6 - 11i - 10i^2$$

Remember that i^2 is really -1, so we have

$$6 - 11i - 10(-1)$$
$$6 - 11i + 10$$

Now, we can combine like terms to get

$$16 - 11i$$

Practice 4

Simplify $(2 + i)(3 - 4i)$

Practice 5

Simplify $(5 - 2i)^2$

Practice 6

Simplify $(4 + 2i)(4 - 2i)$

4.5 Imaginary Numbers

Rationalizing the Denominator When the Denominator has an i-term

Occasionally, you may see a question that requires rationalizing the denominator.

In this case, the denominator has an expression including i.

To rationalize the following, we would simply multiply the number and denominator by i.

$$\frac{3+2i}{4i}$$

$$\frac{i(3+2i)}{i(4i)}$$

$$\frac{3i+2i^2}{4i^2}$$

Remember that i^2 is -1

$$\frac{3i+2(-1)}{4(-1)}$$

$$\frac{3i-2}{-4}$$

We typically wouldn't write a negative number in the denominator, so we should negate the numerator and denominator.

Our final answer is

$$\frac{-3i+2}{4}$$

If we have to write it in $a+bi$ form, we would divide both terms in the numerator by the denominator to get

$$\frac{-3}{4}i+\frac{1}{2}$$

And write the i-term second

$$\frac{1}{2}-\frac{3}{4}i$$

4.5 Imaginary Numbers

Practice 7

Simplify the following

$$\frac{9-i}{3i}$$

Rationalizing the Denominator When the Denominator has a Binomial with an i-term

Sometimes, the denominator is more complex, such as in the example below

$$\frac{3+4i}{4-6i}$$

In this example, rationalizing the denominator is a little more difficult, but not impossible.

We have to multiply the numerator and denominator by something called the conjugate. The name doesn't matter, don't worry about memorizing the name.

The denominator is $4-6i$, so the conjugate is $4+6i$. The conjugate is just the same expression with the opposite sign between the two terms.

For example, if the denominator was $24+2i$, the conjugate would simply be $24-2i$.

Let's rationalize the denominator in the below expression

$$\frac{3+4i}{4-6i}$$

Multiply the numerator and denominator by $(4+6i)$

$$\frac{(3+4i)(4+6i)}{(4-6i)(4+6i)}$$

Remember that we have to distribute (FOIL). We end up with

$$\frac{12+18i+16i+24i^2}{16+24i-24i-36i^2}$$

When we combine like terms, the $i-terms$ in the deonominator ($24i$ and $-24i$) cancel out.

$$\frac{12+34i+24i^2}{16-36i^2}$$

4.5 Imaginary Numbers

Remember that i^2 is -1, so it becomes

$$\frac{12 + 34i - 24}{16 + 36}$$

$$\frac{-12 + 34i}{52}$$

All of the terms can be divided by 2, so we can reduce it to

$$\frac{-6 + 17i}{26}$$

The above can be our final answer, or if the question want the answer in $a + bi$ form, we would split up the fraction and reduce further if we can.

$$\frac{-6 + 17i}{26} = -\frac{6}{26} + \frac{17}{26}i = -\frac{3}{13} + \frac{17}{26}i$$

Our final answer would be

$$-\frac{3}{13} + \frac{17}{26}i$$

Practice 8

Simplify

$$\frac{5 - 3i}{2 + 2i}$$

Practice 9

Simplify

$$\frac{2 + i}{1 - i}$$

4.5 Imaginary Numbers Homework

Homework 1

Simplify $(3 - 2i) + (4 - 5i)$

Homework 2

Simplify $(3 - 2i)(4 - 5i)$

Homework 3

Simplify

$$\frac{4 - i}{3 + 2i}$$

4.5 Answers to Practice Problems (Imaginary Numbers)

Practice 1: $-8 - i$

Simplify $2i + 4 - 3i - 12$.

$$2i + 4 - 3i - 12 = -8 - i$$

Practice 2: $-4 + 8i$

Find the sum of $3 + 2i$ and $-7 + 6i$.

Sum is the answer to an addition problem, so we should add these expressions together.

$$(3 + 2i) + (-7 + 6i)$$
$$3 + 2i - 7 + 6i$$
$$-4 + 8i$$

Practice 3: $-3 + 5i$

Find the difference of $6 + 2i$ and $9 - 3i$.

Difference is the answer to a subtraction problem, so we should subtract the expressions in the order they are written.

$$(6 + 2i) - (9 - 3i)$$

Distribute the negative to get

$$6 + 2i - 9 + 3i$$
$$-3 + 5i$$

Practice 4: $10 - 5i$

Simplify $(2 + i)(3 - 4i)$

$$(2 + i)(3 - 4i) = 6 - 8i + 3i - 4i^2$$

$i^2 = -1$ so we end up with

$$6 - 8i + 3i + 4$$
$$10 - 5i$$

Practice 5: $21 - 20i$

Simplify $(5 - 2i)^2$

$$(5 - 2i)(5 - 2i) = 25 - 10i - 10i + 4i^2$$

$i^2 = -1$ so we end up with

$$25 - 10i - 10i - 4$$
$$21 - 20i$$

Practice 6: 20

Simplify $(4 + 2i)(4 - 2i)$

$$(4 + 2i)(4 - 2i) = 16 - 8i + 8i - 4i^2$$

$i^2 = -1$, so we end up with

$$16 - 8i + 8i + 4$$
$$20$$

4.5 Imaginary Numbers

Practice 7: $\dfrac{-1-9i}{3}$

Simplify the following

$$\dfrac{9-i}{3i}$$

To rationalize this, we should multiply the numerator and denominator by i.

$$\dfrac{i(9-i)}{i(3i)} = \dfrac{9i - i^2}{3i^2}$$

$i^2 = -1$ so we end up with

$$\dfrac{9i + 1}{-3}$$

We should not have a negative in the denominator, so negate the numerator and denominator to get

$$\dfrac{-9i - 1}{3}$$

It is customary to write the i-term last, so we get

$$\dfrac{-1 - 9i}{3}$$

Practice 8: $\dfrac{1-4i}{2}$

Simplify

$$\dfrac{5 - 3i}{2 + 2i}$$

To rationalize this expression, multiply the numerator and denominator by the conjugate of $2 + 2i$, which is $2 - 2i$

$$\dfrac{(5-3i)(2-2i)}{(2+2i)(2-2i)} = \dfrac{10 - 10i - 6i + 6i^2}{4 - 4i + 4i - 4i^2}$$

$i^2 = -1$ so we end up with

$$\dfrac{10 - 16i - 6}{4 - 4i + 4i + 4} = \dfrac{4 - 16i}{8}$$

We can simply further by dividing each term by 4

$$\dfrac{1 - 4i}{2}$$

Practice 9: $\dfrac{1+3i}{2}$

Simplify

$$\dfrac{2 + i}{1 - i}$$

To rationalize this expression, multiply the numerator and denominator by the conjugate of 1-i, which is $1 + i$

$$\dfrac{(2+i)(1+i)}{(1-i)(1+i)} = \dfrac{2 + 2i + i + i^2}{1 + i - i - i^2}$$

$i^2 = -1$, so we end up with

$$\dfrac{2 + 2i + i - 1}{1 + i - i + 1} = \dfrac{1 + 3i}{2}$$

4.5 Imaginary Numbers

Homework 1: $7 - 7i$

$(3-2i) + (4-5i)$

This is just combining like terms

$3 - 2i + 4 - 5i$

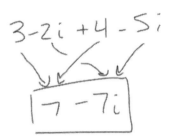

$\boxed{7 - 7i}$

Homework 2: $2 - 23i$

$(3-2i)(4-5i)$

$12 - 15i - 8i + 10i^2$

$12 - 15i - 8i + 10i^2$

$12 - 23i + 10i^2$

$i^2 = -1$

$12 - 23i + 10(-1)$

$12 - 23i - 10$

$\boxed{2 - 23i}$

Homework 3: $\dfrac{10 - 11i}{13}$

$\dfrac{4-i}{3+2i}$

To simplify, multiply the numerator and denominator by the conjugate of the denominator (change the middle sign)

$\dfrac{4-i}{3+2i} \cdot \dfrac{(3-2i)}{(3-2i)}$

$\dfrac{(4-i)(3-2i)}{(3+2i)(3-2i)}$

$\dfrac{12 - 8i - 3i + 2i^2}{9 - 6i + 6i - 4i^2}$

4.5 Imaginary Numbers

$$\frac{12 - 11i + 2(-1)}{9 - 4(-1)}$$

$$\frac{12 - 11i - 2}{9 + 4}$$

$$\frac{10 - 11i}{13}$$

Lesson 5

Want to break a 1400?

We love working with students who are serious about their SAT scores - that means you!

Special Tutoring & Test Prep Offer for You

 caddellprep.com/sboffer

5.1 Circles

Basic Formulas

A couple of basic formulas are given on the SAT for circles: area and circumference.

$$A = \pi r^2$$

$$C = 2\pi r$$

Also, remember that diameter is the width of a circle. It is a chord drawn from one point on the circle to another, passing through the center. It is twice the length of radius, and the radius is half the length of the diameter.

With the two formulas, you will be able to find circumference if you are given the area and vice-versa, because you can find the radius if you are given one.

Example

The circumference of a circle is 8π. What is the area of the circle?

$$C = 8\pi \qquad A = \pi r^2$$

Need r

$$C = 2\pi r \qquad A = \pi r^2$$
$$\frac{8\pi}{\pi} = \frac{2\pi r}{\pi} \qquad A = \pi 4^2$$
$$\frac{8}{2} = \frac{2r}{2} \qquad \boxed{A = 16\pi}$$
$$4 = r$$

5.1 Circles

However, these two formulas don't cover all of the formulas that need to be memorized. You will need to know the center-radius form of the circle equation and the proportions that exists between the central angle and arc length/sector area.

Practice 1

Circle A has an area of $36\pi \ in^2$. What is the circumference of the circle?

Proportions in Circles

The ratio between the central angle and a full circle ($360°$ or 2π radians) is equal to the ratio between the arc length and the full circumference.

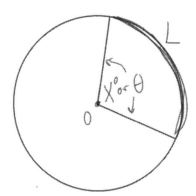

$$\frac{X}{360} = \frac{L}{C}$$

X is the central angle in degrees, L represents the arc length, and C is the circumference

$$\frac{\theta}{2\pi} = \frac{L}{C}$$

θ is the central angle in radians, L represents the arc length, and C is the circumference

5.1 Circles

Also, the ratio between the central angle and a full circle ($360°$ or 2π radians) is equal to the ratio between the sector area and the full area.

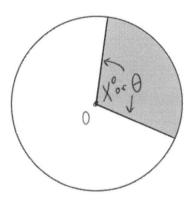

$$\frac{X}{360} = \frac{S}{A}$$

X is the central angle in degrees, S represents the sector area, and A is the area

$$\frac{\theta}{2\pi} = \frac{S}{A}$$

θ is the central angle in radians, S represents the sector area, and A is the area

Example

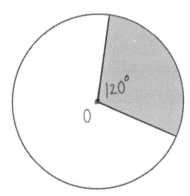

Circle O, shown above, has a radius of 6 inches. What is the area of the shaded portion of the circle?

5.1 Circles

$$\frac{x}{360} = \frac{S}{A}$$

$$A = \pi r^2 = \pi(6)^2 = 36\pi$$

$$\frac{120}{360} = \frac{S}{36\pi}$$

reduce

$$\frac{1}{3} = \frac{S}{36\pi}$$

cross multiply

$$36\pi = 3S$$

$$12\pi = S$$

Practice 2

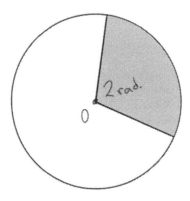

Circle O, shown above has a radius of 4 and a central angle of 2 radians. What is the area of the shaded portion of the circle?

Practice 3

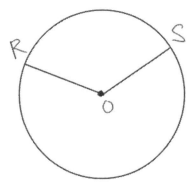

The measure of angle ROS in circle O above is $140°$. What is the length of minor arc RS if the diameter is 4? *Keep you answer in terms of π and reduce if necessary.*

5.1 Circles

Center-Radius Form of the Circle Equation

$$(x - h)^2 + (y - k)^2 = r^2$$

where the center of the circle is (h, k) and the radius is r

For example, if the center of a circle is $(2, -5)$ and the radius is 8, the equation would be $(x - 2)^2 + (y + 5)^2 = 64$.

If the equation of a circle is $(x + 3)^2 + (y - 5)^2 = 8$, then the center of the circle is $(-3, 5)$ and the radius is $\sqrt{8}$, which could be reduced to $2\sqrt{2}$.

Practice 4

Write the equation of a circle with the center $(-4, 4)$ and radius 5.

Practice 5

What is the center of the circle $(x + 2)^2 + (y - 9)^2 = 24$?

5.1 Circles

SUPER TIP
For some questions, a quick sketch can help you get the answer.

Example

The endpoint of the diameter in the circle with equation $(x-2)^2 + (y+3)^2 = 9$ is $(-1, -3)$. What are the coordinates of the other endpoint?

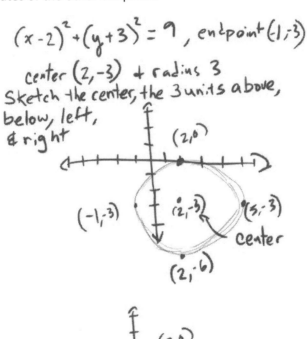

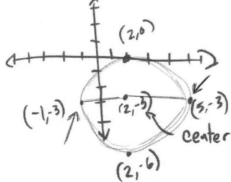

5.1 Circles

> Sketch in the circle. We can see that if one endpoint of the diameter is (-1,-3), then the other endpoint is (5,-3).

Circle Questions Involving Completing the Square

Sometimes we cannot immediately determine the center and radius of a circle from the equation because it's not in center-radius form.

For example, if we were given the equation of circle $x^2 + y^2 - 6x + 2y = 4$, the center and radius aren't readily identifiable.

To get the equation in center-radius form, we need to complete the square twice.

$$x^2 + y^2 - 6x + 2y = 4$$

First we have to organize the x-terms together and y-terms together.

$$x^2 + y^2 - 6x + 2y = 4$$

$$x^2 - 6x + y^2 + 2y = 4$$

Now, we have to complete the square, by first halving and squaring the coefficients in front of the variables raised to the first power (the coefficients of x and y)

$$x^2 - 6x + y^2 + 2y = 4$$

$$\left(\frac{-6}{2}\right)^2 = 9 \qquad \left(\frac{2}{2}\right)^2 = 1$$

9 will complete the square for the x-terms and 1 will complete the square for the y-terms. We have to add the numbers into the equation, but make sure to add them on the right side of the equation also.

5.1 Circles

$$\left(-\frac{6}{2}\right)^2 = 9 \quad \left(\frac{2}{2}\right)^2 = 1$$

$$x^2 - 6x + 9 + y^2 + 2y + 1 = 4 + 9 + 1$$

We can now factor $x^2 - 6x + 9$ and $y^2 + 2y + 1$. We will end up with the circle equation in center-radius form.

$$x^2 - 6x + 9 + y^2 + 2y + 1 = 4 + 9 + 1$$

$$(x-3)(x-3) + (y+1)(y+1) = 14$$

$$(x-3)^2 + (y+1)^2 = 14$$

Practice 6

What is the center of the circle with the equation $x^2 + 6x + y^2 - 8y - 4 = 0$?

Practice 7

What is the radius of the circle with the equation $x^2 - 3x + y^2 - 7y = 1.5$?

5.1 Circles Homework

Homework 1

An XXL pizza has a radius of 14 inches. The pizza is cut into slices of various sizes. The area of one of the slices is $\frac{98}{3}\pi$. What is the central angle that produced a slice with that area?

Homework 2

What is the radius of the circle with the equation $x^2 + 4x + y^2 - 6y = 8$?

Homework 3

How many solutions are there to the system of equations $(x - 4)^2 + (y + 2)^2 = 37$ and $y = 4$?

5.1 Answers to Practice Problems (Circles)

Practice 1: 12π

Circle A has an area of $36\ in^2$. What is the circumference of the circle?

$C = 2\pi r$
↑
need r

given: area = 36π

We can solve for r, then solve for C

$A = \pi r^2$
$36\pi = \pi r^2$
$\dfrac{36\pi}{\pi} = \dfrac{\pi r^2}{\pi}$
$36 = r^2$
$\sqrt{36} = \sqrt{r^2}$
$6 = r$

Now, we can solve for the circumference.

$C = 2\pi r$
$C = 2\pi(6)$
$C = 12\pi$

Practice 2: 16

Calculate the total area of the circle, then use a proportion to find the shaded area.

$A = \pi r^2$
$A = \pi(4)^2$
$A = 16\pi$

$\dfrac{\theta}{2\pi} = \dfrac{S}{A}$

$\dfrac{2}{2\pi} = \dfrac{S}{16\pi}$

$32\pi = 2\pi S$

$\dfrac{32\pi}{2\pi} = \dfrac{2\pi S}{2\pi}$

$\boxed{16 = S}$

5.1 Circles

Practice 3: $\frac{14}{9}\pi$

Calculate the full circumference, then use a proportion to find a portion of it.

$d = 4 \rightarrow r = 2$

$C = 2\pi r = 2\pi(2) = 4\pi$

$$\frac{x}{360} = \frac{L}{C}$$

$$\frac{140}{360} = \frac{L}{4\pi}$$

↳ reduce

$$\frac{7}{18} \bowtie \frac{L}{4\pi}$$

$28\pi = 18L$

$$\frac{28\pi}{18} = \frac{18L}{18}$$

$\frac{14}{9}\pi = L$

Practice 4

$(x+4)^2 + (y-4)^2 = 25$

Practice 5

$(-2, 9)$

Practice 6: (-3, 4)

$x^2 + 6x + y^2 - 8y - 4 = 0$
$ +4 \ +4$

$x^2 + 6x + y^2 - 8y = 4$

Complete the square using $\left(\frac{b}{2}\right)^2$

$\left(\frac{6}{2}\right)^2 = 9 \qquad \left(\frac{-8}{2}\right)^2 = 16$

$x^2 + 6x + 9 + y^2 - 8y + 16 = 4$
$ +9$
$ +16$

$(x+3)^2 + (y-4)^2 = 29$

center: $(-3, 4)$

Practice 7: 4

$x^2 - 3x + y^2 - 7x = 1.5$

Complete the square using $\left(\frac{b}{2}\right)^2$

$\left(\frac{-3}{2}\right)^2 = 2.25 \qquad \left(\frac{-7}{2}\right)^2 = 12.25$

$x^2 - 3x + 2.25 + y^2 - 7y + 12.25 = 1.5$
$ + 2.25$
$ 12.25$

$x^2 - 3x + 2.25 + y^2 - 7y + 12.25 = 16$

It isn't necessary to factor and find the center, we have enough information to find the radius.

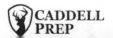

5.1 Circles

$r^2 = 16$
$r = 4$

Homework 1: 60

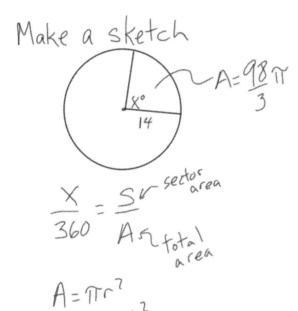

Make a sketch

$\dfrac{x}{360} = \dfrac{sr}{A\pi}$ — sector area / total area

$A = \pi r^2$
$A = \pi(14)^2$
$A = 196\pi$

$\dfrac{x}{360} = \dfrac{S}{A}$

$\dfrac{x}{360} = \dfrac{\frac{98\pi}{3}}{196\pi}$

$196\pi x = 11{,}760\pi$

$\dfrac{196\pi x}{196\pi} = \dfrac{11{,}760\pi}{196\pi}$

$x = 60$

Homework 2: $\sqrt{21}$

$x^2 + 4x + y^2 - 6y = 8$

complete the square

$\left(\dfrac{4}{2}\right)^2 = 4 \qquad \left(\dfrac{-6}{2}\right)^2 = 9$

$x^2 + 4x + 4 + y^2 - 6y + 9 = 8$
$ +4$
$ +9$

$x^2 + 4x + 4 + y^2 - 6y + 9 = 21$

$r^2 = 21$, so $r = \sqrt{21}$

5.1 Circles

Homework 3: 2

$(x-4)^2 + (y+2)^2 = 37$

center: $(4, -2)$

radius = $\sqrt{37}$

$\sqrt{37}$ is a little more than 6

Sketch

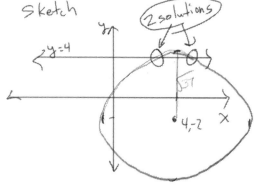

5.2 Angles, Polygons & 3-D Shapes

Naming Angles

An angle can be named based simply by its vertex or by a point on each of its rays and its vertex, with the vertex in the middle.

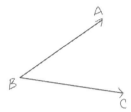

The angle above can be named ∠B, ∠ABC or ∠CBA.

If multiple angles share a vertex, the angles should be named using the vertex and a point on each ray to avoid confusion.

For example, in the diagram below, it would be unclear to refer to any of the angles as ∠X because many angles share X as a vertex.

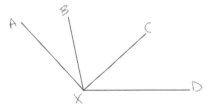

Here are some of the angles that exist in the diagram above.

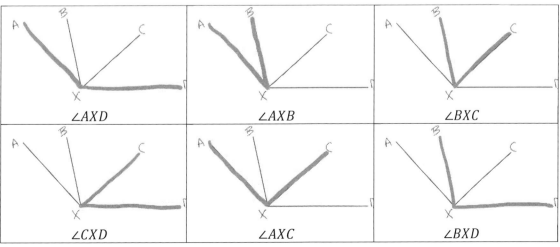

5.2 Angles, Polygons & 3-D Shapes

Supplementary and Complementary

Supplementary Angles

A pair or set of angles that can be combined to form a straight angle add up to $180°$. A pair of angles that add up to $180°$ and called supplementary angles.

In the figure below, $x°$ and $44°$ combine to equal $180°$.

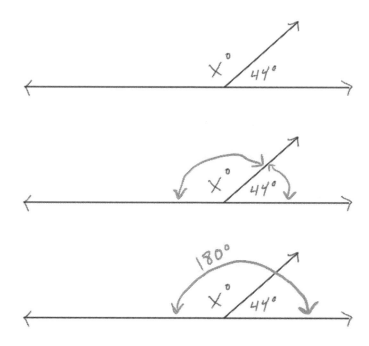

We can set up an equation to solve for x.

$$x + 44 = 180$$
$$-44 \quad -44$$
$$x = 136$$

Below is a slightly modified diagram. Another angle with a measurement of $30°$ is added. What is the value of x now?

5.2 Angles, Polygons & 3-D Shapes

x is still 134. The angle to the left has no effect on the pair of angles on the right.

Angles combined at a vertex add up to $180°$ if they form a straight angle.

Refer to the diagram below.

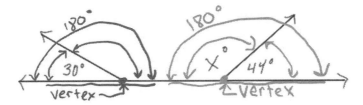

Practice 1

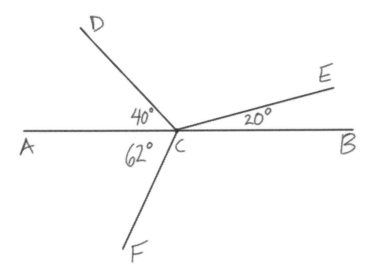

In the diagram above, AB is a straight line that passes through point C. What is the measure of angle DCE?

5.2 Angles, Polygons & 3-D Shapes

Complementary Angles

A pair of angles that add up to 90° is known as complementary angles.

In the diagram below, right angle ABC is split by line segment BD to form complementary angles.

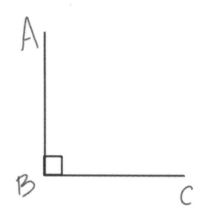
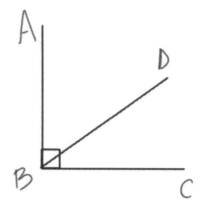

Example

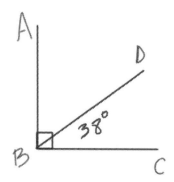

What is the measure of $\angle ABD$ in the diagram above?

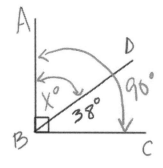

$x + 38 = 90$
$-38-38$
$x = 52$

5.2 Angles, Polygons & 3-D Shapes

SUPER TIP
The two angles in a right triangle other than the right angle are complementary.

In the diagram below, ∠A and ∠B are complementary.

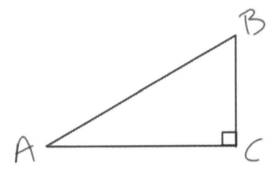

Practice 2

In triangle DEF, angle E is a right angle. If $m\angle D$ is $3x°$ and $m\angle F$ is $(2x - 15)°$, what is the value of x?

5.2 Angles, Polygons & 3-D Shapes

Vertical Angles

When two lines intersect, they form vertical angles which are congruent to each other.

In the diagram below, lines AB and CD intersect at E.

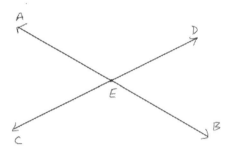

When the two lines intersect, it forms two pairs of congruent angles.

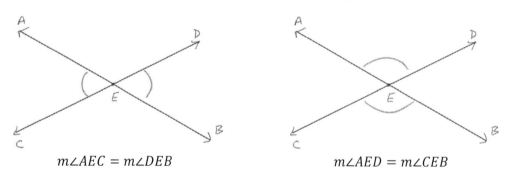

$m\angle AEC = m\angle DEB$ $m\angle AED = m\angle CEB$

Practice 3

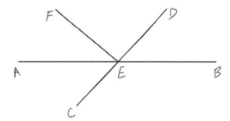

Line segments AB and CD intersect at E. The measure of $\angle AEC$ is $50°$ and the measure of $\angle FED$ is $85°$. What is the measure of angle AEF in the diagram above?

5.2 Angles, Polygons & 3-D Shapes

Parallel Lines Cut by a Transversal

When two parallel lines are intersected by another line, a number of relationships are formed.

In the diagram below line AB is parallel to line CD. Both lines are intersected by line EF.

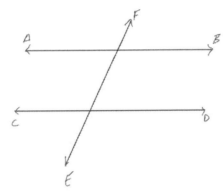

Vertical angles are formed. A pair of vertical angles are show in the diagram below.

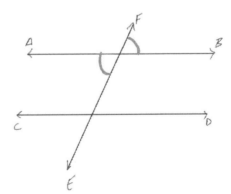

In fact those vertical angles are congruent to the corresponding angles in the bottom part of the diagram.

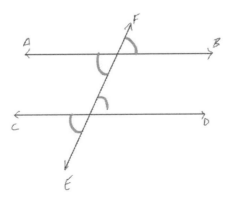

5.2 Angles, Polygons & 3-D Shapes

The other set of four angles are also congruent.

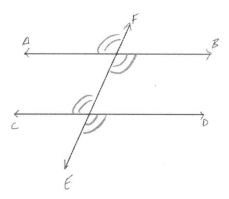

Example

If AE is parallel to CD, what is the value of x?

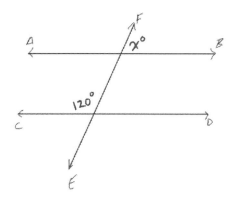

In the diagram above. The angle adjacent to the one measuring $x°$ is also $120°$.

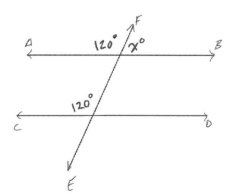

5.2 Angles, Polygons & 3-D Shapes

The adjacent angles form a straight angle, so they add up to $180°$.

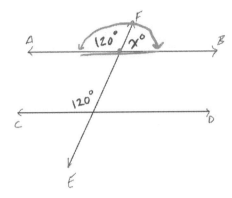

$120 + x = 180$
$-120 \quad\quad -120$
$x = 60$

On the SAT, it is likely that you will have to use the relationships in a more complex diagram.

Practice 4

AB is parallel to CD. Solve for x in the diagram below.

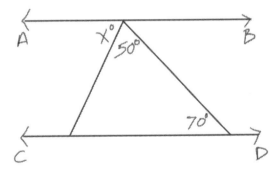

5.2 Angles, Polygons & 3-D Shapes

Area of a Triangle
$A = \frac{1}{2}bh$

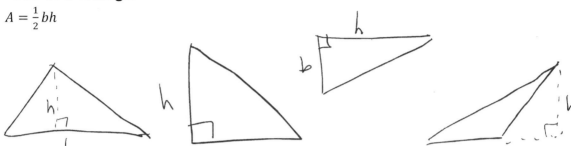

Example

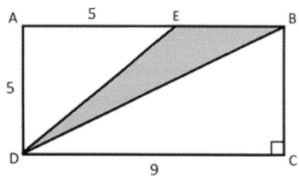

ABCD is a rectangle. What is the area of triangle EBD?

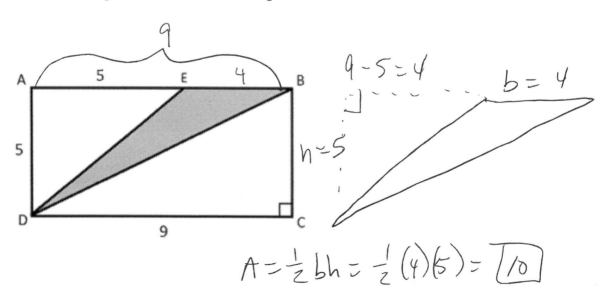

$A = \frac{1}{2}bh = \frac{1}{2}(4)(5) = \boxed{10}$

5.2 Angles, Polygons & 3-D Shapes

Sum of Angles of a Triangle

The sum of the angles of a triangle is 180°.

Example

What is the value of x in the triangle below?

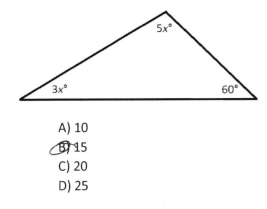

A) 10
B) 15
C) 20
D) 25

$5x + 3x + 60 = 180$

$8x + 60 = 180$

$8x = 120$

$x = 15$

Practice 5

Two angles in an isosceles triangle each have a measure of $3x°$ and the third angle is twice the measure of one of those. What is the measure of the largest angle?

Side Length Inequality in a Triangle

The sum of the 2 smaller sides of a triangle must be greater than the largest side.

Example

Two sides of a triangle are 7 and 10. Which of the following could be the length of the third side?

I. 3
II. 5
III. 17

A. None
B. I only
C. II only ✓
D. II and III only

Two small > biggest
I. $3 + 7 > 10$ NO
II. $5 + 7 > 10$ Yes
III. $7 + 10 > 17$ NO

Practice 6

Which of the following could be the lengths of the sides of a triangle?

A. 4, 5, and 6
B. 3, 4, and 7
C. 3, 4, and 12
D. 2, 4, and 8

Exterior Angle of a Triangle

The sum of 2 angles in a triangle equals the measure of the exterior angle of the third vertex.

Example

In the figure below, what is the average of x and y?

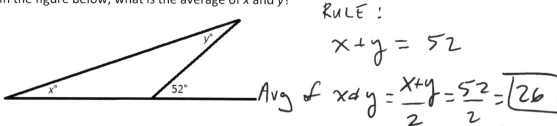

RULE:
$x + y = 52$

Avg of x & $y = \dfrac{x+y}{2} = \dfrac{52}{2} = \boxed{26}$

5.2 Angles, Polygons & 3-D Shapes

Practice 7

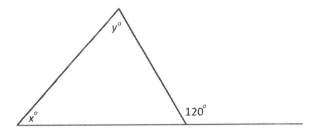

What is the value of $2x + 2y$?

Pythagorean Theorem

Pythagorean Theorem relates the sides of a right triangle.
$$a^2 + b^2 = c^2$$
c must be the length of the hypotenuse, a and b are either leg

Example

In right triangle ABC, angle C is a right angle, side AB is 5 and side AC is 4. What is the length of side BC?

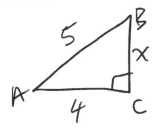

$a^2 + b^2 = c^2$
$4^2 + x^2 = 5^2$
$16 + x^2 = 25$
$-16 \qquad -16$
$x^2 = 9$
$\sqrt{x^2} = \sqrt{9}$
$x = 3$

3

Practice 8

5.2 Angles, Polygons & 3-D Shapes

In triangle ABC, angle C is a right angle, side AB is 9 and side BC is 4. What is the length of side AC?

   A. $2\sqrt{5}$
   B. 5
   C. $\sqrt{42}$
   D. $\sqrt{65}$

Similar Triangles

Similar triangles are in proportion to each other and have congruent angles.

Therefore, if triangle ABC is similar to triangle RST
$$angle\ A = angle\ R, angle\ B = angle\ S, and\ angle\ C = angle\ T$$

And
$$\frac{AB}{RS} = \frac{BC}{ST} = \frac{AC}{RT}$$

Example

Triangle ABC is similar to Triangle DEF. $\overline{AB}$ is 5cm, and $\overline{BC}$ is 8cm. If $\overline{EF}$ is 10 cm, how long is $\overline{DE}$?

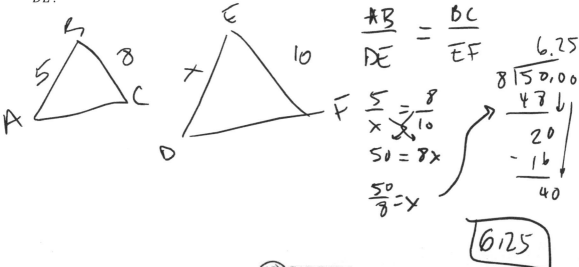

5.2 Angles, Polygons & 3-D Shapes

Practice 9

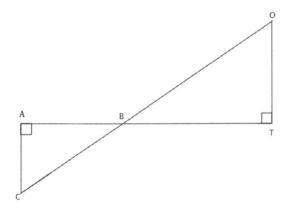

In the diagram above, $\overline{AB}$ is 5cm and $\overline{AC}$ is 12 cm. If $\overline{OT}$ is 7.5cm, what is the length of $\overline{OB}$?

Common Right Triangles/Pythagorean Triplets (not given on SAT, must memorize)

3-4-5 and 5-12-13

3-4-5

5-12-13

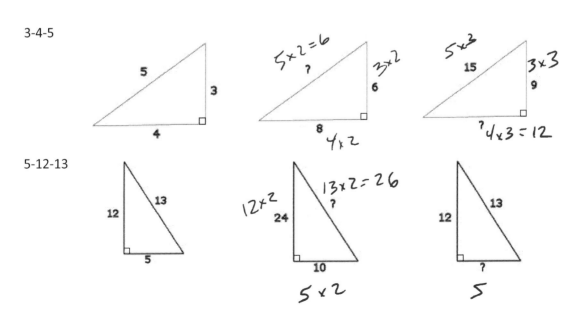

5.2 Angles, Polygons & 3-D Shapes

Example

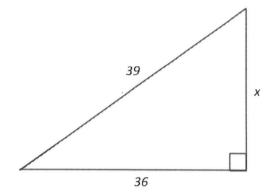

Note: figure not drawn to scale

What is the value of x in the diagram above?

using the sides that are given, this is a 5-12-13 right triangle with a scale-factor of 3

$x = 5 \cdot 3 = 15$

Example

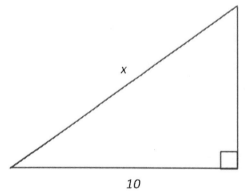

Note: figure not drawn to scale

What is the value of x in the diagram above?

This is a trap.
It looks like a 5-12-13 right $\triangle$ with a scale factor of 2, but the 13 must be the hypotenuse.
We must use pythagorean theorem for this.

$a^2 + b^2 = c^2$
$10^2 + 26^2 = x^2$
$100 + 676 = x^2$
$776 = x^2$
$\sqrt{776} = x$
$\sqrt{4}\sqrt{194} = x$
$2\sqrt{194} = x$

5.2 Angles, Polygons & 3-D Shapes

Practice 10

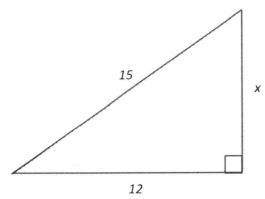

Note: figure not drawn to scale

What is the value of x in the diagram above?

Common Right Triangles (given on SAT)

45°-45°-90°

30°-60°-90°

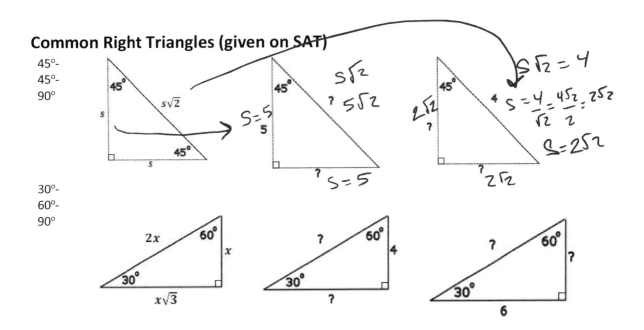

Example

5.2 Angles, Polygons & 3-D Shapes

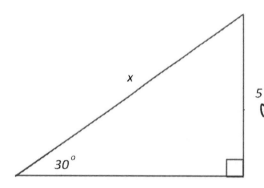

Note: figure not drawn to scale

What is the value of x in the diagram above?

The hypotenuse, $2x$, is $2(5) = 10$

$\boxed{10}$

Example

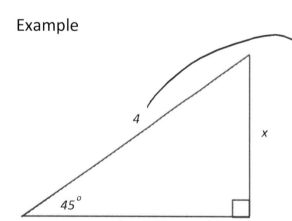

Note: figure not drawn to scale

What is the value of x in the diagram above?

$4 = s\sqrt{2}$

$\dfrac{4}{\sqrt{2}} = s$

simplify

$\dfrac{4}{\sqrt{2}} \cdot \dfrac{\sqrt{2}}{\sqrt{2}} = \dfrac{4\sqrt{2}}{2} = 2\sqrt{2}$

$x = s = \boxed{2\sqrt{2}}$

5.2 Angles, Polygons & 3-D Shapes

Practice 11

In the figure below, what is the perimeter of triangle ABC?

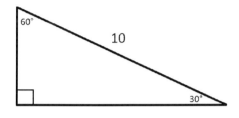

A. $5 + 5\sqrt{3}$
B. $10 + 10\sqrt{3}$
C. $15 + 5\sqrt{3}$
D. $15 + 10\sqrt{3}$

Isosceles Triangles

Isosceles triangles have a pair of congruent angles and the sides opposite the congruent angles are also congruent.

Example

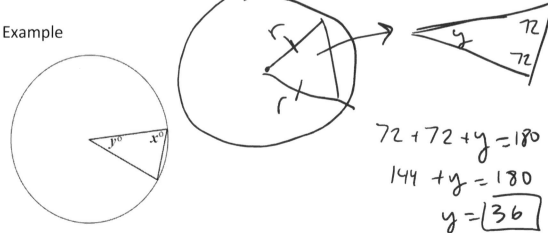

If $x = 72°$, what is the value of y?

5.2 Angles, Polygons & 3-D Shapes

Practice 12

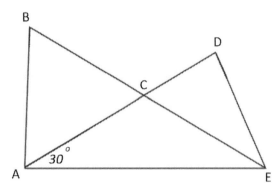

In the diagram above, $\overline{AC}$ and $\overline{CE}$ are congruent. What is the measure of angle ACE?

Equilateral Triangles

All sides of an equilateral triangle are congruent. All angles are congruent (60°).

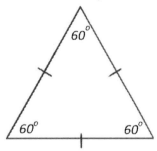

Example

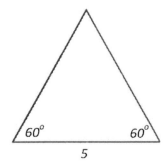

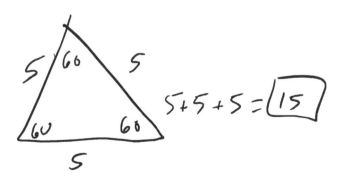

What is the perimeter of the triangle above?

5.2 Angles, Polygons & 3-D Shapes

Practice 13

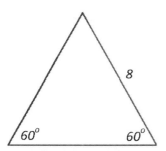

What is the perimeter of the triangle above?

Area of Equilateral Triangle

$$A = \frac{s^2\sqrt{3}}{4}$$

Example

What is the area of an equilateral triangle whose sides are 8?

A. 8
B. $8\sqrt{3}$
C. 16
D. $16\sqrt{3}$ ← (circled)

$A = \dfrac{s^2\sqrt{3}}{4} = \dfrac{8^2\sqrt{3}}{4} = \dfrac{64\sqrt{3}}{4} = 16\sqrt{3}$

5.2 Angles, Polygons & 3-D Shapes

Practice 14

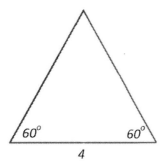

What is the area of the triangle above?

Rectangles

Opposite sides are parallel and congruent.
All four angles are right angles.

When diagonals are drawn, special right triangles are created.

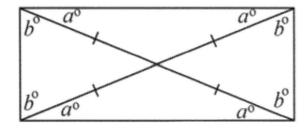 

5.2 Angles, Polygons & 3-D Shapes

Example

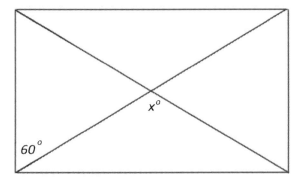

What is the value of x in the diagram above?

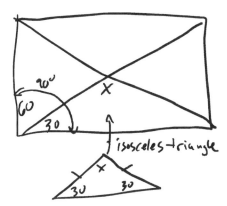

Practice 15

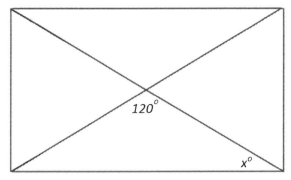

What is the value of x in the diagram above?

5.2 Angles, Polygons & 3-D Shapes

Squares

All sides are congruent.
Opposite sides are parallel.
All four angles are right angles.

When diagonals are drawn, special right triangles are created.

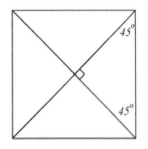

Example

If one side of a square is 8 cm, what is the measure of the diagonal?

A. $8\sqrt{2}$ cm
B. 16 cm
C. 64 cm
D. 128 cm

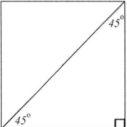
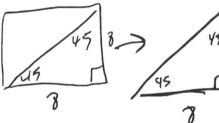
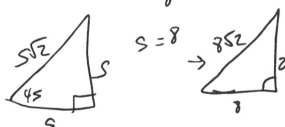

Practice 16

What is the area of square whose diagonal is 6?

A. 9
B. $9\sqrt{2}$
C. 18
D. $18\sqrt{2}$

5.2 Angles, Polygons & 3-D Shapes

Parallelograms

Opposite sides are parallel and congruent.
Opposite angles are congruent.
Adjacent angles are supplementary.

$a + b = 180°$

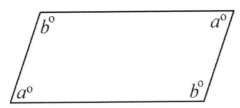

Example

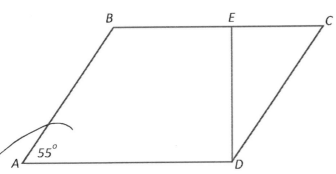

In parallelogram ABCD above, angle A is 55 degrees. What is the measure of angle C?

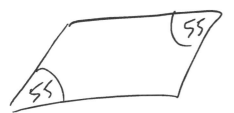

You can ignore DE

5.2 Angles, Polygons & 3-D Shapes

Practice 17

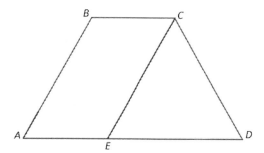

Triangle CDE is an equilateral triangle, and quadrilateral ABCE is a parallelogram. What is the measure of angle A?

Sum of Exterior Angles

The sum of exterior angles is 360°.

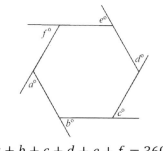

$$a + b + c + d + e + f = 360$$

Sum of Interior Angles

3 sides: 180°
4 sides: 360°
5 sides: 540°
6 sides: 720°
Rule: add 180° for each additional side.

Note: A "regular" polygon has congruent angles and congruent sides.

5.2 Angles, Polygons & 3-D Shapes

Example

What is the measure of an exterior angle of a regular pentagon?

All 5 exterior angles add up to 360

360 ÷ 5 = 72   **72**

Practice 18

What is the measure of an interior angle of a regular octagon?

Area of a Regular Hexagon

$$A = \frac{3\sqrt{3}}{2} s^2$$

s is length of a side

This is not a commonly needed formula, but it does show up sometimes. Memorizing it makes solving this type of problem much easier. If you don't memorize it, you can solve for the area by making six equilateral triangles in the hexagon and finding the area of those.

Example

A regular hexagon has a side with a length of 4 cm. What is the area of the hexagon?

$A = \frac{3\sqrt{3}}{2} s^3 = \frac{3\sqrt{3}(4)^3}{2} = \frac{3\sqrt{3}(64)}{2} = \frac{3\sqrt{3}(64)^{32}}{2} = 96\sqrt{3}$

Practice 19

A regular hexagon has a side with a length of 4 cm. What is the area of the hexagon?

5.2 Angles, Polygons & 3-D Shapes

Volume of a Rectangular Prism

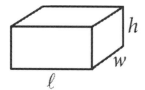

$V = \ell w h$

Example

A box has a height of 3 inches, width of 2 ft, and length of 4 ft. What is the volume of the box in cubic feet?

all measurements must be in feet

$h = 3 \text{ in} = \frac{3}{12} \text{ ft} = \frac{1}{4} \text{ ft}$
$w = 2$
$\ell = 4$

$V = \ell w h$
$V = (4)(2)(\frac{1}{4}) = \boxed{2}$

Practice 20

A crate has a length of 5 ft, width of 3 feet, and a height of 6 inches. What is the volume of the crate?

Volume of a Cube

A cube is a rectangular prism in which the length, width and height are the same.

Therefore $V = lwh = sss = s^3$

$$V = s^3$$

Example

What is the volume of a cube with a side length of 3 cm?

$V = s^3 = 3^3 = \boxed{27}$

5.2 Angles, Polygons & 3-D Shapes

Practice 21

The volume of a cube is 64 cubic centimeters. What is the length of one of its sides?

Volume of a Cylinder

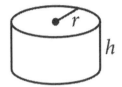

$$V = \pi r^2 h$$

Example

A cylindrical container has a radius of 10 ft and a height of 20 ft. If the container is filled with water to a height of 12 ft, what is the volume of water in the container in cubic feet? Keep your answer in terms of π.

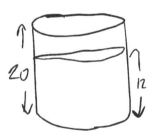

$$V = \pi r^2 h$$
$$V = \pi (10)^2 (12)$$
$$V = 1200\pi$$

Practice 22

What is the volume of a cylinder with a radius of 4 inches and a height of 6 inches? Keep your answer in terms of π.

5.2 Angles, Polygons & 3-D Shapes

Volume of a Sphere

$$V = \frac{4}{3}\pi r^3$$

Example

A spherical balloon had a radius of 3 inches. If someone added more add to the balloon so it had a radius of 6 inches, what volume of air was added to the balloon?

A. $3\pi \ in^3$
B. $9\pi \ in^3$
C. $27\pi \ in^3$
D. $252\pi \ in^3$ ← (circled)

$V = \frac{4}{3}\pi r^3$

START $V = \frac{4}{3}\pi (3)^3 = 36\pi$

END $V = \frac{4}{3}\pi (6)^3 = 288\pi$

Difference $= 288\pi - 36\pi = 252\pi$

Practice 23

A spherical container has an inner radius of 3 inches. What is the greatest volume of water can it hold? Keep your answer in terms of π.

5.2 Angles, Polygons & 3-D Shapes

Volume of a Cone

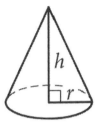

$$V = \frac{1}{3}\pi r^2 h$$

Example

A conical vessel for holding rainwater is 12 feet tall with a radius of 4 feet. It is upside down with an open base for collecting rainwater. If the depth of the water in the vessel is 9 feet, what is the volume of water in the conical vessel, in cubic feet?

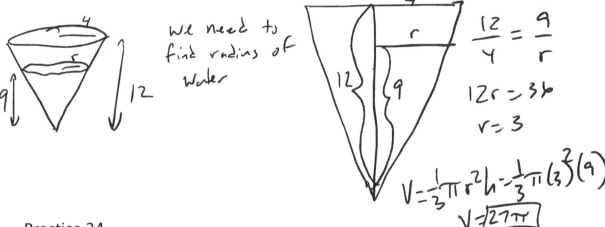

Practice 24

The density of water is 1 gram per cubic centimeter. A cone with a height of 5 cm and a base with a radius of 2 cm is filled with water. What is the mass of the water in the cone, in grams? Round to the nearest gram.

5.2 Angles, Polygons & 3-D Shapes

Volume of a Pyramid

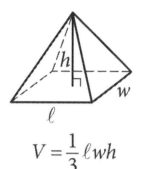

$$V = \frac{1}{3}\ell wh$$

Example

The base of a pyramid is a square with a side length of 4 inches. The height of the pyramid is 9 inches. What is the volume of the pyramid?

$$V = \frac{1}{3}\ell wh = \frac{1}{3}(4)(4)(9) = \boxed{48 \text{ in}^3}$$

Practice 25

The base of a pyramid is a rectangular with a width of 2 cm and length of 3 cm. If the height of the pyramid is 5 cm, what is the volume?

5.2 Angles, Polygons & 3-D Shapes Homework

Homework 1

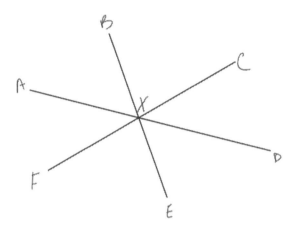

In the diagram above, angle AXB is $48°$, angle CXD is $44°$, and the measure of angle FXE is $9x - 2$ degrees, what is the value of x?

Homework 2

Line segment AB is perpendicular to CD at B. What is the value of x?

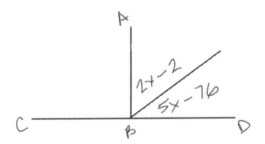

Homework 3

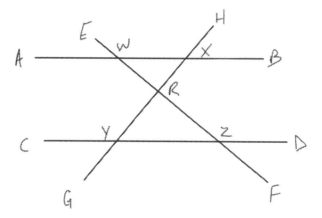

In the diagram above, AB is parallel to CD. The measure of angle XWR is $35°$ and the measure of angle YRZ if $94°$. What is the measure of angle CYR?

Homework 4

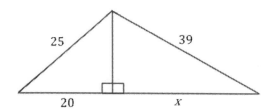

Note: figure not drawn to scale

What is the value of x in the diagram above?

Homework 5

The water from a full conical cup with a radius of 2 inches and a height of 6 inches will be poured into a cylindrical cup with a radius of 1 inch and a height of 10 inches. What will the height of the water be in the cylindrical cup?

5.2 Angles, Polygons & 3-D Shapes

5.2 Answers to Practice Problems (Angles)

Practice 1: 120

To solve this, we have to look for a relationship or relationships that relate angle DCE to the other angles. In this case, since AB is a straight line, angle ACB is 180°.

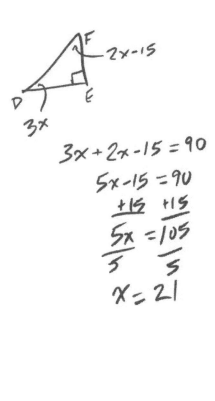

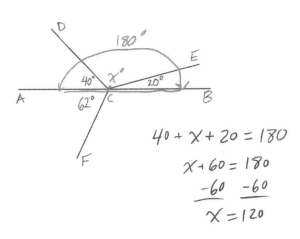

Practice 2: 21

In a right triangle, the two angles other than the right angle add up to 90 degrees.

5.2 Angles, Polygons & 3-D Shapes

Practice 3: $45°$

Let's first add the given information to the diagram.

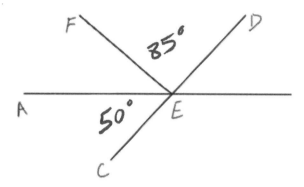

Notice that angles CEA, AEF, and FED combine to form a straight angle (180 degrees).

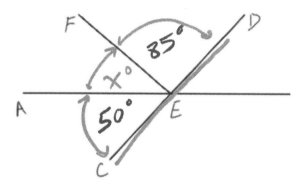

We can create an equation based on the angles adding up to 180 and solve for the missing angle.

$$50 + x + 85 = 180$$
$$135 + x = 180$$
$$-135 \quad -135$$
$$x = 45$$

Practice 4: 60

There are a number of ways to solve this problem. Here is one of them.

The two angles marked below are congruent because they are alternate interior angles.

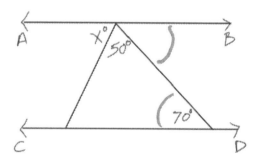

Both of them are $70°$.

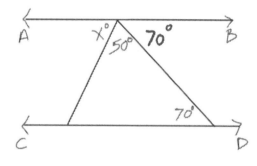

The three angles form a straight angle, which is $180°$.

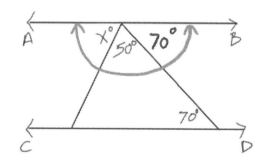

5.2 Angles, Polygons & 3-D Shapes

$x + 50 + 70 = 180$

$x + 120 = 180$

$x = 60$

Practice 5: 90

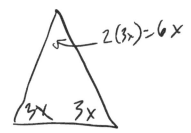

$3x + 3x + 6x = 180$
$12x = 180$
$x = 15$

large $= 6x = 6(15) = 90$

Practice 6: A

The sum of the two smaller sides must be greater than the largest side.

$4 + 5 > 6$
$9 > 6$ ✓

Practice 7: 240

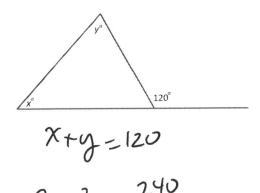

$x + y = 120$

$2x + 2y = 240$

Practice 8: D

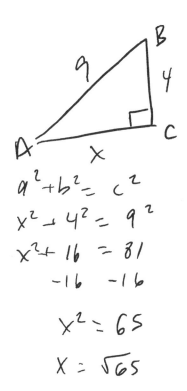

$a^2 + b^2 = c^2$
$x^2 + 4^2 = 9^2$
$x^2 + 16 = 81$
$ -16 -16$
$x^2 = 65$
$x = \sqrt{65}$

5.2 Angles, Polygons & 3-D Shapes

Practice 9: 19.5

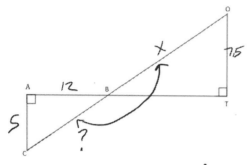

We don't have enough info to set up a proportion and solve for x

△ABC is a 5-12-13 right △

Practice 10: 9

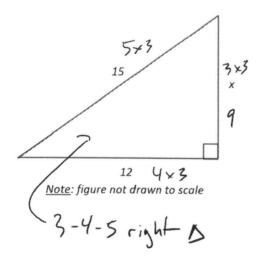

3-4-5 right △

Practice 11: C

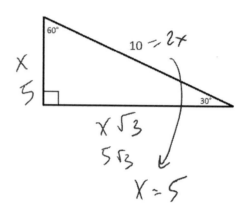

$10 = 2x$

$x\sqrt{3}$
$5\sqrt{3}$
$x = 5$

$5 + 10 + 5\sqrt{3}$
$15 + 5\sqrt{3}$

Practice 12: 120

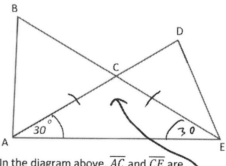

In the diagram above, $\overline{AC}$ and $\overline{CE}$ are congruent.
Triangle ACE is an isosceles triangle.

$30 + 30 = 60$

$180 - 60 = 120$

5.2 Angles, Polygons & 3-D Shapes

Practice 13: 24

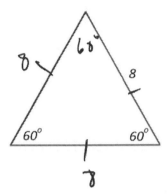

$8 + 8 + 8 = 24$

Practice 14: $4\sqrt{3}$

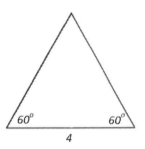

$A = \dfrac{s^2\sqrt{3}}{4} = \dfrac{4^2\sqrt{3}}{4}$

$= \dfrac{16\sqrt{3}}{4} = 4\sqrt{3}$

Practice 15: 30

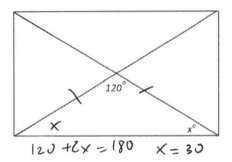

$120 + 2x = 180 \quad x = 30$

Practice 16: C

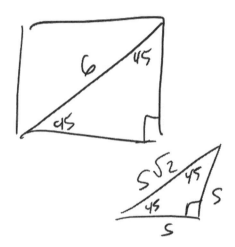

$s\sqrt{2} = 6$

$s = \dfrac{6}{\sqrt{2}}$

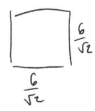

5.2 Angles, Polygons & 3-D Shapes

$$A = \frac{6}{\sqrt{2}} \cdot \frac{6}{\sqrt{2}} = \frac{36}{2} = 18$$

Practice 17: 60

Triangle CDE is an equilateral triangle

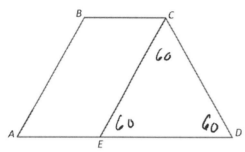

Triangle CDE is an equilateral triangle

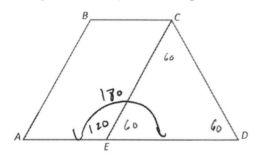

Since ABCE is a parallelogram, angle A and angle AEC are supplementary. Therefore, angle A is 60°

Practice 18: 135

Sides	degrees
3	180
4	360
5	540
6	720
7	900
8	1080

$$\frac{1080}{8} = 135$$

OR

exterior angle

$$\frac{360}{8} = 45$$

interior angle

$$180 - 45 = 135$$

Practice 19: $24\sqrt{3}$

$A = \dfrac{3\sqrt{3}}{2} s^2 = \dfrac{3\sqrt{3}(4)^2}{2}$

$A = \dfrac{3\sqrt{3}(16)}{2} = \dfrac{3\sqrt{3}\,\overset{8}{\cancel{(16)}}}{\cancel{2}}$

$A = 24\sqrt{3}$

Practice 20: 7.5

$V = \ell \cdot w \cdot h$

6 inches = ½ ft

$V = 5 \cdot 3 \cdot \dfrac{1}{2} = \boxed{7.5\ ft^3}$

Practice 21: 4

$V = s^3$
$64 = s^3$
$\sqrt[3]{64} = \sqrt[3]{s^3}$
$\boxed{4} = s$

Practice 22: 96π

$V = \pi r^2 h$
$V = \pi (4)^2 (6)$
$V = 96\pi$

Practice 23: 36π

$V = \dfrac{4}{3}\pi r^3$
$V = \dfrac{4}{3}\pi (3)^3$
$V = \dfrac{4}{3}\pi (27)$
$V = \dfrac{4}{\cancel{3}}\pi (\overset{9}{\cancel{27}}) = 36\pi$

Practice 24: 21

$V = \dfrac{1}{3}\pi r^2 h$
$V = \dfrac{1}{3}\pi (2)^2 (5)$
$V = 20.94\ cm^3$

$1g = 1cm^3$

$20.94 \approx 21$

5.2 Angles, Polygons & 3-D Shapes

Practice 25: 10

$$V = \frac{1}{3}\ell w h$$

$$V = \frac{1}{3}(3)(2)(5)$$

$$V = 10$$

Homework 1: 10

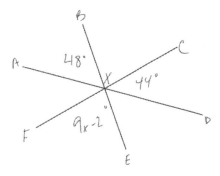

Angle FXE and angle BXC are vertical angles, so they equal each other. We can label angle BXC as $9x - 2$ degrees.

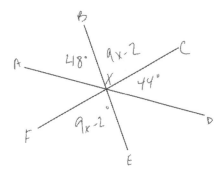

AD is a straight line, so it forms a straight angle, which is $180°$.

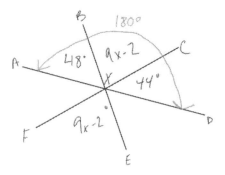

We can set up an equation in which the three angles add up to $180°$ then solve for x.

$$48 + 9x - 2 + 44 = 180$$
$$9x + 90 = 180$$
$$ -90 -90$$
$$9x = 90$$
$$\frac{9x}{9} = \frac{90}{9}$$
$$x = 10$$

Homework 2: 24

Since segment AB is perpendicular to CD at B, angle ABC and angle ABD are both right angles and are $90°$.

5.2 Angles, Polygons & 3-D Shapes

them. Angle RZY is also $35°$ because angle RZY and angle RWX are alternate interior angles.

The angles in triangle YRZ add up to $180°$, so we can solve for angle RYZ.

$$2x-2 + 5x-76 = 90$$
$$7x - 78 = 90$$
$$+78 \quad +78$$
$$7x = 168$$
$$\frac{7x}{7} = \frac{168}{7}$$
$$x = 24$$

$$35 + 94 + x = 180$$
$$129 + x = 180$$
$$-129 \quad -129$$
$$x = 51$$

Now, that we know the measure of angle RYZ, we can solve for angle CYR.

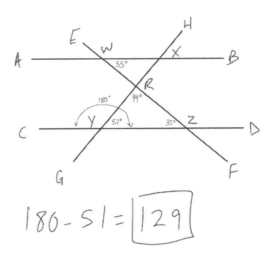

$$180 - 51 = \boxed{129}$$

Homework 3: 129

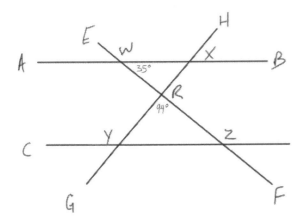

Since AB is parallel to CD, sets of congruent angles are formed when EF intersects

5.2 Angles, Polygons & 3-D Shapes

Homework 4: 36

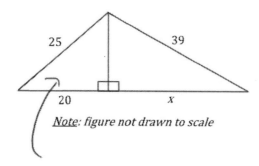

Note: figure not drawn to scale

3-4-5 △

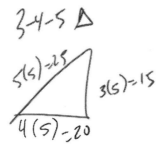

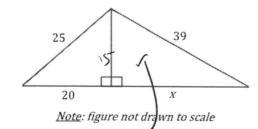

Note: figure not drawn to scale

5-12-13 △

$5(3)$ $13(3) = 39$
$12(3) = 36$

Homework 5: 8

$V_{cone} = \frac{1}{3}\pi r^2 h$
$= \frac{1}{3}\pi (2)^2 (6)$
$= 8\pi$

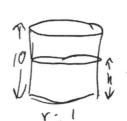

$r = 1$

$V = \pi r^2 h$
$8\pi = \pi (1)^2 h$
$\dfrac{8\pi}{\pi} = \dfrac{\pi h}{\pi}$
$8 = h$

5.3 Trigonometry

Sine, Cosine and Tangent

The trigonometric ratios sine, cosine and tangent, can be remembered by the acronym SOHCAHTOA.

SOH	CAH	TOA
$sinA = \dfrac{opposite}{hypotenuse}$	$cosA = \dfrac{adjacent}{hypotenuse}$	$tanA = \dfrac{opposite}{adjacent}$

Hypotenuse: the longest side of a right triangle. It is always across from the right angle.

Opposite: the side opposite the angle.

Adjacent: the side next to the angle that isn't the hypotenuse.

Here are some examples labeled in reference to angle A.

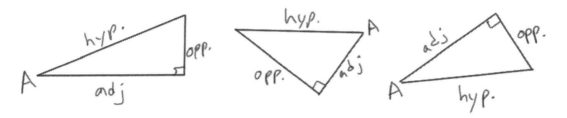

Example

In triangle ABC, angle C is a right angle. If the length of side AC is 3 and the length of side BC is 4, what is $sinB$?

It will help to make a sketch.

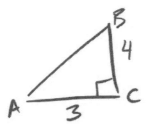

To find $sinB$, we need to find the length of side AB.

5.3 Trigonometry

We can use Pythagorean theorem to solve for the missing length.

$$a^2 + b^2 = c^2$$
$$3^2 + 4^2 = c^2$$
$$9 + 16 = c^2$$
$$25 = c^2$$
$$\sqrt{25} = \sqrt{c^2}$$
$$5 = c$$

Now, we have all of the side lengths.

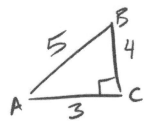

Let's label the sides in reference to angle B then find $sinB$.

$$sinB = \frac{opp}{hyp}$$

$$sinB = \frac{3}{5}$$

5.3 Trigonometry

Practice 1

In triangle PQR, angle Q is a right angle. If the length of side PQ is 5 and the length of PR is 13, what is $sinP$?

Sine, Cosine, and Tangent are Ratios

If $cosA = \frac{2}{5}$, it doesn't mean that the length of the adjacent side is 2 and the length of the hypotenuse is 5, it just means that the ratio of length of the adjacent side to the length of the hypotenuse is $2:5$.

If two triangles are similar, they have congruent angles and their side lengths are proportionate. Also, Sine of one angle will equal sine of the corresponding angle in the other triangle.

For example, If triangle ABC is similar to triangle DEF, it means:

$$\angle A \cong \angle D$$
$$\angle B \cong \angle E$$
$$\angle C \cong \angle F$$

The order that the vertices are written match up with each other.

Since the angles are congruent, then

$$sinA = sinD$$
$$sinB = sinE$$
$$sinC = sinF$$

And the same is true for the other trigonometric ratios also, such as $cosA = cosD$.

5.3 Trigonometry

Example

Triangle ABC has a right angle at C. Triangle ABC is similar to triangle RST. If $tanA = \frac{4}{3}$, what is $cosS$?

$$tanA = \frac{4}{3} = \frac{opp}{adj}$$

[Triangle ABC with right angle at C, side BC = 4, side AC = 3, AB = 5]

$$AB = 5$$

$$cosS = ?$$
$$cosS = cosB = \frac{adj}{hyp} = \frac{3}{5}$$

Practice 2

Triangle ABC and triangle XYZ are similar. If $sinB = 0.2$, what is $sinY$?

$$SinA^o = Cos(90^o - A^o)$$

The SAT tends to question students on these concepts:

$$\sin(x^o) = \cos(90^o - x^o)$$

In other words, sine of an angle is equal to cosine of the complement.

Let's look at why.

Also, if $sinA = cosB$, then $A + B = 90$

5.3 Trigonometry

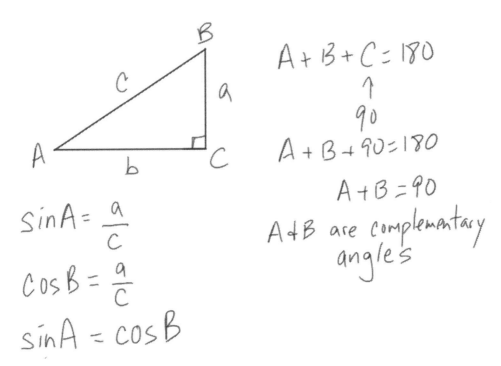

When you do $sinA$, the opposite side is BC, with length a. When you find $cosB$, the adjacent side is BC, with length a.

Example

In right triangle ABC, angle C is a right angle. If $sinA = 0.24$, what is $cosB$?

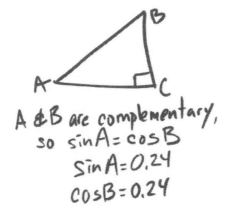

Practice 3

Angle A measures $40°$, and $sinA = cosB$. What is the measure, in degrees, of angle B, if angle B is an acute angle?

5.3 Trigonometry Homework

Homework 1

In right triangle RST, angle R is a right angle. If $sinS = 0.8$, what is $cosT$?

Homework 2

In right triangle DEF, angle E is a right angle. If $cosD = 0.2$, what is $sinD$?

5.3 Answers to Practice Problems (Trigonometry)

Practice 1: 12/13

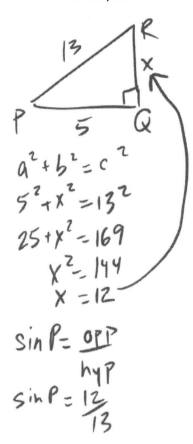

Practice 2: 0.2

$\triangle ABC \sim \triangle XYZ$

$\angle B \cong \angle Y$

$\sin Y = \sin B = 0.2$

Practice 3: 50

If $\sin A = \cos B$, A and B are complementary angles. If A is $40°$, then B is $50°$.

Homework 1: 0.8

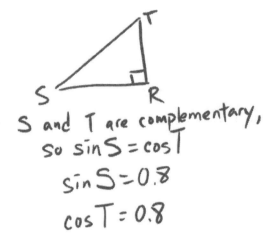

S and T are complementary, so $\sin S = \cos T$

$\sin S = 0.8$

$\cos T = 0.8$

Homework 2: $\frac{2\sqrt{6}}{5}$

$\cos D = 0.2$. There is no direct rule to immediately find $\sin D$. We can sketch a triangle and use Pythagorean theorem to find $\sin D$.

$0.2 = \frac{2}{10} = \frac{1}{5}$, so we can label the adjacent side 1 and the hypotenuse 5.

5.3 Trigonometry

Triangle DEF with right angle at E, DF = 5 (hypotenuse), EF = 1, DE = x.

$a^2 + b^2 = c^2$

$1^2 + x^2 = 5^2$

$1 + x^2 = 25$

$x^2 = 24$

$x = \sqrt{24} = \sqrt{4}\sqrt{6} = 2\sqrt{6}$

$\cos D = \dfrac{adj}{hyp} = \boxed{\dfrac{2\sqrt{6}}{5}}$

5.4 Simplifying Rational Expressions

Sometimes to simplify an expression we need to get common denominators, so we can add the expressions together.

Example

$$\frac{x}{x+4} + \frac{5}{x+4}$$

In the expression above, the two fractions have the same denominator, so we just add the numerators.

$$\frac{x}{x+4} + \frac{5}{x+4}$$

$$\frac{x+5}{x+4}$$

The final answer is

$$\frac{x+5}{x+4}$$

Example

$$\frac{1}{x+3} + \frac{3}{5}$$

In the example above, the denominators are different, so we need to get a common denominator before adding.

In this case, the least common denominator will just be the product of the two denominators: $5(x+3)$.

To do that, we should multiply the numerator and denominator of the first term by 5 and multiply the numerator and denominator of the second term by $x+3$.

5.4 Simplifying Rational Expressions

$$\frac{1}{x+3} + \frac{3}{5}$$

$$\frac{1(5)}{(x+3)(5)} + \frac{3(x+3)}{5(x+3)}$$

$$\frac{5}{5(x+3)} + \frac{3x+9}{5(x+3)}$$

$$\frac{3x+14}{5(x+3)}$$

The final answer is

$$\frac{3x+14}{5(x+3)}$$

Example

$$\frac{2}{x^2-16} - \frac{5}{x+4}$$

The two terms in the example above don't have common denominators. To determine what the least common denominator is, we should factor the denominators as much as we can.

$$\frac{2}{x^2-16} - \frac{5}{x+4}$$

$$\frac{2}{(x+4)(x-4)} - \frac{5}{x+4}$$

The least common denominator is $(x+4)(x-4)$. The denominator of the first term is already $(x+4)(x-4)$. The denominator of the second terms already has $x+4$, so we just need to multiply it by $x-4$.

5.4 Simplifying Rational Expressions

$$\frac{2}{(x+4)(x-4)} - \frac{5(x-4)}{(x+4)(x-4)}$$

$$\frac{2}{(x+4)(x-4)} - \frac{5x-20}{(x+4)(x-4)}$$

We can now subtract the two numerators. Remember that since it is subtraction, we will have to distribute the negative to each of the terms in the second numerator.

$$\frac{2}{(x+4)(x-4)} - \frac{5x+20}{(x+4)(x-4)}$$

$$\frac{2-(5x+20)}{(x+4)(x-4)}$$

$$\frac{2-5x-20}{(x+4)(x-4)}$$

$$\frac{-5x-18}{(x+4)(x-4)}$$

The final answer is

$$\frac{-5x+22}{(x+4)(x-4)}$$

5.4 Simplifying Rational Expressions

> **SUPER TIP**
> Don't forget about our math tricks! We can substitute a value in for the variables and evaluate the expression in the question and then evaluate the answer choices to see which answer choice has the same value as the expression in the question. Review Lesson 1.1

Practice 1

What is the sum of $\frac{5}{x-3}$ and $\frac{2x}{x^2-9}$?

A. $\frac{2x+5}{x^2+x-12}$

B. $\frac{2x+5}{x^2-9}$

C. $\frac{7x+15}{x^2-9}$

D. $\frac{7x}{x^2-9}$

Complex Rational Expressions

If we have a complex fraction with fractions in the numerator and denominator, we can simply it by multiplying all terms by the least common denominator of all of the expressions.

Example

Simplify the following expression.

$$\frac{\frac{1}{x}+\frac{1}{y}}{\frac{1}{x^2}-\frac{1}{y^2}}$$

In the example above, we have four different denominators: x, y, x^2, and y^2.

The least common denominator is x^2y^2 because all of the denominators can multiply to equal it.

5.4 Simplifying Rational Expressions

We will multiply each term by x^2y^2.

$$\frac{(x^2y^2)\frac{1}{x} + \frac{1}{y}(x^2y^2)}{(x^2y^2)\frac{1}{x^2} + \frac{1}{y^2}(x^2y^2)}$$

$$\frac{\frac{x^2y^2}{x} + \frac{x^2y^2}{y}}{\frac{x^2y^2}{x^2} + \frac{x^2y^2}{y^2}}$$

We can reduce each of the fractions now.

$$\frac{\frac{x^2y^2}{x} + \frac{x^2y^2}{y}}{\frac{x^2y^2}{x^2} + \frac{x^2y^2}{y^2}}$$

$$\frac{xy^2 + x^2y}{y^2 + x^2}$$

The final answer is

$$\frac{xy^2 + x^2y}{y^2 + x^2}$$

Practice 2

Simplify the following expression.

$$\dfrac{\dfrac{1}{x}-\dfrac{1}{y}}{\dfrac{x}{y}}$$

A. $\dfrac{xy}{x^2y}$

B. $\dfrac{y-x}{x^2}$

C. $\dfrac{x-y}{x^2}$

D. $\dfrac{x}{xy-x}$

5.4 Simplifying Rational Expressions Homework

Homework 1

Simplify

$$\frac{2x}{5} - \frac{x-2}{5x}$$

A. $\dfrac{2x^2-x-2}{5x}$

B. $\dfrac{2x^2-x+2}{5x}$

C. $\dfrac{x-2}{5x}$

D. $-\dfrac{2x^2-4x}{25x}$

Homework 2

Simplify

$$\frac{3x}{x-2} + \frac{x+3}{x^2-4}$$

A. $\dfrac{3x^2+7x+3}{x^2-4}$

B. $\dfrac{4x+3}{x^2+x-6}$

C. $\dfrac{4x+3}{x^2-4}$

D. $\dfrac{3x^2+9x}{x^2-4}$

Homework 3

Simplify the following expression.

$$\frac{\dfrac{1}{x-y} - \dfrac{1}{x+y}}{\dfrac{x}{x^2-y^2}}$$

A. $\dfrac{2y}{x}$

B. $\dfrac{-xy}{x^2-y^2}$

C. $\dfrac{-xy}{x+y}$

D. $x-y$

Homework 4

Simplify the following expression.

$$\frac{\dfrac{1}{2x} - \dfrac{1}{2y}}{\dfrac{x}{xy}}$$

A. $\dfrac{4xy}{x-y}$

B. $\dfrac{2x+2y}{y}$

C. $\dfrac{xy}{x-y}$

D. $\dfrac{y-x}{2x}$

5.4 Answers to Practice Problems (Simplifying Rational Expressions)

Practice 1: C

What is the sum of $\frac{5}{x-3}$ and $\frac{2x}{x^2-9}$?

$$\frac{5}{x-3} + \frac{2x}{x^2-9}$$

We need common denominators.

Factor the denominators to find the common denominator.

$$\frac{5}{x-3} + \frac{2x}{(x+3)(x-3)}$$

The least common denominator is

$$(x+3)(x-3)$$

We have to multiply the first time by

$$\frac{x+3}{x+3}$$

$$\frac{5(x+3)}{(x-3)(x+3)} + \frac{2x}{(x-3)(x+3)}$$

$$\frac{5x+15}{(x-3)(x+3)} + \frac{2x}{(x-3)(x+3)}$$

$$\frac{7x+15}{(x-3)(x+3)} \text{ OR } \frac{7x+15}{x^2-9}$$

Practice 2: B

$$\frac{\frac{1}{x} - \frac{1}{y}}{\frac{x}{y}}$$

Multiply each term by the LCD: xy

$$\frac{(xy)\frac{1}{x} - \frac{1}{y}(xy)}{\frac{x}{y}(xy)}$$

Reduce

$$\frac{(xy)\frac{1}{x} - \frac{1}{y}(xy)}{\frac{x}{y}(xy)}$$

$$\frac{y-x}{x^2}$$

5.4 Simplifying Rational Expressions

Homework 1: B

$$\frac{2x}{5} - \frac{x-2}{5x}$$

$$\frac{2x(x)}{5(x)} - \frac{x-2}{5x}$$

$$\frac{2x^2}{5x} - \frac{x-2}{5x}$$

$$\frac{2x^2 - (x-2)}{5x}$$

$$\frac{2x^2 - x + 2}{5x}$$

Homework 2: A

$$\frac{3x}{x-2} + \frac{x+3}{x^2-4} \text{ factor}$$

$$\frac{3x}{x-2} + \frac{x+3}{(x+2)(x-2)}$$

LCD is $(x+2)(x-2)$

We need to multiply the first term by

$$\frac{x+2}{x+2}$$

$$\frac{3x(x+2)}{(x-2)(x+2)} + \frac{x+3}{(x+2)(x-2)}$$

$$\frac{3x^2+6x}{(x+2)(x-2)} + \frac{x+3}{(x+2)(x-2)}$$

$$\frac{3x^2+7x+3}{(x+2)(x-2)}$$

$$\frac{3x^2+7x+3}{x^2-4}$$

Homework 3: A

$$\frac{\frac{1}{x-y} - \frac{1}{x+y}}{\frac{x}{x^2-y^2}} = \frac{\frac{1}{x-y} - \frac{1}{x+y}}{\frac{x}{(x+y)(x-y)}} \text{ FACTOR}$$

LCD is $(x+y)(x-y)$, so multiply each term by $(x+y)(x-y)$ to simplify

$$\frac{(x+y)(x-y)\frac{1}{x-y} - \frac{1}{x+y}(x+y)(x-y)}{\frac{x}{(x+y)(x-y)}(x+y)(x-y)}$$

5.4 Simplifying Rational Expressions

$$\frac{(x+y)-(x-y)}{x}$$

$$\frac{x+y-x+y}{x}$$

$$\frac{2y}{x}$$

Homework 4: D

$$\frac{\dfrac{1}{2x}-\dfrac{1}{2y}}{\dfrac{x}{xy}}$$

LCD is $2xy$, so multiply each term by $2xy$.

$$\frac{(2xy)\dfrac{1}{2x}-\dfrac{1}{2y}(2xy)}{\dfrac{x}{xy}(2xy)}$$

$$\frac{y-x}{2x}$$

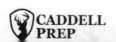

Lesson 6

Need to improve 200 points?

We love working with students who are serious about their SAT scores - that means you!

Special Tutoring & Test Prep Offer for You

 caddellprep.com/sboffer

6.1 Equating Coefficients

Equating Coefficients

Equating coefficients is used to determine the values of coefficients by creating equations.

Let's say we are given the following equation and we have to solve for a.

$$5x - 4 = ax - 4$$

We can simply match up the coefficients of like terms on both sides of the equation

$$5x-4 = ax-4$$

x-terms: $5 = a$

\#: $-4 = -4$

We can find very easily that $a = 5$.

Most of the time on the SAT, there will be more steps, such as simplifying one or both sides.

Example

In the equation below a and b are constants. What is the value of b in the equation below?

$$(2x - 4)(x + 3) = ax^2 + bx - 12$$

$$(2x-4)(x+3) = ax^2 + bx - 12$$
$$2x^2 + 6x - 4x - 12 = ax^2 + bx - 12$$
$$2x^2 + 2x - 12 = ax^2 + bx - 12$$

x^2-terms: $2 = a$

x-terms: $2 = b$

\#: $-12 = -12$

System of Equations from Equating Coefficients

It is possible that we will end up with a system of equations after equating coefficients on the SAT.

Example

In the equation below a and b are constants. What is the value of b?

$$(6x - 4)(2x + 1) = (4x + 2)(ax + b)$$

$$(6x-4)(2x+1) = (4x+2)(ax+b)$$
$$12x^2 + 6x - 8x - 4 = 4ax^2 + 4bx + 2ax + 2b$$
$$12x^2 - 2x - 4 = 4ax^2 + 4bx + 2ax + 2b$$

$$\underline{x^2} \qquad \underline{x} \qquad \underline{\#}$$
$$12 = 4a \qquad -2 = 4b + 2a \qquad -4 = 2b$$
$$3 = a \qquad \text{(solve these 2)} \qquad -2 = b$$

Practice 1

$$a(x^2 + 4x - 5) + bx = 2x^2 + 11x - 10$$

In the equation above, a and b are constants. What is the value of b?

6.1 Equating Coefficients Homework

Homework 1

$$3(ax + 2y) - 5(3x + by) = -9x - 29y$$

In the equation above, a and b are constants. What is the value of b?

Homework 2

$$a(x^2 - 5x + 7) = bx^2 + 3$$

In the equation above, a and b are constants. What is the value of b?

6.1 Answers to Practice Problems (Equating Coefficients)

Practice 1: 3

$a(x^2+4x-5)+bx = 2x^2+11x-10$

$ax^2+4ax-5a+bx = 2x^2+11x-10$

$\underline{x^2 \text{ coefficients}}$

$a = 2$

$\underline{x \text{ coefficients}}$

$4a + b = 11$

$\quad \downarrow 2$

$8 + b = 11$

$-8 \quad\quad -8$

$\quad\quad b = \boxed{3}$

Homework 1: 7

$3(ax+2y)-5(3x+by) = -9x-29y$

$3ax+6y-15x-5by = -9x-29y$

$\underline{x \text{ coefficients}} \quad \underline{y \text{ coefficients}}$

$3a - 15 = -9 \quad\quad 6 - 5b = -29$

Solve for b:

$6 - 5b = -29$

$-6 \quad\quad -6$

$\quad -5b = -35$

$\dfrac{-5b}{-5} = \dfrac{-35}{-5}$

$b = \boxed{7}$

Homework 2: 3

$a(x^2-5x+7)-bx^2+3 = x^2-20x+31$

$ax^2-5ax+7a-bx^2+3 = x^2-20x+31$

$\underline{x^2 \text{ coefficients}}$

$a - b = 1$

$\underline{x \text{ coefficients}}$

$-5a = -20$

$\dfrac{-5a}{-5} = \dfrac{-20}{-5}$

$a = 4$

Now, we can solve for b

$a = 4$

$\underline{x^2 \text{ coefficients}}$

$a - b = 1$

$4 - b = 1$

$-4 \quad\quad -4$

$\quad -b = -3$

$\dfrac{-b}{-1} = \dfrac{-3}{-1}$

$b = \boxed{3}$

6.2 Dividing Polynomials

Factoring & Reducing

Sometimes on the SAT, you will be asked to find an expression that is equivalent to a fraction with x-terms in the numerator and the denominator. If the numerator or denominator has a quadratic expression, it is likely that you'll need to factor and reduce.

Example

Which of the following is equivalent to $\dfrac{x^2+3x+2}{x^2+6x+8}$?

A) $\dfrac{x+2}{2x+4}$

B) $\dfrac{1}{3x+4}$

C) $\dfrac{x+1}{x+4}$

D) $\dfrac{x+3}{x+4}$

$$\frac{x^2+3x+2}{x^2+6x+8} = \frac{(x+2)(x+1)}{(x+4)(x+2)} = \frac{\cancel{(x+2)}(x+1)}{(x+4)\cancel{(x+2)}} = \frac{x+1}{x+4}$$

The correct answer is C.

Practice 1

Which of the following is equivalent to $\dfrac{x^2-x-20}{x^2-8x+15}$?

A. $\dfrac{x+4}{x-3}$

B. $\dfrac{1}{7x-5}$

C. $\dfrac{x-5}{x+4}$

D. $\dfrac{x-20}{x+7}$

6.2 Dividing Polynomials

Long Division

On the SAT, you will likely see a question that asks you to identify which expression is equivalent to a given expression.

If the answer choices look like this $x + 5 - \frac{2}{x+2}$, it likely means you must use long division to answer the question.

Example

Which of the following is equivalent to $\frac{x^2+4x-2}{x+3}$?

A. $x - 5$

B. $x + 2$

C. $x + 1 - \frac{2}{x+3}$

D. $x + 1 - \frac{5}{x+3}$

First, check to see if the numerator and denominator can be factored and reduced.

In this case, they can't be, so we should do long division and see if we get answer choice C or D.

Set up the problem for division.

$$\frac{x^2+4x-2}{x+3}$$

$$x+3 \overline{\smash{\big)}\, x^2+4x-2}$$

We are dividing by a binomial $(x + 3)$, so we should divide it into the first two terms, $x^2 + 4x$.

When we divide, we only care about the terms with the biggest exponents.

$$\boxed{x+3} \overline{\smash{\big)}\, \boxed{x^2}+4x-2}$$

6.2 Dividing Polynomials

x divides into x^2, x times. In other words, to get x^2, we have to multiply x by x.

$$\begin{array}{r} x \\ x+3 \,\overline{\smash{\big)}\, x^2+4x-2} \end{array}$$

Now, just like in regular division, we multiple $x+3$ by x and then subtract.

$$\begin{array}{r} x \\ x+3 \,\overline{\smash{\big)}\, x^2+4x-2} \\ \underline{x^2+3x} \\ x \end{array}$$

Then bring down the -2

$$\begin{array}{r} x \\ x+3 \,\overline{\smash{\big)}\, x^2+4x-2} \\ \underline{x^2+3x\downarrow} \\ x-2 \end{array}$$

Next, we have to again look at the two terms with the greatest exponent, x and x.

$$\begin{array}{r} x \\ \textcircled{x}+3 \,\overline{\smash{\big)}\, x^2+4x-2} \\ \underline{x^2+3x\downarrow} \\ \textcircled{x}-2 \end{array}$$

x goes into x once.

$$\begin{array}{r} x+1 \\ x+3 \,\overline{\smash{\big)}\, x^2+4x-2} \\ \underline{x^2+3x\downarrow} \\ x-2 \end{array}$$

Again, we multiply and subtract.

$$\begin{array}{r} x+1 \\ x+3 \,\overline{\smash{\big)}\, x^2+4x-2} \\ \underline{x^2+3x\downarrow} \\ x-2 \\ \underline{x+3} \\ -5 \end{array}$$

6.2 Dividing Polynomials

There is a remainder of -5, so our final answer is

$$x + 1 - \frac{5}{x+3}$$

The correct answer is D.

Practice 2

Which of the following is equivalent to $\dfrac{x^3+2x^2-8x+12}{x-4}$?

A. $x^2 - 2x - 2$

B. $x^3 + 2x^2 - 8 + \dfrac{3}{x-4}$

C. $x^2 + 6x + 16 + \dfrac{76}{x-4}$

D. $x + 1 - \dfrac{5}{x-4}$

6.2 Dividing Polynomials Homework

Homework 1

Simplify

$$\frac{x^2 - 8x + 12}{x^2 - 3x - 18}$$

- A. $\frac{x-4}{x-6}$
- B. $\frac{x-2}{x+3}$
- C. $x^2 - 5x - 6$
- D. $\frac{x+12}{x-18}$

Homework 2

$$\frac{x^2 + 4x - 8}{x - 2}$$

Use long division to divide the above expression.

Homework 3

$$\frac{x^2 - 2x + 12}{x + 3}$$

Use long division to divide the above expression.

6.2 Answers to Practice Problems (Dividing Polynomials)

Practice 1: A

$$\frac{x^2 - x - 20}{x^2 - 8x + 15}$$

$$\frac{(x-5)(x+4)}{(x-5)(x-3)}$$

$$\frac{x+4}{x-3}$$

Homework 1: B

$$\frac{x^2 - 8x + 12}{x^2 - 3x - 18}$$

$$\frac{(x-6)(x-2)}{(x-6)(x+3)}$$

$$\frac{x-2}{x+3}$$

Practice 2: C

$$\begin{array}{r} x^2 + 6x + 16 \\ x-4 \overline{\smash{)}x^3 + 2x^2 - 8x + 12} \\ \underline{x^3 - 4x^2} \\ 6x^2 - 8x \\ \underline{6x^2 - 24x} \\ 16x + 12 \\ \underline{16x - 64} \\ 76 \end{array}$$

$$\boxed{x^2 + 6x + 16 + \frac{76}{x-4}}$$

Homework 2: $x + 6 + \dfrac{4}{x-2}$

$$\begin{array}{r} x + 6 \\ x-2 \overline{\smash{)}x^2 + 4x - 8} \\ -\underline{x^2 - 2x} \\ 6x - 8 \\ -\underline{6x - 12} \\ 4 \end{array}$$

$$\boxed{x + 6 + \frac{4}{x-2}}$$

6.2 Dividing Polynomials

Homework 3: $x - 5 + \dfrac{27}{x+3}$

$$\require{enclose}
\begin{array}{r}
x - 5 \\
x+3 \enclose{longdiv}{x^2 - 2x + 12} \\
-\underline{(x^2 + 3x)} \downarrow \\
-5x + 12 \\
-\underline{(-5x - 15)} \\
27
\end{array}$$

$$\boxed{\,x - 5 + \dfrac{27}{x+3}\,}$$

6.3 Transforming Functions

Translating Functions

Adding a number to the end of a function will move it up that many units and subtracting a number from the end of a function will move it down that many units.

For example, the graph of $y = x^2 + 4$ is 4 units higher than the graph of $y = x^2 + 4$.

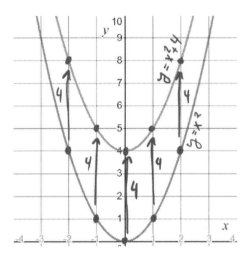

If the function $y = x^2 - 2x + 2$ had 3 added to the end of it, it would become $y = x^2 - 2x + 5$, and it would be 3 units higher.

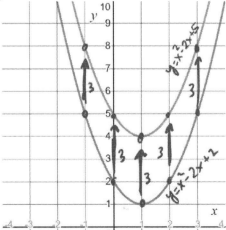

Addition or subtraction done directly to x moves the function left or right. Adding a number to x would translate the function left and subtracting a number from x would move the function right.

6.3 Transforming Functions

For example, the function $y = (x-3)^2$ is the function $y = x^2$ translated right 3 units.

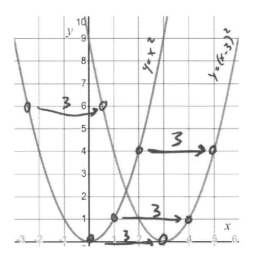

Compared to the function $y = x^2$, the function $y = (x+2)^2 - 5$ is shifted left 2 units and down 5 units.

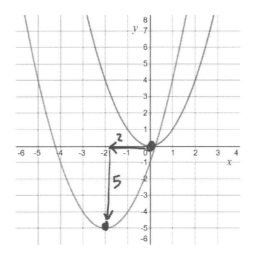

The same can be applied to any function. In function notation, shifting $f(x)$ right 3 units and down 5 units is written $f(x-3) - 5$.

6.3 Transforming Functions

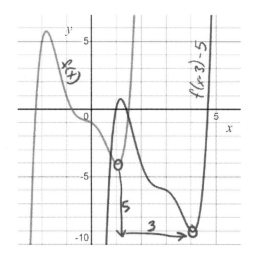

Example

The maximum value of the function $f(x)$ is 4. If $g(x) = f(x-5) + 2$, what is the maximum value of $g(x)$?

$g(x) = f(x-5) + 2$

$g(x)$ is $f(x)$ translated right 5 units and up 2 units.

If the max of $f(x)$ is 4, the max of $g(x)$ will be 2 higher: $\boxed{6}$

6.3 Transforming Functions

Practice 1

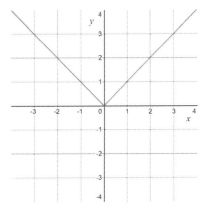

Given the function $f(x)$ above. Which of the following could be the graph of $f(x+1) - 3$?

A)
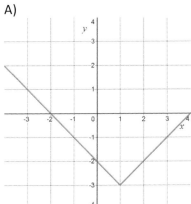

B)
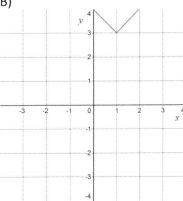

C)
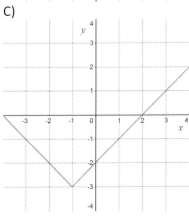

D)
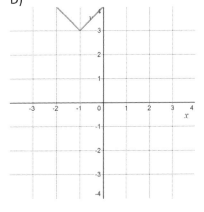

6.3 Transforming Functions

Flipping Functions

Negating a function will flip it vertically.

For example, here is a graph of $y = x^2$ and $y = -x^2$.

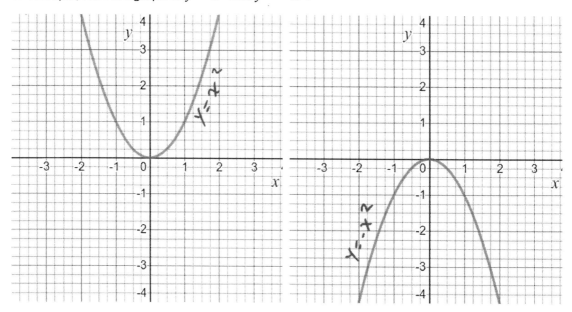

The function $y = -(x-3)^2 + 2$ is the graph of $y = -x^2$ translated right 3 and up 2.

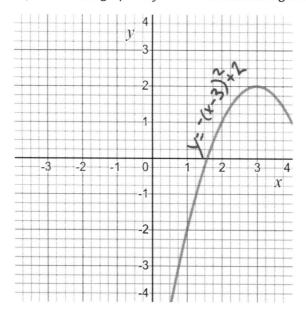

Practice 2

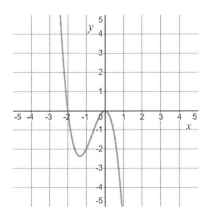

Given the graph of the function $h(x)$ above. Which of the following could be the graph of $-h(x-4)+3$?

A)
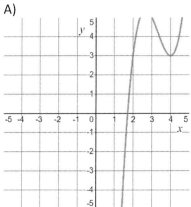

B)
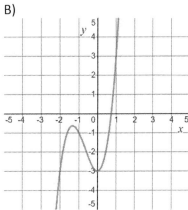

C)
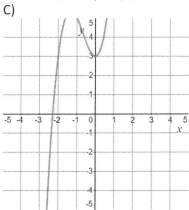

D)
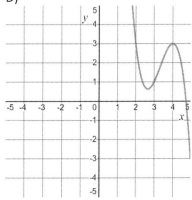

Practice 3

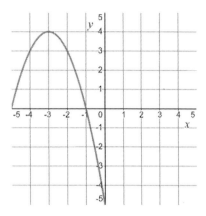

Given the graph, $g(x) = -(x+3)^2 + 4$, above, what is the minimum value of $-g(x) + 3$?

6.3 Transforming Functions Homework

Homework 1

Which of the following equations is greater than or equal to 1 for all x-values?

A) $y = (x-1)^2$
B) $y = |x+1|$
C) $y = (x-3)^2 + 1$
D) $y = x^3 + 1$

Homework 2

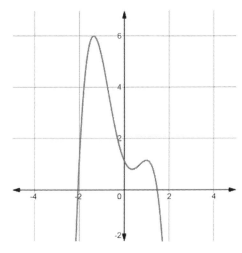

Above is a graph of $f(x)$. What is the maximum value of $f(x) - 3$?

Homework 3

x	$f(x)$
-3	7
2	6
5	2
8	13

Some value for the function $f(x)$ are given in the table above. If $g(x) = f(x) - 4$, what is the value of $g(2)$?

6.3 Answers to Practice Problems (Transforming Functions)

Practice 1: C

Choice C

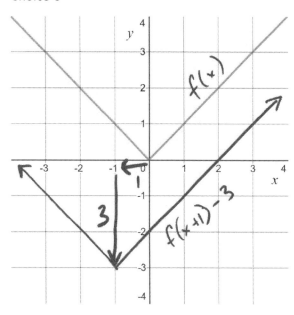

Practice 2: A

Choice A

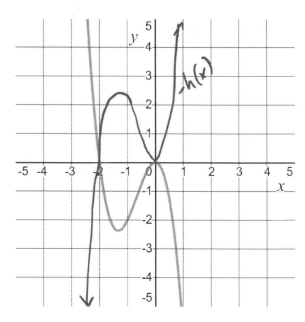

Now, we have to translate $-h(x)$ 4 units right and 3 units up.

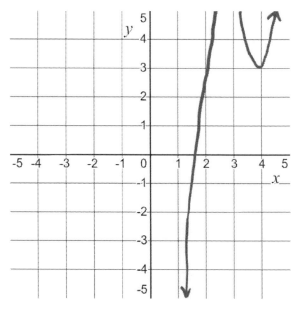

6.3 Transforming Functions

Practice 3: -1

The answer is -1.

The maximum value of $g(x)$ is 4. When $g(x)$ is negated and becomes $-g(x)$, the graph flips and the maximum value of 4 becomes a minimum value of -4.

$-g(x) + 3$ translates the graph up 3 units, so the minimum value also increases by 3 units. The minimum value becomes -1.

Homework 1: C

Which of the following equations is greater than or equal to 1 for all x-values?

- A) $y = (x - 1)^2$
- B) $y = |x + 1|$
- C) $y = (x - 3)^2 + 1$
- D) $y = x^3 + 1$

The value of a function refers to it's y-values. Therefore, we need to examine the y-values.

Choice A is a parabola that is shifted right one unit, so the lowest value, its vertex, will be a (1,0).

Choice B is an absolute value function (V) translated left 1 unit, so the lowest value, its vertex, will be at (-1,0)

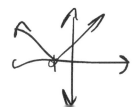

Choice C is a parabola that is shifted right 3 and up 1, so the lowest point, the vertex, is at (3,1). Therefore, all values are equal to or greater than 1.

Choice D is based on the function x^3 which continuously goes up to infinity and down to negative infinity. This function is simply shifted up 1.

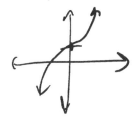

6.3 Transforming Functions

Homework 2: 3

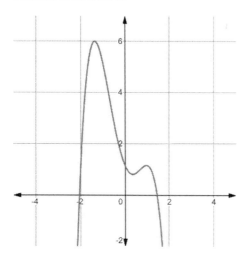

What is the maximum value of $f(x) - 3$?

The maximum value of f(x) is 6 (the greatest y-value).

The function f(x)-3 would be shifted down 3, so the maximum value would be 3.

Homework 3: 2

x	$f(x)$
-3	7
2	6
5	2
8	13

$g(x) = f(x) - 4$, what is the value of $g(2)$?

The y-values of g(x) are all 4 less than the y-values of f(x).

$f(2) = 6$

So $g(2) = 2$

6.4 Solving for a Variable in Terms of Another

Treat variables like numbers and terms like numbers.

One-Step Problems

Here is a relatively simple example

Solve for x in $x + y = 8$

In the equation $x + y = 8$, y Is being added to x. To solve for x, we should subtract y on both sides.

$$x + y = 8$$
$$-y \quad -y$$
$$\overline{}$$
$$x = 8 - y$$

This might seem confusing but consider the equation $x + 4 = 8$. If you had to solve for x, you would simply subtract 4 from both sides.

$$x + 4 = 8$$
$$-4 \quad -4$$
$$\overline{}$$
$$x = 4$$

Well, y represents a number, so it should be treated the same way. The only difference is we can't combine 8 and y since they aren't like terms, so it stays as $x = 8 - y$.

Multiple-Step Problem

Let's look at a more complicated example.

Solve for x in the equation $2x - y = 12$.

In this case, x is being multiplied by 2 and y is being subtracted from the x-term.

6.4 Solving for a Variable in Terms of Another

We should solve for x by first getting the x-term by itself. That means add y to both sides.

$$2x - y = 12$$
$$+y \quad +y$$
$$2x = 12 + y$$

Now, the x-term, $2x$, is by itself. When determining what to do next, completely ignore the right side of the equation and just focus on the x-term.

We want to get x by itself, so divide both sides of the equation by 2 to isolate the x.

$$\frac{2x}{2} = \frac{12 + y}{2}$$
$$x = \frac{12 + y}{2}$$

The final answer is

$$x = \frac{12 + y}{2}$$

Practice 1

$3x + 4 = 9 - y$

Solve for x in the equation above.

- A) $x = -\frac{1}{3}y - 1$
- B) $x = -\frac{1}{3}y + \frac{5}{3}$
- C) $x = y + 5/3$
- D) $x = -3y + 31$

6.4 Solving for a Variable in Terms of Another

Multiple x-terms

A problem that trips up a lot of students is when they have to solve for x and there is an x-term on both sides of the equation that can't be combined.

The trick is to get all of the x-terms alone on one side of the equation first and then factor out the x.

Here is an example.

Solve for x in the equation below.

$5x - 7 = 2xy + z$

To solve this, let's get all of the terms that have a x onto the left side of the equation by subtracting $2xy$ on both sides.

$$\begin{array}{r} 5x - 7 = 2xy + z \\ -2xy \quad -2xy \\ \hline 5x - 2xy - 7 = z \end{array}$$

At this point all of the x-terms are on the left side.

We want to get the x-terms alone, so we should get rid of the -7 by adding 7 to both sides.

$$\begin{array}{r} 5x - 2xy - 7 = z \\ +7 \quad +7 \\ \hline 5x - 2xy = z + 7 \end{array}$$

Now that we only have x-terms on the left side of the equation, we can factor out an x.

6.4 Solving for a Variable in Terms of Another

$$5x - 2xy = z + 7$$

$$x(5 - 2y) = z + 7$$

Since x is being multiplied by the expression $5 - 2y$, we should divide both sides by $5 - 2y$ to isolate the x.

$$\frac{x(5-2y)}{(5-2y)} = \frac{z+7}{5-2y}$$

$$x = \frac{z+7}{5-2y}$$

The final answer is

$$x = \frac{z+7}{5-2y}$$

Practice 2

$5x + 4y = 3xy + 4$

Solve for x in the equation above.

A) $x = \frac{4-4y}{5-3y}$
B) $x = \frac{7-4y}{5}$
C) $x = y + 2$
D) $x = \frac{-y+4}{4}$

6.4 Solving for a Variable in Terms of Another

Complex but Simple Problem

The last example we will go over has the impression of being very difficult. However, it is actually pretty easy.

Solve for x in the equation below

$$r = \frac{P_1 + P_2}{t^2} x$$

The equation above can be intimidating. Before we try and solve that equation, let's try a simpler equation.

Solve for x in the equation below

$$y = \frac{3}{4} x$$

In this equation, x is being multiplied by $\frac{3}{4}$. To solve for x, divide both sides by $\frac{3}{4}$. Remember that when you divide by a fraction you use keep-change-flip, so really we should multiply both sides by $\frac{4}{3}$.

$$y = \frac{3}{4} x$$

$$\left(\frac{4}{3}\right) y = \frac{3}{4} x \left(\frac{4}{3}\right)$$

$$\frac{4}{3} y = x$$

Let's try the other equation now.

$$r = \frac{P_1 + P_2}{t^2} x$$

In the equation x is being multiplied by $\frac{P_1+P_2}{t^2}$, so we should multiple both sides by $\frac{t^2}{P_1+P_2}$.

6.4 Solving for a Variable in Terms of Another

$$r = \frac{P_1 + P_2}{t^2} x$$

$$\left(\frac{t^2}{P_1+P_2}\right) r = \frac{P_1+P_2}{t^2} x \left(\frac{t^2}{P_1+P_2}\right)$$

$$\frac{t^2}{P_1+P_2} r = x$$

The final answer is

$$x = \frac{t^2}{P_1 + P_2} r$$

Practice 3

$$F = \frac{3kqv}{2r}$$

Solve for v in the equation above.

A) $v = \frac{3kqF}{2r}$
B) $v = \frac{3kq}{2Fr}$
C) $v = 6Fkqr$
D) $v = \frac{2Fr}{3kq}$

6.4 Solving for a Variable in Terms of Another

Solve for a Variable and then Simplify

Sometimes after we solve for a variable, we have to simplify the expression to match one of the answer choices.

Example

If the expression $\frac{9x^2}{3x-1}$ is written in the equivalent form $\frac{1}{3x-1} + A$, what is A in terms of x?

A) $3x + 1$

B) $3x - 1$

C) $9x^2$

D) $9x^2 - 1$

The question states $\frac{9x^2}{3x-1}$ is equivalent to $\frac{1}{3x-1} + A$, so let's set them equal to each other.

$$\frac{9x^2}{3x-1} = \frac{1}{3x-1} + A$$

We have to solve for A, so let's subtract $\frac{1}{3x-1}$ from both sides.

6.4 Solving for a Variable in Terms of Another

$$\frac{9x^2}{3x-1} = \frac{1}{3x-1} + A$$

$$-\frac{1}{3x-1} \quad -\frac{1}{3x-1}$$

$$\frac{9x^2}{3x-1} - \frac{1}{3x-1} = A$$

Since the two fractions have the same denominator, we can subtract the numerators to get

$$\frac{9x^2 - 1}{3x-1} = A$$

The numerator can be factored because it is the difference of perfect squares.

$$\frac{9x^2 - 1}{3x-1} = A$$

$$\frac{(3x-1)(3x+1)}{3x-1} = A$$

Reduce to get your final answer.

$$\frac{\cancel{(3x-1)}(3x+1)}{\cancel{3x-1}} = A$$

$$3x + 1 = A$$

The final answer is

$$A = 3x + 1$$

6.4 Solving for a Variable in Terms of Another Homework

Homework 1

$$F = \frac{Gm_1m_2}{r^2}$$

Solve for r^2 in the equation above.

A) $r^2 = \frac{Gm_1m_2}{F}$
B) $r^2 = \frac{Gm_1m_2}{r^2}$
C) $r^2 = \frac{F}{Gm_1m_2}$
D) $r^2 = \frac{Gm_1m_2}{\sqrt{F}}$

Homework 2

$$F = \frac{1}{2}kx^2$$

Solve for x in the equation above.

A) $x = \frac{2\sqrt{F}}{k}$
B) $x = \sqrt{2kf}$
C) $x = \sqrt{\frac{2F}{k}}$
D) $x = 2k\sqrt{F}$

Homework 3

$$P = \frac{1}{2}x + \frac{1}{3}y + \frac{1}{4}z$$

Solve for y in the equation above.

A) $z = 4P - 2x - \frac{4}{3}y$
B) $z = 4P - \frac{1}{2}x - \frac{1}{3}y$
C) $z = \frac{1}{4}(P - \frac{1}{2}x - \frac{1}{3y})$
D) $z = \frac{1}{4}P - \frac{1}{12}x - \frac{1}{16}y$

6.4 Answers to Practice Problems (Solving for a Variable in Terms of Another)

Practice 1: B

$3x + 4 = 9 - y$

Solve for x in the equation above.

$$3x + 4 = 9 - y$$
$$-4 -4$$
$$3x = 5 - y$$
$$\frac{3x}{3} = \frac{5-y}{3}$$
$$x = -\frac{1}{3}y + \frac{5}{3}$$

Practice 2: A

$5x + 4y = 3xy + 4$

Solve for x in the equation above.

Get all of the x-terms on the same side.

$$5x + 4y = 3xy + 4$$
$$-3xy -3xy$$
$$5x - 3xy + 4y = 4$$
$$ -4y -4y$$
$$5x - 3xy = 4 - 4y$$

Factor out the x

$$x(5 - 3y) = 4 - 4y$$

$$\frac{x(5-3y)}{5-3y} = \frac{4-4y}{5-3y}$$

$$x = \frac{4-4y}{5-3y}$$

Practice 3: D

$$F = \frac{3kqv}{2r}$$

Solve for v in the equation above.

$$F = \frac{3kq}{2r}v$$

$$\left(\frac{2r}{3kq}\right)F = \frac{3kq}{2r}v\left(\frac{2r}{3kq}\right)$$

$$\frac{2Fr}{3kq} = v$$

6.4 Solving for a Variable in Terms of Another

Homework 1: A

$$F = \frac{Gm_1m_2}{r^2}$$

Solve for r^2 in the equation above.

Let's start by getting r^2 out of the denominator.

$$(r^2)F = \frac{Gm_1m_2}{r^2}(r^2)$$

$$Fr^2 = Gm_1m_2$$

$$\frac{Fr^2}{F} = \frac{Gm_1m_2}{F}$$

$$r^2 = \frac{Gm_1m_2}{F}$$

Homework 2: C

$$F = \frac{1}{2}kx^2$$

Solve for x in the equation above.

$$(2)F = \frac{1}{2}kx^2(2)$$

$$2F = kx^2$$

$$\frac{2F}{k} = \frac{kx^2}{k}$$

$$\frac{2F}{k} = x^2$$

$$\sqrt{\frac{2F}{k}} = \sqrt{x^2}$$

$$\sqrt{\frac{2F}{k}} = x$$

Homework 3: A

$$P = \frac{1}{2}x + \frac{1}{3}y + \frac{1}{4}z$$

Let's use a trick to make this easier. Multiply all terms by the LCD, 12, to get rid of the denominators.

$$P(12) = \frac{1}{2}x(12) + \frac{1}{3}y(12) + \frac{1}{4}z(12)$$

$$12P = 6x + 4y + 3z$$

Now, solve for z

6.4 Solving for a Variable in Terms of Another

$$12P = 6x + 4y + 3z$$
$$\underline{-6x \quad -6x}$$
$$12P - 6x = 4y + 3z$$
$$\underline{-4y \quad -4y}$$
$$12P - 6x - 4y = 3z$$

$$\frac{12P}{3} - \frac{6x}{3} - \frac{4y}{3} = \frac{3z}{3}$$

$$4P - 2x - \frac{4}{3}y = z$$

6.5 Absolute Value

Evaluating Expressions with Absolute Value

Absolute value is the distance from 0 to the value, which is always positive.

Essentially, whatever value is inside the absolute value bars will be positive. If it's already positive, it remains positive, and if it's negative, it becomes positive.

For example,

$$|5| = 5 \qquad\qquad |-5| = 5$$

When evaluating an expression inside the absolute value bars, completely evaluate it and then take the absolute value of it.

Example

What is the value of $|2x + 4|$ if $x = -3$?

$$|2x+4|, \quad x = -3$$

$$|2(-3)+4|$$

↳ Do **NOT** change -3 to 3.
Evaluate the expression

$$|-6+4|$$
$$|-2| \leftarrow \text{Now, take the absolute value of } -2$$
$$2$$

6.5 Absolute Value

Practice 1

What is the value of $|5x - 19|$ if $x = 2$?

Practice 2

What is the value of $|x^2 + 2x - 5|$ if $x = -2$?

Practice 3

What is the value of $-2|x - 5| + 3$ if $x = -4$?

6.5 Absolute Value

Solving an Equation that Includes Absolute Value

If an equation is given that includes an expression an absolute value, isolate the absolute value expression first. After it is isolated, make two equations: one where the expression inside the absolute value bars equals the other side of the equation as is and one where it equals the negated other side of the equation.

Example

Solve for x in the equation below.

$|2x - 5| - 3 = 6$

$|2x-5| - 3 = 6$
↑ isolate this first

$|2x-5| - 3 = 6$
$+3 +3$
$|2x-5| = 9$

Now, set up 2 equations

$2x - 5 = 9 \qquad\qquad 2x - 5 = -9$
$ +5 +5 \qquad\qquad +5 +5$
$2x = 14 \qquad\qquad 2x = -4$
$\dfrac{2x}{2} = \dfrac{14}{2} \qquad\qquad \dfrac{2x}{2} = \dfrac{-4}{2}$
$x = 7 \qquad\qquad x = -2$

Practice 4

Solve for x in the equation below.

$|x - 9| + 7 = 8$

6.5 Absolute Value

Using Absolute Value to Describe a Distance or a Range

Sometimes on the SAT, an inequality involving an absolute value expression is used to express a range.

For example, a ride at an amusement park may only all riders who are no more than 6 inches taller or shorter than five feet tall. Five feet is 60 inches, so the rider must be between 54 inches and 66 inches tall.

We can write the height constraint at $54 \leq h \leq 66$.

However, it can also be represented with an absolute value, $|h - 60| \leq 6$.

It states that the difference between the person's height, h, and 60 must be less than 6. It's absolute value because the difference has to be less than 6 and we will think about the distance as a positive number.

If the person is 64 inches tall, $64 - 60 = 4$, which is less than 6, so it is good.

If the person is 57 inches tall, $57 - 60 = -3$, but the difference is really 3 inches in height, which is why we take the absolute value.

Here's the real reason the absolute value is necessary:

If the person is 40 inches tall, $40 - 60 = -20$. -20 is less than 6, so if there was no absolute value, a rider who is 40 inches tall would be allowed on the ride. However, $|40 - 60| = 20$. 20 is not less than 6, so the person is not allowed on the ride.

Note that both $|h - 60| \leq 6$ or $|60 - h| \leq 6$ is acceptable.

SUPER TIP
If the range is given, the average of the range is middle value used to find the difference between the variable and the middle value. The difference between the middle value and the lower value is the allowance in either direction.

6.5 Absolute Value

Example

A machinist must create a cylindrical rod that is $3cm$ in diameter. He is allowed a margin of error of $0.01cm$. Which of the following represents the allowable diameters, d, of the cylindrical rod?

A) $|d + 0.01| = 3$
B) $|3 - d| \leq 0.01$
C) $|d - 0.01| \leq 3$
D) $|3 - 0.01| \leq d$

3cm, within 0.01
The difference between the actual diameter, d, and 3 must be less than 0.01

$|3-d| \leq 0.01$
OR
$|d-3| \leq 0.01$

Practice 5

A machine produces 100,000 parts per day. A certain number of defects are expected each day. Each day a machine is considered to be working at an acceptable level if it produces between 0 and 8 defects each day. Which of the following represents the allowable number of defects, n, each day?

A) $0 \leq |n + 4| \leq 8$
B) $|100,000 - n| \leq 8$
C) $|n - 4| \leq 4$
D) $|n - 8| \leq 4$

6.5 Absolute Value Homework

Homework 1

What is the value of $|-x + 6| + 3$ if $x = 3$?

Homework 2

What is the value of $-2|x + 9| - 1$ if $x = -4$?

Homework 3

Solve for x in the equation below.

$3|2x - 5| + 6 = 12$

Homework 4

To ride on the rollercoaster at the amusement park, riders muse be at least 36 inches tall and no more than 60 inches tall. Which inequality correctly represents this constraint for height h?

    A) $|60 - h| \geq 36$
    B) $|h - 48| \leq 12$
    C) $|h - 12| \leq 48$
    D) $|h - 36| \leq 60$

6.5 Absolute Value

6.5 Absolute Value

Answers to Practice Problems (Absolute Value)

Practice 1: 9

What is the value of $|5x - 19|$ if $x = 2$?

$|5x - 19|$, $x = 2$

$|5(2) - 19|$

$|10 - 19|$

$|-9|$

$\boxed{9}$

Practice 2: 5

What is the value of $|x^2 + 2x - 5|$ if $x = -2$?

$|(-2)^2 + 2(-2) - 5|$

$|4 - 4 - 5|$

$|-5|$

$\boxed{5}$

Practice 3: -15

What is the value of $-2|x - 5| + 3$ if $x = -4$?

$-2|x - 5| + 3$, $x = -4$

$-2|(-4) - 5| + 3$

$-2|-9| + 3$

$-2(9) + 3$

$-18 + 3$

$\boxed{-15}$

Practice 4: 10 or 8

Solve for x in the equation below.

$|x - 9| + 7 = 8$

Isolate the absolute value expression.

$|x - 9| + 7 = 8$
$\underline{-7 \quad -7}$
$|x - 9| = 1$

Set $x - 9$ equal to 1 and -1.

$x - 9 = 1 \qquad x - 9 = -1$
$\underline{+9 \ +9} \qquad \underline{+9 \ +9}$
$x = 10 \qquad x = 8$

6.5 Absolute Value

Practice 5: C

A machine produces 100,000 parts per day. A certain number of defects are expected each day. Each day a machine is considered to be working at an acceptable level if it produces between 0 and 8 defects each day. Which of the following represents the allowable number of defects, n, each day?

A) $0 \leq |n + 4| \leq 8$
B) $|100{,}000 - n| \leq 8$
C) $|n - 4| \leq 4$
D) $|n - 8| \leq 4$

Lowest: 0
Highest: 8

Middle: $\dfrac{0+8}{2} = 4$

difference between middle number and the highest or lowest is 4

difference ≤ 4

$|4 - n| \leq 4$

OR

$|n - 4| \leq 4$

Homework 1: 6

What is the value of $|-x + 6| + 3$ if $x = 3$?

$|-x + 6| + 3$

$|-(3) + 6| + 3$

$|3| + 3$

$3 + 3$

6

Homework 2: -11

What is the value of $-2|x + 9| - 1$ if $x = -4$?

$-2|x + 9| - 1$

$-2|(-4) + 9| - 1$

$-2|5| - 1$

$-2(5) - 1$

$-10 - 1$

-11

6.5 Absolute Value

Homework 3: $\frac{7}{2}$ or $\frac{3}{2}$

Solve for x in the equation below.

$$3|2x - 5| + 6 = 12$$

isolate the absolute value expression

$$3|2x-5|+6 = 12$$
$$-6 \quad -6$$
$$\overline{3|2x-5| = 6}$$
$$\frac{3|2x-5|}{3} = \frac{6}{3}$$
$$|2x-5| = 2$$

Set the expression equal to 2 and -2

$$2x-5 = 2 \qquad 2x-5 = -2$$
$$+5 \quad +5 \qquad +5 \quad +5$$
$$2x = 7 \qquad 2x = 3$$
$$\frac{2x}{2} = \frac{7}{2} \qquad \frac{2x}{2} = \frac{3}{2}$$
$$x = 7/2 \qquad x = 3/2$$

Homework 4: B

To ride on the rollercoaster at the amusement park, riders muse be at least 36 inches tall and no more than 60 inches tall. Which inequality correctly represents this constraint for height h?

A) $|60 - h| \geq 36$
B) $|h - 48| \leq 12$
C) $|h - 12| \leq 48$
D) $|h - 36| \leq 60$

$$36 \leq h \leq 60$$

The middle height is
$$\frac{36+60}{2} = 48$$

Heights can be 12 greater or 12 less than 48, so the difference between the height and 48 must be less than or equal to 12.

$$|h-48| \leq 12 \text{ or}$$
$$|48-h| \leq 12$$

Math Practice Test 1

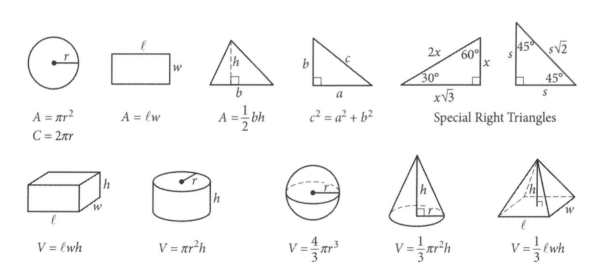

The number of degrees of arc in a circle is 360.

The number of radians of arc in a circle is 2π.

The sum of the measures in degrees of the angles of a triangle is 180.

Want to break a 1400?

We love working with students who are serious about their SAT scores - that means you!

Special Tutoring & Test Prep Offer for You

 caddellprep.com/sboffer

Math Practice Test 1

1.
A baker uses the equation $T = cdL + a$ to calculate the total cost T to bake L loaves of bread with c cups of flour that cost d dollars per cup using equipment which costs a to run. The bakery switches to a different, cheaper brand of flour. Which of the factors will change?

- A) c
- B) d
- C) a
- D) L

2.
If $5z = 25$ what is the value of $12z + 7$?

- A) 12
- B) 20
- C) 67
- D) 74

3.
Which of the following is equal to $b^{4/5}$ power for all values of b?

- A) $\sqrt{b^{2/5}}$
- B) $\sqrt{b^5}$
- C) $\sqrt[5]{b^4}$
- D) $\sqrt[4]{b^5}$

4.
The number of waterfalls in the United States is three times the number of waterfalls in England. If there are 315 waterfalls in the United States, and x waterfalls in England, which of the following equations is true?

- A) $315x = 3$
- B) $3x = 315$
- C) $\frac{x}{3} = 315$
- D) $x + 3 = 315$

5.
If $\frac{3}{x} = \frac{9}{x+24}$, what is the value of $\frac{x}{3}$?

- A) 10
- B) 4
- C) 3
- D) 1

6.
$$-2y - 3x = 12$$
$$y = -4x - 1$$

If (x, y) is a solution to the system of equations above, what is the value of $x - y$?

- A) 11
- B) 7
- C) 2
- D) -11

7.

x	$f(x)$
0	-6
1	0
4	30
5	44

The function f is defined by a polynomial. Some values of x and $f(x)$ are given in the table above. Which of the following must be a factor of $f(x)$?

A) $(x + 6)$
B) $(x + 1)$
C) $(x - 1)$
D) $(x - 6)$

8.
The line $y = 4x + b$, where b is a constant, is graphed in the xy-plane. If the line contains point (c, d) where $c \neq 0$ and $d \neq 0$. What is the y-intercept of the line in terms of c and d?

A) $d - 4c$
B) $d - \frac{c}{4}$
C) $c - 4d$
D) $c + 4d$

9.
$$3y - kx = 9$$
$$4y - 6x = 28$$

In the system of equations above, k is a constant. For what value of k will the system of equations have no solution?

A) $\frac{9}{2}$
B) $\frac{14}{3}$
C) $-\frac{9}{2}$
D) $-\frac{14}{3}$

10.
In the xy-plane the equation of $y = (x + 2)^2$ intersects the equation $y = 36$ at two points, A and B. What is the length of line AB?

A) 12
B) 8
C) 4
D) 2

11.

Note: Figure not drawn to scale.

In the figure above, four lines intersect at a point. If $h + f = d + e$, which of the following must be true?

I. $f = a$
II. $h + d = f + e$
III. $a = d$

A) I only
B) I & II only
C) I & III only
D) II & III only

12. In the quadratic equation $y = a(x+2)(x-b)$, the vertex is located at $(-3, c)$. Which of the following is equal to c?

A) $-3a$
B) $4a$
C) $-a$
D) $2a$

13.
The equation $\frac{8x^2+2x+4}{ax+1} = 4x - 1 + \frac{5}{ax+1}$ is true for all values of $x \neq -\frac{1}{a}$, where a is a constant. What is the value of a?

A) 1
B) 2
C) 4
D) 8

14.
What are the solutions to the equation $7x^2 + 12x - 3 = 0$?

A) $x = -\frac{6}{7} \pm \frac{\sqrt{57}}{7}$
B) $x = \frac{6}{7} \pm \sqrt{228}$
C) $x = \frac{12 \pm \sqrt{228}}{14}$
D) $x = \frac{-12 \pm \sqrt{228}}{-14}$

15.

$$K = \frac{5}{9}(F - 32) + 273.15$$

The equation above shows how to convert a temperature F, measured in degrees Fahrenheit, to a temperature K, measured in degrees Kelvin.

Based on the equation, which of the following must be true?

I. A temperature decrease of 1 degree Fahrenheit is equivalent to a temperature decrease of $\frac{5}{9}$ degree Kelvin.

II. A temperature increase of 1 degree Kelvin is equivalent to a temperature increase of $\frac{9}{5}$ degrees Fahrenheit.

III. A temperature increase of $\frac{5}{9}$ Fahrenheit is equivalent to a temperature increase of 1 degree Kelvin.

A) I only
B) III only
C) I & III only
D) I & II only

16.

$$4x(x - 8)(x + 3) = 0$$

If $x > 0$, what is one possible value of x in the equation above?

17.

$$\frac{1}{12}x + \frac{1}{18}x = \frac{2}{9} + \frac{1}{18}$$

What is the value of x in the equation above?

18.

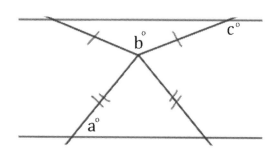

Note: Figure not drawn to scale

If $2b + 3a = 360$ and $a = 40$, what is the value of c?

19.

A baby store sells large boxes of baby diapers and small boxes of diapers. The large boxes have 30 more diapers than the small boxes. 6 small boxes and 5 large boxes combine for a total of 612 diapers. How many diapers are in a small box?

20.
In triangle QRS, the measure of $\angle R = 90°$ and QR=16. If $\sin Q = 0.28$, what is $\cos S$?

1.

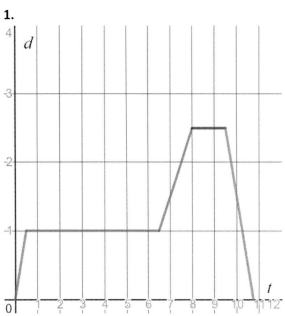

The graph above shows Amanda's distance from her home on a typical school day starting from when she is in the car with her mom driving to school. She spends 6 hours at school and then goes to her friend's house before going home. About how many hours does she spend at her friend's house?

A) 1
B) 1.5
C) 2.5
D) 9.5

2.

	Older than 6 years	Younger than 6 years	Total
Cats	5	12	17
Dogs	12	31	43
Total	17	43	60

The table above shows the number of pets who entered a pet show and organizes them by age and species. If you were to select a contestant at random, what are the odds that the pet will be either a cat older than 6 or a dog younger than 6?

A) $\dfrac{1}{12}$
B) $\dfrac{3}{5}$
C) $\dfrac{31}{60}$
D) $\dfrac{17}{60}$

Math Practice Test 1

3.

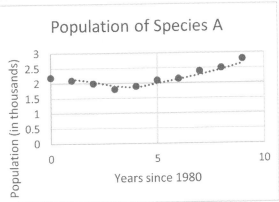

The graph above shows the population, in thousands, of species A in a small town each year from 1980 through 1989. Based on the graph, which of the following best describes the trend in the population for species A from 1980 through 1989?

A) Population generally increased each year since 1980.
B) Population generally decreased each year since 1980.
C) Population generally remained steady from 1980 through 1989.
D) Population decreased until 1983 and then generally increased.

4.

n	1	4	5	7
$f(n)$	11	23	27	35

The table above shows some values for linear function f. Which of the following defines f?

A) $f(n) = 2n$
B) $f(n) = 3n + 8$
C) $f(n) = 4n + 7$
D) $f(n) = 12n - 1$

5.

At a supermarket one year, $33\frac{1}{3}$ percent of the clerks and 25 percent of cashiers received outstanding performance reports at least once. If there are 21 clerks and 12 cashiers, what is the total number of employees who received outstanding performance reports?

A) 10
B) 11
C) 15
D) 20

6.

$4x^2 - 7x + 9$
$2x^2 + 4x + 6$

Which of the following is the sum of the two polynomials shown above?

A) $6x^2 - 3x + 15$
B) $6x^2 + 11x + 15$
C) $6x^4 + 11x^2 + 15$
D) $8x^4 + 28x^2 + 54$

7.

If $\frac{5}{7}w = \frac{3}{4}$, what is the value of w?

A) $\frac{20}{21}$
B) $\frac{15}{28}$
C) $\frac{1}{28}$
D) $\frac{21}{20}$

8.

The average number of locations per U.S. state of a popular fast food chain is modelled by the equation $y = .42x + 16$ where x represents the number of years since 1998. Which of the following best describes the meaning of 16 in the equation?

A) The total number of locations in the U.S. in 1998
B) The estimated increase in the average number of locations per U.S. state each year.
C) The average number of locations per U.S. state in 1998.
D) The estimated difference between the number of locations per U.S. state in 1998 and 2018.

9.

Katie runs 150 inches in 1 second. If she keeps this pace, how many feet can she run in a minute?

A) 12.5 feet
B) 750 feet
C) 9,000 feet
D) 9,012.5 feet

Questions 10 and 11 refer to the following information.

	Conversion Factor, k
Euro	0.89
British Pound	0.76
Indian Rupee	71.32
Swiss Franc	0.97
Japanese Yen	108.89

The chart above shows approximate conversion factors used to convert US dollars to other currencies. The value of any dollar amount can be estimated using the formula $\frac{c}{d} = k$, where c is the value in the other currency, d is the value in US dollars, and k is the conversion factor.

10.

What is the approximate value, in Swiss francs, of 240 US dollars?

A) 206.40
B) 232.80
C) 239.03
D) 247.42

11.

A one-ounce Gold America Eagle coin is currently worth $1,356. In which of the listed currencies is the coin worth about $1,030?

   A) Euro
   B) British Pound
   C) Swiss Franc
   D) Japanese Yen

12.

If the function f has one distinct zero, which of the following could represent the complete graph of f in the xy-plane?

A)
B)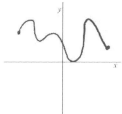
C)
D)
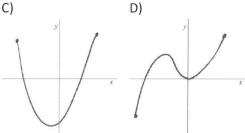

13.

$$K = \frac{1}{2}mv^2$$

The equation above gives the kinetic energy, K, of an object of mass m moving at the speed v feet per second. Which of the following gives v in terms of m and K?

   A) $\frac{2K}{m} + 2$
   B) $\sqrt{\frac{1}{2}Km}$
   C) $\sqrt{\frac{2K}{m}}$
   D) $\frac{1}{2}Km + 2$

14.

The cost of running a widget machine is $5 per hour. Which equation models the cost, c, in dollars for m minutes of the machine running?

   A) $c = 5(60m)$
   B) $c = 5m$
   C) $c = 60m/5$
   D) $c = 5m/60$

15.

To test the effectiveness of a cold medicine, 300 patients with the common cold were surveyed. Of those surveyed, half were given Treatment Z while the other half were given nothing. After a week, the number of patients who were given Treatment Z and still had a cold was much less than the number of patients who were given nothing and still had a cold. Based on the design and result of the study, which of the following is an appropriate conclusion?

A) Treatment Z may help a patient get over a common cold.
B) Treatment Z will help a patient get over a common cold better than any other medication.
C) Treatment Z will cure a common cold.
D) Treatment Z will help any patient get over a common cold.

16.

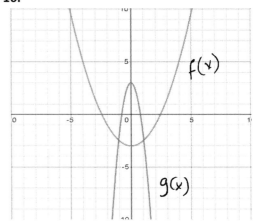

Graphs of the functions $f(x)$ and $g(x)$ are shown above. For which of the following values of x does $f(x) + g(x) = 0$?

A) -1
B) 0
C) 1
D) 2

Questions 17 and 18 refer to the following information.

$$S(P) = \frac{1}{3}P + 30$$

$$D(P) = 380 - \frac{1}{2}P$$

The quantity of a product supplied and the quantity of the product demanded in an economic market are functions of the price of the product. The functions above are the estimated supply and demand functions for a certain product. The function $S(P)$ gives the quantity of the product supplied to the market when the price is P dollars, and the function $D(P)$ gives the quantity of the product demanded when the price is P dollars.

17.
How will the quantity of the product supplied to the market change if the price of the product is increased by $30?
  A) The quantity supplied will decrease by 15 units.
  B) The quantity supplied will increase by 15 units.
  C) The quantity supplied will decrease by 10 units.
  D) The quantity supplied will increase by 10 units.

18.
At what price will the quantity of the product supplied to the market equal the quantity of the product demanded by the market?
  A) $170
  B) $350
  C) $380
  D) $420

19.
A one-pound bag of grass seeds can cover 1,500 square feet. A football field is 120 yards long and $53\frac{1}{3}$ yards wide. How many one-pound bags of grass seeds would you need to cover a football field twice?
  A) 9
  B) 27
  C) 39
  D) 77

20.

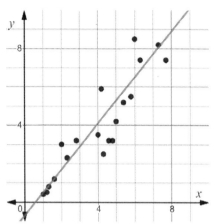

Data from a chemistry report was recorded and plotted on the graph above. The line of best fit for the data is also shown. For the x-value of 6, how much greater is the actual y-value than the y-value predicted by the line of best fit?

    A) 1
    B) 1.5
    C) 2
    D) 2.5

21.
Of the following four types of savings account plans, which option would **not** yield exponential growth of the money in the account?

    A) Each successive year, $\frac{1}{30}$ of the current value is added to the value of the account.
    B) Each successive year, 2.4% of the current value is added to the value of the account.
    C) Each successive year, 5% of the initial deposit is added to the value of the account.
    D) Each successive year, the new value is 103% of the current value.

22.
The average of three numbers is 75. One of the numbers, z, is 20 percent less than the sum of the other two. What is the value of z?

    A) 62.5
    B) 100
    C) 125
    D) 75

23.

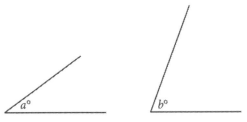

The complementary angles a and b are shown above. $\sin(a) = 3k + 3$ and $\cos(b) = 5k - 7$. Which of the following is the value of k?

A) 3
B) 4
C) 5
D) 6

24.
Mrs. Tennerman has a box of n cookies to distribute to her students. If she gives 2 cookies to each student, she will have 8 left over. In order to give each student 3 cookies, she would need 20 more cookies. How many students are in the class?

A) 18
B) 28
C) 32
D) 64

25.
A cone shaped container is used to collect rainwater. The overall height of the container is 12 feet and the diameter at the top base of the container is 6 feet. The container is partially filled. There is 4 feet from the top of the container to the top of the water in the container. What is the volume of water in the container?

A) $\frac{32}{3}\pi\ ft^3$
B) $\frac{128}{3}\pi\ ft^3$
C) $96\pi\ ft^3$
D) $144\pi\ ft^3$

26.
In the xy-plane, the line determined by the points $(2, t)$ and $(t, 18)$ passes through the origin. Which of the following could be the value of t?

A) 0
B) 4
C) 6
D) 9

27.
A right triangle was altered by increasing one leg by 20% and decreasing the other by 30%. This resulted in a decrease in the area of p percent. What is the value of p?

A) 10
B) 50
C) 16
D) 26

28.
A chemist expects a colony of bacteria to increase its population by 60% every 4 hours. If there are currently 16,000 bacteria, which of the following expressions models the chemist's predictions of total population p in t hours?

A) $16{,}000(.60)^{t/4}$
B) $16{,}000(.60)^{4t}$
C) $16{,}000(1.6)^{4t}$
D) $16{,}000(1.6)^{t/4}$

29.

	Pink	Blue
Male		
Female		
Total	76	76

The table above summarizes the number of students who prefer blue or green by gender for the 6th grade students at Logico Middle School. There are 5 times as many male students who like blue than there are male students who like pink. There are 4 times as many female students who like pink that there are female students who like blue. If there is a total of 76 students who like pink and 76 students who like blue, which of the following is closest to the probability that a male student chosen at random likes pink?

A) 0.079
B) 0.158
C) 0.167
D) 0.200

30.
$5x + 4b = 2x + 3$
$5y + 4c = 2y + 2$

In the equations above, b and c are constants. If the value of b minus c is $\frac{7}{4}$, what is the value of $x - y$?

A) -2
B) -1
C) 0
D) 1

31.
At a bake sale, cookies are $2 each and brownies are $3 each. If Nichelle spends at least $13 but no more than $17 on n cookies and 1 brownie, what is one possible value of n?

32.

10 students participated in a project to grow a plant during the school year. The heights of their plants at the end of the school year are shown in the table below. According to the table, what was the mean height, in inches, of these plants at the end of the school year? (Round your answer to the nearest tenth.)

Student	Plant Height (inches)	Student	Plant Height (inches)
Anne	54	Favrol	44
Ben	42	Guy	47
Charlie	36	Helen	51
Desean	61	Indira	58
Edna	48	Jaqueline	39

33.

$$(-5x^2 + 2x - 9) - 3(x^2 - 4x + 1)$$

If the expression above is rewritten in the form $ax^2 + bx + c$, where a, b, and c are constants, what is the value of b?

34.

In a circle with center O, central angle AOB has a measure of $80°$. The area of the sector formed by central angle AOB is what fraction of the area of the circle?

35.

Michael will compete in 20 archery contests this year. Each contest is scored out of a maximum of 80 points. It's his goal to finish the year with an average of 60 points per contest. So far, he already competed in 10 contests with an average of 56 points. What is the least score he can receive in the 11th contest and still be able to accomplish his goal for the 20 contests?

36.

$$y \leq 4x$$
$$y \leq -20x + 60$$

In the xy-plane, if a point with coordinates (a, b) lies in the solution set of the system of inequalities above, what is the maximum value of b?

Questions 37 and 38 refer to the following information.

The total distance travelled, d, by a vehicle can be found by multiplying the average speed, $\bar{s}$, by time, t. For example, a truck dispatcher can estimate the distance travelled by one of the drivers using known average speeds in different parts of the country at different times of day. He can estimate that Brett should have travelled 110 miles over the last two hours, because traffic typically allows for the truck to be driven at an average speed of 55 miles per hour.

37.
The dispatcher used this formula to estimate the total number of miles driven by the one of the truck drivers, Alex, over the last 8 hours. The dispatcher estimates that the average speed of the driver is 44 miles per hour while he is actively driving. During the 8-hour shift, the driver stopped for a 45-minute lunch break. Based on this information, what is the estimated number of miles driven?

38.
The dispatcher used the formula to estimate the total number of miles driven by a different driver, Brad, in a different part of the country. The dispatcher estimates an average speed of 40 miles per hour while the driver is actively driving. During the 8-hous shift, the driver stopped for a 30-minute lunch break. Based on this information, the estimated number of miles driven by Brad is what percent less than the estimated number of miles driven by Alex? (Note: Ignore the percent symbol when entering your answer. For example, if the answer is 53.4%, enter 53.4)

Math Practice Test 1

Math Practice Test 1, Section 3 Explanations

1. B

Linear Functions

d represents the cost per cup of flour, so if a flour with a different price is used, d will change.

2. C

System of Equations

$$5z = 25$$
$$\frac{5z}{5} = \frac{25}{5}$$
$$z = 5$$
$$12z + 7$$
$$12(5) + 7$$
$$60 + 7$$
$$\boxed{67}$$

3. C

Exponents

$b^{4/5}$ — 4 power, 5 root

$\sqrt[5]{b^4}$

4. B

Combining Like Terms & Solving Equations

\# in U.S. = 3 × (\# in Eng.)
$$315 = 3(x)$$
$$315 = 3x$$

5. B

Ratios & Proportions

$$\frac{3}{x} = \frac{9}{x+24}$$
$$3(x+24) = 9x$$
$$3x + 72 = 9x$$
$$-3x \qquad -3x$$
$$72 = 6x$$
$$\frac{72}{6} = \frac{6x}{6}$$
$$12 = x$$

$$\frac{x}{3} = \frac{12}{3} = \boxed{4}$$

6. A

System of Equations

$$x - y = ?$$

Try to solve for $x-y$ directly

$$-2y - 3x = 12$$
$$y = -4x - 1$$

$$y = -4x - 1$$
$$+4x \quad +4x$$
$$y + 4x = -1$$

Now, we have

Math Practice Test 1

$-2y - 3x = 12$
$y + 4x = -1$
Add them together to get $x - y$.

$-2y - 3x = 12$
$y + 4x = -1$
―――――――――
$-y + x = 11$ reorder
$x - y = 11$ $x + y$

7. C

Quadratics Functions

Factors of a function are used to help find the zeros of a function. For example, if the factor of a function was $(x + 5)$, the value of the function would be zero at $x = -5$.

From the table, we can see that the function is zero when $x = 1$, so a factor would be $(x - 1)$.

8. A

Linear Functions, Solving for a Variable

(c, d) is a point on the line $y = 4x + b$, so c & d can be substituted in for x and y.

(c, d)
 ↑ ↑
 x y   y-int

$d = 4c + b$
$-4c \; -4c$
―――――――
$d - 4c = b$

9. A

No Solution & Infinite Solutions

$3y - kx = 9$

$4y - 6x = 28$

These are linear functions, so they will have no solution when they have the same slope and different y-intercepts. Solve for y in both equations to get them into $y = mx + b$ form, so we can easily identify the slopes.

$3y - kx = 9$
$\;\;\; +kx \;\; +kx$
―――――――
$3y = kx + 9$

$\dfrac{3y}{3} = \dfrac{kx}{3} + \dfrac{9}{3}$

$y = \boxed{\dfrac{k}{3}} x + 3$
        ↑ slope

$4y - 6x = 28$
$\;\;\; +6x \;\; +6x$
―――――――
$4y = 6x + 28$

$\dfrac{4y}{4} = \dfrac{6x}{4} + \dfrac{28}{4}$

$y = \boxed{\dfrac{3}{2}} x + 7$
        ↑ slope

Math Practice Test 1

Set the slopes equal to solve for k

$$\frac{k}{3} = \frac{3}{2}$$

$$2k = 9$$

$$\frac{2k}{2} = \frac{9}{2}$$

$$k = \boxed{\frac{9}{2}}$$

10. A

Quadratic Functions

Find where they intersect

$$(x+2)^2 = 36$$

$$\sqrt{(x+2)^2} = \sqrt{36}$$

$$x + 2 = \pm 6$$

$$x = -2 \pm 6$$

$$x = -2+6, \quad x = -2-6$$

$$x = 4, \quad x = -8$$

Sketch

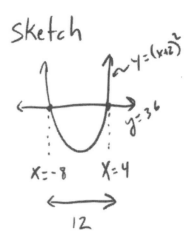

11. A

Angles, Polygons, & 3-D Shapes

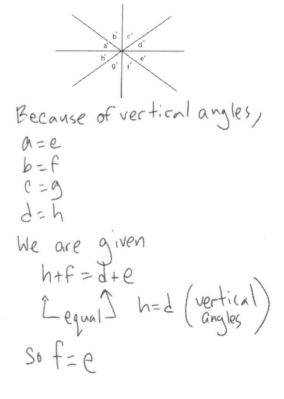

Because of vertical angles,

$a = e$
$b = f$
$c = g$
$d = h$

We are given

$h + f = d + e$
 ↳ equal ↲ $h = d$ (vertical angles)

So $f = e$

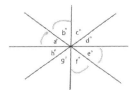

$f = b$ and $a = e$
so $f = b = a = e$
I. $f = a$ is true
II. Doesn't have to be true.
III. can't be proven.

12. C

Quadratic Functions

$y = a(x+2)(x-b)$
$\downarrow$
zeros
$x = -2 \quad x = b$

vertex at $(-3, c)$,
so axis of symmetry: $x = -3$

b must equal -4

$y = a(x+2)(x-b)$
becomes
$y = a(x+2)(x-(-4))$
$y = a(x+2)(x+4)$

c is the y-value of the vertex.
Substitute the x-value of the vertex in.

$y = a(-3+2)(-3+4)$
$y = a(-1)(1)$
$y = \boxed{-a}$

13. B

Dividing Polynomials

$\dfrac{8x^2 + 2x + 4}{ax+1} = 4x - 1 + \dfrac{5}{ax+1}$

To get this we do long division

$\; 4x - 1 + 5/{ax+1}$
$ax+1 \,\overline{)\, 8x^2 + 2x + 4}$

Look at the circled terms

$\; \boxed{4x} - 1 + 5/{ax+1}$
$\boxed{ax+1} \,\overline{)\, \boxed{8x^2} + 2x + 4}$

$8x^2 \div ax = 4x$, so $a = 2$

Math Practice Test 1

14. A

Quadratic Functions

The answer choices show us that we will have to use the quadratic formula.

$$x = \frac{-b \pm \sqrt{b^2 - 4ac}}{2a}$$

$a = 7, b = 12, \text{ and } c = -3$

$$\frac{-12 \pm \sqrt{(12)^2 - 4(7)(-3)}}{2(7)}$$

$$\frac{-12 \pm \sqrt{144 + 84}}{14}$$

$$\frac{-12 \pm \sqrt{228}}{14}$$

$$\frac{-12 \pm \sqrt{4}\sqrt{57}}{14}$$

$$\frac{-12 \pm 2\sqrt{57}}{14}$$

Reduce by 2

$$\frac{-6 \pm \sqrt{57}}{7}$$

15. D

Linear Functions

$$K = \frac{5}{9}(F - 32) + 273.15$$

$$K = \frac{5}{9}F \underbrace{- \frac{160}{9} + 273.15}_{\text{combine to equal the y-int}}$$

$\uparrow$ slope (rate of change)

I. True. $\uparrow \frac{5}{9}K$ for every $\uparrow 1F$ and $\downarrow \frac{5}{9}K$ for every $\downarrow 1F$

II. True. If you solve for F, will end up with $\frac{9}{5}$ as the coefficient of K.

III. False

16. 8

Quadratic Functions

$$4x(x-8)(x+3) = 0$$

Already factored!
set each factor equal to 0 and solve.

$4x = 0 \quad\quad x - 8 = 0 \quad\quad x + 3 = 0$
$\frac{4x}{4} = \frac{0}{4} \quad\quad +8 +8 \quad\quad -3 -3$
$x = 0 \quad\quad x = 8 \quad\quad x = -3$

$x > 0$, so x can only be 8.

Math Practice Test 1

17. 2

Combining Like Terms & Solving Equations

$$\frac{1}{12}x + \frac{1}{18}x = \frac{2}{9} + \frac{1}{18}$$

Multiply by the LCD, 36

$$(36)\frac{1}{12}x + (36)\frac{1}{18}x = (36)\frac{2}{9} + (36)\frac{1}{18}$$

$$3x + 2x = 8 + 2$$
$$5x = 10$$
$$\frac{5x}{5} = \frac{10}{5}$$
$$x = 2$$

18. 150

Angles, Polygons, & 3-D Shapes

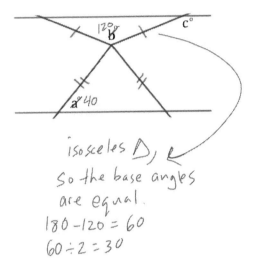

isosceles △,
so the base angles
are equal.
$180 - 120 = 60$
$60 \div 2 = 30$

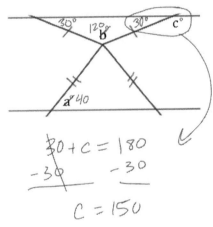

$30 + c = 180$
$-30 \quad -30$
$c = 150$

$a = 40$
$2b + 3a = 360$
$2b + 3(40) = 360$
$2b + 120 = 360$
$\quad -120 \quad -120$
$2b = 240$
$\frac{2b}{2} = \frac{240}{2}$
$b = 120$

Math Practice Test 1

19. 42

System of Equations

L = # of diapers in a large box
S = # of diapers in a small box

$L = \boxed{S + 30}$

$6S + 5L = 612$
$6S + 5(S+30) = 612$
$6S + 5S + 150 = 612$
$11S + 150 = 612$
$-150 \quad -150$
$11S = 462$
$S = \boxed{42}$

20. 0.28 or .28

Trigonometry

sketch of △

$\sin Q = 0.28$
$\cos S = ?$

S & Q are complementary angles, so sine of one of them equals cosine of the other.

$\cos S = \boxed{0.28}$

Math Practice Test 1, Section 4 Explanations

1. B

Data & Probability

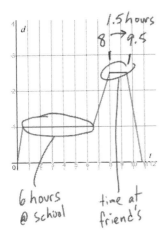

6 hours @ school
1.5 hours
8 → 9.5
time at friend's

2. B

Data & Probability

	Older than 6 years	Younger than 6 years	Total
Cats	(5)	12	17
Dogs	12	(31)	43
Total	17	43	60

either a cat older than 6 (5) or a dog younger than 6 (31):

36 options out of 60 total

$\frac{36}{60} = \boxed{\frac{3}{5}}$

3. D

Data & Probability

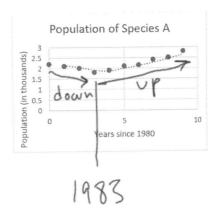

down up

1983

4. C

Evaluating Functions

n	1	4	5	7
$f(n)$	11	23	27	35

The table above shows some values for linear function f. Which of the following defines f?

A) $f(n) = 2n$
B) $f(n) = 3n + 8$
C) $f(n) = 4n + 7$
D) $f(n) = 12n - 1$

$n = 1$
$4(1) + 7 = 11$
$n = 4$
$4(4) + 7 = 23$
$n = 5$
$4(5) + 7 = 27$
$n = 7$
$4(7) + 7 = 35$

Math Practice Test 1

5. A

Percent

$33\frac{1}{3}\%$ of 21 clerks
$(.33\overline{3}) \times (21) = 7$

25% of 12 cashiers
$(.25) \times (12) = 3$

$7 + 3 = 10$

6. A

Combining Like Terms & Solving Equations

Sum → add

$4x^2 - 7x + 9 + 2x^2 + 4x + 6$

$6x^2 - 3x + 15$

7. D

Combining Like Terms & Solving Equations

$\frac{5}{7}w = \frac{3}{4}$

$\left(\frac{7}{5}\right)\frac{5}{7}w = \frac{3}{4}\left(\frac{7}{5}\right)$

$w = \frac{21}{20}$

8. C

Linear Functions

$y = 0.42x + 16$

↑ slope (rate of change)   ↑ y-int (initial value)

used to estimate avg. number per state, so 0.42 is avg increase each year per state

16 is avg initial number in each state

9. B

Ratios & Proportions

$\frac{150 \text{ in.}}{1 \text{ sec}} \times \frac{1 \text{ ft}}{12 \text{ in}} \times \frac{60 \text{ sec.}}{1 \text{ min.}}$

$\frac{(150)(60)}{12} \frac{\text{ft}}{\text{min}} = \frac{(150)(\cancel{60}^5)}{\cancel{12}_1} \frac{\text{ft}}{\text{min}}$

750 ft/min

Math Practice Test 1

10. B

Combining Like Terms & Solving Equations

	Conversion Factor, k
Euro	0.89
British Pound	0.76
Indian Rupee	71.32
Swiss Franc	0.97
Japanese Yen	108.89

$240 = X$ Swiss Franc

$$\frac{c}{d} = k$$

$$\frac{x}{240} = 0.97$$

$$x = (0.97)(240)$$

$$x = 232.8$$

11. B

Combining Like Terms & Solving Equations

	Conversion Factor, k
Euro	0.89
British Pound	0.76
Indian Rupee	71.32
Swiss Franc	0.97
Japanese Yen	108.89

$d = 1,356$

$c = 1,030$

$$\frac{c}{d} = k$$

$$\frac{1030}{1356} = k$$

$$0.76 = k$$

British Pound

12. B

Quadratic Functions

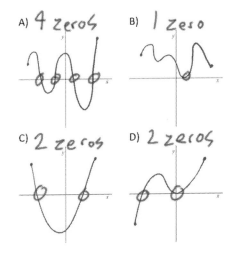

A) 4 zeros
B) 1 zero
C) 2 zeros
D) 2 zeros

Math Practice Test 1

13. C

Solving for a Variable in terms of Another

$$K = \frac{1}{2}mv^2$$

$$(2)K = \frac{1}{2}mv^2(2)$$

$$2K = mv^2$$

$$\frac{2K}{m} = \frac{mv^2}{m}$$

$$\frac{2K}{m} = v^2$$

$$\sqrt{\frac{2K}{m}} = v$$

14. D

Linear Functions, Ratios & Proportions

$\$5/hr$

m minutes

Convert m minutes to hours

m minutes $\times \dfrac{1 \, hr}{60 \, min} = \dfrac{m}{60} hr$

$$C = 5\left(\frac{m}{60}\right)$$

$$C = \frac{5m}{60}$$

15. A

Data & Probability

Based on the results, more people recovered from the common cold when they were given the treatment than those who didn't get the treatment. We can conclude that the treatment may help people get over the common cold. We cannot choose B because choice B states that the treatment will definitively help patients recover. However, everyone in the study who received the treatment did not recover. For the same reason, we cannot choose choices C and D.

16. B

Evaluating Functions

In order for $f(x) + g(x)$ to equal 0, one must be the negative value of the other. We can see that happens when $x = 0$. $f(0) = 3$ and $g(0) = -3$. The values add up to 0.

Math Practice Test 1

17. D

Linear Functions

$$S(P) = \frac{1}{3}P + 30$$

↑ Product supplied   ↑ rate of change

The slope, rate of change, is $\frac{1 \text{ product supplied}}{\$3}$.

For every $3 in price change, the number of products supplied will increase by 1.

$30↑ then 10 prod↑

18. D

System of Equations

$$S(P) = D(P)$$
$$\frac{1}{3}P + 30 = 380 - \frac{1}{2}P$$

Get rid of fractions by multiplying by LCD: 6

$$(6)\frac{1}{3}P + (6)30 = (6)380 - (6)\frac{1}{2}P$$

$$2P + 180 = 2{,}280 - 3P$$
$$+3P \qquad\qquad +3P$$
$$5P + 180 = 2280$$
$$-180 \quad -180$$
$$5P = 2100$$
$$P = 420$$

19. D

Ratios & Proportions

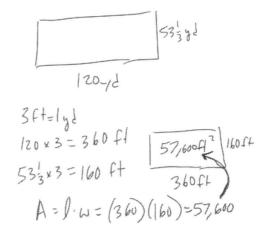

$3ft = 1yd$
$120 × 3 = 360 ft$
$53\frac{1}{3} × 3 = 160 ft$

$A = l \cdot w = (360)(160) = 57{,}600$

57,600 ft² | 160 ft
360 ft

Math Practice Test 1

$$\frac{1 \text{ bag}}{1,500 \text{ ft}^2} = \frac{x \text{ bags}}{57,600 \text{ ft}^2}$$

$$57,600 = 1,500x$$

$$\frac{57,600}{1,500} = \frac{1,500x}{1,500}$$

$$38.4 \text{ bags} = x$$

Cover twice

$$38.4(2) = 76.8$$

77 bags

20. C

Data & Probability

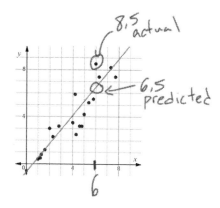

$$8.5 - 6.5 = 2$$

21. C

Exponential Growth & Decay

Since it will increase by 5% of the initial deposit each year, it will increase by the same number each year. Therefore, it is will have linear growth, not exponential.

22. B

Combining Like Terms & Solving Equations, Data & Probability

Avg of 3 #s is 75

Sum = (Avg)(#)

Sum = (75)(3)

Sum = 225

3 numbers add up to 225

let the #s be $x, y, +z$

z is 20% less than the sum of x and y means

z is 80% of the sum of x and y

$$z = 0.8(x+y)$$

$$x+y+z = 225$$

$$x+y+.8(x+y) = 225$$

$$x+y+.8x+.8y = 225$$

$$1.8x + 1.8y = 225$$

$$\frac{1.8x}{1.8} + \frac{1.8y}{1.8} = \frac{225}{1.8}$$

$$x+y = 125$$

$$z = .8(x+y)$$

$$z = .8(125)$$

$$z = 100$$

23. C

Trigonometry

If a and b are complementary, then $\sin a = \cos b$.

$$\sin a = \cos b$$
$$3k + 3 = 5k - 7$$
$$-3k \qquad -3k$$
$$3 = 2k - 7$$
$$+7 \qquad +7$$
$$10 = 2k$$
$$\frac{10}{2} = \frac{2k}{2}$$
$$5 = k$$

24. B

System of Equations

$n = $ # of cookies
$x = $ # of students

$$2x + 8 = n$$
$$3x = n + 20$$
$$3x = 2x + 8 + 20$$
$$3x = 2x + 28$$
$$-2x \quad -2x$$
$$x = 28$$

25. A

Angles, Polygons, & 3-D Shapes

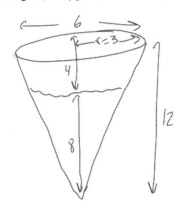

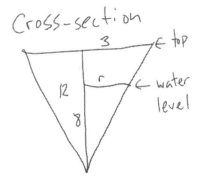

We can use a proportion to find the radius at the water-level.

Math Practice Test 1

$$\frac{3}{12} = \frac{r}{8}$$

$$24 = 12r$$

$$2 = r$$

Water in cone:
$r = 2$, $h = 8$

$$V = \frac{1}{3}\pi r^2 h$$

$$V = \frac{1}{3}\pi (2)^2 (8)$$

$$V = \frac{32}{3}\pi \text{ ft}^3$$

$(2, t)$ $(t, 18)$

$\frac{y}{x} = m$ $\frac{y}{x} = m$

$\frac{t}{2} = m$ $\frac{18}{t} = m$

$\frac{t}{2} = \frac{18}{t}$

$t^2 = 36$

$t = \pm 6$

Or just try the answer choices.

A. 0 $(2, 0)$ $(0, 18)$
         $\times 0$
         $2 \times 0 = 0$ $0 \times 0 \ne 18$ ✗

B. 4 $(2, 4)$ $(4, 18)$
         $\times 2$
         $2 \times 2 = 4$ $4 \times 2 \ne 18$ ✗

C. 6 $(2, 6)$ $(6, 18)$
         $\times 3$
         $2 \times 3 = 6$ $6 \times 3 = 18$ ✓

D. 9 $(2, 9)$ $(9, 18)$
         $\times 4.5$
         $2 \times 4.5 = 9$ $9 \times 4.5 \ne 18$ ✗

26. C

Linear Functions, Common Math Tricks

If the line passes through the origin, it has the equation $y = mx$. Therefore, $\frac{y}{x} = m$. There is a constant ratio between y and x.

Math Practice Test 1

27. C

Ratios & Proportions

↑b by 20% = 1.2b
↓h by 30% = 0.7h

$A = \frac{1}{2}(1.2b)(0.7h)$

$A = (0.84)\frac{1}{2}bh$

0.84 = 84%
a 16% decrease

28. D

Exponential Growth & Decay

↑60% means 160%

160% = 1.6

t = hours
increases by 60% every 4 hours
For example, in 8 hours it will increase by 60% twice, so t must be divided by 2

$16,000(1.6)^{t/4}$

29. C

Data & Probability

male pink = x
male blue = 5x
female blue = y
female pink = 4y

	Pink	Blue
Male	x	5x
Female	4y	y
Total	76	76

$x + 4y = 76$
$5x + y = 76$

use elimination

Math Practice Test 1

$$-5(x+4y=76)$$
$$5x+y=76$$

$$-5x-20y=-380$$
$$5x+y=76$$
_____
$$-19y=-304$$

$$\frac{-19y}{-19}=\frac{-304}{-19}$$

$$y=16$$

$$x+4y=76$$
$$x+4(16)=76$$
$$x=12$$

	Pink	Blue
Male	x	5x
Female	4y	y
Total	76	76

$$x=12$$
$$y=16$$

	Pink	Blue	Total
Male	12	60	72
Female	64	16	
Total	76	76	

$$\frac{\#\text{ males who like pink}}{\#\text{ males}}$$

$$\frac{12}{72}$$

$$\frac{1}{6}=0.167$$

30. A

System of Equations, Common Math Tricks

$$5x+4b=2x+3$$
$$5y+4c=2y+2$$
$$b-c=7/4,\ x-y=?$$

Based on the given information and objective, it seems like we should subtract the equations.

Let's reorganize first

$$5x+4b=2x+3 \qquad 5y+4c=2y+2$$
$$-2x \quad -2x \qquad\qquad -2y \quad -2y$$
$$3x+4b=3 \qquad\qquad 3y+4c=2$$

$$3x+4b=3$$
$$-(3y+4c=2)$$

$$3x-3y+4b-4c=1$$
$$3(x-y)+4(b-c)=1$$
$$3(x-y)+4(7/4)=1$$
$$3(x-y)+7=1$$
$$\qquad\qquad -7\ -7$$
$$3(x-y)=-6$$

$$\frac{3(x-y)}{3}=\frac{-6}{3}$$

$$x-y=-2$$

Math Practice Test 1

31. 5, 6, or 7

System of Equations

cookies = $2
brownies = $3

$13 \leq 2n + 3 \leq 17$

$ -3 -3 -3$

$10 \leq 2n \leq 14$

$\dfrac{10}{2} \leq \dfrac{2n}{2} \leq \dfrac{14}{2}$

$5 \leq n \leq 7$

$\boxed{5, 6, \text{ or } 7}$

32. 48

Data & Probability

Add them up to get

Sum = 480

Avg = $\dfrac{\text{Sum}}{\#}$

Avg = $\dfrac{480}{10}$

Avg = 48

33. 14

Equating Coefficients

$(-5x^2 + 2x - 9) - 3(x^2 - 4x + 1)$

$-5x^2 + 2x - 9 - 3x^2 + 12x - 3$

$-8x^2 + 14x - 12$

$ \uparrow$

$ax^2 + bx + c$

$b = 14$

34. $\dfrac{2}{9}$ or .222

Circles

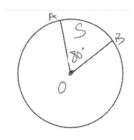

$\dfrac{80}{360} = \dfrac{S}{A}$

$\dfrac{8}{36} = \dfrac{S}{A}$

$\boxed{\dfrac{2}{9}} = \dfrac{S}{A}$

Math Practice Test 1

35. 0

Data & Probability

20 contests
Avg = 60
Sum = (Avg)(#)
Sum = (60)(20)
Sum = 1200

The 20 contests must add up to 1,200 for a 60 average

First 10, Avg = 56
Sum = (56)(10) = 560

Remaining 10 must add up to 1200 − 560 = 640

To find the least possible score for the 11th, we have to assume the highest possible for the other 9.

Sum = (80)(9)
Sum = 720

He only needs 640, so he can get a 0 on his 11th and still get a 60 average.

36. 10

System of Equations

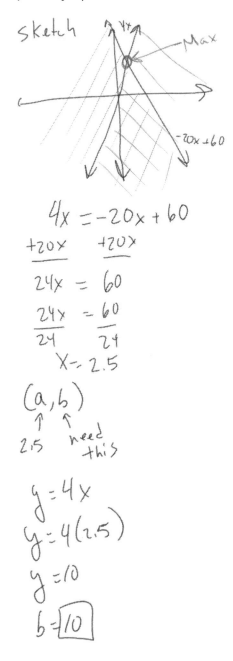

$4x = -20x + 60$

$+20x \quad +20x$

$24x = 60$

$\dfrac{24x}{24} = \dfrac{60}{24}$

$x = 2.5$

(a, b)
 ↑   ↑
 2.5 need this

$y = 4x$
$y = 4(2.5)$
$y = 10$
$b = \boxed{10}$

Math Practice Test 1

37. 319

Combining Like Terms & Solving Equations

$d = st$

$45 \text{ min} = 0.75 \text{ hr}$

$8 - 0.75 = 7.25 \text{ hrs driving}$

$d = (44)(7.25)$

$d = 319$

38. 5.95 or 5.96

Percent, Combining Like Terms & Solving Equations

$d = st$

$30 \text{ min} = 0.5 \text{ hr}$

$8 - 0.5 = 7.5 \text{ hrs driving}$

$d = (40)(7.5)$

$d = 300$

$\dfrac{\text{change}}{\text{original}} \times 100\%$

$\dfrac{319 - 300}{319} \times 100$

$5.95\% \text{ or } 5.96\%$

Math Practice Test 2

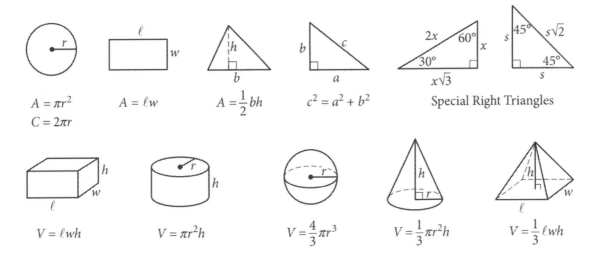

The number of degrees of arc in a circle is 360.

The number of radians of arc in a circle is 2π.

The sum of the measures in degrees of the angles of a triangle is 180.

Need to improve 200 points?

We love working with students who are serious about their SAT scores - that means you!

Special Tutoring & Test Prep Offer for You

 caddellprep.com/sboffer

Math Practice Test 2

1.

Which of the following expressions is equal to 0 for some value of x?

A) $|x - 2| + 1$
B) $|x - 2| - 2$
C) $|x + 2| + 1$
D) $|x - 2| + 2$

2.

$$\frac{3x}{2y} = 6$$
$$2(y + 4) = 16$$

If (x, y) is the solution to the system of equations above, what is the value of y?

A) 2
B) 4
C) 19
D) 75

3.

$$f(x) = \frac{2}{3}x + b$$

In the function above, b is a constant. If $f(3) = 7$, what is the value of $f(-1)$?

A) -5
B) $-\frac{8}{3}$
C) $\frac{13}{3}$
D) 7

4.

If $f(x) = -2x + 9$, what is $f(-5x)$ equal to?

A) $10x + 9$
B) $-10x + 9$
C) $20x - 9$
D) $20x + 9$

5.

$$4(3x + 2)(x + 1)$$

Which of the following is equivalent to the expression above?

A) $43x$
B) $24x^2 + 3$
C) $16x^2 + 20x + 1$
D) $12x^2 + 20x + 8$

6.

If $\frac{a-b}{b} = \frac{5}{8}$, which of the following must also be true?

A) $\frac{a}{b} = \frac{21}{8}$
B) $\frac{a}{b} = \frac{14}{8}$
C) $\frac{a+b}{b} = \frac{21}{8}$
D) $\frac{a-b}{b} = -\frac{1}{8}$

7.

To prepare for a marathon, Lisa created a training schedule in which the distance of her longest run every week increased by a constant amount. If Lisa's training schedule requires that her longest run in week 3 is a distance of 9 miles and her longest run in week 15 is a distance of 27 miles, which of the following best describes how the distance Amelia runs changes between week 3 and week 15 of her training schedule?

A) Lisa increases the distance of her longest run by 3 miles each week.
B) Lisa decreases the distance of her longest run by 1.5 miles a week.
C) Lisa increases the distance of her longest run by 3 miles every 2 weeks.
D) Lisa increases the distance of her longest mile by 1.8 miles each week.

8.

Which of the following equations represents a line that is parallel to the line with equation $y = -6x + 5$?

A) $6x + 2y = 8$
B) $18x + 3y = 4$
C) $3x - y = 10$
D) $x + 12y = 0$

9.

$\sqrt{x - a} = \frac{1}{2}x - 6$

If $a = 4$, what is the solution set of the equation above?

A) $\{20\}$
B) $\{8, 20\}$
C) $\{8\}$
D) $\{0\}$

10.

If $\frac{t+7}{t-7} = 14$, what is the value of t?

A) $\frac{105}{13}$
B) $\frac{13}{105}$
C) $\frac{7}{2}$
D) $\frac{100}{15}$

11.

$x = 2y + 3$
$y = (2x - 1)(x + 1)$

How many ordered pairs (x, y) satisfy the system of equations shown above?

A) 0
B) 1
C) 2
D) Infinitely many

12.

Ria and Olivia each ordered a salad at a restaurant. The price of Ria's salad was x dollars, and the price of Olivia's salad was $2 more than the price of Ria's salad. If Ria and Olivia split the cost of the salads evenly and each paid a 10% tip, which of the following expressions represents the amount, in dollars, each of them paid?

A) $0.2x + 2.4$
B) $2.1x + 0.7$
C) $1.2x + 0.6$
D) $1.1x + 1.1$

13.

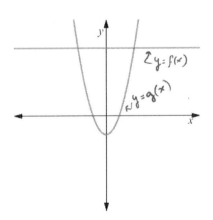

The functions f and g, defined by $f(x) = 7$ and $g(x) = x^2 - 2$, are graphed in the xy-plane above. The graphs of f and g intersect at the points $(-k, 7)$ and $(k, 7)$. What is the value of k?

A) 2
B) 3
C) 4.5
D) 7

14.

$$\frac{7 - i}{3 - 2i}$$

If the expression above is rewritten in the form of $a + bi$, where a and b are real numbers, what is the value of a? (Note: $i = \sqrt{-1}$)

A) 2
B) $\frac{23}{13}$
C) $\frac{32}{3}$
D) $\frac{31}{25}$

15.

$$x^2 - \frac{k}{3}x = 2p$$

In the quadratic equation above, k and p are constants. What are the solutions for x?

A) $x = \frac{k}{3} \pm \frac{\sqrt{k^2 + 3p}}{3}$

B) $x = \frac{k}{3} \pm \frac{\sqrt{k^2 + 8p}}{12}$

C) $x = \frac{k}{6} \pm \frac{\sqrt{k^2 + 72p}}{6}$

D) $x = \frac{k}{6} \pm \frac{\sqrt{k^2 + 18p}}{4}$

16.
Max has three chains of different lengths. They are all attached together, end to end, to make a chain that is 8 feet long. The second longest chain is twice as long as the shortest one, and the longest chain is three times as long as the shortest one. What is the length of the shortest chain, in inches?

17.
$x^3 - 6x^2 + 6x - 36 = 0$
For what real value of x is the equation above true and $x > 3$?

18.

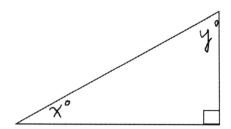

Note: Not drawn to scale.
In the triangle above, the cosine of $x°$ is 0.4. What is the sine of $y°$?

19.
$-2x + 5y = 20$
$4x + y = 15$
If (x, y) is the solution to the systems of equations above, what is the value of x?

20.
Alberto works in an Italian restaurant. To make a small pot of sauce he must use 3 ounces of parmesan cheese with 10 cans of tomatoes. If makes a big pot of sauce he must use 8 ounces of parmesan with 24 cans of tomatoes. For every additional 21 cans of tomatoes he must use n ounces of parmesan. What is the value of n?

1.
The monthly membership fee for an online movie service is $9.50 but there is an additional fee of $1.20 to rent each movie online. For one month, Kayla's membership and movie rental fees were $13.10. How many movies did Kayla rent online that month?

    A) 1
    B) 2
    C) 3
    D) 4

2.
To become the fastest typist in his class, a student has to be able to type 250 words per minute. Kai can currently type 135 words per minute and believes that with practice, he can increase his typing speed by 10 words per minute each month. Which of the following represents the number of words per minute Kai believes he will be able to type m months from now?

    A) $135 + 10m$
    B) $250 - 10m$
    C) $115 - 10m$
    D) $250 + 10m$

3.
If a 6-pound cake is sliced into thirds and each third is sliced into halves, what is the weight, in ounces, of each of the slices? (1 pound = 16 ounces)

    A) 4
    B) 6
    C) 8
    D) 16

4.
Yana surveyed a random sample of Band students at her school to determine whether they thought the piano counted as a legitimate band instrument or not. Of the 80 students surveyed, 35.3% said yes. Based on this information, about how many of the 225 total Band students in the entire school would be expected to also agree that the piano counts as a legitimate band instrument?

    A) 55
    B) 65
    C) 70
    D) 80

5.

The density of an object is equal to the mass of the object divided by the volume of the object. What is the volume, in milliliters, of an object with a mass of 60 grams and a density of 5 grams per milliliter?

   A) 300
   B) $\frac{1}{12}$
   C) 12
   D) 560

6.

Last week, Nina studied for 13 more hours than Larry did. If they studied for a combined total of 63 hours, how many hours did Larry study last week?

   A) 35
   B) 20
   C) 25
   D) 50

7.

Movies with Greatest Ticket Sales in 2012

MPAA Rating	Action	Animated	Comedy	Drama	Total
PG	2	7	2	5	16
PG-13	9	0	5	5	19
R	7	0	2	6	15
Total	18	7	9	16	50

The table above represents the 50 movies that had the greatest ticket sales in 2012, categorized by movie genre and Motion Picture Association of America (MPAA) rating. What proportion of the movies are dramas with a R rating?

   A) $\frac{2}{25}$
   B) $\frac{3}{25}$
   C) $\frac{3}{50}$
   D) $\frac{16}{50}$

8.

Line ℓ in the xy-plane contains points from each of Quadrants I, III, and IV, but no points from Quadrant II. Which of the following must be true?

   A) The slope of line ℓ is undefined.
   B) The slope of line ℓ is zero.
   C) The slope of line ℓ is positive.
   D) The slope of line ℓ is negative.

9.

Number of Registered Voters in the United States in 2012, in thousands

Region	Age 18 to 24	Age 25 to 44	Age 45 to 64	Age 65 to 74	75 & Older	Total
Northeast	2,713	8,159	10,986	3,342	2,775	27,975
Midwest	3,453	11,237	13,865	4,221	3,350	36,126
South	5,210	18,072	21,346	7,272	4,969	56,869
West	3,390	10,428	11,598	3,785	2,986	32,187
Total	14,766	47,896	57,795	18,620	14,080	153,157

The table above shows the number of registered voters in 2012, in thousands, in four geographic regions and five age groups. Based on the table, if a registered voter who was 45 to 64 years old in 2012, is chosen at random, which of the following is closest to the probability that the registered voter was from the South region?

A) 0.29
B) 0.30
C) 0.35
D) 0.37

Questions 10 and 11 refer to the following information.

A teacher plotted the test results of 11 students against the number of hours spent studying for the test by each student.

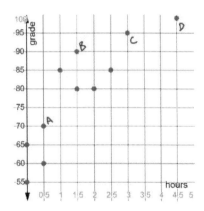

10.
Of the 11 students represented in the above, what was the longest number of hours spent studying?
A) 99
B) 5
C) 4.5
D) 3

11.
Of the labeled points, which represents the student for which the ratio of grade to time spent studying is greatest?
A) A
B) B
C) C
D) D

12.
In the xy-plane, the graph of function f has x-intercepts at $-4, -2$, and 1. Which of the following could define f?
A) $f(x) = (x + 4)(x + 2)(x - 1)$
B) $f(x) = (x - 4)(x - 1)(x + 2)$
C) $f(x) = (x + 4)(x - 2)(x + 1)$
D) $f(x) = (x - 4)(x - 2)(x - 1)$

13.
The population of rabbits in a meadow is estimated over the course of 20 weeks, as shown in the table.

Time (weeks)	Population
0	5
5	25
10	125
15	625
20	3125

Which of the following best describes the relationship between time and the estimated population of rabbits during the twenty weeks?
A) Increasing linear
B) Decreasing linear
C) Exponential growth
D) Exponential decay

14.

$$1{,}000\left(1 + \frac{r}{1{,}200}\right)^{12}$$

The expression above gives the amount of money, in dollars, generated in a year by $1,000 deposit in a bank account that pays an annual interest rate of r%, compounded monthly. Which of the following expressions shows how much additional money is generated at an interest rate of 10% than at an interest rate of 6%?

A) $1{,}000\left(1 + \frac{10-6}{1{,}200}\right)^{12}$

B) $1{,}000\left(1 + \frac{\frac{10}{6}}{1{,}200}\right)^{12}$

C) $\dfrac{1{,}000\left(1 + \frac{10}{1{,}200}\right)^{12}}{1{,}000\left(1 + \frac{6}{1{,}200}\right)^{12}}$

D) $1{,}000\left(1 + \frac{10}{1{,}200}\right)^{12} - 1{,}000\left(1 + \frac{6}{1{,}200}\right)^{12}$

15.

Which of the following scatterplots shows a relationship that is appropriately modeled with the equation $y = ax^b$, where a is negative and b is positive?

A)

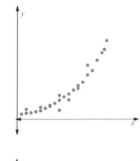

B)

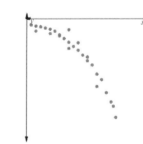

C)

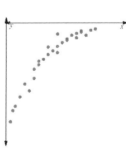

D)

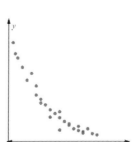

Questions 16 and 17 refer to the following information.

Mr. Wilson is building a concrete patio in his backyard and is deciding where to buy the materials and rent the tools needed for the project. The table below shows the materials' cost and daily rental costs for three different stores.

Store	Materials Cost, M (dollars)	Rental cost of wheelbarrow, W (dollars per day)	Rental cost of concrete mixer, K (dollars per day)
A	750	15	65
B	600	25	80
C	700	20	70

The total cost, y, for buying the materials and renting the tools in terms of the number of days, x, is given by $y = M + (W + K)x$.

16.
For what number of days, x, will the total cost of buying the materials and renting the tools from Store B be greater than or equal to the total cost of buying the materials and renting the tools from Store A?

A) $x \geq 6$
B) $x \leq 6$
C) $x \leq 7.3$
D) $x \geq 7.3$

17.
If the relationship between the total cost, y, of buying the materials and renting the tools at Store C, and the number of days, x, for which the tools are rented is graphed in the xy-plane, what does the y-intercept of the line represent?

A) The total cost of the project
B) The total cost of materials
C) The total daily cost of the project
D) The total daily rental costs of the tools

18.
Sara has identical drinking glasses each in the shape of a right circular cylinder with an internal diameter of 4 inches. She pours milk from a gallon jug into each glass until it is full. If the height of milk in each glass is about 9 inches, what is the largest number of full milk glasses he can pour from one gallon of milk? (Note: There are 231 cubic inches in 1 gallon)

A) 2
B) 4
C) 5
D) 6

19.
If $4p - 5 \geq 3$, what is the least possible value of $4p + 2$?

A) 5
B) 8
C) 10
D) 12

20.

A species has been introduced to an environment where there aren't any natural predators. An environmentalist predicts that the population will triple each year. Which of the following graphs could morel the population, y, of the species as a function of time, x?

A)
B)
C)
D)

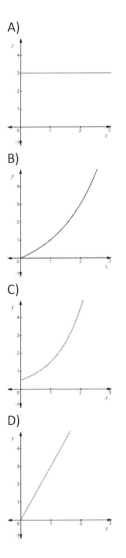

_____▽_____

Questions 21 and 22 refer to the following information.

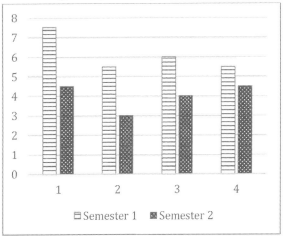

A teacher recorded the average daily hours spent by her students on their phones during Semester 1 and Semester 2. The bar graph above shows the results for the four classes: Class 1, Class 2, Class 3, and Class 4. The students in the class made a conscious effort to reduce the amount of time they spend on the phone each day during Semester 2.

Math Practice Test 2

21.

In a scatterplot of this data, where Semester 1 is plotted along the x-axis and Semester 2 is plotted along the y-axis, for each of the classes, how many data points would be above the line $y = x$?

A) 0
B) 1
C) 3
D) 4

22.

Which of the four classes had the greatest percent change in the average daily number of hours spent on phone from Semester 1 to Semester 2?

A) Class 1
B) Class 2
C) Class 3
D) Class 4

23.

Students in two classes were tested to see how many US presidents they could name. The results are shown below.

Class A

Number of Presidents	Frequency
2	6
3	3
4	4
5	2
6	3
7	4

Class B

Number of Presidents	Frequency
2	1
3	5
4	10
5	4
6	1
7	1

Which of the following is true about the data shown regarding these students?

A) The standard deviation of number of presidents named is the same for both classes.
B) The standard deviation of number of presidents named is the greater for Class A than for Class B.
C) The standard deviation of number of presidents named is greater for Class B than for Class A

D) Since both classes had students who names 2 presidents and 7 presidents there is no standard deviation

24.

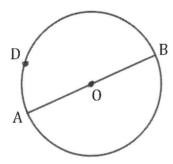

In the circle above, segment AB is a diameter. If the length of arc ADB is 10π, what is the length of the radius of the circle?

A) 6
B) 2
C) 10
D) 20

25.
$f(x) = 2x^3 + 5x^2$
$g(x) = x + 2$
The polynomials $f(x)$ and $g(x)$ are defined above. Which of the following polynomials is divisible by $x^2 + 4$?

A) $h(x) = f(x) + g(x)$
B) $p(x) = f(x) + 8g(x)$
C) $r(x) = 2f(x) + 3g(x)$
D) $s(x) = 3(x) = 4g(x)$

26.
Let x and y be number such that $-y < x < y$. Which of the following must be true?

I. $|x| < y$
II. $x = 0$
III. $y > 0$

A) I only
B) I and II only
C) I and III only
D) I, II, and III

Math Practice Test 2

27.

Josie plotted the value of a stock each year since 2000. The scatterplot below reflects the price of the stock t years after 2000.

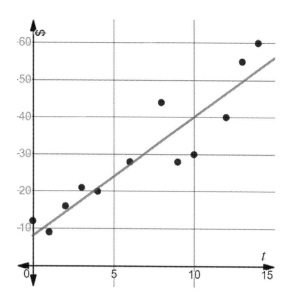

The line of best fit is also shown and has equation $y = 3.2t + 8$. Which of the following best explains the number 8 in the equation as it relates to the scatterplot.

A) In the year 2000, the price of the stock was $8.
B) Since the year 2000, the price of the stock increased by approximately $8 per year.
C) $8 is the price Josie would have paid for the stock if she purchased it in 2000.
D) The estimated price of the stock in 2000 is $8, but the actual price was over $10.

28.

$f(x) = (x + 4)(x - 2)$

Which of the following is an equivalent form of the function f above in which the minimum value of f appears as a constant or coefficient?

A) $f(x) = x^2 + 2x + 2$
B) $f(x) = (x - 1)^2 - 5$
C) $f(x) = x(x + 2) + 2$
D) $f(x) = (x + 1)^2 - 9$

29.

If x is the average (arithmetic mean) of m and 8, y is the average of $2m$ and 16, and z is the average of $3m$ and 20, what is the average of x, y, and z in terms of m?

A) $m + 8$
B) $m + \frac{14}{3}$
C) $6m + 22$
D) $m + \frac{22}{3}$

30.

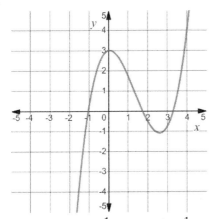

The function $f(x) = \frac{1}{2}x^2 - 2x^2 + \frac{1}{4}x + 3$ is graphed in the xy-plane above. If k is a constant such that $f(x) = k$ has exactly 2 real solutions, which of the following could be the value of k?

A) -2
B) 0
C) 1
D) 3

31.
A partially filled pool contains 530 gallons of water. A hose is turned on, and water flows into the pool at the rate of 6 gallons per minute. How many gallons of water will be in the pool after 70 minutes?

32.
The normal blood pressure, P, in milliliters for iron, for an adult male x years old can be modeled by the equation $P = \frac{x + 420}{3}$. According to the model, for every increase of 1 year in age, by how many milliliters of iron will the normal blood pressure for an adult male increase?

33.
The pes, a Roman measure of length, is approximately equal to 11.65 inches. It is also equivalent to 16 smaller Roman units called digits. Based on these relationships, 92 Roman digits is equivalent to how many feet, to the nearest hundredth? (12 inches = 1 foot)

34.
In a study of bat migration habits, 320 male bats and 180 female bats have been tagged. If 100 more female bats are tagged, how many more male bats must be tagged so that ⅗ of the total number of bats in the study are male?

35.

$$q = \frac{1}{2}nv^2$$

The dynamic pressure q generated by a fluid moving with velocity v can be found using the formula above, where n is the constant density of the fluid. An aeronautical engineer uses the formula to find the dynamic pressure of a fluid moving with velocity v and the same fluid moving with velocity $2v$. What is the ratio of the dynamic pressure of the faster fluid to the dynamic pressure of the slower fluid?

36.

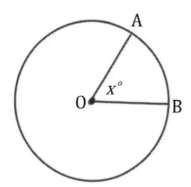

Note: Figure not drawn to scale

In the figure above, the circle has center O and has a radius 8. If the length of arc AB is between 3 and 4, what is one possible integer value of x?

Questions 37 and 38 refer to the following information.

The stock price of one share in a certain company is worth $430 today. A stock analyst believes that the stock will lose 26 percent of its value each week for the next 3 weeks. The analyst uses the equation $V = 430(r)^t$ to model the value, V, of the stock after t weeks.

37.
What value should the analyst use for r?

38.
To the nearest dollar, what does the analyst believe the value of the stock will be at the end of three weeks? (Note: Disregard the $ sign when gridding your answer.)

Math Practice Test 2, Section 3 Explanations

1. B

Absolute Value

The absolute value of an expression is always positive, so in order to get a negative answer it is necessary to subtract a positive number from it. Only choice B does that.

2. B

System of Equations

Solve for y in the equation below since there's no x-term

$$2(y+4) = 16$$
$$2y + 8 = 16$$
$$\underline{-8 -8}$$
$$2y = 8$$
$$\frac{2y}{2} = \frac{8}{2}$$
$$y = 4$$

3. C

Evaluating Functions

$$f(x) = \frac{2}{3}x + b$$

To solve for $f(-1)$, we need to know what b is.

Use $f(3) = 7$ to solve for b.

$$7 = \frac{2}{3}(3) + b$$
$$7 = 2 + b$$
$$5 = b$$

Now, we know

$$f(x) = \frac{2}{3}x + 5$$

We can evaluate $f(-1)$

$$f(-1) = \frac{2}{3}(-1) + 5$$
$$= -\frac{2}{3} + 5$$

get common denominators

$$= -\frac{2}{3} + \frac{5(3)}{1(3)}$$
$$= -\frac{2}{3} + \frac{15}{3}$$
$$= \boxed{\frac{13}{3}}$$

Math Practice Test 2

4. A

Evaluating Functions

$f(x) = -2x + 9$

To evaluate $f(-5x)$, substitute $-5x$ in for x.

$f(-5x) = -2(-5x) + 9$

$\boxed{= 10x + 9}$

5. D

Combining Like Terms & Solving Equations

$4(3x+2)(x+1)$

$(12x + 8)(x+1)$

$12x^2 + 12x + 8x + 8$

$12x^2 + 20x + 8$

6. C

Ratios & Proportions

Pick #s

$\dfrac{\overset{13}{\cancel{a}} - \overset{8}{\cancel{b}}}{\underset{8}{b}} = \dfrac{5}{8}$

Try Ans. choices

A. $\dfrac{13}{8} = \dfrac{21}{8}$ ✗

B. $\dfrac{13}{8} = \dfrac{14}{8}$ ✗

C. $\dfrac{13+8}{8} = \dfrac{21}{8}$ ✓

D. $\dfrac{13-8}{8} = -\dfrac{1}{8}$ ✗

Math Practice Test 2

7. B

Linear Functions

Week 3, 9 miles

Week 15, 27 miles

Avg rate of change
(similar to slope)

$$\frac{27-9}{15-3} = \frac{18}{12} = \frac{3}{2} \text{ or } 1.5$$

$$\frac{3 \text{ miles}}{2 \text{ wks}} \text{ or } 1.5 \frac{\text{miles}}{\text{wk}}$$

8. B

Linear Functions

Parallel → same slope

$y = -6x + 5$
       ↑ slope = -6

Solve each Ans for y to find each slope

A) $6x + 2y = 8$
   $2y = -6x + 8$
   $y = -3x + 4$
   $m = -3$ ✗

B) $18x + 3y = 4$
   $3y = -18x + 4$
   $y = -6x + 4/3$
   $m = -6$ ✓

C) $3x - y = 10$
   $-y = -3x + 10$
   $y = 3x - 10$
   $m = 3$ ✗

D) $x + 12y = 0$
   $12y = -x$
   $y = -\frac{x}{12}$
   $m = -\frac{1}{12}$ ✗

Math Practice Test 2

9. A

Combining Like Terms & Solving Equations

$\sqrt{x-a} = \frac{1}{2}x - 6$

$a = 4$

$\sqrt{x-4} = \frac{1}{2}x - 6$

Try the Ans. choices

$\sqrt{20-4} = \frac{1}{2}(20) - 6$

$\sqrt{16} = 10 - 6$

$4 = 4$ ✓

20 works, so it could be A or B.

We have to check if 8 also works.

$\sqrt{x-a} = \frac{1}{2}x - 6$

$\sqrt{8-4} = \frac{1}{2}(8) - 6$

$\sqrt{4} = 4 - 6$

$2 = -2$ ✗

8 doesn't work, so A is the answer.

10. A

Combining Like Terms & Solving Equations

$\frac{t+7}{t-7} = 14$

Write 14 as $\frac{14}{1}$ and cross multiply

$\frac{t+7}{t-7} = \frac{14}{1}$

$t+7 = 14(t-7)$

$t+7 = 14t - 98$

$-t \quad\quad -t$

$7 = 13t - 98$

$+98 \quad\quad +98$

$105 = 13t$

$\frac{105}{13} = \frac{13t}{13}$

$\frac{105}{13} = t$

Math Practice Test 2

11. A

Quadratic Functions

Simplify
$$y = (2x-1)(x+1)$$
$$y = 2x^2 + 2x - x - 1$$
$$y = \boxed{2x^2 + x - 1}$$

substitute into the other equation

$$x = 2y + 3$$
$$x = 2(2x^2 + x - 1) + 3$$
simplify
$$x = 2(2x^2 + x - 1) + 3$$
$$x = 4x^2 + 2x - 2 + 3$$
$$x = 4x^2 + 2x + 1$$

Solve for x
$$x = 4x^2 + 2x + 1$$
$$\underline{-x \qquad\quad -x}$$
$$0 = 4x^2 + x + 1$$

Use quadratic formula
$$x = \frac{-b \pm \sqrt{b^2 - 4ac}}{2a}$$
$$x = \frac{-1 \pm \sqrt{(1)^2 - 4(4)(1)}}{2(1)}$$
$$x = \frac{-1 \pm \sqrt{1 - 16}}{2}$$
$$x = \frac{-1 \pm \sqrt{-15}}{2}$$
← imaginary, so no real solutions

12. D

Percent

Cost of Ria's = x
Cost of Olivia's = $x + 2$
Total = $x + x + 2$
       = $2x + 2$

Total with tip:
10% ↑ so 110%
110% = 1.10
$$1.10(2x + 2)$$
$$2.2x + 2$$

They will split it evenly, so divide by 2
$$\frac{2.2x}{2} + \frac{2}{2}$$
$$1.1x + 1$$

Math Practice Test 2

13. B

Quadratic Functions

If $f(x)$ and $g(x)$ intersect at $(-k, 7)$ and $(k, 7)$, then the x-value k makes the two functions equal each other.

Set the functions equal to each other and solve for x.

$$x^2 - 2 = 7$$
$$-7 \quad -7$$
$$x^2 - 9 = 0$$
$$(x-3)(x+3) = 0$$
$$x = 3 \quad x = -3$$

k can be 3 or -3

14. B

Imaginary Numbers

Multiply the numerator & denominator by conjugate of the denominator

$$\frac{7-i}{3-2i} \cdot \frac{(3+2i)}{(3+2i)} \quad \text{Distribute}$$

$$\frac{21 + 14i - 3i - 2i^2}{9 + 6i - 6i - 4i^2}$$

combine like terms

$$\frac{21 + 11i - 2i^2}{9 - 4i^2}$$

$$i^2 = -1$$

$$\frac{21 + 11i - 2(-1)}{9 - 4(-1)}$$

$$\frac{21 + 11i + 2}{9 + 4}$$

$$\frac{23 + 11i}{13}$$

Write in $a + bi$ form

$$\frac{23}{13} + \frac{11}{13}i$$

$$a = \frac{23}{13}$$

15. C

Quadratic Functions

$$x^2 - \frac{k}{3}x = 2p$$

Get one side equal to 0, so we can use the quadratic formula.

$$x^2 - \frac{k}{3}x - 2p = 0$$

$$a = 1, \; b = \frac{-k}{3}, \; c = -2p$$

$$\frac{-b \pm \sqrt{b^2 - 4ac}}{2a}$$

$$\frac{-\left(\frac{-k}{3}\right) \pm \sqrt{\left(\frac{-k}{3}\right)^2 - 4(1)(-2p)}}{2(1)}$$

$$\frac{\frac{k}{3} \pm \sqrt{\frac{k^2}{9} + 8p}}{2}$$

None of the answer choices have $\frac{k^2}{9}$, so it seems that $\sqrt{\frac{1}{9}}$ was factored out.

$$\frac{\frac{k}{3} \pm \sqrt{\left(\frac{1}{9}\right)\left(k^2 + 72p\right)}}{2}$$

$\frac{1}{9} \cdot \frac{?}{1} = \frac{72}{1}$

$$\frac{\frac{k}{3} \pm \sqrt{\frac{1}{9}} \sqrt{k^2 - 72p}}{2}$$

$$\frac{\frac{k}{3} \pm \frac{1}{3}\sqrt{k^2 - 72p}}{2}$$

$$\frac{\frac{k}{3}}{2} \pm \frac{\frac{1}{3}\sqrt{k^2 - 72p}}{2}$$

$$\frac{k}{6} \pm \frac{\sqrt{k^2 - 72p}}{6}$$

16. 16

Ratios & Proportions

The answer must be in inches, so convert 8ft to inches.

$$8 \text{ ft} \times \frac{12 \text{ in}}{1 \text{ ft}} = 96 \text{ inches}$$

Short: x
2nd longest: $2x$
longest: $3x$

$\longleftarrow$ 96 in $\longrightarrow$

$$x + 2x + 3x = 96$$
$$6x = 96$$
$$\frac{6x}{6} = \frac{96}{6}$$
$$x = 16$$

17. 6

Quadratic Functions

$x^3 - 6x^2 + 6x - 36 = 0$

Factor by grouping

$x^3 - 6x^2 + 6x - 36 = 0$

$x^2(x-6) + 6(x-6) = 0$

$(x^2+6)(x-6) = 0$

Set each factor equal to zero and solve

$x^2 + 6 = 0 \qquad x - 6 = 0$
$x^2 = -6 \qquad \boxed{x = 6}$
$x = \sqrt{-6}$
↑ imaginary

18. 0.4, .4 or $\frac{2}{5}$

Trigonometry

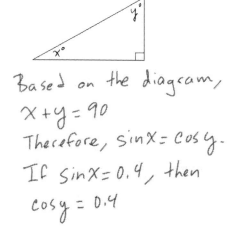

Based on the diagram,

$x + y = 90$

Therefore, $\sin x = \cos y$.

If $\sin x = 0.4$, then

$\cos y = 0.4$

19. 2.5 or $\frac{5}{2}$

System of Equations

We can use elimination to solve for x. Eliminate y.

$-2x + 5y = 20$
$-5(4x + y = 15)$

$-2x + 5y = 20$
$-20x - 5y = -75$
───────────────
$-22x = -55$

$\frac{-22x}{-22} = \frac{-55}{-22}$

$x = 2.5$

20. 7.5 or $\frac{14}{2}$

Linear Functions

10 cans, 3 oz. p

24 cans, 8 oz p

Find the rate

$$\frac{8oz - 3oz}{24 \, cans - 10 \, cans} = \frac{5 oz}{14 \, cans}$$

We need to find how many ounces for every 21 cans

$$\frac{5 oz}{14 \, cans} = \frac{n}{21}$$

$$105 = 14n$$

$$\frac{105}{14} = \frac{14n}{14}$$

$$7.5 = n$$

Math Practice Test 2, Section 4 Explanations

1. C

$13.10 ← Total
− $9.50 ← monthly fee
———
$3.60 ← rented movies

$$\frac{\$3.60}{\$1.20} = \boxed{3}$$
↑ cost per rented movie

2. A

Increases by 10 $\frac{words}{month}$, a constant rate, so this is a linear function

$y = mx + b$
↑ slope (rate)   ↑ y-int (initial value)
↓
$y = 10x + 135$

$10m + 135$
or
$135 + 10m$

3. D

thirds:

then halved:

there will be 6 pieces

$\frac{6 \text{ pounds}}{6} = 1$ pound each

1 pound = $\boxed{16 \text{ oz}}$

4. D

35.3% said yes in the survey, so we would expect 35.3% of all the students to say yes.

35.3% = .353

225
$\times .353$
———
79.425

About 80

Math Practice Test 2

5. C

$$\text{density} = \frac{\text{mass}}{\text{volume}}$$

Volume = ?
mass = 60g
density = 5 g/mL

$$5 = \frac{60}{x}$$

write 5 as $\frac{5}{1}$, then cross multiply

$$\frac{5}{1} \times \frac{60}{x}$$

$$5x = 60$$

$$\frac{5x}{5} = \frac{60}{5}$$

$$x = 12$$

6. C

x = # of hours Larry studied
$x + 13$ = # of hours Nina studied

Their hours add up to 63

$$x + x + 13 = 63$$
$$2x + 13 = 63$$
$$-13 -13$$
$$2x = 50$$
$$\frac{2x}{2} = \frac{50}{2}$$
$$x = 25$$

7. B

MPAA Rating	Action	Animated	Comedy	Drama	Total
PG	2	7	2	5	16
PG-13	9	0	5	5	19
R	7	0	2	6	15
Total	18	7	9	16	50

Dramas with an R rating

$$\frac{6}{50} = \frac{3}{25}$$

Math Practice Test 2

8. C

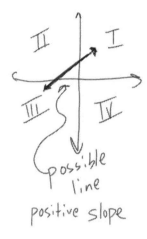

possible line
positive slope

9. D

Region	Age 18 to 24	Age 25 to 44	Age 45 to 64	Age 65 to 74	75 & Older	Total
Northeast	2,713	8,159	10,986	3,342	2,775	27,975
Midwest	3,453	11,237	13,865	4,221	3,350	36,126
South	5,210	18,072	21,346	7,272	4,969	56,869
West	3,390	10,428	11,598	3,785	2,986	32,187
Total	14,766	47,896	57,795	18,620	14,080	153,157

chosen from 45-64

from 45-64 & South region

$\frac{21346}{57795} = 0.3693 \approx 0.37$

10. C

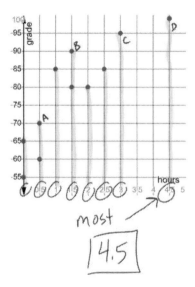

most
$\boxed{4.5}$

11. A

$\frac{grade}{time}$

A $\frac{70}{0.5} = 140$

B $\frac{90}{1.5} = 60$

C $\frac{95}{3} = 31.67$

D $\frac{99}{4.5} = 22$

greatest: A

Math Practice Test 2

12. A

x-intercepts at $-4, -2,$ and 1
x-intercepts are zeros
We can solve for the factors

$x = -4 \quad | \quad x = -2 \quad | \quad x = 1$
$+4 \;+4 \quad | \quad +2 \;+2 \quad | \quad -1 \;-1$
$x+4 = 0 \quad | \quad x+2 = 0 \quad | \quad x-1 = 0$

$(x+4)(x+2)(x-1)$

13. C

Time (weeks)	Population
0	5
5	25
10	125
15	625
20	3125

(differences: 20, 100, 500, 2,500; time increments of 5)

Not linear because it does not increase at a constant rate.

The population is multiplied by 5 every 5 years, so it's <u>exponential</u>.

Increasing → <u>growth</u>

exponential growth

14. D

at 10%
$1000\left(1 + \dfrac{10}{1200}\right)^{12}$

at 6%
$1000\left(1 + \dfrac{6}{1200}\right)^{12}$

Difference
$1000\left(1 + \dfrac{10}{1200}\right)^{12} - 1000\left(1 + \dfrac{6}{1200}\right)^{12}$

15. B

Try it in your calculator. According to the question, a is negative and b is positive. Try $y = -2x^3$.

16. A

Store A's cost
$y = M + (W + K)x$
$y = 750 + (15 + 65)x$
$y = 750 + 80x$

Store B's cost
$y = M + (W + K)x$
$y = 600 + (25 + 80)x$
$y = 600 + 105x$

Math Practice Test 2

Store B ≥ Store A
$600 + 105x \geq 750 + 80x$
$-80x -80x$
$600 + 25x \geq 750$
$-600 -600$
$25x \geq 150$
$\dfrac{25x}{25} \geq \dfrac{150}{25}$
$x \geq 6$

17. B

$y = M + (W+K)x$

rewrite

$y = (W+K)x + M$

$y = mx + b$
   (slope) (y-int)

y-int: M, Materials' cost

18. A

Sara has 231 in³ of milk.
Cylindrical glasses
$V = \pi r^2 h$
$h = 9$ in
$d = 4$, so $r = 2$
$V = \pi (2)^2 (9) = 113.1$ in³

$231 \div 113.1 = 2.04$

$\boxed{2}$

19. C

$4p - 5 \geq 3$
$+5 +5$
$4p \geq 8$

We want the least possible value of $4p + 2$, so use the least possible value of $4p$: 8

$4p + 2$
$8 + 2$
10

Math Practice Test 2

20. C

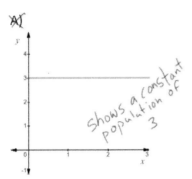
A) Shows a constant population of 3

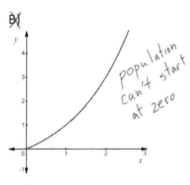
B) population can't start at zero

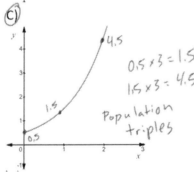
C) $0.5 \times 3 = 1.5$
$1.5 \times 3 = 4.5$
Population triples

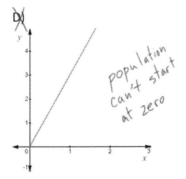
D) population can't start at zero

21. A

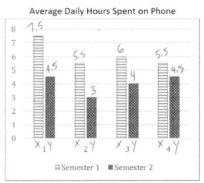

Class 1: (7.5, 4.5)
Class 2: (5.5, 3)
Class 3: (6, 4)
Class 4: (5.5, 4.5)

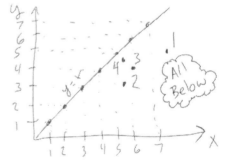
All Below

Math Practice Test 2

22. B

Percent Change

$$\frac{\text{Change}}{\text{Original}} \times 100\%$$

Class 1
$7.5 \to 4.5$
$\frac{3}{7.5} \times 100\% = 40\%$

Class 2
$5.5 \to 3$
$\frac{2.5}{5.5} \times 100\% = 45.5\%$

Class 3
$6 \to 4$
$\frac{2}{6} \times 100\% = 33.3\%$

Class 4
$5.5 \to 4.5$
$\frac{1}{5.5} \times 100\% = 18.2\%$

23. B

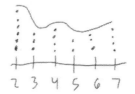

Class A has a relatively high standard deviation because none of the values are clustered together.

Class B

Number of Presidents	Frequency
2	1
3	5
4	10
5	4
6	1
7	1

Class B has a relatively small standard deviation since most of the numbers are 4 (there are ten 4s) and nine numbers are within one of 4 (there are five 3s and four 5s).

A dot plot would look like this:

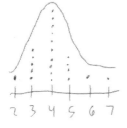

24. C

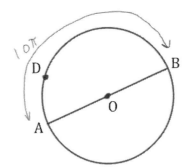

Arc ADB is 10π and half of the circumference, so the full circumference is 20π.

$$C = 2\pi r$$
$$20\pi = 2\pi r$$
$$\frac{20\pi}{2\pi} = \frac{2\pi r}{2\pi}$$
$$10 = r$$

Math Practice Test 2

25. B

$f(x) = 2x^3 + 5x^2$
$g(x) = x + 2$

B) $f(x) + 8g(x)$

$2x^3 + 5x^2 + 8(x+2)$
$2x^3 + 5x^2 + 8x + 16$

Factor by grouping

$2x^3 + 5x^2 + 8x + 16$
$x^2(2x+5) + 4(2x+5)$
$(x^2 + 4)(2x + 5)$

$x^2 + 4$ is a factor

26. C

$-y < x < y$

Try Numbers, $y = 5$

$-5 < x < 5$

x could be negative, positive or zero, so test all possibilities.

Test $x = -3, 3, 0$

I. $|-3| < 5$ ✓
   $|3| < 5$ ✓   } True
   $|0| < 5$ ✓

II. $-3 = 0$ False

III. $y > 0$ True

27. D

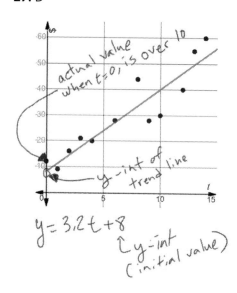

actual value when $t=0$ is over 10

y-int of trend line

$y = 3.2t + 8$

↳ y-int (initial value)

28. D

The minimum value can be seen when the quadratic function is in vertex-form

$y = (x-a)^2 + b$
    vertex: (a, b)

Eliminate answer choices not in vertex form

A) $f(x) = x^2 + 2x + 2$ ✗
B) $f(x) = (x-1)^2 - 5$ → vertex $(1, -5)$
C) $f(x) = x(x+2) + 2$ ✗
D) $f(x) = (x+1)^2 - 9$ → vertex $(-1, -9)$

Let's find the actual vertex

$y = (x+4)(x-2)$
So the zeros are
$x = -4, 2$
the vertex is in the middle of them, so at $x = -1$.
Substitute -1 in for x to find the y-value
$y = (-1+4)(-1-2)$
$y = -9$
$y = (x+1)^2 - 9$

29. D

The avg. of m and 8 is x
$$\frac{m+8}{2} = x$$
The avg. of $2m$ and 16 is y
$$\frac{2m+16}{2} = y$$
The avg. of $3m$ and 20 is z.
$$\frac{3m+20}{2} = z$$
Avg of $x, y,$ and z:
$$\frac{x+y+z}{3}$$

$$\frac{\frac{m+8}{2} + \frac{2m+16}{2} + \frac{3m+20}{2}}{3}$$

$$\frac{\frac{6m+44}{2}}{3} = \frac{3m+22}{3} = \boxed{\frac{m+22}{3}}$$

30. D

$f(x) = k$ will be a horizontal line
Solutions are where the functions intersect

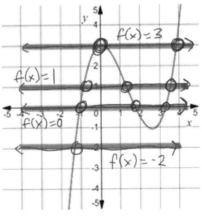

$f(x) = 3 \rightarrow 2$ solutions
$f(x) = 1 \rightarrow 3$ solutions
$f(x) = 0 \rightarrow 3$ solutions
$f(x) = -2 \rightarrow 1$ solution

Math Practice Test 2

31. 890

Initial: 530 gallons
Rate: 6 gallons/minute
60 minutes

$$\begin{array}{r} 60 \\ \times\ 6 \\ \hline 360 \end{array}$$ gallons added

$$\begin{array}{r} 530 \\ +360 \\ \hline 890 \end{array}$$ total gallons

32. $\frac{1}{3}$ or .333

$$P = \frac{x + 420}{3}$$

rewritten as

$$P = \frac{x}{3} + \frac{420}{3}$$

$$P = \frac{1}{3}x + 140$$

↳ rate

$$\boxed{\frac{1}{3} \text{ or } .333}$$

33. 5.58

1 pes = 11.65 in
1 pes = 16 digits
Therefore,
11.65 in = 16 digits

$$92 \text{ digits} \times \frac{11.65 \text{ in}}{16 \text{ digits}} \times \frac{1 \text{ ft}}{12 \text{ in}}$$

$$\frac{1,071.8}{192} = 5.58229$$

$$\boxed{5.58}$$

34. 100

320 male, 180 female
$$\begin{array}{r} +100 \\ \hline 280 \text{ female} \end{array}$$

$$\frac{3}{5} = \frac{\text{males}}{\text{total}}$$

male = 320 + x
total = female + male
= 280 + 320 + x
= 600 + x

$$\frac{3}{5} = \frac{320+x}{600+x}$$

$3(600+x) = 5(320+x)$

$1800 + 3x = 1600 + 5x$

$-3x -3x$

$1800 = 1600 + 2x$

$-1600 -1600$

$200 = 2x$

$\dfrac{200}{2} = \dfrac{2x}{2}$

$100 = x$

35. 4

$q = \frac{1}{2}nv^2$

v becomes 2v, so v is doubled. However, in the formula, v is squared, so 2v is squared.

$(2v)^2 = 4v^2$

The expression becomes multiplied by 4.

$\boxed{4}$

Math Practice Test 2

36. 22, 23, 24, 25, 26, 27, or 28

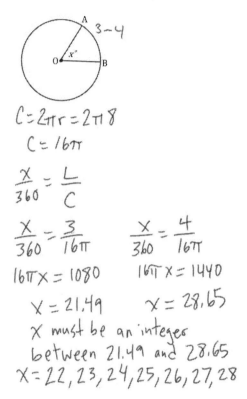

$C = 2\pi r = 2\pi 8$
$C = 16\pi$

$\dfrac{x}{360} = \dfrac{L}{C}$

$\dfrac{x}{360} = \dfrac{3}{16\pi}$ $\dfrac{x}{360} = \dfrac{4}{16\pi}$

$16\pi x = 1080$ $16\pi x = 1440$

$x = 21.49$ $x = 28.65$

x must be an integer between 21.49 and 28.65

$x = 22, 23, 24, 25, 26, 27, 28$

37. 0.74 or .74

Decrease by 26%, so each week the stock will have 74% of its value

$74\% = .74$

0.74 or $.74$

38. 174

From question 37,
$r = 0.74$

$V = 430(0.74)^t$

$V = 430(0.74)^3$

$V = 174.25$

$\boxed{174}$

Additional Practice

Want to break a 1400?

We love working with students who are serious about their SAT scores - that means you!

Special Tutoring & Test Prep Offer for You

 caddellprep.com/sboffer

Common Math Tricks: Practice 1

1. Given the system of equations below, what is the value of $x + y$?
   $4x + 3y = 17$
   $2x + y = 3$

2. Given the system of equations below, what is the average of x and y?
   $2x + 3y = 12$
   $4x = 18 - 3y$

3. $x^2 - y^2 = 63$ and the sum of x and y is 9. What is the value of $x - y$?

4. If $x^2 + y^2 = 8$ and $xy = 6$, what is the value of $(x + y)^2$?

5. <u>Try to solve this problem by using the answer choices.</u>
   After a 40% markup, the price of a shirt is $18.90. What was the original price of the shirt before the markup?
   A) $11.34
   B) $13.50
   C) $15.75
   D) $18.50

6. <u>Try to solve this problem by using the answer choices.</u>
   The sum of three consecutive even numbers is 108. What is the least of these numbers?
   A) 32
   B) 34
   C) 36
   D) 38

Common Math Tricks: Practice 1

7. <u>Try to solve this problem by using the answer choices.</u>
   The product of two consecutive odd numbers is 8,099. What is the larger of the two numbers?
   A) 79
   B) 81
   C) 87
   D) 91

8. <u>Try to solve this problem by picking numbers for the variables.</u>
   Which of the following is equivalent to the expression below?
   $$\frac{3}{t-4} - \frac{t+1}{t+3}$$
   A) $\dfrac{-t+2}{2t-1}$
   B) $\dfrac{-t^2+6t+13}{(t-4)(t+3)}$
   C) $\dfrac{-t+2}{t^2-12}$
   D) $\dfrac{-t^2-6t-13}{t^2-t-12}$

9. <u>Try to solve this problem by picking numbers for the variables.</u>
   Which of the following is equivalent to the expression below?
   $$\frac{\frac{x}{x+y}}{\frac{2}{x}}$$
   A) $\dfrac{2x^2}{x+y}$
   B) $\dfrac{2x}{x^2+y}$
   C) $\dfrac{x^2}{2x+2y}$
   D) $\dfrac{2}{x+y}$

Common Math Tricks: Practice 1

10. <u>Try to estimate the missing value. (You aren't provided with enough information to actually solve for the missing value).</u>
    In the diagram below, what is the value of x?

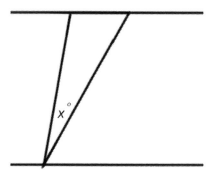

11. <u>Try to estimate the missing value. (You aren't provided with enough information to actually solve for the missing value).</u>
    In the diagram below, the length of AB is 18 and the length of BC is 12. What is the length of AD?

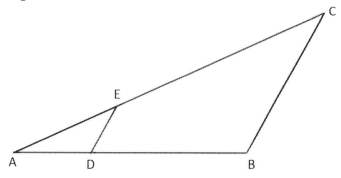

Common Math Tricks: Practice 2

1. Given the system of equations below, what is the value of $x + y$?
   $7x + 3y = 12$
   $2x = 15 - 6y$

2. Given the system of equations below, what is the average of x and y?
   $5x + 3y = 15$
   $4x = 9 - 2y$

3. $x - y = 6$ and the sum of x and y is 12. What is the value of $x^2 - y^2$?

4. If $x + y = 8$ and $x^2 - y^2 = 32$, what is the value of $x - y$?

5. <u>Try to solve this problem by using the answer choices.</u>
   After a 30% discount, the price of a tablet is $682.70. What was the original price of the tablet before the discount?
   A) $477.89
   B) $652.70
   C) $887.50
   D) $975.29

6. <u>Try to solve this problem by using the answer choices.</u>
   The product of three consecutive numbers is 2,184. What is the greatest of these numbers?
   A) 12
   B) 14
   C) 46
   D) 47

Common Math Tricks: Practice 2

7. <u>Try to solve this problem by using the answer choices.</u>
   The sum of four consecutive odd integers is 72. What is the smallest of the numbers?
   A) 11
   B) 15
   C) 19
   D) 23

8. <u>Try to solve this problem by picking numbers for the variables.</u>
   Which of the following is equivalent to the expression below?
   $$\frac{x-3}{x+4} - \frac{3}{x-3}$$

   A) $\frac{3x-9}{x^2-12}$

   B) $\frac{x}{x+1}$

   C) $\frac{3}{x+4}$

   D) $\frac{x^2-3x+21}{(x-3)(x+4)}$

9. <u>Try to solve this problem by picking numbers for the variables.</u>
   Which of the following is equivalent to the expression below?
   $$\frac{\frac{x+2y}{2}}{\frac{x+y}{3}}$$

   A) $\frac{3x+6y}{2x+2y}$

   B) $\frac{x^2+2y^2}{6}$

   C) $\frac{2x+4y}{3x+3y}$

   D) $\frac{6x+3y}{4xy}$

Common Math Tricks: Practice 2

10. <u>Try to estimate the missing value. (You aren't provided with enough information to actually solve for the missing value).</u>
    In the diagram below, what is the value of x?

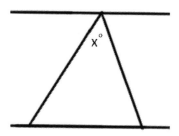

11. <u>Try to estimate the missing value. (You aren't provided with enough information to actually solve for the missing value).</u>
    In the diagram below, the length of BC is 6 and the length of DE is 3. What is the length of AB?

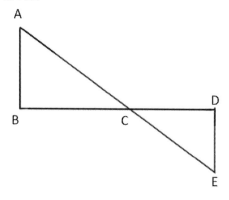

Common Math Tricks Explanations

Common Math Tricks 1

1. 7

$$4x + 3y = 17$$
$$-(2x + y = 3)$$
$$\overline{2x + 2y = 14}$$

Divide by 2

$$x + y = 7$$

$$2x + 3y = 12$$
$$+ \; 4x + 3y = 18$$
$$\overline{6x + 6y = 18}$$

divide by 6

$$x + y = 3$$

$$Avg = \frac{x+y}{2} = \frac{3}{2} \text{ or } 1.5$$

2. 3/2 or 1.5

Avg of x and y means

$$\frac{x+y}{2}$$

$2x + 3y = 12$

$4x = 18 - 3y$

Set up the equations so they line up for addition or subtraction.

$$4x = 18 - 3y$$
$$+3y \qquad +3y$$
$$\overline{4x + 3y = 18}$$

Now, we can set up the equations for addition or subtraction.

3. 7

The sum of x and y is 9, so $x + y = 9$.

$x + y$ is a factor of $x^2 - y^2$ and $x - y$ is the other factor.

$$x^2 - y^2 = 63$$
$$(x+y)(x-y) = 63$$
$$(9)(x-y) = 63$$
$$\frac{(9)(x-y)}{9} = \frac{63}{9}$$
$$x - y = 7$$

Common Math Tricks Explanations

4. 20

$(x+y)^2 = (x+y)(x+y)$

$x^2 + xy + xy + y^2$

$\underline{x^2 + y^2} + \underline{2xy}$

$8 + 2(6)$

$8 + 12$

20

5. B

Try one of the answer choices to be the original price.

```
  13.50         13.50
×   .40       +  5.40
────────       ──────
 5.4000         18.90
     ↑
   markup
```

6. B

Try one of the answer choices to be the least of the consecutive even numbers.

```
A.  32        B.  34
    34            36
    36            38
   ───           ───
   102            108 ✓
   wrong
```

7. D

Try the answer choices to be the larger of the consecutive odd numbers.

A. $79 \times 77 = 6083$

B. $81 \times 79 = 6399$

C. $87 \times 85 = 7395$

D. $91 \times 89 = 8099$

8. B

Pick 3 for t, and substitute it into the original expression.

$$\frac{3}{3-4} - \frac{3+1}{3+3} = \frac{3}{-1} - \frac{4}{6}$$

$$\frac{-3}{1} - \frac{2}{3}$$

get common denominators

$$\frac{-9}{3} - \frac{2}{3} = \frac{-11}{3}$$

Now, check the answer choices by substitution 3 in for t

$$\frac{-(3)^2 + 6(3) + 13}{(3-4)(3+3)}$$

$$\frac{-9 + 18 + 13}{(-1)(6)}$$

$$\frac{22}{-6} \text{ reduces to } \frac{-11}{3}$$

We got the same value as the original expression, so B is the answer.

9. C

Pick 3 for x and 4 for y, and substitute it into the original expression.

$$\frac{\frac{3}{3+4}}{\frac{2}{3}} = \frac{\frac{3}{7}}{\frac{2}{3}}$$

Keep-change-flip

$$\frac{3}{7} \div \frac{2}{3} = \frac{3}{7} \times \frac{3}{2} = \frac{9}{14}$$

Now, check the answer choices by plugging in 3 for x and 4 for y.

C.

$$\frac{x^2}{2x+2y} = \frac{(3)^2}{2(3)+2(4)} = \frac{9}{6+8}$$

$$\frac{9}{14}$$

We got the same value as the original expression, so C is the answer.

10. 10

11. 6

Common Math Tricks 2

1. 3

$7x + 3y = 12$

$2x = 15 - 6y$

Common Math Tricks Explanations

Set up the equations so they line up for addition or subtraction.

$$2x = 15 - 6y$$
$$+6y \quad +6y$$
$$2x + 6y = 15$$

Now, we can set up the equations for addition or subtraction.

$$7x + 3y = 12$$
$$+ 2x + 6y = 15$$
$$\overline{9x + 9y = 27}$$

divide by 9

$$x + y = 3$$

2. 3

Avg of x and y means $\dfrac{x+y}{2}$

$5x + 3y = 15$

$4x = 9 - 2y$

Set up the equations so they line up for addition or subtraction.

$$4x = 9 - 2y$$
$$+2y \quad +2y$$
$$4x + 2y = 9$$

Now, we can set up the equations for addition or subtraction.

$$5x + 3y = 15$$
$$-(4x + 2y = 9)$$
$$\overline{x + y = 6}$$

$$Avg = \dfrac{x+y}{2} = \dfrac{6}{2} = 3$$

3. 72

The sum of x and y is 12 means $x + y = 12$.

We also are given that $x - y = 6$.

$x + y$ and $x - y$ are both factors of $x^2 - y^2$.

$$x^2 - y^2$$
$$(x+y)(x-y)$$
$$(12)(6) = 72$$

$x + y = 8$ and $x^2 - y^2 = 32$.

Common Math Tricks Explanations

$x^2 - y^2 = 32$
$(x+y)(x-y) = 32$
$8(x-y) = 32$

$$\frac{8(x-y)}{8} = \frac{32}{8}$$

$x - y = 4$

5. D

Try one of the answer choices to be the original price.

D.
```
  975.29          975.29
×    .30      −  292.59
─────────     ─────────
29 25870         682.70
    ↑               ↑
 discount        sale price
```

6. B

Try the answer choices to be the greatest consecutive number.

A $12 \cdot 11 \cdot 10 = 1,320$
B $14 \cdot 13 \cdot 12 = 2,184$
C $46 \cdot 45 \cdot 44 = 91,080$
D $47 \cdot 46 \cdot 45 = 97,290$

7. B

Try the answer choices to be the smallest consecutive odd number.

A $11 + 13 + 15 + 17 = 56$
B $15 + 17 + 19 + 21 = 72$
C $19 + 21 + 23 + 25 = 88$
D $23 + 25 + 27 + 29 = 104$

8. C

For this problem, we can't pick 3 for x because we will end up with 0 in the for $x - 3$.

Pick 4 for x, and substitute it into the original expression.

$$\frac{4-3}{4+4} - \frac{3}{4-3}$$

$$\frac{1}{8} - \frac{3}{1}$$

get common denominators

$$\frac{1}{8} - \frac{24}{8} = \frac{-23}{8}$$

Now, check the answer choices by plugging in 4 for x.

Common Math Tricks Explanations

C.

$$\frac{4^2 - 9(4) + 3}{(4-3)(4+4)} = \frac{16 - 36 + 3}{(1)(8)} = \frac{-23}{8}$$

9. A

Pick 3 for x and 4 for y, and substitute it into the original expression.

$$\frac{\frac{3 + 2(4)}{2}}{\frac{3+4}{3}} = \frac{\frac{11}{2}}{\frac{7}{3}}$$

$$\frac{11}{2} \div \frac{7}{3} = \frac{11}{2} \times \frac{3}{7} = \frac{33}{14}$$

Now, check the answer choices by plugging in 3 for x and 4 for y.

A.

$$\frac{3(3) + 6(4)}{2(3) + 2(4)} = \frac{9 + 24}{6 + 8}$$

$$\frac{33}{14}$$

10. 53
11. 4

Combining Like Terms & Solving Equations: Practice 1

1. Which of the following is equivalent to the expression below?
$$2x^2y^2 - 3xy^2 + 2y^2 - (y^2 - 3xy^2 + x^2y^2)$$
   A) $y^2(x^2 + 1)$
   B) $3x^2y^2 + 6xy^2 + 3y^2$
   C) $x^2y^2 + 3y^2$
   D) $3x^2y^2 - 2xy^2 + y^2$

2. If $x \leq 4$, which of the following is equivalent to
$$\frac{1}{\frac{1}{3x+1} + \frac{1}{x-4}}$$
   A) $\frac{3x^2-4}{4x-3}$
   B) $\frac{3x^2+13x-4}{4x-3}$
   C) $4x - 3$
   D) $\frac{3x^2-11x-4}{4x-3}$

3. If $2\left(\frac{x+4}{3}\right) = k$ and $k = 8$, what is the value of x?
   A) 4
   B) 6
   C) 8
   D) 9

4. If $a = 2\sqrt{2}$ and $3a = \sqrt{3x}$, what is the value of x?
   A) 48
   B) 38
   C) 36
   D) 24

5. If $24 - 3x$ is double 9, what is the value of $2(x+1)$?
   A) 5
   B) 6
   C) 7
   D) 8

Combining Like Terms & Solving Equations: Practice 1

6. Which of the following is NOT a solution of the inequality?
$$\frac{1+16x}{7} \geq \frac{5x-4}{2}$$
   A) 11
   B) 10
   C) 9
   D) 8

7. A freight elevator can carry a maximum weight of 4500 lbs. A delivery man weighing 210 lbs. and x number of air conditioning unit weighing 360 lbs. each will be transported from the ground floor up to the 12th floor. What is the maximum possible value for x that will keep the total weight below the limit?
   A) 12
   B) 11
   C) 10
   D) 9

8. If $7m + 8 = 50$, what is $\frac{8m+8}{7}$?
   A.) 5
   B.) 6
   C.) 7
   D.) 8

9. If $\frac{3}{1-2x} = \frac{2}{4x-10}$, what is the value of $\frac{x}{2}$?
   A) $\frac{3}{2}$
   B) 2
   C) 1
   D) $\frac{2}{3}$

10. If $\frac{7}{8}x - \frac{3}{16}x = \frac{7}{16} + \frac{1}{4}$, what is the value of x?
    A) 5.5
    B) 11
    C) 1
    D) 5

Combining Like Terms & Solving Equations: Practice 1

11. Which of the following is the sum of the two polynomials shown below?

$$9x^2 + 6x - 7$$
$$4x^2 - 2x + 8$$

  A) $13x^2 + 4x + 1$
  B) $5x^2 + 4x - 1$
  C) $13x^2 + 8x + 15$
  D) $5x^2 + 8x - 15$

12. If $\frac{4}{5}x = \frac{1}{2}$, what is the value of x?

  A) $\frac{8}{5}$
  B) $\frac{5}{8}$
  C) 8
  D) 5

13. The table below shows approximations of the density of common fluids. The pressure at a given height/depth can be found by using the formula $P = \rho g h$, where P is the pressure in Pascal (Pa), ρ is the density in $\frac{kg}{m^3}$, g is the acceleration due to gravity in $\frac{m}{s^2}$, and h is the height/depth in meters.

Fluid	Density ($\frac{kg}{m^3}$)
Water, 4°C	1000
Gasoline	711
Ethyl Alcohol	789
Olive Oil	911
Sea water	1022
Milk	1020
Glycerin	1259

What is the pressure, in Pa, in sea water at a depth of 100 meters and if acceleration (g) is $9.8 \frac{m}{s^2}$?

  A) 980,000 Pa
  B) 1,022,000 Pa
  C) 1,001,560 Pa
  D) 1,010,220 Pa

14. The pressure of a specific fluid is 439,000 Pa at a depth of 63 meters. What fluid could this be? (Acceleration is $9.8 \frac{m}{s^2}$)

  A) Ethyl Alcohol
  B) Gasoline
  C) Glycerin
  D) Olive Oil

Combining Like Terms & Solving Equations: Practice 2

1. In the equation, $\sqrt{k-5} + x = 0$, k is a constant. If $x = -12$, what is the value of k?
   A) -149
   B) 149
   C) 64
   D) 36

2. Which of the following is equivalent to the sum of the expressions $2a^2 + 6a - 5$ and $a^2 - 7$?
   A) $a^2 + 6a - 12$
   B) $a^2 - 6a + 12$
   C) $3a^2 + 6a - 12$
   D) $3a^2 + 6a + 12$

3. If $9x^2 + 16y^2 = a$ and $2xy = b$, which of the following is equivalent to $a + 12b$?
   A) $(4x - 3y)^2$
   B) $(4x + 3y)^2$
   C) $(3x - 4y)^2$
   D) $(3x + 4y)^2$

4. What value of c is the solution to the equation $4(c + 3) - 9(c - 2) = c$?
   A) 6
   B) 5
   C) 4
   D) 3

5. In the expression $\frac{5x+1}{(x-4)^2} - \frac{5x-8}{(x-4)^2} = \frac{a}{(x-4)^2}$, where a is a constant and $x \neq 4$. What is the value of a?
   A) -7
   B) 7
   C) -9
   D) 9

6. If $10(a - b) = 15$, what is the value of $a - b$?
   A) $\frac{3}{2}$
   B) $\frac{2}{3}$
   C) 10
   D) 2

Combining Like Terms & Solving Equations: Practice 2

7. Which of the following is the equivalent form of $(1.2x + 3.8)^2 - (4.7x^2 + 7.8)$?
   A) $-3.26x^2 + 9.12x + 6.64$
   B) $6.14x^2 + 9.12x + 22.24$
   C) $-3.26x^2 + 9.12x + 22.24$
   D) $6.14x^2 + 9.12x + 6.64$

8. What is the product of $x - 4$ and $x + 3$?
   A) $x^2 - 12$
   B) $2x - 1$
   C) $x^2 - 7x - 12$
   D) $x^2 - x - 12$

9. If $x = \frac{4}{5}y - 8$ and $y = 20$, what is the value of $6x - 9$?
   A) 38
   B) 39
   C) 40
   D) 41

10. If $2\sqrt{x} - \sqrt{16} = \sqrt{100}$, what is the value of x?
    A) $2\sqrt{14}$
    B) 9
    C) 49
    D) 6

11. Which of the following is equivalent to $(2a^2 - \frac{b}{3})^2$?
    A) $4a^4 - \frac{4}{3}a^2b + \frac{b^2}{9}$
    B) $4a^4 + 4a^2b + \frac{b^2}{9}$
    C) $2a^4 - \frac{4}{3}a^2b - \frac{b^2}{9}$
    D) $4a^4 + \frac{4}{3}a^2b + \frac{b^2}{9}$

12. What is the value of t is the solution of the equation $\frac{7}{8}t = \frac{4}{3}$?
    A) $\frac{21}{32}$
    B) $\frac{3}{4}$
    C) $\frac{32}{21}$
    D) 21

Combining Like Terms & Solving Equations: Practice 2

13. Which expression is equivalent to $(7x^2 - 8x + 3) - (4x^2 - 5x + 7)$?
    A) $3x^2 - 3x - 4$
    B) $3x^2 - 13x - 4$
    C) $11x^2 - 3x + 4$
    D) $11x^2 - 13x - 4$

14. What value of x satisfies the equation $4(2x + 8) - 3(5 + 7x) = 4$?
    A) $-\frac{13}{28}$
    B) 1
    C) $\frac{43}{28}$
    D) 2

Combining Like Terms & Solving Equations Explanations

Combining Like Terms & Solving Equations 1

1. A

$2x^2y^2 - 3xy^2 + 2y^2 - (y^2 - 3xy^2 + x^2y^2)$

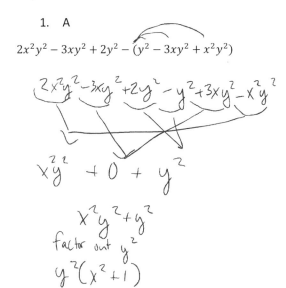

2. D

If $x \le 4$, which of the following is equivalent to

$$\dfrac{1}{\dfrac{1}{3x+1} + \dfrac{1}{x-4}}$$

A) $\dfrac{3x^2-4}{4x-3}$
B) $\dfrac{3x^2+13x-4}{4x-3}$
C) $4x-3$
D) $\dfrac{3x^2-11x-4}{4x-3}$

Try the answer choices.
Plug in 3 for x in the question and answer choices to see which is equal.

$\dfrac{1}{\dfrac{1}{3(3)+1} + \dfrac{1}{3-4}} = \dfrac{1}{\dfrac{1}{10} + \dfrac{1}{-1}} = \dfrac{1}{\dfrac{1}{10} - 1} = \dfrac{1}{\dfrac{1}{10} - \dfrac{10}{10}} = \dfrac{1}{\dfrac{-9}{10}}$

$1 \div \dfrac{-9}{10} = 1 \times \dfrac{10}{-9} = \dfrac{-10}{9}$

See which answer $= \dfrac{-10}{9}$

D) $\dfrac{3(3)^2 - 11(3) - 4}{4(3) - 3} = \dfrac{27 - 33 - 4}{12 - 3} = \dfrac{-10}{9}$

3. C

If $2\left(\dfrac{x+4}{3}\right) = k$ and $k = 8$, what is the value of x?

$\dfrac{\cancel{2}\left(\dfrac{x+4}{3}\right)}{\cancel{2}} = \dfrac{8}{2}$

$\dfrac{x+4}{3} = 4$

$(3)\dfrac{x+4}{\cancel{3}} = 4(3)$

$x + 4 = 12$
$ -4 -4$
$x = 8$

4. D

If $a = 2\sqrt{2}$ and $3a = \sqrt{3x}$, what is the value of x?

$3(2\sqrt{2}) = \sqrt{3x}$
$6\sqrt{2} = \sqrt{3x}$
$(6\sqrt{2})^2 = (\sqrt{3x})^2$
$36(2) = 3x$
$\dfrac{72}{3} = \dfrac{3x}{3}$
$24 = x$

Combining Like Terms & Solving Equations Explanations

5. B
If $24 - 3x$ is double 9, what is the value of $2(x+1)$?

$24 - 3x = 18$
$-24 \quad -24$
$-3x = -6$
$\overline{-3} \quad \overline{-3}$
$x = 2$

$2(x+1)$
$2(2+1)$
$2(3)$
6

6. A
$\dfrac{1+16x}{7} \geq \dfrac{5x-4}{2}$

$2(1+16x) \geq 7(5x-4)$
$2 + 32x \geq 35x - 28$
$-32x \quad -32x$
$2 \geq 3x - 28$

$2 \geq 3x - 28$
$+28 \quad +28$
$30 \geq 3x$
$\overline{3} \quad \overline{3}$
$10 \geq x$

→ x must be less than 10, so 11 is **NOT** a solution

7. B
man's weight + AC weight $\leq 4,500$
$210 + 360x \leq 4,500$
$-210 \quad\quad -210$
$360x \leq 4,290$
$\overline{360} \quad\quad \overline{360}$
$x \leq 11.9$

8. D
If $7m + 8 = 50$, what is $\dfrac{8m+8}{7}$?

$7m + 8 = 50$
$-8 \quad -8$
$7m = 42$
$\overline{7} \quad \overline{7}$
$m = 6$

$\dfrac{8m+8}{7}$
$\dfrac{8(6)+8}{7}$
$\dfrac{56}{7}$
8

9. C
If $\dfrac{3}{1-2x} = \dfrac{2}{4x-10}$, what is the value of $\dfrac{x}{2}$?

$3(4x-10) = 2(1-2x)$
$12x - 30 = 2 - 4x$
$+4x \quad\quad +4x$
$16x - 30 = 2$
$+30 \quad +30$
$16x = 32$
$\overline{16} \quad \overline{16}$
$x = 2$

10. C
$\dfrac{7}{8}x - \dfrac{3}{16}x = \dfrac{7}{16} + \dfrac{1}{4}$

make the equation simpler by multiplying by the LCD to eliminate the fractions. LCD = 16

$\dfrac{(16)7}{8}x - \dfrac{(16)3}{16}x = \dfrac{(16)7}{16} + \dfrac{1(16)}{4}$

$\dfrac{(16)7}{8}x - \dfrac{(16)3}{16}x = \dfrac{(16)7}{16} + \dfrac{(16)1}{4}$

$14x - 3x = 7 + 4$

Combining Like Terms & Solving Equations Explanations

$11x = 11$
$x = 1$

11. A
$9x^2 + 6x - 7$
$4x^2 - 2x + 8$
$\overline{13x^2 - 4x + 1}$

12. B
$\frac{4}{5}x = \frac{1}{2}$

$\frac{4}{5}x = \frac{1}{2}$

$\left(\frac{5}{4}\right)\frac{4}{5}x = \frac{1}{2}\left(\frac{5}{4}\right)$

$\left(\frac{5}{4}\right)\frac{4}{5}x = \frac{1}{2}\left(\frac{5}{4}\right)$

$x = \frac{5}{8}$

13. C

$P = \rho g h$
ρ for sea water is $1,022$

$P = (1,022)(9.8)(100)$
$P = 1,001,560$

14. B

$P = \rho g h$
$439,000 = \rho(9.8)(63)$
$439,000 = 617.4 \rho$
$\frac{439,000}{617.4} = \frac{617.4 \rho}{617.4}$

$711 = \rho$
Gasoline has a density of $711 \, \text{kg}/\text{m}^3$

Combining Like Terms & Solving Equations 2

1. B
$\sqrt{k-5} + x = 0$, k is a constant. $x = -12$

$\sqrt{k-5} + 12 = 0$
$\phantom{\sqrt{k-5}} +12 +12$

$\sqrt{k-5} = 12$
$\sqrt{k-5}^2 = 12^2$
$k - 5 = 144$
$ +5 +5$
$k = 149$

2. C
$2a^2 + 6a - 5 + (a^2 - 7)$
$2a^2 + 6a - 5 + a^2 - 7$

$3a^2 + 6a - 12$

3. D
If $9x^2 + 16y^2 = a$ and $2xy = b$
$a + 12b$
$9x^2 + 16y^2 + 12(2xy)$
$9x^2 + 16y^2 + 24xy$

D. $(3x + 4y)^2$
$(3x + 4y)(3x + 4y)$
$9x^2 + 12xy + 12xy + 16y^2$
$9x^2 + 24xy + 16y^2$

Combining Like Terms & Solving Equations Explanations

4. B

$4(c+3) - 9(c-2) = c$

$4c + 12 - 9c + 18 = c$

$-5c + 30 = c$
$+5c \quad\quad +5c$

$\dfrac{30}{6} = \dfrac{6c}{6}$

$5 = c$

5. D

$$\dfrac{5x+1}{(x-4)^2} - \dfrac{5x-8}{(x-4)^2} = \dfrac{a}{(x-4)^2}$$

The denominators are the same, so we can drop them. Be careful with the minus signs.

$5x + 1 - (5x - 8) = a$

$5x + 1 - 5x + 8 = a$

$9 = a$

6. A

$\dfrac{10(a-b)}{10} = \dfrac{15}{10}$

$a - b = \dfrac{15}{10} = \dfrac{3}{2}$

7. A

$(1.2x + 3.8)^2 - (4.7x^2 + 7.8)$

$(1.2x + 3.8)(1.2x + 3.8) - 4.7x^2 - 7.8$

$1.44x^2 + 4.56x + 4.56x + 14.44 - 4.7x^2 - 7.8$

$-3.26x^2 + 9.12x + 6.64$

8. D

$(x-4)(x+3)$

$x^2 + 3x - 4x - 12$

$x^2 - x - 12$

9. B

$x = \dfrac{4}{5}(20) - 8 \quad\quad 6x - 9$

$x = 16 - 8 \quad\quad\quad\quad 6(8) - 9$

$x = 8 \quad\quad\quad\quad\quad\quad 48 - 9$

$\quad\quad\quad\quad\quad\quad\quad\quad\quad 39$

10. C

$2\sqrt{x} + 4 = 10$

$\quad\quad -4 \quad -4$

$\dfrac{2\sqrt{x}}{2} = \dfrac{14}{2}$

$\sqrt{x} = 7$

$\sqrt{x}^2 = 7^2$

$x = 49$

11. A

$\left(2a^2 - \dfrac{b}{3}\right)\left(2a^2 - \dfrac{b}{3}\right)$

$4a^4 - \dfrac{2a^2 b}{3} - \dfrac{2a^2 b}{3} + \dfrac{b^2}{9}$

$4a^4 - \dfrac{4a^2 b}{3} + \dfrac{b^2}{9}$

Combining Like Terms & Solving Equations Explanations

12. C

$$\left(\frac{8}{7}\right)\frac{7}{8}t = \frac{4}{3}\left(\frac{8}{7}\right)$$

$$t = \frac{32}{21}$$

13. A

$$(7x^2 - 8x + 3) - (4x^2 - 5x + 7)$$

$$7x^2 - 8x + 3 - 4x^2 + 5x - 7$$

$$3x^2 - 3x - 4$$

14. B

$$4(2x+8) - 3(5+7x) = 4$$

$$8x + 32 - 15 - 21x = 4$$

$$-13x + 17 = 4$$
$$ -17 -17$$

$$\frac{-13x}{-13} = \frac{-13}{-13}$$

$$x = 1$$

Systems of Equations: Practice 1

$$5x + 5y = -50$$
$$2y - x = -23$$

1. What is the solution (x, y) to the system of equations above?
    A) $(11, 1)$
    B) $(1, -11)$
    C) $(5, -11)$
    D) $(11, 5)$

$$a = 1.30 + 0.25x$$
$$o = 1.50 + 0.15x$$

2. In the equation above, a and o represent the price per pound, in dollars, of apple and orange, respectively, x weeks after July 1 during last summer. What was the price per pound of orange when it was equal to the price per pound of apple?
    A) $1,80
    B) $3.30
    C) $3.50
    D) $4.30

$$x + 2y = 10$$
$$x - y = -11$$

3. According to the system of equations above, what is the value of y?

System of Equations: Practice 1

$$y > x + a$$
$$y < x + b$$

4. In the xy-plane, if $(2, -2)$ is a solution to the system of inequalities above, which of the following relationships between a and b must be true?
   A) $a > b$
   B) $b > a$
   C) $|a| > |b|$
   D) $|b| > |a|$

5. A restaurant sells chicken burgers for $5.50 each and soda for $1.50 each. The food truck's revenue from selling a total of 210 burgers and sodas in one day was $855. How many chicken burgers were sold that day?
   A) 75
   B) 100
   C) 135
   D) 200

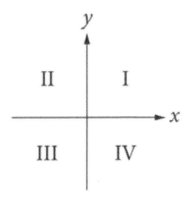

6. If the system of inequalities $y > 3x + 2$ and $y > \frac{1}{3}x - 5$ is graphed on the xy-plane above, which of the following quadrant contains no solutions in the system?
   A) Quadrant II
   B) Quadrant III
   C) Quadrant IV
   D) There are solutions in all four quadrants.

System of Equations: Practice 1

$$3x - 2y = 16$$
$$4x - 3y = 19$$

7. If (x, y) is a solution to the system of equations above, what is the value of $x - y$?
   A) 35
   B) 16
   C) 7
   D) 5

8. At a salad stand, each fruit salad has 30 more calories than each order of green salad. If 5 fruit salads and 6 green salads have a total of 1008 calories, how many calories does a fruit salad have?

$$S(P) = \frac{1}{2}P - 200$$
$$D(P) = 500 - 3P$$

9. The quantity of a product supplied and the quantity of the product demanded in an economic market are functions of the price of the product. The functions above are the estimated supply and demand functions for a certain product. The function $S(P)$ gives the quantity of the product supplied to the market when the price is P dollars, and the function $D(P)$ gives the quantity of the product demanded by the market when the price is P dollars.

   At what price will the quantity of the product supplied to the market equal the quantity of the product demanded by the market?
   A) $80
   B) $130
   C) $200
   D) $500

System of Equations: Practice 1

10. Mr. Parker has a jar containing j jellybeans to distribute to his students. If he gives each student 5 jellybeans, he will have 10 jellybeans left over. In order to give each student 6 jellybeans, he will need an additional 12 jellybeans. How many students are in the class?
    A) 10
    B) 12
    C) 22
    D) 26

$$5x + b = 8x - 10$$
$$5y + c = 8y - 10$$

11. In the equations above, b and c are constants. If b is c minus $\frac{1}{4}$, which of the following is true?
    A) x is y plus $\frac{1}{4}$.
    B) x is y minus $\frac{1}{4}$.
    C) x is y plus $\frac{1}{12}$.
    D) x is y minus $\frac{1}{12}$.

$$y \geq 10x + 500$$
$$y \leq 50x + 1000$$

12. In the xy-plane, if a point with coordinates (a, b) lies in the solution set of the system of inequalities above, what is the maximum possible value of b?

System of Equations: Practice 1

$$2(x + 3y) = \frac{28}{3}$$

$$y = 2x$$

13. The system of equations above has solutions (x, y). What is the value of x?

14. A comic bookstore sells Marvel and DC comics. Each Marvel comic book cost $8, and each DC comic book cost $6. If Rachel purchased a total of 10 Marvel and DC comics that have a combined selling price of $70, how many Marvel comics did she purchase?
    A) 3
    B) 4
    C) 5
    D) 10

$$\frac{1}{2}x = 6$$

$$x - y = 7$$

15. The system of equations above has solution (x, y). What is the value of y?
    A) 5
    B) 6
    C) 7
    D) $\frac{1}{2}$

Systems of Equations: Practice 2

$$y \geq \frac{1}{2}x + 3$$

$$x - y < 3$$

1. Which of the following ordered pairs (x, y) satisfies the system of inequalities above?
   A) $(0, 2)$
   B) $(12, 9)$
   C) $(-6, 0)$
   D) $(-2, -3)$

$$x = \frac{1}{2}y - 5$$

$$\frac{x}{4} - 2y = 10$$

2. Which ordered pair (x, y) satisfies the system of equations shown above?
   A) $(-8, 6)$
   B) $(-8, -6)$
   C) $(-6, -8)$
   D) $(6, 8)$

$$3x - y = 9$$

$$x + 3y = 13$$

3. For the system of equations above, what is the value of $x + y$?
   A) 3
   B) 4
   C) 5
   D) 7

System of Equations: Practice 2

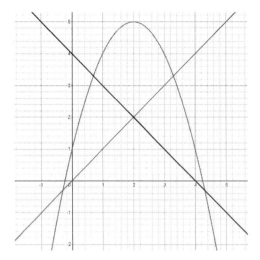

4. A system of three equations is graphed in the xy-plane above. How many solutions does the system have?
   A) None
   B) Two
   C) Four
   D) Five

System of Equations: Practice 2

$$y \geq 2x + 3$$
$$3x + 4y \leq 8$$

5. In which of the following does the shaded regions represent the solution set in the xy-plane to the system of inequalities above?

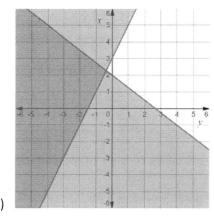
A)

B)

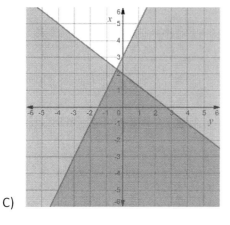
C)

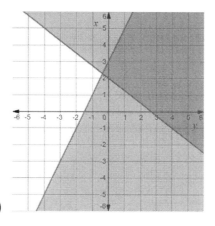
D)

6. If $x + 3y = 15$ and $3x + 5y = 23$, what is the value of $2x + 4y$?
   A) 9.5
   B) 8
   C) 19
   D) 38

System of Equations: Practice 2

$$5x + 6y = 1050$$
$$6x + 5y = 1500$$

7. Based on the system of equations above, what is the value of $11x + 11y$?

$$2.8x - 2.4y = 1.2$$
$$1.8x + 0.6y = 1.6$$

8. The system of equations above is graphed in the xy-plane. What is the x-coordinate of the intersection point (x, y) of the system?
   A) -0.5
   B) -0.25
   C) 0.28
   D) 0.76

$$4x + 5y = -24$$
$$y + 2x = -18$$

9. What is the solution (x, y) to the system of equations above?
   A) $(4, -11)$
   B) $(-11, 4)$
   C) $(4, 5)$
   D) $(-5, 4)$

$$a = 2.75 + 0.30x$$
$$o = 3.35 + 0.20x$$

10. In the equations above, a represents the price of one box of apple juice x weeks after April 1 during last spring. o represents the price of one box of orange juice x weeks after April 1 during last spring. What was the price of one box of apple juice when it was equal to the price of one box of orange juice?
    A) $2.55
    B) $4.35
    C) $4.45
    D) $4.55

System of Equations: Practice 2

$$3x + y = -11$$
$$x - y = -25$$

11. According to the system of equations above, what is the value of y?

$$y < -x + a$$
$$y > -x + b$$

12. In the xy-plane, if $(1, 2)$ is a solution to the system of inequalities above, which of the following relationship between a and b must be true?
    A) $a > b$
    B) $b > a$
    C) $|a| > |b|$
    D) $a = -b$

13. A deli sells beef sandwich for $2.50 each and a cup of coffee for $1.00 each. The deli's revenue from selling a total of 124 beef sandwich and cups of coffee in one day was $227.50. How many cups of coffee was sold that day?
    A) 55
    B) 69
    C) 124
    D) 228

System of Equations: Practice 2

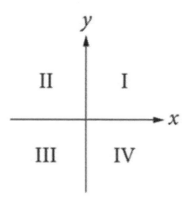

14. In the system of inequalities $y > \frac{1}{2}x + 5$ and $2y - x \leq -12$ is graphed in the xy-plane above, which quadrant contains solutions to the system?
    A) Quadrant III
    B) Quadrant IV
    C) There are solutions in all four quadrants.
    D) There are no solutions in any quadrant.

$$6x - 3y = -19$$

$$4x - 7y = 17$$

15. If (x, y) is a solution to the system of equations above, what is the value of $5x - 5y$?
    A) 2
    B) -0.2
    C) -0.4
    D) -1

System of Equations Explanations

System of Equations 1

1. B

$$5x + 5y = -50$$
$$5(-x + 2y = -23)$$

$$5x + 5y = -50$$
$$-5x + 10y = -115$$
$$\overline{15y = -165}$$

$$\frac{15y}{15} = \frac{-165}{15}$$
$$y = -11$$

$$5x + 5y = -50$$
$$5x + 5(-11) = -50$$
$$5x - 55 = -50$$
$$+55 \quad +55$$
$$5x = 5$$
$$x = 1$$

2. A

$$1.30 + .25x = 1.50 + .15x$$
$$\quad -.15x \qquad -.15x$$
$$1.30 + .10x = 1.50$$
$$-1.30 \qquad -1.30$$
$$.10x = .20$$

$$\frac{.10x}{.10} = \frac{.20}{.10}$$
$$x = 2$$

$$a = 1.30 + .25(2)$$
$$a = 1.80$$

3. 7

$$x + 2y = 10$$
$$-(x - y = -11)$$
$$\overline{3y = 21}$$
$$y = 7$$

4. B

$$y > x + a \qquad y < x + b$$
$$-2 > 2 + a \qquad -2 < 2 + b$$
$$\underline{-2 \; -2} \qquad \underline{-2 \; -2}$$
$$-4 > a \qquad -4 < b$$

$$b > a$$

5. C

$$5.5B + 1.5S = 855$$
$$B + S = 210$$
$$S = 210 - B$$

System of Equations Explanations

$5.5B + 1.5(210-B) = 855$
$5.5B + 315 - 1.5B = 855$
$4B + 315 = 855$
$ -315 \quad -315$
$\dfrac{4B}{4} = \dfrac{540}{4}$
$B = 135$

8. 108

$F = G + 30$
$5F + 6G = 1008$
$5(G+30) + 6G = 1008$
$5G + 150 + 6G = 1008$
$11G + 150 = 1008$
$ -150 \quad -150$
$\dfrac{11G}{11} = \dfrac{858}{11}$
$G = 78$

$F = G + 30$
$F = 78 + 30$
$F = 108$

6. C

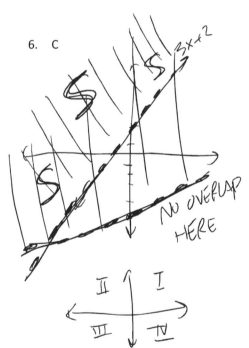

NO OVERLAP HERE

7. D

$-(3x - 2y = 16)$
$4x - 3y = 19$

$-3x + 2y = -16$
$4x - 3y = 19$
$\overline{x - y = 3}$

9. C

$\tfrac{1}{2}P - 200 = 500 - 3P$
$2(\tfrac{1}{2}P - 200) = 2(500 - 3P)$
$P - 400 = 1000 - 6P$
$+6P +6P$
$7P - 400 = 1000$
$ +400 \quad +400$
$7P = 1400$
$\dfrac{7P}{7} = \dfrac{1400}{7}$
$P = 200$

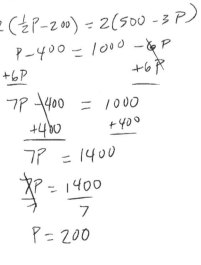

10. C

students $= x$

$5x + 10 = j$

$6x - 12 = j$

$5x + 10 = 6x - 12$

$-5x \quad -5x$

$10 = x - 12$

$+12 \quad +12$

$22 = x$

11. D

$b = c - 1/4$

$5x + b = 8x - 10$

$5y + c = 8y - 10$

$5x + c - 1/4 = 8x - 10$

$-(5y + c = 8y - 10)$

$5x - 5y - 1/4 = 8x - 8y$

$-5x + 5y \quad -5x + 5y$

$-1/4 = 3x - 3y$

$\overline{3} \quad \overline{3} \quad \overline{3}$

$-1/12 = x - y$

$+y \quad +y$

$y - \frac{1}{2} = x$

12. 375

For this question, the max will occur at the intersection

$10x + 500 = 50x + 1000$

$-10x \quad -10x$

$500 = 40x + 1000$

$-1000 \quad -1000$

$-500 = 40x$

$\frac{-500}{40} = \frac{40x}{40}$

$-12.5 = x$

$y = 10(-12.5) + 500$

$y = -125 + 500$

$y = 375$

13. 2/3

$y = 2x$

$2(x + 3y) = \frac{28}{3}$

$2(x + 6x) = \frac{28}{3}$

$2(7x) = \frac{28}{3}$

System of Equations Explanations

$$14x = \frac{28}{3}$$

$$\frac{14x}{14} = \frac{28}{3} \cdot \frac{1}{14}$$

$$x = \frac{2}{3}$$

14. C

$$8M + 6D = 70 \qquad M+D = 10$$
$$D = 10 - M$$

$$8M + 6(10-M) = 70$$
$$8M + 60 - 6M = 70$$
$$2M + 60 = 70$$
$$2M = 10$$
$$M = 5$$

15. A

$$(8)\frac{1}{8}x = 6(2)$$

$$x = 12$$

$$x - y = 7$$
$$12 - y = 7$$
$$-12 \qquad -12$$
$$-y = -5$$
$$y = 5$$

System of Equations 2

1. C

check answers

c) $0 \geq \frac{1}{2}(-6) + 3$
$0 \geq -3 + 3$
$0 \geq 0$ ✓

$-6 - 0 < 3$
$-6 < 3$ ✓

2. B

$$4\left(\frac{x}{4}\right) - (2y)4 = (10)4$$

$$x - 8y = 40$$
$$x = 40 + 8y$$

$$40 + 8y = \frac{1}{2}y - 5$$
$$2(40 + 8y) = 2\left(\frac{1}{2}y - 5\right)$$
$$80 + 16y = y - 10$$
$$\quad -y \quad -y$$
$$80 + 15y = -10$$
$$-80 \qquad -80$$
$$\frac{15y}{15} = \frac{-90}{15}$$

System of Equations Explanations

$y = -6$

$x = \frac{1}{2}(-6) - 5$

$x = -8$

$(-8, -6)$

3. D

$3x - y = 9$
$+y \quad +y$

$3x = 9 + y$
$-9 \quad -9$

$3x - 9 = y$

$x + 3y = 13$

$x + 3(3x - 9) = 13$

$x + 9x - 27 = 13$

$10x - 27 = 13$

$10x - 27 = 13$
$+27 \quad +27$

$10x = 40$

$x = 4$

$4 + 3y = 13$
$-4 \quad -4$

$3y = 9$

$y = 3$

find $x + y$

$4 + 3 = 7$

4. A

All 3 graphs don't intersect at a single point, so there is no solution.

5. A

$3x + 4y \leq 8$
$-3x \qquad -3x$

$4y \leq -3x + 8$

$\frac{4y}{4} \leq \frac{-3x}{4} + \frac{8}{4}$

$y \leq -\frac{3}{4}x + 2$

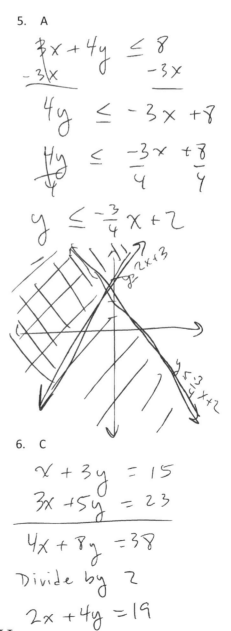

6. C

$x + 3y = 15$
$3x + 5y = 23$

$4x + 8y = 38$

Divide by 2

$2x + 4y = 19$

System of Equations Explanations

7. 2550

$$5x + 6y = 1050$$
$$6x + 5y = 1500$$
$$11x + 11y = 2550$$

8. D

$$2.8x - 2.4y = 1.2$$
$$4(1.8x + 0.6y = 1.6)$$

$$2.8x - 2.4y = 1.2$$
$$7.2x + 2.4y = 6.4$$

$$10x = 7.6$$
$$x = .76$$

9. B

$$y + 2x = -18$$
$$\underline{} -2x -2x$$
$$y = -2x - 18$$

$$4x + 5y = -24$$

$$4x + 5(-2x - 18) = -24$$

$$4x - 10x - 90 = -24$$
$$-6x - 90 = -24$$
$$ +90 +90$$
$$-6x = 66$$

$$x = -11$$

$$y + 2x = -18$$
$$y + 2(-11) = -18$$
$$y - 22 = -18$$
$$y = 4$$

10. D

$$2.75 + .30x = 3.35 + .20x$$
$$ -.20x -.20x$$

$$2.75 + .10x = 3.35$$
$$-2.75 -2.75$$

$$.10x = .60$$
$$\overline{.10} \overline{.10}$$

$$x = 6$$

$$a = 2.75 + .30(6)$$
$$a = 4.55$$

11. 16

$$3x + y = -11$$
$$x - y = -25$$

$$4x = -36$$
$$x = -9$$

System of Equations Explanations

$x - y = 25$
$+9 - y = -25$
$+9 \qquad +9$
$-y = -16$
$y = 16$

12. A

$y < -x + a$
$2 < -1 + a$
$3 < a$

$y > -x + b$
$2 > -1 + b$
$3 > b$

$a > b$

13. A

$s + c = 124$
$s = 124 - c$

$2.5s + 1c = 277.50$
$2.5(124 - c) + c = 277.50$
$310 - 2.5c + c = 277.50$
$310 - 1.5c = 277.50$
$-310 \qquad -310$
$-1.5c = -82.5$
$c = 55$

14. D

$2y - x \leq -12$
$2y \leq x - 12$
$y \leq \frac{1}{2}x - 6$

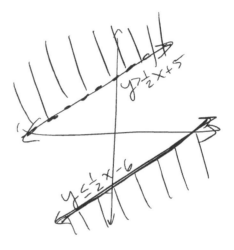

15. D

$6x - 3y = -19$
$4x - 7y = 17$
———————
$10x - 10y = -2$
Divide by 2
$x - y = -1$

Ratios & Proportions: Practice 1

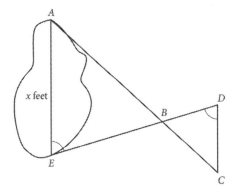

1. A summer camp counselor wants to find a length, x, in feet, across a lake as represented in the sketch, above. The lengths represented by AB, EB, BD, and CD on the sketch was determined to be 1600 feet, 1200 feet, 600 feet, 900 feet, respectively. Segments AC and DE intersect at B, and ∠AEB and ∠CDB have the same measure. What is the value of x?

1 decagram = 10 grams

1,000 milligrams = 1 gram

2. A hospital stores one type of medicine in 5-decagram containers. Based on the information given in the box above, how many 1-milligram doses are there in one 5-decagram container?
   A) 0.005
   B) 500
   C) 5,000
   D) 50,000

Ratios & Proportions: Practice 1

3. A square field measures 10 meters by 10 meters. Ten students each mark off a randomly selected one meter by one meter region of the field, and no two regions overlap. The students count the earthworms contained in the soil to a depth of 5 centimeters beneath the ground's surface in each region. The results are shown in the table below.

Region	Number of earthworms	Region	Number of earthworms
A	115	F	131
B	137	G	160
C	156	H	144
D	105	I	166
E	143	J	177

Which of the following is a reasonable approximation of the number of earthworms to a depth of 5 centimeters beneath the ground's surface in the entire field?
A) 140
B) 1,400
C) 14,000
D) 140,000

4. James can husk at least 12 dozen ears of corn per hour and at most 16 dozen ears of corn per hour. Based on this information, what is a possible integer number of hours that it could take James to husk 96 dozen ears of corn?

5. Tom walks 30 meters in 15.9 seconds. If he walks at this same rate, which of the following is closest to the distance he will walk in 5 minutes?
A) 270 meters
B) 470 meters
C) 570 meters
D) 1,700 meters

Ratios & Proportions: Practice 1

6. The cost of using a telephone in a hotel meeting room is $0.30 per minute. Which of the following equations represent in the total cost, c, in dollars, for h hours of phone use?
   A) $c = 0.30(60h)$
   B) $c = 0.30h + 60$
   C) $c = \dfrac{60h}{0.30}$
   D) $c = \dfrac{0.30h}{60}$

7. Graphene, which is used in the manufacture of integrated circuits, is so thin that a sheet weighing one ounce can cover up to 7 football fields. If a football field has an area of approximately $1\dfrac{1}{3}$ acres, about how many acres could 72 ounces of graphene cover?
   A) 370
   B) 470
   C) 570
   D) 670

8. To make a bakery's signature banana muffins, a baker needs 1.5 ounces of banana for each muffin. How many pounds of banana are needed to make 24 signature banana muffins? (1 pound = 16 ounces)
   A) 2.25
   B) 9
   C) 153.6
   D) 576

9. Horsepower and watts are units of measure of power. They are directly proportional such that 5 horsepower is equal to 3,730 watts. How much power, in watts, is equal to 1 horsepower?

10. The painting *The Starry Night* by Vincent van Gogh is rectangular in shape with height 29 inches and width 36.25 inches. If a reproduction was made where each dimension is $\dfrac{1}{2}$ the corresponding original dimension, what is the height of the reproduction, in inches?

Ratios & Proportions: Practice 2

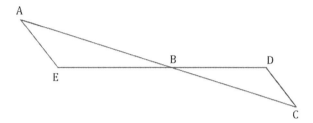

Note: Figure not drawn to scale.

1. The lengths represented by *AB*, *EB*, *BD*, and *CD* on the diagram above measure 1500 feet, 1000 feet, 400 feet, 800 feet, respectively. Segments AC and DE intersect at B, and ∠AEB and ∠CDB have the same measure. What is the perimeter of triangle ABE?

1 decameter = 10 meter

100 centimeter = 1 meter

2. Riley walks 5 decameters every morning to get her mail. Based on the information given in the box above, how many centimeters does she walk in a week?
    A) 0.035
    B) 50
    C) 5,000
    D) 35,000

Ratios & Proportions: Practice 2

3. A square area of the beach measures 20 meters by 20 meters. Ten students each mark off a randomly selected square meter of the field, and no two regions overlap. The students count the seashells contained in the sand to a depth of 50 centimeters beneath the beach's surface in each region. The results are shown in the table below.

Region	Number of seashells	Region	Number of seashells
A	123	F	129
B	139	G	165
C	163	H	101
D	125	I	189
E	155	J	173

Which of the following is a reasonable approximation of the number of seashells to a depth of 50 centimeters beneath the ground's surface in the entire field?
A) 580
B) 5,800
C) 58,000
D) 580,000

4. Kevin can bake at least 15 dozen muffins per hour and at most 20 dozen muffins per hour. Based on this information, what is a possible integer number of hours that it could take Kevin to bake 180 dozen muffins?

5. Tom walks 6 meters in 10 seconds. If he walks at this same rate, which of the following is closest to the distance he will walk in 1 hour?
A) 216 meters
B) 316 meters
C) 516 meters
D) 2,160 meters

Ratios & Proportions: Practice 2

6. The cost of using a telephone in a hotel meeting room is $0.15 per minute. Which of the following equations represent in the total cost, c, in dollars, for s seconds of phone use?
   A) $c = 0.15(60s)$
   B) $c = 0.15s + 60$
   C) $c = \dfrac{60s}{0.15}$
   D) $c = \dfrac{0.15s}{60}$

7. Graphene, which is used in the manufacture of integrated circuits, is so thin that a sheet weighing one ounce can cover up to 7 football fields. If a football field has an area of approximately $1\dfrac{1}{3}$ acres, about how many acres could 0.5 ounces of graphene cover?
   A) $\dfrac{2}{3}$
   B) 1
   C) $1\dfrac{1}{3}$
   D) $4\dfrac{2}{3}$

8. To make a bakery's signature ice cream cake, a baker needs 7 ounces of ice cream for each cake. About how many grams of ice cream are needed to make 3 signature ice cream cake? (1 ounce = 28.35 grams)
   A) 2.1
   B) 21
   C) 198
   D) 595

9. Horsepower and watts are units of measure of power. They are directly proportional such that 5 horsepower is equal to 3,730 watts. About how much power, in horsepower, is equal to 1,000 watts?

10. The painting *The Starry Night* by Vincent van Gogh is rectangular in shape with height 29 inches and width 36.25 inches. If a reproduction was made where each dimension is twice the corresponding original dimension, what is the width of the reproduction, in inches?

Ratios & Proportions 1

1. 1800

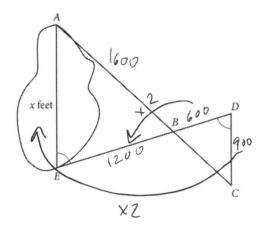

$900 \times 2 = 1800$

2. D

$\dfrac{deca}{gram}$ $\dfrac{1}{10} = \dfrac{5}{x}$

$x = 50$

$\dfrac{milli}{gram}$ $\dfrac{1{,}000}{1} = \dfrac{x}{50}$

$50{,}000 = x$

Ratios & Proportions Explanations

3. C

$10 \times 10 = 100 \text{ m}^2$ total area

each 1×1 area has about 140,

so $140 \times 100 = 14{,}000$

4. 6 or 7 or 8

$96 \div 12 = 8$ hours

$96 \div 16 = 6$ hours

fastest is 6
slowest is 8

5. C

5 min = 300 seconds

$\dfrac{meters}{sec}$ $\dfrac{30}{15.9} = \dfrac{x}{300}$

$9000 = 15.9x$

$566 = x$

6. A

$\dfrac{\$.30}{minute} \cdot \dfrac{60 \text{ minutes}}{hr} \cdot h \text{ hrs}$

left with dollars ($)

Ratios & Proportions Explanations

7. D

$$\frac{1 \text{ ounce}}{7 \text{ fields}} = \frac{72}{x}$$

$x = 504 \text{ fields}$

$$504 \times 1.33 = 670.32$$

8. A

$$\frac{\text{ounces}}{\text{muffin}} \quad \frac{1.5}{1} = \frac{x}{24}$$

$36 = x$

$$\frac{\text{ounces}}{\text{pound}} \quad \frac{16}{1} = \frac{36}{x}$$

$16x = 36$

$x = 2.25$

9. 746

$$\frac{HP}{W} \quad \frac{5}{3730} = \frac{1}{x}$$

$5x = 3730$

$x = 746$

10. 14.5

$$\frac{h}{w} \quad \frac{29}{36.25} = \frac{x}{18.125}$$

$525.625 = 36.25x$

$14.5 = x$

Ratios & Proportions 2

1. 4500

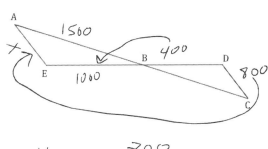

$$\frac{400}{1000} = \frac{800}{x}$$

$400x = 800,000$

$x = 2000$

$P = 2000 + 1500 + 1000$

$P = 4500$

2. D

$$\frac{\text{deca}}{\text{meter}} \quad \frac{1}{10} = \frac{5}{x}$$

$x = 50$

Ratios & Proportions Explanations

$\dfrac{\text{meter}}{\text{cm}} \quad \dfrac{1}{100} = \dfrac{50}{x}$

$x = 5000$

$5,000 \times 7 = 35,000$

3. C

$20m \times 20m = 400 m^2$ total area

From the table, each square meter has about 150 seashells

$400 \times 150 = 60,000$

approximately 58,000

4. 9, 10, 11, or 12

$180 \div 15 = 12$ hours

$180 \div 20 = 9$ hours

fastest is 9 hours
slowest is 12 hours

5. D

1 hr = 60 minutes

60 minutes = 3,600 seconds

meters

$\dfrac{6}{\text{sec.}} \quad \dfrac{6}{10} \times \dfrac{x}{3600}$

$21,600 = 10x$

$2,160 = x$

6. D

$\dfrac{\$0.15}{\text{minute}} \cdot \dfrac{1 \text{ minute}}{60 \text{ seconds}} \cdot 5 \text{ seconds}$

left with dollars ($)

7. D

$\dfrac{\text{ounce}}{\text{field}} \quad \dfrac{1}{7} = \dfrac{0.5}{x}$

$x = 3.5$

3.5 fields

3.5×1.33

$4.655 \to 4\dfrac{2}{3}$

8. D

$\dfrac{\text{ounces}}{\text{cake}} \quad \dfrac{7}{1} = \dfrac{x}{3}$

$21 = x$

21 ounces of ice cream

Ratios & Proportions Explanations

$$\frac{\text{ounces}}{\text{grams}} \quad \frac{1}{28.35} = \frac{21}{x}$$

$$x = 595.35$$

9. 1.34

$$\frac{HP}{W} \quad \frac{5}{3730} = \frac{x}{1000}$$

$$5000 = 3730x$$

$$1.34 = x$$

10. 72.5

$$\begin{array}{r} 36.25 \\ \times \quad 2 \\ \hline 72.5 \end{array}$$

Data & Probability: Practice 1

1. Which of the following graphs best shows a strong positive correlation between x and y?

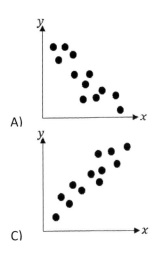

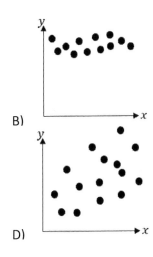

Data & Probability: Practice 1

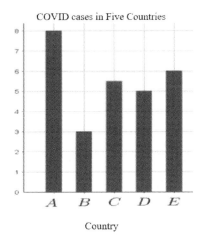

2. The number of COVID cases in 5 countries is shown in the graph above. If the total number of covid cases is 275,000, what is an appropriate label for the vertical axis of the graph?

A) Number of COVID cases (in hundreds)
B) Number of COVID cases (in thousands)
C) Number of COVID cases (in tens of thousands)
D) Number of COVID cases (in hundreds of thousands)

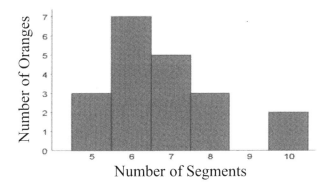

3. Based on the histogram above, of the following, which is closest to the average (arithmetic mean) number of segments per orange?

A) 5
B) 6
C) 7
D) 8

Data & Probability: Practice 1

		Course			Total
		Algebra	Geometry	Calculus	
Gender	Male	57	65	79	201
	Female	64	70	75	209
	Total	121	135	154	410

4. A group tenth-grade students responded to a survey that asked which math course they were currently enrolled in. The survey data were broken down as shown in the table above. Which if the following categories accounts for approximately 14 percent of all the survey respondents?
A) Females taking Algebra
B) Males taking Geometry
C) Females taking Calculus
D) Males taking Algebra

Lengths of Fish (in inches)							
24	29	37	38	35	26	35	56
35	35	28	36	27	33	30	41
36	40	35	32	26	32	35	22

5. The table above list the lengths, to the nearest inch, of a random sample of 24 rainbow trout fish. The outlier measurement of 56 inches is an error. Of the mean, median, mode, and range of the values listed, which will change the most if the 56-inch measurement is removed from the data?
A) Mean
B) Median
C) Mode
D) Range

Data & Probability: Practice 1

Dreams Recalled During One Week

	None	1 to 3	4 or more	Total
Group A	32	55	63	150
Group B	41	72	37	150
Total	73	127	100	300

6. The data in the table above were produced by a sleep researcher studying the number of dreams people recall when asked to record their dreams for one week. Group A consisted of 150 people who observed early bedtimes, and Group Y consisted of 150 people who observed later bedtimes. If a person is chosen at random from those who recalled at most 3 dreams, what is the probability that the person belonged to Group A?

A) $\frac{87}{200}$

B) $\frac{118}{150}$

C) $\frac{113}{200}$

D) $\frac{87}{227}$

Annual Budgets for Different Programs in Wyoming, 2015 to 2018

	Year			
	2015	2016	2017	2018
General Government	17,542,246	16,873,014	15,219,752	18,570,012
Education	6,218,670	6,542,870	6,008,513	6,952,167
Agriculture/Natural Resources	785,314	813,654	843,740	879,524
Highways and Transportation	3,567,842	3,722,547	3,426,018	3,982,673
Human Resources	8,655,853	8,922,753	9,221,057	9,621,104
Public Safety	542,900	593,752	607,843	658,024

7. The table above list the annual budget, in thousands of dollars, for each of the six different state programs in Wyoming from 2015 to 2018. Of the following, which program's ratio of its 2015 budget to its 2018 budget is closest to the education program's ratio of its 2015 budget to its 2018 budget?

A) Public Safety
B) Highways and Transportation
C) General Government
D) Human Resources

Data & Probability: Practice 1

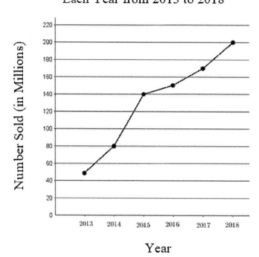

8. According to the line graph above, the number of phones sold in 2014 is what fraction of the number sold in 2018?

	Age		Total
Gender	Under 35	35 or older	
Male	10	7	17
Female	8	5	13
Total	18	12	30

9. The table above shows the distribution of age and gender for 30 people who entered a raffle contest. What is the probability that the winner will be either a male under 35 or female age 35 or older?

A) $\dfrac{18}{30}$

B) $\dfrac{12}{30}$

C) $\dfrac{15}{30}$

D) $\dfrac{17}{30}$

Data & Probability: Practice 1

10. The graph below shows the total sales of an album, in thousands, each year from 2008 through 2020.

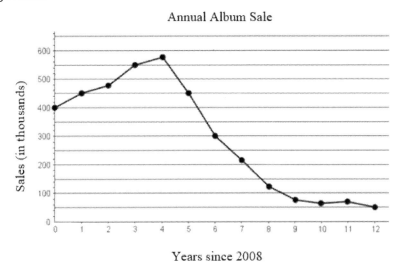

Based on the graph, which of the following best describes the general trend in the album sales from 2008 through 2020?
A) Sales generally increased until 2020.
B) Sales generally decreased since the release of the album.
C) Sales increased until 2012 and then generally decreased.
D) Sales increased half of the time then decreased.

11. Students in two high school classrooms were given two versions of the same test. Test A is arranged from easier to more difficult questions and Test B is arranged in reversed order. The resulting data showed that students who took Test A scored significantly higher than those who took Test B. Based on the design and results of the study, which of the following is an appropriate conclusion?
A) Test A is easier than Test B.
B) If another group of students were given test A and a second group of students were given test B, the students who took test A are likely to score higher than the students who took test B.
C) If another group of students were given test A and a second group of students were given test B, the students who took test A are will definitely score higher than the students who took test B.
D) Students who took Test B will fail.

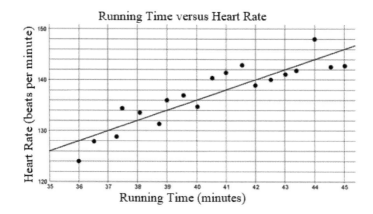

12. Gabriel ran 4,000 yards on each of nineteen days. The scatterplot above shows his run time for and corresponding heart rate after each run. The line of best fit for the data is also shown. For the run that took 44 minutes, Gabriel's actual heart rate was about how many beats per minute more than the rate predicted by the line of best fit?

A) 2
B) 3
C) 4
D) 5

	Subject	
Gender	Chemistry	Biology
Female		
Male		
Total	31	47

13. The incomplete table above summarizes the number of male and female students enrolled in Chemistry and Biology. There are 4 times as many female students enrolled in Biology as there are enrolled in Chemistry, and there are 3 times as many male students enrolled in Chemistry as there are enrolled in Biology. If there are a total of 31 students enrolled in Chemistry and 47 students enrolled in Biology, which of the following is the probability that a student enrolled in Chemistry selected at random is male? (Note: Assume that none of the students are enrolled in both Chemistry and Biology subjects.)

A) 0.323
B) 0.362
C) 0.677
D) 0.851

Ages of the Latest 12 United States Presidents at the Beginning of Their Terms in Office

President	Age	President	Age
Biden	78	Carter	52
Trump	70	Ford	61
Obama	47	Nixon	56
Bush	54	Johnson	55
Clinton	46	Kennedy	43
Bush	64	Eisenhower	62

14. The table above lists the ages of the latest 12 United States presidents when they began their terms in office. According to the table, what was the mean age, in years, of these presidents at the beginning of their terms? (Round your answer to the nearest tenth)

A) 57.3
B) 57.6
C) 58.3
D) 58.6

15. An online store receives customer satisfaction ratings between 0 and 100, inclusive. In the first 10 ratings the store received, the average (arithmetic mean) of the rating was 80. What is the least value the store can receive for the 11th rating and still be able to have an average of at least 85 for the first 15 ratings?

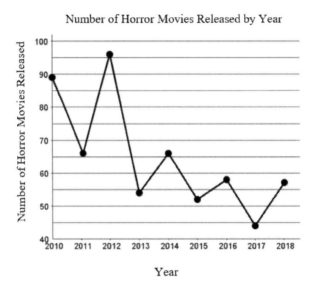

16. According to the line graph above, between which consecutive years was there the greatest drop in the number of horror movies released?
A) 2010-2011
B) 2012-2013
C) 2014-2015
D) 2017-2018

Data & Probability: Practice 2

Type of surgeon	Major Professional Activity		Total
	Teaching	Research	
General	186	204	390
Pediatric	127	112	239
Cardiac	64	215	279
Total	377	531	908

1. In a survey, 908 general surgeons, pediatric surgeons, and cardiac surgeons indicated their major professional activity. The results are summarized in the table above. If one of the surgeons is selected at random, which of the following is closest to the probability that the selected surgeon is a pediatric surgeon whose indicated professional activity is teaching?

   A) 0.140
   B) 0.182
   C) 0.424
   D) 0.490

2. A polling agency recently surveyed 1,500 voters who were selected randomly from a large city and asked each of the adults, "Are you satisfied with the performance of the president?" Of those surveyed, 72 percent responded that they were satisfied with the performance of the president. Based on the results of the survey, which of the following statements must be true?

   I. Of all the voters in the city, 28 percent are not satisfied with the performance of the president.
   II. If another 1,000 voters selected at random from the city were surveyed, 720 voters would respond that they are satisfied with the performance of the president.
   III. If 1,500 voters selected at random from another state were surveyed, 72 percent of them would respond that they are satisfied with the performance of the president.

   A) II only
   B) II and III only
   C) II only
   D) None

Data & Probability: Practice 2

3. In the state of California, Mr. Right's tenth-grade class consisting of 29 students was surveyed and 24.1 percent of the students reported that they are an only child. The average tenth-grade class size in the state is 29. If the students in Mr. Right's class are representative of the students in the state's tenth-grade class and there are 1,500 tenth-grade classes in the state, which of the following best estimates the number of tenth-grade students in the state who have 1 or more siblings?
   A) 26,400
   B) 33,000
   C) 36,500
   D) 41,200

4. John's mean grade in his 8 subjects is 90.5. If the subject with the highest grade is removed, the mean grade of the remaining subjects becomes 90. What is John's highest grade?
   A) 91
   B) 92
   C) 93
   D) 94

5. Carter walks daily to lose weight. His goal is to walk an average of at least 18 miles per week for 4 weeks. He walked 14 miles the first week, 21 miles the second week, and 22 miles the third week. Which inequality can be used to represent the number of miles, x, Carter could walk on the 4th week to meet his goal?

   A) $\frac{14+21+22}{4} + x \geq 18$
   B) $14 + 21 + 22 + x \geq 18$
   C) $\frac{14}{4} + \frac{21}{4} + \frac{22}{4} + x \geq 18$
   D) $12 + 21 + 22 + x \geq 72$

Data & Probability: Practice 2

6. A new car model is tested in an experiment. The experiment starts when the car, at rest, accelerates for about 15 minutes then maintains its speed for about 20 minutes. If after 35 minutes from the start of the experiment, the car accelerates twice as fast than the start, which of the following graphs best represent the speed of the car versus time?

A)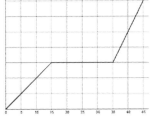

C)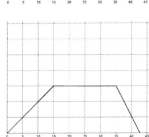

B)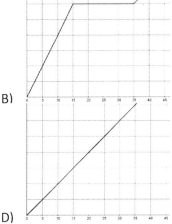

D)

7. The members of a city council wanted to assess the opinions of all city residents about converting an open field into an elderly care facility. The council surveyed a sample of 450 elderly residents. The survey showed that majority of those sampled were in favor of the elderly care facility. Which of the following is true about the city council's survey?

A) It shows that most city residents are in favor of the elderly care facility.
B) The survey sample should have included more elderly residents.
C) The survey sample should have consisted entirely of teenager residents.
D) The survey sample is biased because it is not representative of all city residents.

Data & Probability: Practice 2

		Flavor	
		Strawberry	Cookies N' Cream
Topping	Sprinkles	7	13
	Chocolate Chips	9	8

8. The table above shows the flavors of ice cream and the toppings chosen by the people at a party. Each person chose one flavor of ice cream and one topping. Of the people who chose cookies n' cream ice cream, what fraction chose chocolate chips as a topping?

A) $\frac{8}{21}$

B) $\frac{8}{21}$

C) $\frac{8}{37}$

D) $\frac{8}{13}$

Data & Probability: Practice 2

Sunflower Growth	
Day	Height (cm)
0	0.00
7	17.93
14	36.36
21	67.76
28	98.10
35	131.00
42	169.50
49	205.50
56	228.30
63	247.10
70	250.50
77	253.80
84	254.50

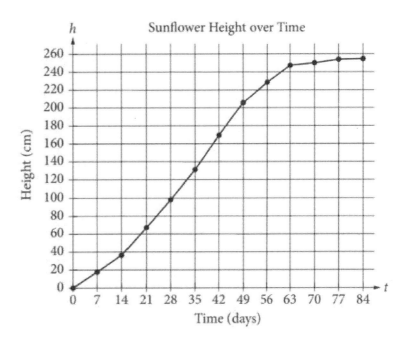

In 1919, H. S. Reed and R. H. Holland published a paper on the growth of sunflowers. Included in the paper were the table and graph above, which show the height h, in centimeters, of a sunflower t days after the sunflower begins to grow.

9. Which of the following best describes the growth rate of the sunflower from day 63 to day 84?
A) The sunflower stopped growing.
B) The average growth rate of the sunflower is the least.
C) The average growth rate of the sunflower is the greatest.
D) The average growth rate is constant.

10. A study was done on the lengths of different types of fish in a pond. A random sample of fish were caught and marked in order to ensure that none were measured more than once. The sample contained 120 black bullheads, of which 25% measured more than 12 inches. Which of the following conclusions is best supported by the sample data?
A) The majority of all fish in the pond measured less than 12 inches.
B) The average length of all fish in the pond is approximately 12 inches.
C) Approximately 25% of all fish in the pond measured more than 12 inches.
D) Approximately 25% of all black bullheads in the pond measured more than 12 inches.

Data & Probability: Practice 2

Number of States with 10 or More Electoral Votes in 2020

Electoral Votes	Frequency
10	4
11	4
12	1
13	1
14	1
15	1
16	2
18	1
20	2
29	2
38	1
55	1

11. In 2020, there are 21 states with 10 or more electoral votes, as shown in the table above. Based on the table, what was the median number of electoral votes for the 21 states?

A) 13
B) 14
C) 15
D) 16

	Distance (in miles)						
Alex	2.3	3.0	2.9	2.2	2.4	2.0	2.7
Beth	x	2.7	3.1	2.3	1.9	2.5	2.9

12. Alex and Beth each walked daily for 1 week, and the distance they walked are shown in the table above. The mean of the distances walked by Beth is 0.2 mi greater than the mean of the distances walked by Alex. What is the value of x?

	Chicken Flavor	Tuna Flavor	Total
Dogs	13	6	19
Cats	9	22	31
Total	22	28	50

13. The table above shows the preferred food flavor by dogs and cats currently boarded at a pet care facility. What fraction of cats preferred tuna flavor?

A) $\frac{9}{31}$

B) $\frac{9}{19}$

C) $\frac{22}{31}$

D) $\frac{22}{28}$

Data & Probability: Practice 2

Questions 14 & 15 refer to the information below

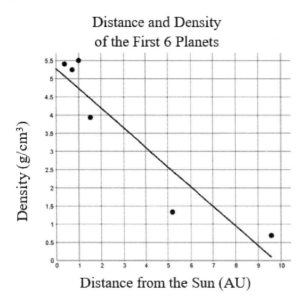

14. The scatterplot above shows the densities of the first 6 planets in the solar system, in grams per cubic centimeter, with respect to their average distances from the Sun in astronomical units (AU). The line of best fit is also shown. According to the scatterplot, which of the following statements is true about the relationship between a planet's average distance from the Sun and its density?

A) Planets that are more distant from the Sun tend to have greater densities.
B) Planets that are closer to the Sun tend to have lesser densities.
C) Planets with lesser densities tend to be more distant from the Sun.
D) The distance from a planet to the Sun is unrelated to its density.

15. According to the line of best fit, if a hypothetical planet is discovered about 7 AU from the Sun, which of the following best approximates the density of the planet, in grams per cubic centimeter?

A) 1.2
B) 1.5
C) 2.4
D) 3.7

Data & Probability: Practice 2

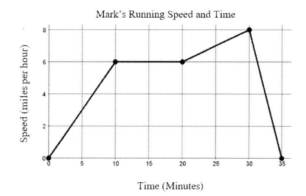

16. Mark ran on a treadmill for thirty-five minutes, and his time and speed are shown on the graph above. According to the graph, which of the following is true concerning Mark's run?
A) Mark is at rest for ten minutes.
B) Mark's speed is decreasing for a longer period than it was increasing.
C) Mark's speed reached its maximum during the last ten minutes.
D) Mark's speed is constant for more than ten minutes.

Data & Probability Explanations

Data & Probability 1

1. C

A) It trends down, so negative correlation

B) The y-values don't change, so there is no correlation

C) It trends up and the points are close together, so it's strong positive correlation

D) The points trend up, but the points aren't close together, so it's weak positive correlation

2. C

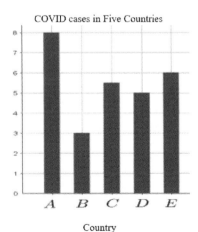

All of the cases have to add up to 275,000. The bars in the graph add up to 27.5, so it must be 10,000 times as much. The units of the vertical axis must be in tens of thousands.

3. C

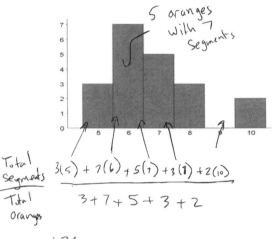

5 oranges with 7 segments

Total Segments: $3(5) + 7(6) + 5(7) + 3(8) + 2(10)$

Total Oranges: $3 + 7 + 5 + 3 + 2$

$\frac{136}{20} = 6.8$

4. D

14% of all

$(.14)(410) = 57.4$

Male – Algebra

5. D

If the largest number decreases by from 56 to 35, the range will decrease by 21. The mean will reduce but not by as much since the total gets divided. The median won't change as much because even if it does change, it will change to a number next to it, while range is the difference of greatest and least values. The mode will not change.

Data & Probability Explanations

6. A

Dreams Recalled During One Week

	None	1 to 3	4 or more	Total
Group A	32	55	63	150
Group B	41	72	37	150
Total	73	127	100	300

At most 3 includes "None" and "1 to 3".

$$\frac{\text{Group A, at most 3}}{\text{at most 3}} = \frac{32+55}{73+127} = \frac{87}{200}$$

7. B

$$EDU \quad \frac{6,218,670}{6,952,167} = .894$$

A) $\frac{542,900}{658,024} = .825$

B) $\frac{3,567,842}{3,982,673} = .8958$

C) $\frac{17,542,246}{18,570,012} = .944$

D) $\frac{8,655,853}{9,621,104} = .899$

8. 2/5

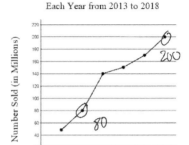

2014
2018

$\frac{80}{200} = \frac{8}{20} = 2/5$

9. C

	Age		Total
Gender	Under 35	35 or older	
Male	10	7	17
Female	8	5	13
Total	18	12	30

$\frac{10+5}{30} = \frac{15}{30}$

10. C

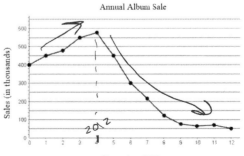

Data & Probability Explanations

11. B

When a test or survey is done, we can use the results to determine what may happen, not what will definitely happen. Choice B is correct because it states that students who take test A are "more likely" to score higher.

	Subject	
Gender	Chemistry	Biology
Female	x	$4x$
Male	$3y$	y
Total	31	47

12. C

HR of run that took 44 mins (148)

predicted HR for 44 mins (144)

$148 - 144 = 4$

$x + 3y = 31$
$4x + y = 47$

use elimination to solve

$x + 3y = 31$
$-3(4x + y = 47)$

$x + 3y = 31$
$-12x - 3y = -141$
_____
$-11x = -110$

$\dfrac{-11x}{-11} = \dfrac{-110}{-11}$

$x = 10$

Solve for y

$x + 3y = 31$
$10 + 3y = 31$
$-10 \quad -10$
_____
$3y = 21$
$y = 7$

13. A

Female + Chem = x
Female + Bio = $4x$
Male + Bio = y
Male + Chem = $3y$

Male + Chem = $3y = 21$

$\dfrac{21}{31} = .667$

Data & Probability Explanations

14. A

$$\frac{Sum}{\#} = \frac{688}{12} = 57.3$$

15. 75

15 ratings, Avg of 85

sum = Avg · #
sum = 85 · 15
sum = 1,275

all 15 ratings must add up to 1,275

First 10 → Avg of 80
sum = Avg · #
sum = 80 · 10
sum = 800

The first 10 add up to 800

1,275 − 800 = 475

The last 5 have to add up to at least 475 to get an average of at least 85

To find what the lowest rating one of them can be, we would need the other ratings to be as high as possible

475 total

? | 100 | 100 | 100 | 100

low as possible ← → high as possible

$x + 100 + 100 + 100 + 100 = 475$
$x + 400 = 475$
$x = 75$

16. B

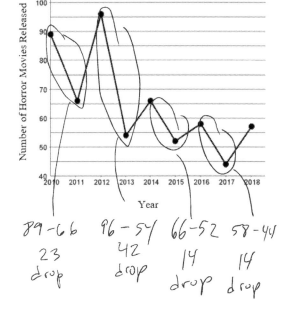

89−66   96−54   66−52   58−44
  23   42   14   14
 drop   drop   drop   drop

Data & Probability 2

1. A

Type of surgeon	Major Professional Activity		Total
	Teaching	Research	
General	186	204	390
Pediatric	127	112	239
Cardiac	64	215	279
Total	377	531	908

a surgeon is selected at random, so we are choosing from all 908. There are 127 pediatric surgeons whose main profession is teaching.

$$\frac{127}{908} = .1398 = .140$$

2. D
    I. No. There are two main reasons: First, if 72% are satisfied, it doesn't mean the other 28% are not satisfied. Some could be indifferent. Second, the results of a sample survey can only give us an idea of what might be true for the whole population (in this case all voters in a specific city), but not tell us definitively how the whole population feels.
    II. No. Based on the first sample survey, we would expect there to be similar results, but not definitive.
    III. No. Results from a survey of one population cannot be used for assumptions about another population.

3. B

24.1% → only child
1500 classes × 29 students/class
43,500 students

$$\begin{array}{r} 43500 \\ \times .241 \\ \hline 10,484 \end{array}$$ are only childs

$$\begin{array}{r} 43,500 \\ -10,484 \\ \hline 33,016 \end{array}$$ have a sibling

approx 33,000

4. D

Sum = Avg · #
Sum = 90.5 · 8
Sum = 724

John's tests add up to 724

One test is removed and the Avg becomes 90 (7 tests)

Sum = Avg · #
Sum = 90 · 7
Sum = 630

Total of tests dropped from 724 to 630

724 − 630 = 94

94 was removed

Data & Probability Explanations

5. D

$$\text{Avg} \geq 18$$

$$\frac{14+21+22+x}{4} \geq 18$$

$$(4)\frac{14+21+22+x}{4} \geq 18(4)$$

$$14+21+22+x \geq 72$$

6. A

accelerates → increase in speed

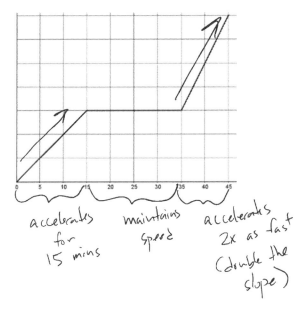

accelerates for 15 mins | maintains speed | accelerates 2x as fast (double the slope)

7. D
The survey is biased. The city council wanted to assess the opinions of all city residents, but only surveyed elderly residents.

8. B

		Flavor	
		Strawberry	Cookies N' Cream
Topping	Sprinkles	7	13
	Chocolate Chips	9	8

The probability is out of the people who chose cookies n' cream, so it is out of 21 people (13+8). Out of those people, 8 chose Choc. chip.

$$\frac{8}{21}$$

9. B

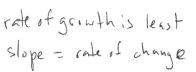

smallest slope

rate of growth is least
slope = rate of change

10. D

The sample only included black bullheads, so we cannot apply the findings to fish other than black bullheads.

Data & Probability Explanations

11. B

There are 21 states in the table
The position of the median is $\frac{n+1}{2}$

$\frac{21+1}{2} = \frac{22}{2} = 11$, so the 11th
Count down to the 11th

Number of States with 10 or More Electoral Votes in 2020

Electoral Votes	Frequency
10	4
11	4
12	1
13	1
14	1
15	1
16	2
18	1
20	2
29	2
38	1
55	1

12. 3.5 or 7/2

Alex's Avg = $\frac{2.3 + 3 + 2.9 + 2.2 + 2.4 + 2 + 2.7}{7}$

= 2.5

Beth's Avg = 2.5 + 0.2 = 2.7

Sum = Avg · #
Sum = 2.7 · 7
Sum = 18.9
Beth's total is 18.9 miles

$X + 2.7 + 3.1 + 2.3 + 1.9 + 2.5 + 2.9 = 18.9$
$X + 15.4 = 18.9$
$X = 3.5$

13. C

There are 31 cats.
Out of the 31 cats, 22 like tuna flavor

$\frac{22}{31}$

14. C

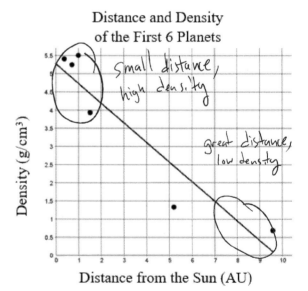

Distance and Density of the First 6 Planets

Based on the graph above, as distance from the sun increases, the density decreases. Likewise, as distance from the sun decreases, the density increases.

Data & Probability Explanations

15. B

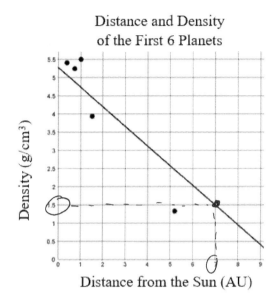

16. C

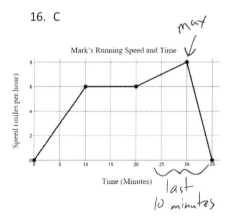

Evaluating Functions: Practice 1

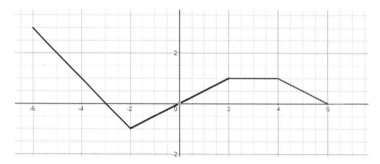

1. The complete graph of the function f is shown in the xy-plane above. For what value of x is the value of $f(x)$ at its minimum?
   A) -6
   B) -2
   C) 2
   D) 6

$$g(x) = ax^2 + 8x + 8$$

2. For the function g defined above, a is a constant and $g(-1) = 2$. What is the value of $g(1)$?
   A) 0
   B) 2
   C) 8
   D) 18

$$a = 2.10t + 2030$$

3. The speed of a sound wave in air depends on the air temperature. The formula above shows the relationship between a, the speed of a sound wave, in feet per second, and t, the air temperature, in degrees Fahrenheit (°F). At which of the following air temperatures will the speed of a sound wave be closest to 2,000 feet per second?
   A) -14°F
   B) -15°F
   C) -16°F
   D) -17°F

Evaluating Functions: Practice 1

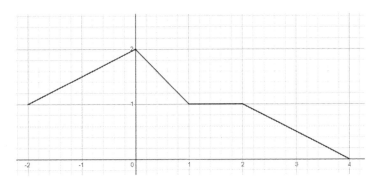

4. The complete graph of the function f is shown in the xy-plane above. Which of the following are equal to 1?

   i. $f(-2)$
   ii. $f\left(\frac{3}{2}\right)$
   iii. $f(3)$

   A) iii only
   B) i and iii only
   C) i and ii only
   D) i, ii, and iii

Questions 5 and 6 refer to the following information.

A farmer is planting crops for the current harvest season. He currently has 500 crops. The number of crops that the farmer expects to grow next year, $N_{next\ year}$, can be estimated from the number of plants this year, $N_{this\ year}$, by the equation below.

$$N_{next\ year} = N_{this\ year} + 0.5(N_{this\ year})(1 - \frac{N_{this\ year}}{K})$$

The constant K in this formula is the number of crops the environment is able to support.

5. According to the formula, what will be the number of crops two years from now if $K = 1000$? (Round your answer to the nearest whole number.)

6. The farmer would like to increase the number of crops the environment can support so that he can grow a larger number of crops. If the farmer's goal is that the number of crops will increase from 500 this year to 700 next year, about how many crops must the modified environment support?

Evaluating Functions: Practice 1

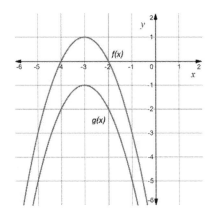

7. Graphs of the function f and g are shown in the xy-plane above. For which of the following values of x does $f(x) + g(x) = 0$?
   A) -4
   B) -3
   C) -2
   D) -1

8. If $f(x) = -5x + 10$, what is $f(3x)$ equal to?
   A) $5(3x + 2)$
   B) $-5(3x - 2)$
   C) $-5(3x + 2)$
   D) $5(3x - 2)$

Evaluating Functions: Practice 1

$$f(x) = \left(\frac{1}{2}\right)^x + 1$$

9. The function f is defined by the equation above. Which of the following is the graph of $y = -f(x)$ in the xy-plane?

A)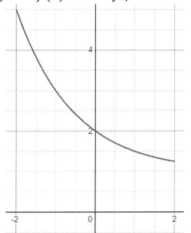

B)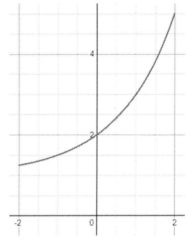

C)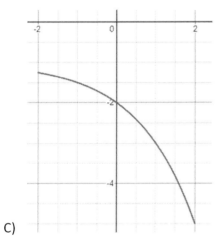

D)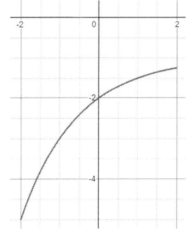

Evaluating Functions: Practice 1

x	$w(x)$	$t(x)$
1	-5	-6
2	-2	-2
3	1	2
4	4	6
5	7	10

10. The table above shows some values of the functions w and t. For which value of x is $w(x) + t(x) = x$?
    A) 1
    B) 2
    C) 3
    D) 4

Evaluating Functions: Practice 2

x	1	2	3	4	5
y	$\frac{2}{3}$	$\frac{7}{3}$	4	$\frac{17}{3}$	$\frac{22}{3}$

1. Which of the following equations relates y to x for the values in the table above?
   A) $y = \frac{5}{3}x - 1$
   B) $y = \frac{5}{3}x - 2$
   C) $y = \frac{5}{3}x - \frac{7}{3}$
   D) $y = \left(\frac{3}{5}\right)^x$

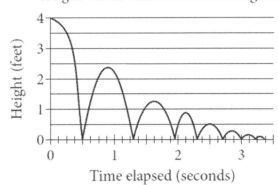

2. As part of a science experiment, a group of students dropped a ball at a height of 4 feet. The ball repeatedly bounces off the ground until it came to a rest. The graph above represents the relationship between the time elapsed after the ball was dropped and the height of the ball above the ground. After it was dropped, how many times was the ball at a height of 1 foot?
   A) Two
   B) Three
   C) Four
   D) Five

Evaluating Functions: Practice 2

3. If $f(x) = \dfrac{x^2+5x-7}{x-3}$, what is $f(2)$?
   A) -8
   B) -7
   C) 6
   D) 7

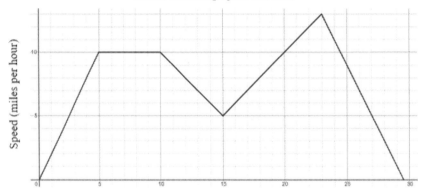

4. Serena ran on a treadmill for about thirty minutes, and her time and speed are shown on the graph above. According to the graph, which of the following statements is true concerning Serena's run?
   A) Serena ran at a constant speed for the first five minutes of her run.
   B) Serena's speed increased, stay constant, and decreased for the first 15 minutes.
   C) Serena's speed was decreasing from 15 minutes to 23 minutes.
   D) Serena's speed was decreasing for a longer period of time than it was increasing,

$$g(x) = \dfrac{1}{2}x - 2$$
$$h(x) = 3 - g(x)$$

5. The functions g and h are defined above. What is the value of $h(6)$?
   A) 0
   B) 1
   C) 2
   D) 3

Evaluating Functions: Practice 2

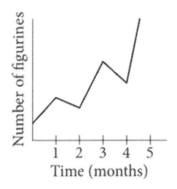

6. Samuel collects, sells, and trades figures, and he tracks the number of figurines in her collection on the graph below. On what interval did the number of figurines increase the fastest?
   A) Between 1 and 2 months
   B) Between 2 and 3 months
   C) Between 3 and 4 months
   D) Between 4 and 5 months

Evaluating Functions: Practice 2

7. The range of the polynomial function f is the set of all real numbers greater than or equal to -1. If the zeros of f are -6 and -4, which of the following could be the graph of $y = f(x)$ in the xy-plane?

A)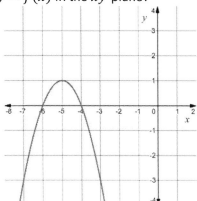

B)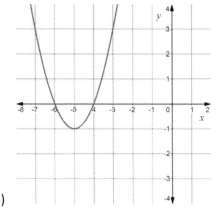

C)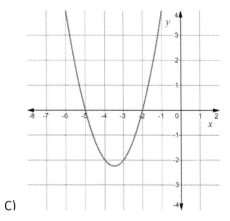

D)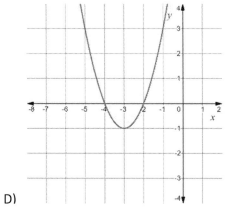

Evaluating Functions: Practice 2

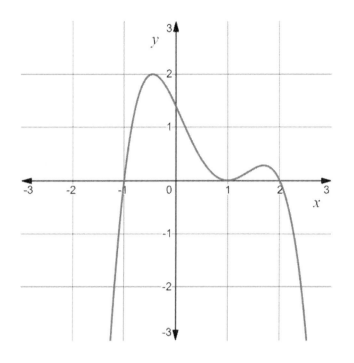

x	$g(x)$
-2	0
-1	2
0	4
1	6
2	8
3	10
4	12

8. The complete graph of the function f and a table of values for the function g are shown above. The maximum value of f is k. What is the value of $g(k)$?
   A) -2
   B) -1
   C) 0
   D) 8

Evaluating Functions: Practice 2

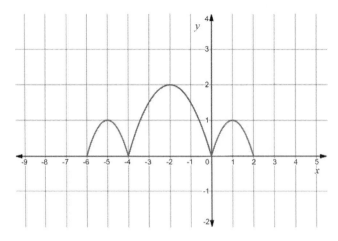

9. The figure above shows the complete graph of the function f in the xy-plane. The function g (not shown) is defined by $g(x) = f(x) - 5$. What is the maximum value of the function g?

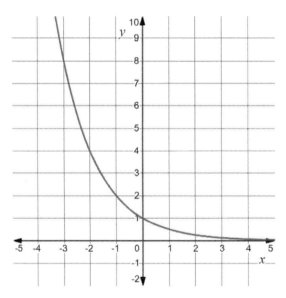

10. The graph of $y = f(x)$ is shown in the xy-plane. What is the value of $f(-3)$?
    A) 8
    B) 4
    C) 1
    D) 0

Evaluating Functions Explanations

Evaluating Functions 1

1. B

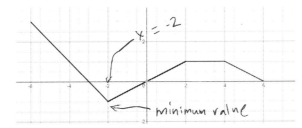

2. D

$g(x) = ax^2 + 8x + 8$

$2 = a(-1)^2 + 8(-1) + 8$

$2 = a - 8 + 8$

$2 = a$

3. A

$a = 2.10t + 2030$

$2000 = 2.10t + 2030$

$-30 = 2.10t$

$-14.2 = t$

4. B

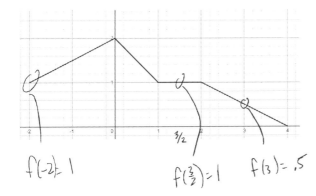

5. 742

$N = 500 + .5(500)\left(1 - \frac{500}{1000}\right)$

$N = 625 \leftarrow$ in 1 year

$N = 625 + .5(625)\left(1 - \frac{625}{1000}\right)$

$N = 742.18 \leftarrow$ in 2 years

round to 742

6. 2500

$700 = 500 + .5(500)\left(1 - \frac{500}{K}\right)$

$700 = 500 + 250\left(1 - \frac{500}{K}\right)$

$200 = 250\left(1 - \frac{500}{K}\right)$

$\frac{200}{250} = \frac{250\left(1 - \frac{500}{K}\right)}{250}$

$.8 = 1 - \frac{500}{K}$

$-1 \quad -1$

$-.2 = -\frac{500}{K}$

$-.2(K) = -\frac{500(K)}{K}$

$-.2K = -500$

$\frac{-.2K}{-.2} = \frac{-500}{-.2}$

$K = 2500$

Evaluating Functions Explanations

7. B

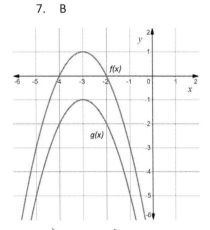

A) $f(-4) + g(-4)$
$0 + -2 = -2$

B) $f(-3) + g(-3)$
$1 + -1 = 0$

C) $f(-2) + g(-2)$
$0 + -2 = -2$

D) $f(-1) + g(-1)$
$-3 + -5 = -8$

8. B

$f(x) = -5x + 10$

$f(3x) = -5(3x) + 10$

$f(3x) = -15x + 10$

can factor out -5

$-5(3x - 2)$

9. D

$y = \frac{1}{2}^x + 1$

$f(0) = \frac{1}{2}^0 + 1 = 1 + 1 = 2 ; (0, 2)$

$= \frac{1}{2}^1 + 1 = \frac{1}{2} + 1 = 1.5 ; (1, 1.5)$

if $-f(x)$, negate the y-values
$(0, -2)$ and $(1, -1.5)$

10. C

x	w(x)	t(x)
1	-5	-6
2	-2	-2
3	1	2
4	4	6
5	7	10

Evaluating Functions 2

1. A

x	1	2	3	4	5
y	$\frac{2}{3}$	$\frac{7}{3}$	$\frac{12}{3}$	$\frac{17}{3}$	$\frac{22}{3}$

$+\frac{5}{3}$ $+\frac{5}{3}$ $+\frac{5}{3}$ $+\frac{5}{3}$

Evaluating Functions Explanations

slope = $\frac{5}{3}$

find the y-int

x	1	2	3	4	5
y	$\frac{2}{3}$	$\frac{7}{3}$	4	$\frac{17}{3}$	$\frac{22}{3}$

0, $-\frac{3}{3}$, $-\frac{5}{3}$

y-int = $-\frac{3}{3}$ = -1

$y = mx + b$
$y = \frac{5}{3}x - 1$

4. B

constant, decrease, increase

15 minutes

2. D

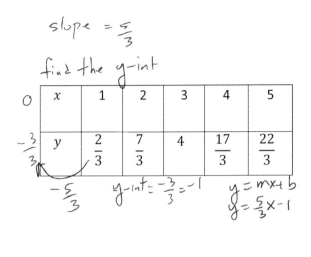

5. C

$h(x) = 3 - g(x)$
$h(6) = 3 - g(6)$

we need to calculate $g(6)$

$g(x) = \frac{1}{2}x - 2$
$g(6) = \frac{1}{2}(6) - 2$
$g(6) = 1$

$h(6) = 3 - g(6)$
$h(6) = 3 - 1$
$h(6) = 2$

3. B

$f(x) = \dfrac{x^2 + 5x - 7}{x - 3}$

$f(2) = \dfrac{(2)^2 + 5(2) - 7}{2 - 3}$

$f(2) = \dfrac{4 + 10 - 7}{-1}$

$f(2) = -7$

Evaluating Functions Explanations

6. D

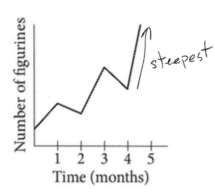
steepest

8. D

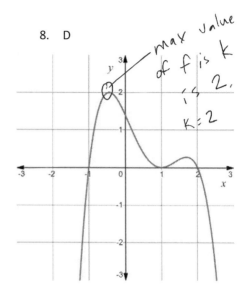

max value of f is k is 2.
k = 2

7. B

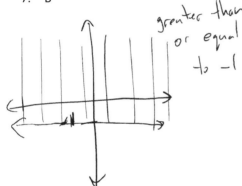
greater than or equal to −1

$g(k) = g(2)$
       ↑ x = 2

x	g(x)
-2	0
-1	2
0	4
1	6
2	8
3	10
4	12

x = 2

g(2) = 8

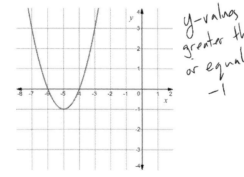
y-values are greater than or equal to −1

Evaluating Functions Explanations

9. 7

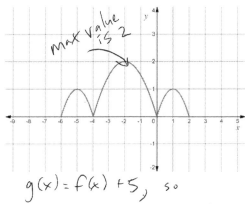

$f(-3) \rightarrow$ y-value when $x = -3$

$f(-3) = 8$

$g(x) = f(x) + 5$, so
$g(x)$ is the same as $f(x)$ but shifted up 5.
All y-values are 5 greater.

If the maximum value of $f(x)$ is 2, then the maximum value of $g(x)$ is $2 + 5 = 7$

10. A

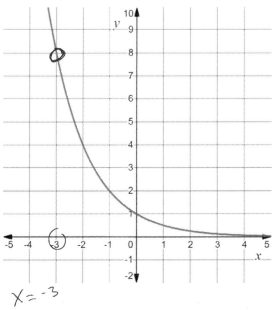

$x = -3$

Linear Functions: Practice 1

1. On a snowy day, the thickness of the snow accumulated on the ground can be estimated using the equation $T = 4.2 + 0.39h$, where T is the thickness of the snow in inches and h is the number of hours that it snowed. What does the value 4.2 represents in the equation?
    A) The initial thickness of the snow before it started snowing on that day.
    B) The number of hours it took for the snow to accumulate.
    C) The amount of snow that falls every hour.
    D) The number of days that it snowed.

2. Due to climate change, a certain lake's water level can be modelled using the equation $L = 3.29 + 2.14T$, where L is the water level of the lake in meters and T is the increase in temperature in degree Celsius. Based on the model, what is the estimated change in the water level per degree Celsius?
    A) 1.15
    B) 2.14
    C) 3.29
    D) 5.43

3. A line in the xy-plane passes through the point $(0, 1)$ and has a slope of -1. Which of the following points lies on the line?
    A) $(-2, 1)$
    B) $(3, 1)$
    C) $(3, 2)$
    D) $(3, -2)$

Linear Functions: Practice 1

4. The frequency recorded by an oscilloscope is shown in the graph below. On which interval is the frequency strictly decreasing then strictly increasing?

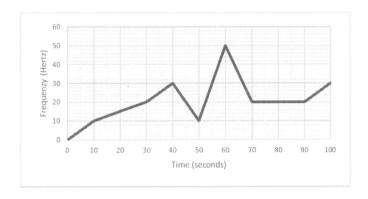

A) Between 50 and 60 seconds
B) Between 60 and 80 seconds
C) Between 40 and 60 seconds
D) Between 0 and 10 seconds

5. If $y = kx + 4$, where k is a constant, and $y = 32$ when $x = 4$, what is the value of y when $x = 8$?
A) 28
B) 45
C) 52
D) 60

Questions 6 & 7 refer to the following information.

A lemon plant was bought at an orchard. The graph below displays the total height (H) of the lemon plant every year (y) since it was bought.

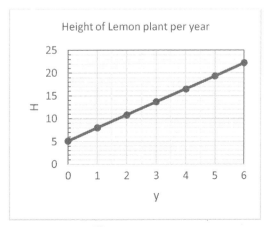

Linear Functions: Practice 1

6. What does the H-intercept represent in the graph?
   A) The initial height of the plant when it was bought.
   B) The height of the plant after 2 years.
   C) The years it took to reach 5 inches.
   D) The increase in height of the plant per year.

7. Which of the following equations best represents the relationship between H and y?
   A) $H = 5.16 - 2.34y$
   B) $H = 5.16 + 2.84y$
   C) $H = 2.84 + 5.16y$
   D) $H = 2.16 + 5.14y$

8. The line $y = kx - 6$, where k is a constant, is graphed in the xy-plane. If the line contains the point (a, b), where $a \neq 0$ and $b \neq 0$, what is the slope of the line in terms of a and b?
   A) $\dfrac{b+6}{a}$
   B) $\dfrac{b-6}{a}$
   C) $\dfrac{-a+6}{b}$
   D) $\dfrac{a-6}{b}$

9. The equation $V_f = V_0 + 9.8t$ is used to compute the final velocity, V_f, of an object at a given initial velocity, V_0, and time, t. If the object starts at 2.5 m/s, which of the following statements must be true?
   I. A one-second increase in t is equivalent to a velocity increase in V_f of 9.8
   II. A one-second increase in t is equivalent to a velocity increase in V_0 of 9.8
   III. A velocity increase of 1 in V_f is equivalent to $\dfrac{5}{49}$ increase in t
   A) I only
   B) II only
   C) III only
   D) I and III only

10. The table below shows some values of the linear function f. Which of the following defines f?

n	1	2	3	4
$f(n)$	3	7	11	15

    A) $f(n) = 3n - 1$
    B) $f(n) = 3n + 6$
    C) $f(n) = 4n - 1$
    D) $f(n) = -4n + 3$

Linear Functions: Practice 1

11. The average number of apples per tree can be estimated using the equation $y = 53.6t + 320$, where y is the estimated number of apples and t is the number of years after the 3rd year of planting. Which of the following best describes the value 53.6 in the equation?
    A) The estimated number of apples per tree after the 3rd year
    B) The estimated increase in the average number of apples per tree per year after the 3rd year
    C) The number of years after the 3rd year
    D) The number of apples per year on the farm

12. In a supermarket, the demand for Good Y is given by the function $Q = 320 - 15p$, where Q is the quantity demanded per month and p is the price of Good Y per unit in dollars. How will the quantity demand change for every $1 increase in price of Good Y?
    A) The quantity demanded will increase by 10 units.
    B) The quantity demanded will increase by 15 units.
    C) The quantity demanded will decrease by 15 units.
    D) The quantity demanded will decrease by 320 units.

13. In a recipe, n pans of caramel custard are made by adding x number of eggs. If $x = 3n + 2$, how many eggs are needed to make an additional pan of custard?
    A) 2
    B) 3
    C) 5
    D) 6

14. A dancer walks an average of 2.5 hours per day. If 30 minutes of walking burns 180 calories and the dancer wants to burn 150 more calories, which of the following equations can she use to determine how many additional hours, t, should she walk every day?
    A) $1050 = 360t + 900$
    B) $1050 = 360t + 2.5$
    C) $150 = 180t - 900$
    D) $150 = 180t + 2.5$

Linear Functions: Practice 1

15. Some values of the linear function f are shown in the table below. Which of the following defines f?

x	$f(x)$
1	11
3	29
5	47

A) $f(x) = 10x - 3$
B) $f(x) = 10x + 1$
C) $f(x) = 9x + 2$
D) $f(x) = 8x + 5$

16. A family home magazine plans to increase its subscribers by n subscribers per month. If there were s subscribers last month, which function best models the total number of subscribers, t, the magazine will have m months from now?
A) $t = mn$
B) $s = mn + t$
C) $t = ms + n$
D) $t = mn + s$

17. In the xy-plane, the graph of which of the following equations is perpendicular to the graph of $4x + y = 2$?
A) $8x - 2y = 7$
B) $8y + 2 = 4$
C) $4y - x = 3$
D) $4x + y = 9$

Linear Functions: Practice 2

Questions 1, 2 & 3 refer to the following information.

1. The table below shows different varieties of cheese and their corresponding moisture factor. In a study conducted, the moisture content (%) of a cheese can be approximated by multiplying the age, in days, by the moisture factor. What is the approximate moisture content of a Mozzarella cheese that is 7 days old?

Variety	Moisture Factor
Romano	1.06
Havarti	2.80
Cheddar	3.14
Colby	3.97
Brick	5.50
Mozzarella	7.37

   A) 51.6%
   B) 38.5%
   C) 27.8%
   D) 19.6%

2. The scatterplot below gives the moisture content % plotted against age for 20 cheeses of a certain variety. The moisture factor of this variety is closest to that of which of the following variety of cheese?

   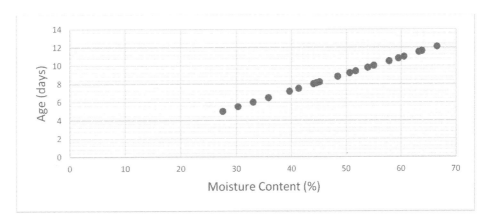

   A) Havarti
   B) Colby
   C) Cheddar
   D) Brick

Linear Functions: Practice 2

3. If a Havarti and a Cheddar cheese each now have a moisture content of approximate 25%. Which of the following will be the closest difference, in days, of their ages?
    A) 1 day
    B) 2 days
    C) 3 days
    D) 10 days

4. A large equipment rental company invested in 5 different machines listed below. The table shows the amount, in dollars, the company paid for each machine P and the corresponding monthly rental price R, in dollars, the company charges for each machine. Which of the following equations best represents the relationship between P and R?

Machine	Purchase Price (P)	Rental Price (R)
Machine A	45,000	8,995
Machine B	20,000	3,995
Machine C	5,700	1,135
Machine D	32,000	6,395
Machine E	17,000	3,395

A) $P = 15R + 35$
B) $P = 20R + 45$
C) $P = 5R + 25$
D) $P = 10R - 15$

Linear Functions: Practice 2

5. The graph of the linear function f is shown in the xy-plane below. The slope of the graph of linear function g is 8 times the slope of graph of f. If the graph of g passes through $(3, 0)$, what is the value of $g(7)$?

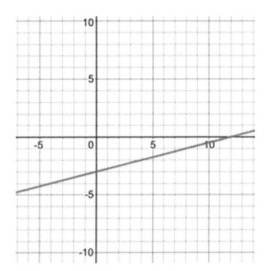

A) 20
B) 17
C) 12
D) 8

6. A restaurant charges a one-time corkage fee for serving bottles of wine in an event on top of the service fee per bottle. The equation $F = 5b + 30$, where F represents the total amount in dollars the guests will pay for b number of bottles. What does 5 represent in the equation?
  A) The total amount for serving the bottles of wine.
  B) The number of bottles of wine.
  C) The corkage fee.
  D) The service fee per bottle of wine.

Linear Functions: Practice 2

7. Which of the following is the graph of $y = 7x - 2$ in the xy-plane?

A)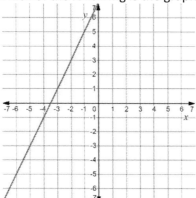

B)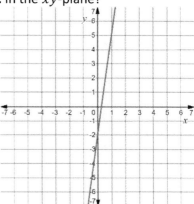

C)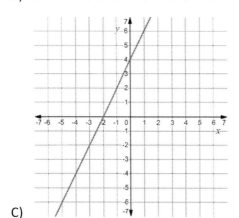

D)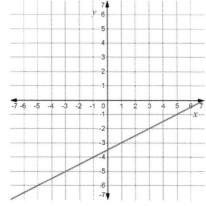

Linear Functions: Practice 2

8. The graph below shows the altitude of 2 balloons, balloon A and balloon B, filled with different gases were that released one after the other. According to the graph, how many seconds apart were the balloons released?

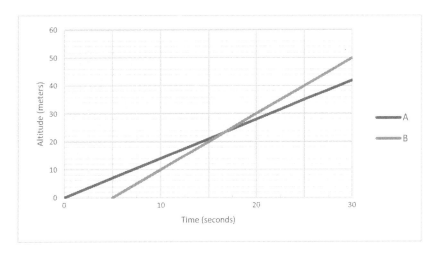

   A) 10 seconds
   B) 30 seconds
   C) 5 seconds
   D) 20 seconds

9. The graph below shows the approximate wingspan of a certain owl specie over the years. The function $w = ay + b$, where a and b are constants, models the wingspan of the owl, in feet, after y years. What does a represents in the equation?

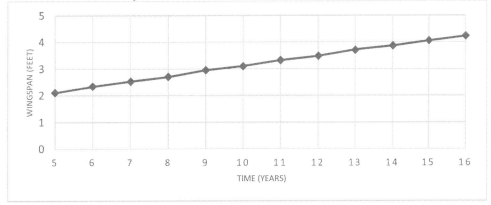

   A) The approximate increase in wingspan of the owl every year
   B) The approximate wingspan of the owl before the 5th year
   C) The approximate increase in wingspan of the owl after 8 years
   D) The approximate wingspan of the owl after 16 years

Linear Functions: Practice 2

10. The data table shows the approximate wingspan of an owl specie over the years. On this interval, which of the following best models the wingspan, w, in feet, of the owl after y years?
    A) $w = 0.36y + 3.4$
    B) $w = 0.29y - 1.9$
    C) $w = 0.24y - 2.8$
    D) $w = 0.19y + 1.2$

11. Some values of the linear function f are shown in the table below. What is the value of $f(4)$?

x	f(x)
0	-4
2	8
6	32

    A) 20
    B) 24
    C) 36
    D) 56

12. The line with equation $\frac{2}{5}x + \frac{1}{4}y = 2$ is graphed in the xy-plane. What is the x-coordinate of the x-intercept of the line?
    A) 6
    B) 5
    C) 3
    D) 2

13. The graph of a line in the xy-plane passes through the point (2,2) and crosses the y-axis at the point (0,6). The line crosses the x-axis at the point (a, 0). What is the value of a?
    A) -3
    B) -1
    C) 2
    D) 3

14. The equation $y = 15x + 60$ models the total amount, y, in dollars, that a ski resort charges a customer to rent a ski gear for x number of hours. The total amount includes a one-time lift fee and the charge per hour of rent. When the equation is graphed in xy-plane, what does the y-intercept of the graph represent in terms of the model?
    A) The charge per hour of $15.
    B) The rental fee of the ski gear of $15.
    C) The one-time lift fee of $60.
    D) The daily charge the customer pays of $75.

Linear Functions: Practice 2

15. The graph below shows the number of calories for every gram of carbohydrate. According to the graph, which of the following is the approximate increase in calories for every 1-gram increase in carbohydrate?

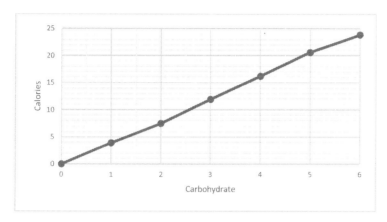

A) 2
B) 4
C) 6
D) 8

16. In the xy-plane, a point with coordinates (a, b) lies on the graph of linear function shown below. If a and b are positive integers, what is the ratio of b to a?

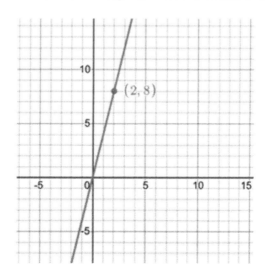

A) 8:1
B) 1:8
C) 4:1
D) 1:4

Linear Functions: Practice 2

17. A linear function is shown in the graph below. What is the approximate slope?

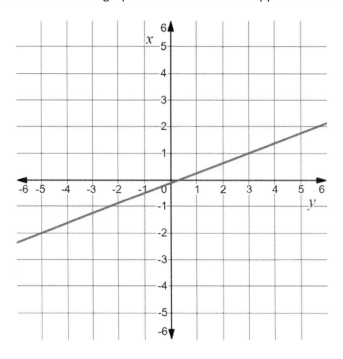

A) $\dfrac{3}{8}$
B) 3
C) $-\dfrac{3}{8}$
D) 8

Linear Functions 1

1. A

$y = mx + b$

m = slope (rate), b = y-int (initial)

$T = 0.39h + 4.2$

2. B

$y = mx + b$

m = slope (rate), b = y-int (initial)

$L = 2.14T + 3.29$

3. D

$y = mx + b$

$(0,1) \Rightarrow$ y-int is 1

slope $= -1$

$y = -x + 1$

check answers

D. $(3, -2)$

$y = -x + 1$

$-2 = -3 + 1$

$-2 = -2$ ✓

4. C

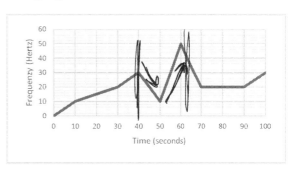

5. D

$y = Kx + 4$

We need to find the value of k

$y = Kx + 4$

$32 = K(4) + 4$

$-4 \quad\quad -4$

$28 = 4K$

$7 = K$

Now, we can find the value of y when $x = 8$

$y = 7x + 4$

$y = 7(8) + 4$

$y = 60$

Linear Functions Explanations

6. A

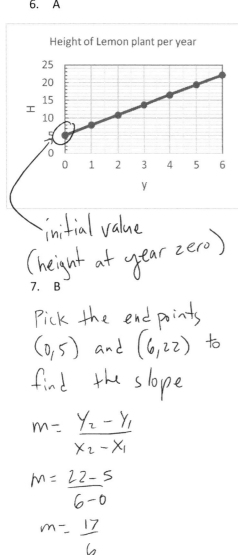

↳ initial value
(height at year zero)

7. B

Pick the end points
$(0,5)$ and $(6,22)$ to
find the slope

$m = \dfrac{y_2 - y_1}{x_2 - x_1}$

$m = \dfrac{22 - 5}{6 - 0}$

$m = \dfrac{17}{6}$

$m = 2.83$

$y = mx + b$
$y = 2.83x + 5$
$H = 5.16 + 2.84y$
is the closest.
It can be rewritten
as $H = 2.84y + 5.16$

8. A

$m = \dfrac{y_2 - y_1}{x_2 - x_1}$

one point is (a, b)

We also know the y-int is -6,
so another point is $(0, -6)$

$\dfrac{b - -6}{a - 0} = \dfrac{b + 6}{a}$

9. D

$V_f = \underset{\uparrow}{9.8} t + V_0$

$\dfrac{\text{change in } V_f}{\text{change in time}} = \dfrac{9.8}{1}$

(choice I)

Also,

$\dfrac{\text{change in } V_f}{\text{change in } t} = \dfrac{9.8 \div 9.8}{1 \div 9.8} = \dfrac{1}{1/9.8}$

$\dfrac{\text{change in } V_f}{\text{change in } t} = \dfrac{1}{5/49}$

(choice III)

Linear Functions Explanations

10. C

n	1	2	3	4
$f(n)$	3	7	11	15

+4 +4 +4

$m = \frac{4}{1} = 4$

go backwards to find y-int

n	0	1	2	3	4
$f(n)$	-1	3	7	11	15

$y = 4x - 1$

11. B

$y = 53.6t + 320$
       ↑
     slope
     (rate)

slope = $\frac{\text{change in } y}{\text{change in } t}$ = $\frac{\text{change in apples}}{\text{change in years}}$

gives change in apples per year

12. C

$Q = 320 - 15P$
      ↑   ↑
   initial slope (rate)

$\frac{\text{change in } Q}{\text{change in } P}$ = $\frac{-15 \text{ demanded}}{\$1 \text{ price change}}$

13. B

eggs   pans
  ↓   ↓
$x = 3n + 2$

rate = $\frac{3 \text{ eggs}}{1 \text{ pan}}$

14. A

$\frac{1}{2}$ hr = 180 calories

$\frac{\text{hour}}{\text{cal}}$ $\frac{0.5}{180} = \frac{2.5}{x}$

$0.5x = 450$
$x = 900$

2.5 hours ⇒ 900 calories

900 is the starting value, the y-int

1 hr = 360 calories

$1050 = 360t + 900$

15. C

x	$f(x)$
1	11
3	29
5	47

2→ }18
2→ }18

slope = $\frac{18}{2} = 9$

Linear Functions Explanations

work backwards to find the y-int

x	f(x)
1	11
3	29
5	47

$y = 9x + 2$

16. D

initial value is s (y-int)
rate is n (slope)

$y = mx + b$
$ \uparrow \uparrow \uparrow$
$t n m s$

$t = nm + s$

17. C

perpendicular lines have slopes that are negative reciprocals, so we need to find the slope

$4x + y = 7$
$-4x -4x$

slope $= y = -4x + 7$

Perpendicular slope $= \frac{1}{4}$

check answers.

c) $4y + x = 3$
$ +x +x$

$\frac{4y}{4} = \frac{x}{4} + \frac{3}{4}$

$y = \frac{1}{4}x + 3$

$m = \frac{1}{4}$

Linear Functions 2

1. A

$7,37$
$\times 7$
$\overline{51,59}$

2. D

moisture content $=$ age $\times$ moisture factor

moisture factor $= \dfrac{\text{moisture content}}{\text{age}}$

Try some points

$\dfrac{33}{6} = 5.5 \leftarrow$ moisture factor

$\dfrac{66}{12} = 5.5 \leftarrow$

Linear Functions Explanations

Brick has a moisture factor of 5.5

3. A

Havarti
$$(M.C) = (age)(M.F.)$$
$$25 = x(2.8)$$
$$8.9 = x$$

Cheddar
$$(M.C.) = (age)(M.F.)$$
$$25 = x(3.14)$$
$$7.9 = x$$

$$8.9 - 7.9 = 1$$

4. C

Find the slope by using 2 points (R, P)

$(8,995, 45,000)$
$(1,135, 5,700)$

$$\frac{45,000 - 5,700}{8,995 - 1,135} = \frac{39,300}{7,860} = 5$$

Only C has a slope of 5

5. D

find the slope of f using the points (12,0) and (0,-3) from the graph

$$\frac{0 - -3}{12 - 0} = \frac{3}{12} = \frac{1}{4}$$

Slope of g is 8 times slope of f

$$8\left(\frac{1}{4}\right) = 2$$

g
$$y = 2x + b$$
find b
$$0 = 2(3) + b$$
$$0 = 6 + b$$
$$-6 = b$$
$$y = 2x - 6$$

$g(7)$
$$y = 2(7) - 6$$
$$y = 8$$

Linear Functions Explanations

6. D

$F = 5b + 30$
   ↑   ↑
  rate   initial

7. B

$y = 7x - 2$ y-int = -2
               $m = 7 = \frac{7}{1}$

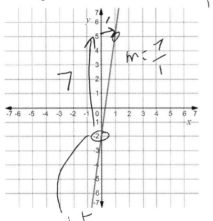

8. y-int

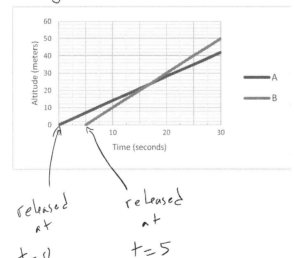

released at $t = 0$ released at $t = 5$

9. A

$a =$ slope $= \dfrac{\text{change in wingspan}}{\text{year}}$

10. D

Find slope using 2 points
$(5, 2.1)$ and $(16, 4.25)$

$\dfrac{4.25 - 2.1}{16 - 5} = \dfrac{2.15}{11} = .195$

$y = mx + b$
$y = .195x + b$ solve for b

$4.25 = .195(16) + b$

$4.25 = 3.12 + b$
$1.13 = b$

$y = .195x + 1.13$

choice D is closest

11. A

linear, so we can find the slope

x	f(x)
0	-4
2	8
6	32

2 ⟨ ⟩ 12

$\dfrac{12}{2} = 6$

Linear Functions Explanations

Fill in the table

x	f(x)
2	8
3	14
4	20
5	26
6	32

(differences of 6)

$f(4) = 20$

12. B

x-int is when $y = 0$

$\frac{2}{5}x + \frac{1}{4}y = 2$

$\frac{2}{5}x + \frac{1}{4}(0) = 2$

$\frac{2}{5}x = 2$

$\left(\frac{5}{2}\right)\frac{2}{5}x = 2\left(\frac{5}{2}\right)$

$x = 5$

13. D

$(2, 2)$ and $(0, 6)$ ← y-int

$\text{Slope} = \frac{y_2 - y_1}{x_2 - x_1} = \frac{6-2}{0-2} = \frac{4}{-2} = -2$

$y = mx + b$
$y = -2x + 6$
at $(a, 0)$

$0 = -2a + 6$
$-6 = -2a$
$3 = a$

14. C

$y = \underset{\underset{\text{(rate)}}{\text{slope}}}{15}x + \underset{\underset{\text{(initial)}}{\text{y-int}}}{60}$

15. B

$\text{Slope} = \frac{\text{calories}}{\text{carbohydrates}}$

$\text{Slope} = \frac{4 \text{ cal.}}{1 \text{ carb.}}$

16. C

$(2, 8)$
(a, b)

b : a
8 : 2
4 : 1

Linear Functions Explanations

17. A

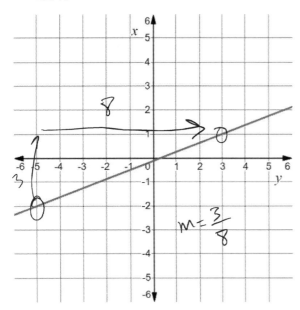

Quadratic Functions: Practice 1

1. If $(ax + 4)(bx + 5) = 10x^2 + cx + 20$ for all values of x, and $a + b = 7$, what are the two possible values of c?

    A) 9 and 15
    B) 20 and 25
    C) 30 and 33
    D) 40 and 42

2. If $t > 0$ and $t^2 - 25 = 0$, what is the value of t?

3. $h = -3.6t^2 + 22t$

    The equation above expresses the approximate height h, in meters, of a ball t seconds after it is launched vertically upward from the ground with an initial velocity of 22 meters per second. After approximately how many seconds will the ball hit the ground?

    A) 4
    B) 6
    C) 8
    D) 10

Quadratic Functions: Practice 1

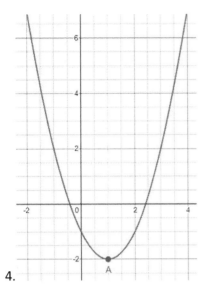

4.

Which of the following is an equivalent form of the equation of the graph $(x^2 - 2x - 1)$ shown in the xy-plane above, from which the coordinates of vertex A can be identified as constants in the equation?

A) $y = (x + 1)(x - 1)$
B) $y = (x - 1)^2 - 2$
C) $y = x(x - 1) - 2$
D) $y = (x + 1)(x + 1)$

5. $h(x) = \dfrac{1}{(x-8)^2 + 6(x-8) + 9}$

For what value of x is the function g above undefined?

6. $y = a(x - 11)(x + 5)$

In the quadratic equation above, a is a nonzero constant. The graph of the equation in the xy-plane is a parabola with vertex (c, d). Which of the following is equal to d?

A) $32a$
B) $-64a$
C) $-96a$
D) $-128a$

Quadratic Functions: Practice 1

7. What are the solutions to $3x^2 + 12x + 6 = 0$
   A) $x = -2 \pm \sqrt{2}$
   B) $x = -2 \pm \frac{\sqrt{64}}{3}$
   C) $x = -4 \pm \sqrt{8}$
   D) $x = -4 \pm \frac{\sqrt{8}}{3}$

8. $x^3(x^2 - 13) = -36x$

If $x > 0$, what is one possible solution to the equation above?

9. If the function f has 6 distinct zeroes, which of the following could represent the complete graph f in the xy-plane?

A)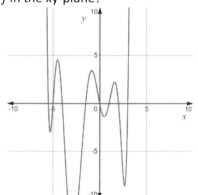

B)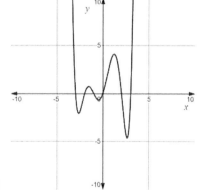

C)

D)

Quadratic Functions: Practice 1

10. What are the solutions of the quadratic equation $3x^2 - 21x - 54 = 0$?

   A) $x = 9$ and $x = 2$
   B) $x = -9$ and $x = -2$
   C) $x = 9$ and $x = -2$
   D) $x = -9$ and $x = 2$

11. What characteristics are true for all linear, exponential, and quadratic functions?
   A) The range of the function is all real numbers.
   B) The graph of the function has no intercepts.
   C) The graph of the function is always increasing.
   D) The domain of the function is all real numbers.

12. $$y = x^2 + 2kx + k^2$$
   In the equation above, a is a positive constant and the graph of the equation in the xy-plane is a parabola. Which of the following is an equivalent form of the equation?

   A) $y = (x + k)(x - k)$
   B) $-y = (x - 1)^2$
   C) $y = (x + k)^2$
   D) $y = (x - \sqrt{k})(x - \sqrt{k})$

13. $9x^2 - 49 = (bx + q)(bx - q)$
   In the equation above, b and q are constants. Which of the following could be the value of q?

   A) 3
   B) 4
   C) 7
   D) 9

Quadratic Functions: Practice 1

14. $$4x^2 - 8x - t = 0$$
In the equation above, t is a constant. If the equation has no real solutions, which of the following could be the value of t?

A) 5
B) 4
C) -4
D) -5

15. What is the positive difference of the solutions to $(x - 5)(x - 3.6) = 0$

A) 1.4
B) 8.6
C) -1.4
D) -8.6

16. The scatterplot below shows corporation's profit over 10 years.

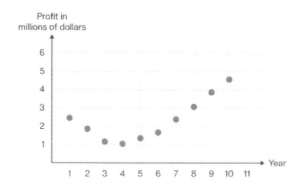

Of the following equations, which best models the data in the scatterplot?

A) $y = -0.1023x^2 + 0.8426x + 3.0767$
B) $y = 0.1023x^2 - 0.8426x + 3.0767$
C) $y = -0.1023^2 - 0.8426x - 3.0767$
D) $y = -0.1023x^2 + .08426x - 3.0767$

Quadratic Functions: Practice 1

17. $x^2 + 10x - 10$

Which of the following is equivalent to the expression above?

A) $(x - 5)^2 - 10$
B) $(x + 5)^2 - 35$
C) $(x + 5)^2 - 15$
D) $(x - 5)^2 + 10$

18. $ax^3 + bx^2 + cx + d = 0$

In the expression above a, b, c, and d are constants. If the equation has roots -4, 5, and 6, which of the following is a factor of $ax^3 + bx^2 + cx + d$?

A) $x - 4$
B) $x + 5$
C) $x + 6$
D) $x + 4$

19. The function f is defined by $f(x) = (x + 6)(x + 4)$. The graph f in the xy-plane is a parabola. Which of the following intervals contains the x-coordinate of the vertex of the graph f?

A) $-1 < x < 4$
B) $-4 < x < 1$
C) $-2 < x < 6$
D) $-6 < x < 2$

20. The expression $\frac{1}{3}x^2 - 3$ can be rewritten as $\frac{1}{3}(x - k)(x + k)$, where k is a positive constant. What is the value of k?

A) 3
A) $\sqrt{3}$
B) 6
C) $\sqrt{6}$

Quadratic Functions: Practice 1

21. In the equation $(ax + 3)^2 = 81$, a is a constant. If $x = -4$ is a solution to the equation, what is a possible value of a?

A) 1
B) 3
C) 9
D) 18

22. $h(t) = -32t^2 + 144t + 64$

The function above models the height h, in meters, of an object above the ground t seconds after being launched straight up in the air. What does the number 64 represent in the function?

A) The maximum height, in meters, of the object

B) The initial height, in meters, of the object

C) The initial speed, in meters per second, of the object

D) The maximum speed, in meters per second, of the object

Quadratic Functions: Practice 1

22. Which of the following could be the equation of the graph above?

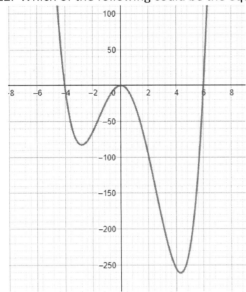

Which of the following could be the equation of the graph above?

A) $y = x(x - 4)(x + 6)$
B) $y = x^2(x + 4)(x - 6)$
C) $y = x(x + 4)(x - 6)$
D) $y = x^2(x - 4)(x + 6)$

24.
$y = x^2 + 6x + 9$
$y = 3x - 5$

How many solutions are there to the system of equations above?

A) There are exactly 2 solutions
B) There is exactly 1 solution
C) There are infinitely many soulutions
D) There are no solutions

25. $x^2 + 3x - 18 = 0$

If a is a solution of the equation above and $a > 0$, what is the value of a?

Quadratic Functions: Practice 1

26. The range of the polynomial function f is the set of real numbers greater than or equal to -9. If the zeros of f are -2 and 4, which of the following could be the graph of $y = f(x)$ in the xy-plane?

A)
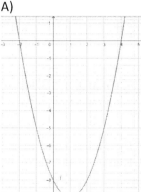

B)
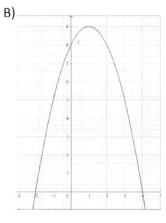

C)

D)

Quadratic Functions: Practice 1

27. The graph of the function f in the xy-plane above is a parabola. Which of the following defines f?

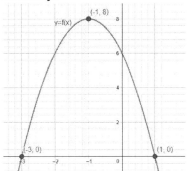

The graph of the function f in the xy-plane above is a parabola. Which of the following defines f?

A) $f(x) = -2(x-1)^2 + 8$
B) $f(x) = 3(x+1)^2 + 8$
C) $f(x) = 3(x-1)^2 + 8$
D) $f(x) = -2(x+1)^2 + 8$

28. $h(x) = -24^2 + 64x + 8$

The quadratic function above models the height above the ground h, in feet, of a projectile x seconds after it had been launched vertically. If $y = h(x)$ is graphed in the xy-plane, which of the following represents the real-life meaning of the positive x-intercept of the graph?

A) The initial height of the projectile
B) The maximum height of the projectile
C) The time at which the projectile hits the ground
D) The time at which the projectile reaches its maximum height

29. In the xy-plane, the graph of the polynomial function f crosses the x-axis at exactly two points, (a,0) and (b,0), where a and b are both negative. Which of the following could define f?

A) $f(x) = (x+a)(x-b)$
B) $f(x) = (x-a)(x-b)$
C) $f(x) = (x-a)(x+b)$
D) $f(x) = (x+a)(x+b)$

Quadratic Functions: Practice 1

30. If $y = 4x^2 + 12x + 3$ is graphed in the xy-plane, which of the following characteristics of the graph is displayed as a constant or coefficient in the equation?

   A) y-coordinate of the vertex
   B) y-intercept
   C) x-intercept(s)
   D) x-intercept of the line of symmetry

31.
$$\frac{x^2+5}{x-2} = -6, x \neq 2$$
What is one value of x that satisfies the equation?

   A) 5
   B) -7
   C) -6
   D) 2

32.

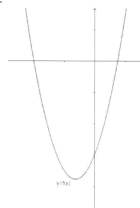

The graph of $y = 4x^2 + 5x - 6$ is shown. If the graph crosses the y-axis at point $(0, k)$, what is the value of k?

   A) -6
   B) -5
   C) 2
   D) 10

Quadratic Functions: Practice 1

33. In the xy-plane, the graph of the function $f(x) = x^2 - 14x + 24$ has two x-intercepts. What is the distance between the x-intercepts?

   A) 12
   B) 14
   C) 10
   D) 8

34. $y = (x - 1)^2 - a$

   In the equation above, a is a constant. The graph of the equation in the xy-plane is a parabola. Which of the following is true about the parabola?

   A) Its minimum occurs at $(-1, -a)$
   B) Its minimum occurs at $(1, -a)$
   C) Its maximum occurs at $(-1, -a)$
   D) Its maximum occurs at $(1, -a)$

Quadratic Functions: Practice 1

35. $f(x) = (x+4)(x-h)$

The function f is defined above. If k is a positive integer, which of the following could represent the graph of $y = f(x)$ in the xy-plane?

A)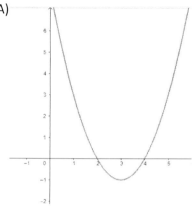

B)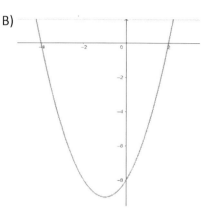

C)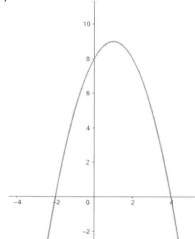

D)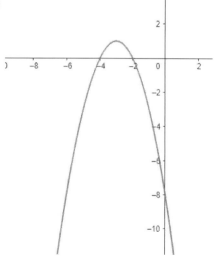

Quadratic Functions: Practice 2

1. If $(ax + 4)(bx + 5) = 14x^2 + cx + 20$ for all values of x, and $a + b = 9$, what are the two possible values of c?

    A) 9 and 15
    B) 20 and 25
    C) 30 and 33
    D) 38 and 43

2. If $t > 0$ and $t^2 - 16 = 0$, what is the value of t?

3. $h = -2.1t^2 + 36t$

    The equation above expresses the approximate height h, in meters, of a ball t seconds after it is launched vertically upward from the ground with an initial velocity of 36 meters per second. After approximately how many seconds will the ball hit the ground?

    A) 9
    B) 11
    C) 17
    D) 19

4. Which of the following is an equivalent form of the equation of the graph $y = x^2 - 12x + 20$ from which the coordinates of vertex can be identified as constants in the equation?

    A) $y = (x - 2)(x - 10)$
    B) $y = (x + 2)(x + 10)$
    C) $y = (x - 6)^2 - 16$
    D) $y = x(x - 6) - 38$

Quadratic Functions: Practice 2

5. $m(x) = \dfrac{1}{(x-6)^2 - 10(x-6) + 25}$

For what value of x is the function m above undefined?

6. $y = a(x - 10)(x + 4)$

In the quadratic equation above, a is a nonzero constant. The graph of the equation in the xy-plane is a parabola with vertex (c, d). Which of the following is equal to d?

A) $21a$
B) $-49a$
C) $-63a$
D) $-72a$

7. What are the solutions to $5x^2 - 10x - 9 = 0$?

A) $x = 1 \pm \dfrac{\sqrt{70}}{5}$
B) $x = -1 \pm 50$
C) $x = -2 \pm \sqrt{10}$
D) $x = -2 \pm \dfrac{\sqrt{45}}{3}$

8. $x^3(x^2 - 20) = -64x$

If x > 0, what is one possible solution to the equation above?

Quadratic Functions: Practice 2

9. If the function f has 8 distinct zeroes, which of the following could represent the complete graph f in the xy-plane?

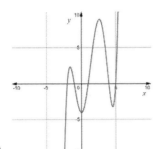
A)

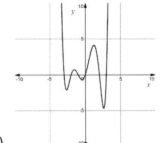
B)

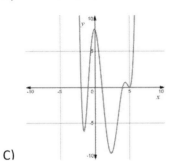
C)

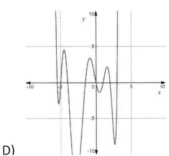
D)

10. What are the solutions of the quadratic equation $2x^2 + 12x - 80 = 0$?

A) $x = 4$ and $x = -10$
B) $x = -4$ and $x = -10$
C) $x = -4$ and $x = 10$
D) $x = 4$ and $x = -10$

Quadratic Functions: Practice 2

11. The graph of a quadratic function does not cross the x-axis, but crosses the y-axis in one place. Which of the following statements is correct?

    A) The quadratic function has two distinct real zeros.
    B) The quadratic function has no real zeros.
    C) The quadratic function has one distinct real zero.
    D) The quadratic function has two y-intercepts.

12. $y = x^2 - k^2$

    In the equation above, a is a positive constant and the graph of the equation in the xy-plane is a parabola. Which of the following is an equivalent form of the equation?

    A) $-y = (x - 1)^2$
    B) $y = (x + k)^2$
    C) $y = (x - \sqrt{k})(x - \sqrt{k})$
    D) $y = (x + k)(x - k)$

13. $36x^2 - 64 = (bx + q)(bx - q)$

    In the equation above, b and q are constants. Which of the following could be the value of q?

    A) 3
    B) 6
    C) 8
    D) 12

14. $3x^2 - 6x - t = 0$

    In the equation above, t is a constant. If the equation has no real solutions, which of the following could be the value of t?

    A) −4
    B) −3
    C) 3
    D) 4

Quadratic Functions: Practice 2

15. What is the positive difference of the solutions to $(x + 11)(x - 3.8) = 0$?

    A) -14.8
    B) -7.2
    C) 7.2
    D) 14.8

16. The scatterplot below shows the height of an object at certain points in time.

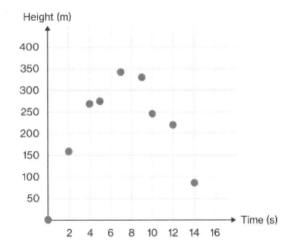

Of the following equations, which best models the data in the scatterplot?

    A) $y = 5.71883x^2 + 85.47x + 6.707$
    B) $y = -5.71883x^2 - 85.47x + 6.707$
    C) $y = -5.71883x^2 + 85.47x + 6.707$
    D) $y = 5.71883x^2 + 85.47x - 6.707$

17. $x^2 - 12x + 17$

    Which of the following is equivalent to the expression above?

    A) $(x - 6)^2 + 11$
    B) $(x + 6)^2 - 11$
    C) $(x + 6)^2 + 19$
    D) $(x - 6)^2 - 19$

18. $ax^3 + bx^2 + cx + d = 0$

In the expression above a, b, c, and d are constants. If the equation has roots -3, 4, and 7, which of the following is a factor of $ax^3 + bx^2 + cx + d$?

A) $x - 3$
B) $x + 3$
C) $x + 4$
D) $x + 7$

19. The function f is defined by $f(x) = (x + 5)(x + 7)$. The graph f in the xy-plane is a parabola. Which of the following intervals contains the x-coordinate of the vertex of the graph f?

A) $5 < x < 7$
B) $-5 < x < 7$
C) $-8 < x < -1$
D) $1 < x < 8$

20. The expression $\frac{1}{2}x^2 - 7$ can be rewritten as $\frac{1}{2}(x - k)(x + k)$, where k is a positive constant. What is the value of k?

A) 14
A) $\sqrt{14}$
B) 7
C) $\sqrt{7}$

21. In the equation $(ax - 6)^2 = 100$, a is a constant. If $x = 4$ is on solution to the equation, what is a possible value of a?

A) 6
B) 5
C) 4
D) 2

Quadratic Functions: Practice 2

22. $h(t) = -28t^2 + 100t + 49$

The function above models the height h, in meters, of an object above the ground t seconds after being launched straight up in the air. What does the number 49 represent in the function?

A) The maximum height, in meters, of the object

B) The initial speed, in meters per second, of the object

C) The initial height, in meters, of the object

D) The maximum speed, in meters per second, of the object

23.

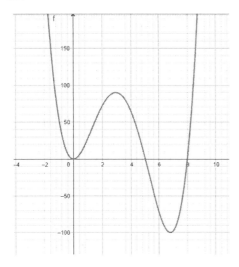

Which of the following could be the equation of the graph above?

A) $y = x(x - 8)(x - 5)$
B) $y = x^2(x + 8)(x + 5)$
C) $y = x(x + 8)(x + 5)$
D) $y = x^2(x - 8)(x - 5)$

Quadratic Functions: Practice 2

24.
$$y = x^2 + 8x + 12$$
$$y = -2x - 4$$
How many solutions are there to the system of equations above?

A) There are exactly 2 solutions
B) There is exactly 1 solution
C) There are infinitely many soulutions
D) There are no solutions

25. $x^2 + 4x - 32 = 0$

If a is a solution of the equation above and $a > 0$, what is the value of a?

26. The range of the polynomial function f is the set of real numbers less than or equal to 16. If the zeros of f are -2 and 6, which of the following could be the graph of $y = f(x)$ in the xy-plane?

A)
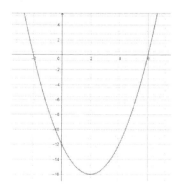

B)
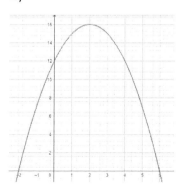

C)
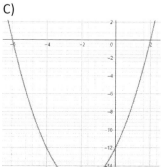

D)
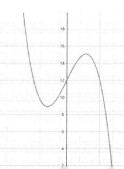

Quadratic Functions: Practice 2

27. The graph of the function f in the xy-plane above is a parabola. Which of the following defines f?

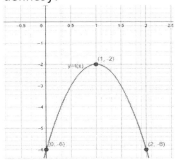

The graph of the function f in the xy-plane above is a parabola. Which of the following defines f?

A) $f(x) = 4(x+1)^2 - 2$
B) $f(x) = -2(x-1)^2 - 6$
C) $f(x) = -4(x-1)^2 - 2$
D) $f(x) = 2(x+1)^2 - 6$

28. $h(x) = -32^2 + 81x + 12$

The quadratic function above models the height above the ground h, in feet, of a projectile x seconds after it had been launched vertically. If $y = h(x)$ is graphed in the xy-plane, which of the following represents the real-life meaning of the positive x-intercept of the graph?

A) The initial height of the projectile
B) The time at which the projectile hits the ground.
C) The maximum height of the projectile
D) The time at which the projectile reaches its maximum height

29. In the xy-plane, the graph of the polynomial function f crosses the x-axis at exactly two points, (a,0) and (b,0), where a positive b is negative. Which of the following could define f?

A) $f(x) = (x+a)(x-b)$
B) $f(x) = (x-a)(x-b)$
C) $f(x) = (x-a)(x+b)$
D) $f(x) = (x+a)(x+b)$

Quadratic Functions: Practice 2

30. If $y = 2x^2 + 8x + 5$ is graphed in the xy-plane, which of the following characteristics of the graph is displayed as a constant or coefficient in the equation?
   A) y-coordinate of the vertex
   B) x-intercept(s)
   C) x-intercept of the line of symmetry
   D) y-intercept

31. $\frac{x^2+6}{x+2} = 3, x \neq -2$
   What are all values if x that satisfy the equation?

   A) −6
   B) −2
   C) 3
   D) 1

32. The graph of $y = 2x^2 + 10x + 15$ crosses the y-axis at point $(0, k)$, what is the value of k?

   A) 5
   B) 7.5
   C) 15
   D) 18

33. In the xy-plane, the graph of the function $f(x) = x^2 - 2x - 3$ has two x-intercepts. What is the distance between the x-intercepts?

   A) 6
   B) 4
   C) 5
   D) 8

34. $y = -2(x - 5)^2 + a$

   In the equation above, a is a constant. The graph of the equation in the xy-plane is a parabola. Which of the following is true about the parabola?

   A) Its minimum occurs at $(-5, a)$
   B) Its minimum occurs at $(5, a)$
   C) Its maximum occurs at $(-5, a)$
   D) Its maximum occurs at $(5, a)$

Quadratic Functions: Practice 2

35. $f(x) = (x - 1)(x - h)$

The function f is defined above. If h is a positive integer, which of the following could represent the graph of $y=f(x)$ in the xy-plane?

A)
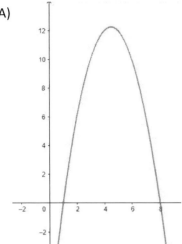

B)
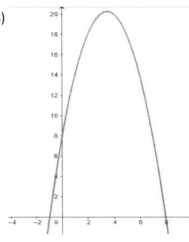

C)
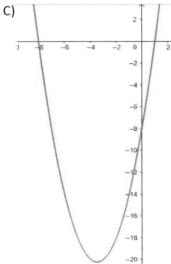

D)
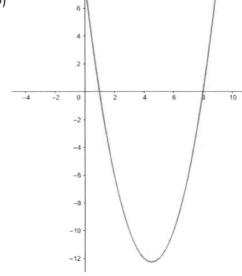

Quadratic Functions Explanations

Quadratic Functions 1

1. C

$(ax+4)(bx+5) = 10x^2 + cx + 20$

This tells us that a times b is 10.

We also know that $a + b = 7$, so a and b have to be 5 and 2.

$(5x+4)(2x+5) = 10x^2 + 25x + 8x + 20$

$= 10x^2 + 33x + 20$
          ↑
          c

The values of a and b could be switched.

$(2x+4)(5x+5) = 10x^2 + 10x + 20x + 20$

$10x^2 + 30x + 20$
        ↑
        c

c could be 33 or 30.

2. 5

$t^2 - 25 = 0$
$(t+5)(t-5) = 0$
$t = -5 \quad t = 5$
$t > 0$, so $t = 5$

3. B

$h = -3.6t^2 + 22t$
$0 = -3.6t^2 + 22t$
$0 = t(-3.6t + 22)$

$t = 0 \qquad -3.6t + 22 = 0$
$\qquad\qquad\qquad t = 6.1$

4. B

Choice B is the only equation in vertex form.

5. 5

An expression is undefined when the denominator is 0.

$(x-8)^2 + 6(x-8) + 9 = 0$

This is pretty complex. Let's use y to represent the term $x - 8$.

$y^2 + 6y + 9 = 0$
$(y+3)(y+3) = 0$
$y = -3$

$x - 8 = -3$
$x = 5$

6. B

$y = a(x-11)(x+5)$
$a(x-11)(x+5) = 0$
      ↓   ↓
   $x = 11$ $x = -5$

Quadratic Functions Explanations

The x-value of the vertex will be exactly in between the zeros.

$$\frac{11+-5}{2} = \frac{6}{2} = 3 \quad \text{(x-coordinate of vertex)}$$

$$y = a(x-11)(x+5)$$
$$y = a(3-11)(3+5)$$
$$y = -64a$$

7. A

Based on the answers, we probably should use the quadratic formula to find the solutions.

We can simplify the problem by dividing all of the terms by 3.

$$\frac{3x^2}{3} + \frac{12x}{3} + \frac{6}{3} = \frac{0}{3}$$

$$x^2 + 4x + 2 = 0$$

$$a=1, \; b=4, \; c=2$$

$$\frac{-b \pm \sqrt{b^2 - 4ac}}{2a}$$

$$\frac{-4 \pm \sqrt{4^2 - 4(1)(2)}}{2(1)}$$

$$\frac{-4 \pm \sqrt{8}}{2} = \frac{-4 \pm \sqrt{4}\sqrt{2}}{2}$$

$$\frac{-4 \pm 2\sqrt{2}}{2} = -2 \pm \sqrt{2}$$

8. 2 or 3

$$x^3(x^2 - 13) = -36x$$
$$x^5 - 13x^3 = -36x$$
$$x^5 - 13x^3 + 36x = 0$$
$$x(x^4 - 13x^2 + 36) = 0$$

$$x(x^4 - 13x^2 + 36) = 0$$
$$x(x^2 - 9)(x^2 - 4) = 0$$
$$x(x+3)(x-3)(x+2)(x-2) = 0$$
$$x=0 \quad x=-3 \quad x=3 \quad x=-2 \quad x=2$$

$$x > 0$$

2 or 3

9. B

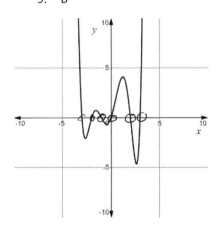

Quadratic Functions Explanations

10. C

$$\frac{3x^2}{3} - \frac{21x}{3} - \frac{54}{3} = \frac{0}{3}$$

$$x^2 - 7x - 18 = 0$$

$$(x-9)(x+2) = 0$$

$$x = 9 \quad x = -2$$

11. D

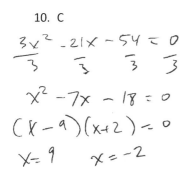

linear

exponential

quadratic

all 3 types of graphs continue infinitely to the left and right. Even if the graphs go up steeply, they are still changing x-value as they go up.

12. C

$$y = x^2 + 2kx + k^2$$

$(x+k)(x+k) \leftarrow$ this is a rule.

You can also check the answers.

A) $(x+k)(x+k) = x^2 + xk + xk + k^2$

$$x^2 + 2xk + k^2 \checkmark$$

13. C

$9x^2 - 49 \leftarrow$ This is the difference of perfect squares

$$9x^2 - 49$$
$$(3x + 7)(3x - 7)$$

14. D

$$4x^2 - 8x - t = 0$$

no real solutions $\Rightarrow \sqrt{\text{negative \#}}$

$$\frac{-b \pm \sqrt{b^2 - 4ac}}{2a}$$

$$\frac{8 \pm \sqrt{(-8)^2 - 4(4)(-t)}}{2(4)} \leftarrow \text{important part}$$

$64 + 16t < 0$ for no solution

$$16t < -64$$
$$t < -4$$

-5 is less than -4

15. A

$$(x-5)(x-3.6) = 0$$
$$x = 5 \quad x = 3.6$$
$$5 - 3.6 = 1.4$$

16. B

$$ax^2 + bx + c$$

Quadratic Functions Explanations

↑ so a is positive, and choices A, C, and D are wrong

17. B

$x^2 + 10x - 10$

complete the square

$\left(\dfrac{b}{2}\right)^2 = \left(\dfrac{10}{2}\right)^2 = 25$

$x^2 + 10x + 25 \quad -10 - 25$

$(x+5)(x+5) \quad -35$

$(x+5)^2 - 35$

Or check the answers

B) $(x+5)^2 - 35$

$(x+5)(x+5) - 35$

$x^2 + 5x + 5x + 25 - 35$

$x^2 + 10x - 10$ ✓

18. D

roots: $-4 \quad 5 \quad 6$

factors: $(x+4)(x-5)(x-6)$

19. D

$f(x) = (x+6)(x+4)$

↓

-6 & -4 are zeros

The x-value of the vertex will be exactly in between the zeros.

$\dfrac{-6 + -4}{2} = -5$ ← x-coordinate of the vertex

20. A

$\dfrac{1}{3}x^2 - 3$

1/3 is factored out, so factor it out first.

$\dfrac{1}{3}(x^2 - 9)$

$\dfrac{1}{3}(x+3)(x-3)$

21. B

$(ax+3)^2 = 81, \quad x = -4$

$(a(-4)+3)^2 = 81$

$(-4a+3)^2 = 81$

$\sqrt{(-4a+3)^2} = \sqrt{81}$

$-4a + 3 = \pm 9$

$\begin{array}{ll} -4a + 3 = 9 & -4a + 3 = -9 \\ \quad -3 \; -3 & \quad -3 \; -3 \\ -4a = 6 & -4a = -12 \\ \dfrac{-4a}{-4} = \dfrac{6}{-4} & \dfrac{-4a}{-4} = \dfrac{-12}{-4} \\ a = -3/2 & a = 3 \end{array}$

22. B

$h(t) = -32t^2 + 144t + 64$

64 is the y-intercept. It is the value of the function, the height, when $t = 0$. It's the initial height.

Quadratic Functions Explanations

23. B

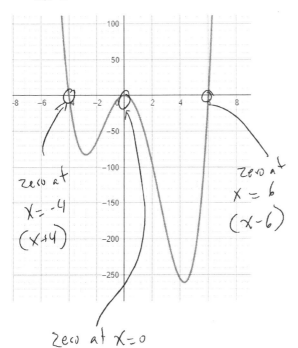

zero at $x = -4$
$(x+4)$

zero at $x = 6$
$(x-6)$

zero at $x = 0$
(x)
but it doesn't cross the x-axis, so there is duplicity $\to (x)^2$

$x^2(x+4)(x-6)$

24. B

$y = x^2 + 6x + 9$

$y = 3x - 5$

set them equal
$x^2 + 9x + 4 = 3x - 5$
solve for x by getting one side equal to 0

$$x^2 + 9x + 4 = 3x + 5$$
$$ +5 +5$$
$$x^2 + 9x + 9 = 3x$$
$$ -3x -3x$$
$$x^2 + 6x + 9 = 0$$
$$(x+3)(x+3) = 0$$
$$x = -3 \quad x = -3$$

One solution, $x = -3$

25. 3

$x^2 + 3x - 18 = 0$
$(x+6)(x-3) = 0$
$x = -6 \quad x = 3$
$a > 0$, so $x = 3$

26. A

zeros at -2 and 4

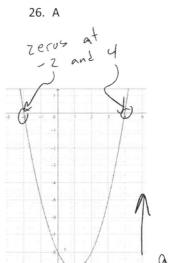

-9

Quadratic Functions Explanations

The range (y-values) of the functions are from −9 and up.

27. D

Vertex is at (-1, 8), so it has to resemble:

$(x+1)^2 + 8$

The parabola is upside down, so there has to be a negative coefficient in front, such as −2.

28. C

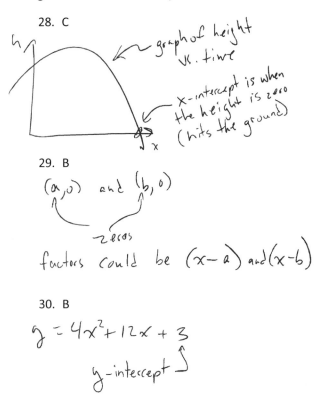

29. B

$(a, 0)$ and $(b, 0)$ — zeros

factors could be $(x-a)$ and $(x-b)$

30. B

$y = 4x^2 + 12x + 3$ ← y-intercept

31. B

$\frac{x^2+5}{x-2} = -6, x \neq 2$

$\frac{(x-2)\,x^2+5}{x-2} = -6(x-2)$

$x^2 + 5 = -6x + 12$
$+6x \quad\quad +6x$

$x^2 + 6x + 5 = 12$
$\quad\quad\quad -12 \;\; -12$

$x^2 + 6x - 7 = 0$

$(x+7)(x-1) = 0$

$\quad -7 \quad\quad 1$

32. A

$y = 4x^2 + 5x - 6$

$(0, k)$
 ↑ ↑
 x y

$k = 4(0)^2 + 5(0) - 6$

$k = -6$

33. C

$x^2 - 14x + 24 = 0$

$(x-12)(x-2) = 0$

 ↓   ↓
 12   2

$12 - 2 = 10$

34. B

$y = 2(x-1)^2 - a$

positive, so ∪ and has a minimum

$(x-1)^2 - a$
↓
$(+1, -a)$ ✓

Quadratic Functions Explanations

$(2x+4)(7x+5) = 14x^2 + 10x + 28x + 20$
$14x^2 + 38x + 20$
↑
c

35. B

$y = (x+4)(x-h)$
  ✓   ✓
-4 & h are zeros

c could be 43 or 38.

2. 4

$t^2 - 16 = 0$
$(t+4)(t-4) = 0$
   ↓   ↓
   -4 4

$t > 0$, so $t = 4$

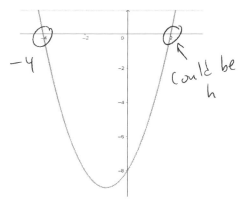

-4 ... could be h

It's not possible to know what h is, but it has to be a positive number.

Quadratic Functions 2

1. D

$(ax+4)(bx+5) = 14x^2 + cx + 20$

This tells us that a times b is 10.

We also know that $a + b = 7$, so a and b have to be 7 and 2.

$(7x+4)(2x+5) = 14x^2 + 35x + 8x + 20$
$14x^2 + 43x + 20$
↑
c

The values of a and b could be switched.

3. C

$h = -2.1t^2 + 36t$
$0 = -2.1t^2 + 36t$
$0 = t(-2.1t + 36)$

$t = 0$ $-2.1t + 36 = 0$
           $t = 17$

4. C

Choice C is the only equation in vertex form.

5. 11

An expression is undefined when the denominator is 0.

$(x-6)^2 - 10(x-6) + 25 = 0$

This is pretty complex. Let's use y to represent the term $x - 6$.

Quadratic Functions Explanations

$y^2 - 10y + 25 = 0$

$(y-5)(y-5) = 0$

$y = 5 \quad y = 5$

$\boxed{x - 6 = 5}$

$x = 11 \quad$ remember $y = x - 6$

6. B

$y = a(x - 10)(x + 4)$

$\quad\quad\quad\quad\downarrow \quad\quad\quad \downarrow$

$\quad\quad\quad\quad 10 \quad\quad -4$

The x-value of the vertex will be exactly in between the zeros.

$\dfrac{10 + -4}{2} = \dfrac{6}{2} = 3 \quad$ x-coordinate of vertex

$y = a(3 - 10)(3 + 4)$

$y = a(-7)(7)$

$y = -49a$

7. A

Based on the answers, we probably should use the quadratic formula to find the solutions.

$\dfrac{-b \pm \sqrt{b^2 - 4ac}}{2a}$

$\dfrac{10 \pm \sqrt{10^2 - 4(5)(-9)}}{2(5)}$

$\dfrac{10 \pm \sqrt{280}}{10} = \dfrac{10 \pm \sqrt{4}\sqrt{70}}{10}$

$\dfrac{10 \pm 2\sqrt{70}}{10} = \dfrac{10}{10} \pm \dfrac{2\sqrt{70}}{10}$

$1 \pm \dfrac{\sqrt{70}}{5}$

8. 2 or 4

$x^3(x^2 - 20) = -64x$

$x^5 - 20x^3 = -64x$

$\quad\quad\quad\quad +64x \quad +64x$

$x^5 - 20x^3 + 64x = 0$

$x(x^4 - 20x^2 + 64) = 0$

$x(x^2 - 16)(x^2 - 4) = 0$

$x(x+4)(x-4)(x+2)(x-2) = 0$

$\downarrow \quad \downarrow \quad \downarrow \quad \downarrow \quad \downarrow$

$0 \quad -4 \quad 4 \quad -2 \quad 2$

$x > 0, \text{ so } x = 2 \text{ or } 4$

Quadratic Functions Explanations

9. D

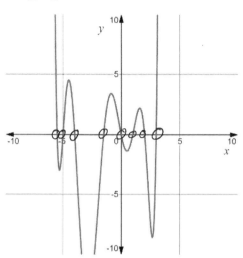

10. D

$$2x^2 + 12x - 80 = 0$$
$$\overline{} \quad \overline{}$$
$$2 2$$

$$x^2 + 6x - 40 = 0$$
$$(x+10)(x-4) = 0$$
$$\downarrow \downarrow$$
$$-10 4$$

11. B

for example
crosses the y-axis, but doesn't cross the x-axis.
No x-intercepts, so no real zeros

12. D

This is the difference of perfect squares.

Just like $x^2 - 9 = (x + 3)(x - 3)$, where 3 is the square root of 9,

$x^2 - k^2 = (x + \sqrt{k})(x - \sqrt{k})$, where $\sqrt{k}$ is the square root of k

13. C

$$36x^2 - 64 = (bx + q)(bx - q)$$

This is the difference of perfect squares.

Just like $x^2 - 9 = (x + 3)(x - 3)$, where x is the square root of x^2 and 3 is the square root of 9,

$36x^2 - 64 = (6x + 8)(6x - 8)$, where $6x$ is the square root of $36x^2$ and 8 is the square root of 64

14. A

$$3x^2 - 6x - t = 0$$

no real solutions → $\sqrt{\text{negative } \#}$

$$\frac{-b \pm \sqrt{b^2 - 4ac}}{2a}$$

$$\frac{6 \pm \sqrt{36 - 4(3)(-t)}}{6}$$

$$\frac{6 \pm \sqrt{36 + 12t}}{6} \quad \leftarrow \text{important part}$$

$36 + 12t < 0$ for no solution

$$36 + 12t < 0$$
$$-36 -36$$

$$\frac{12t}{12} < \frac{-36}{12}$$

$$t < -3$$

Quadratic Functions Explanations

-4 is less than -3

15. D

$(x+11)(x-3.8) = 0$
↓   ↓
-11 3.8

$3.8 - ^-11 = 14.8$

16. B

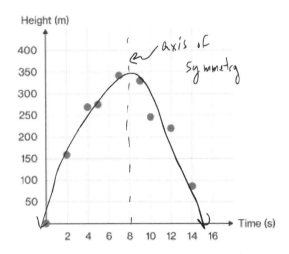

↙ so negative in front of x^2,
so A & D are wrong

The axis of symmetry is found using the formula $x = -\frac{b}{a}$, since the axis of symmetry is a positive number, b must be a negative number.

17. D

$x^2 - 12x + 17$

complete the square

$\left(\frac{b}{2}\right)^2 = \left(\frac{-12}{2}\right)^2 = 36$

$x^2 - 12x + 36 \quad +17 - 36$
$(x-6)(x-6) \quad - 19$
$\boxed{(x-6)^2 - 19}$

or check the answers

D. $(x-6)^2 - 19$
$(x-6)(x-6) - 19$
$x^2 - 6x - 6x + 36 - 19$
$x^2 - 12x + 17$

18. B

roots: -3 4 7
         ↓   ↓   ↓
factors: $(x+3)$ $(x-4)$ $(x-7)$

19. C

$f(x) = (x+5)(x+7)$
         ↓   ↓
        -5 & -7 are zeros

The x-value of the vertex will be exactly in between the zeros.

$\frac{-5 + ^-7}{2} = \frac{-12}{2} = -6$

(x-coordinate of the vertex)

Quadratic Functions Explanations

20. A

$$\frac{1}{2}x^2 - 7$$

1/2 is factored out, so factor it out first.

$$\frac{1}{2}(x^2 - 14)$$

14 isn't a perfect square, but we can still use the difference of perfect squares to factor.

$$\frac{1}{2}(x^2 - 14)$$
$$\frac{1}{2}(x + \sqrt{14})(x - \sqrt{14})$$

21. C

$$(ax - 6)^2 = 100$$
$$(4a - 6)^2 = 100$$
$$\sqrt{(4a-6)^2} = \sqrt{100}$$
$$4a - 6 = \pm 10$$

$4a - 6 = 10$ $4a - 6 = -10$
$+6 \quad +6$ $+6 \quad +6$
$4a = 16$ $4a = -4$

$\frac{4a}{4} = \frac{16}{4}$ $\frac{4a}{4} = \frac{-4}{4}$

$a = 4$ $a = -1$

22. C

$h(t) = -28t^2 + 100t + 49$

49 is the y-intercept. It is the value of the function, the height, when $t = 0$. It's the initial height.

23. D

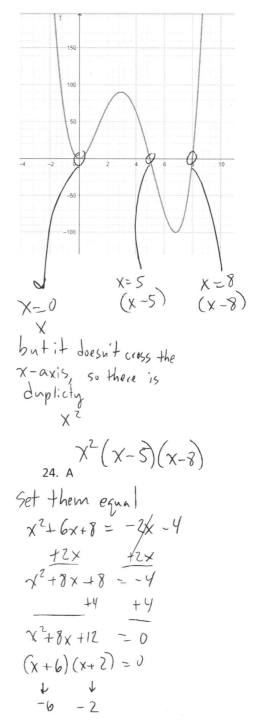

$x = 0$ $x = 5$ $x = 8$
x $(x-5)$ $(x-8)$

but it doesn't cross the x-axis, so there is duplicity

x^2

$x^2(x-5)(x-8)$

24. A

Set them equal

$x^2 + 6x + 8 = -2x - 4$
$\quad\quad +2x \quad\quad\quad +2x$
$x^2 + 8x + 8 = -4$
$\quad\quad\quad\quad +4 \quad\quad +4$
$x^2 + 8x + 12 = 0$
$(x+6)(x+2) = 0$
$\quad\downarrow \quad\quad\quad \downarrow$
$\quad -6 \quad\quad -2$

Quadratic Functions Explanations

25. 4

2 solutions

$$x^2 + 4x - 32 = 0$$
$$(x+8)(x-4) = 0$$
$$\downarrow \qquad \downarrow$$
$$-8 \qquad 4$$

$x > 0$, so $x = 4$

26. B

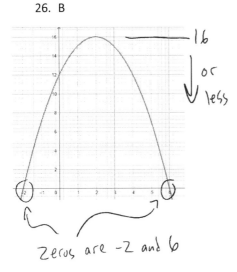

16 or less

Zeros are -2 and 6

27. C

Vertex is at (1, -2), so it has to resemble:

$(x-1)^2 - 2$

The parabola is upside down, so there has to be a negative coefficient in front, such as -4.

28. B

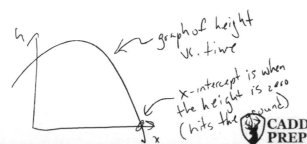

graph of height vs. time

x-intercept is when the height is zero (hits the ground)

29. B

$(a, 0)$ and $(b, 0)$ — zeros

factors could be $(x-a)$ and $(x-b)$

30. D

$y = 2x^2 + 8x + 5$ — y-intercept

31. C

$$(x+2)\frac{x^2 + 6}{x+2} = 3(x+2)$$

$$x^2 + 6 = 3x + 6$$
$$-3x \quad -3x$$

$$x^2 - 3x + 6 = 6$$
$$-6 \quad -6$$

$$x^2 - 3x = 0$$
$$x(x-3) = 0$$
$$\downarrow \quad \downarrow$$
$$0 \quad 3$$

32. C

$$y = 2x^2 + 10x + 15$$
$$(0, k)$$
$$\uparrow \quad \uparrow$$
$$x \quad y$$

$$k = 2(0)^2 + 10(0) + 15$$
$$k = 15$$

Quadratic Functions Explanations

33. B

$$x^2 - 2x - 3$$
$$(x-3)(x+1)$$
$$\downarrow \quad \downarrow$$
$$3 \quad -1$$

$$3 - -1 = 4$$

34. D

$$y = -2(x-5)^2 + a$$

negative so ⌢
and has a maximum

$$y = -2(x-5)^2 + a$$
Vertex: $(5, a)$

35. D

$$y = (x-1)(x-h)$$

1 & h are zeros

$$y = (x-1)(x-h)$$

When you multiply it out, the coefficient of x^2 is positive, so the graph will look like ⌣

No Solution & Infinite Solutions: Practice 1

1) What value of a will result in infinite solutions to the system of equations shown below?

   $3x + 2y = 5$

   $9x + ay = 15$

   A) -9
   B) 3
   C) 6
   D) 8

2) What value of a will result in no solution to the system of equations shown below?

   $6x + 5y = 9$

   $4x + ay = 8$

   A) 3
   B) $\frac{10}{3}$
   C) 4
   D) $\frac{15}{2}$

3) How many solutions does the system of equations shown below have?

   $y = 2x + 5$

   $y = x^2 - x + 9$

   A) 0
   B) 1
   C) 2
   D) 3

No Solution & Infinite Solutions: Practice 1

4) How many solutions does the system of equations shown below have?

$y = -2x + 1$

$y = x^2 + 3x - 2$

A) 0
B) 1
C) 2
D) 3

5) How many solutions does the system of equations shown below have?

$y = 3x - 7$

$y = x^2 - 3x + 2$

A) 0
B) 1
C) 2
D) 3

6) What value of t will result in no real solutions?

$3x = x^2 + t$

A) 3
B) 2
C) 1
D) -1

No Solution & Infinite Solutions: Practice 2

1) What value of a will result in infinite solutions to the system of equations shown below?

   $2x + 5y = 8$

   $4x = ay + 16$

   A) -10
   B) -2
   C) 2
   D) 10

2) What value of a will result in no solution to the system of equations shown below?

   $2y = 3x - 7$

   $5y = ax + 6$

   A) -3
   B) 3
   C) $\frac{6}{5}$
   D) $\frac{15}{2}$

3) How many solutions does the system of equations shown below have?

   $y = -2x + 3$

   $y = x^2 + 6x + 19$

   A) 0
   B) 1
   C) 2
   D) 3

No Solution & Infinite Solutions: Practice 2

4) How many solutions does the system of equations shown below have?

$y + 3 = 4x$

$y = x^2 + x - 1$

A) 0
B) 1
C) 2
D) 3

5) How many solutions does the system of equations shown below have?

$y = -4x + 7$

$y = x^2 - 2x + 10$

A) 0
B) 1
C) 2
D) 3

6) What value of t will result in no real solutions?

$-6x - t = x^2$

A) 3
B) 2
C) 1
D) -1

No Solution & Infinite Solutions Explanations

No Solution & Infinite Solutions 1

1. C

$3x + 2y = 5$

$9x + ay = 15$

The two equations above are linear equations. We will end up with infinite solutions if the two equations are the exact same equations.

To better compare them, let's solve for y in both of them.

First equation:

$3x + 2y = 5$

$-3x \quad\quad -3x$

$2y = -3x + 5$

$\dfrac{2y}{2} = \dfrac{-3x + 5}{2}$

$y = -\dfrac{3}{2}x + \dfrac{5}{2}$

Second equation:

$9x + ay = 15$

$-9x \quad\quad -9x$

$ay = -9x + 15$

$\dfrac{ay}{a} = \dfrac{-9x + 15}{a}$

$y = -\dfrac{9}{a}x + \dfrac{15}{a}$

The slopes of the two linear functions must be equal and the y-intercepts must be the same also.

Solve for the value of a that makes them equal.

Slopes:

$\dfrac{-3}{2} = \dfrac{-9}{a}$

$-3a = -18$

$\dfrac{-3a}{-3} = \dfrac{-18}{-3}$

$a = 6$

The same can be done with the y-intercepts.

y-intercept:

$\dfrac{5}{2} = \dfrac{15}{a}$

$15a = 30$

$\dfrac{15a}{15} = \dfrac{30}{15}$

$a = 2$

No Solution & Infinite Solutions Explanations

2. B

$$6x + 5y = 9$$
$$4x + ay = 8$$

The two equations above are linear equations. We will end up with no solution if the two equations are parallel: have the same slope and different y-intercepts.

To better compare them, let's solve for y in both of them.

First equation:
$$6x + 5y = 9$$
$$-6x \qquad -6x$$
$$5y = -6x + 9$$
$$\frac{5y}{5} = \frac{-6x + 9}{5}$$
$$y = -\frac{6}{5}x + \frac{9}{5}$$

Second Equation:
$$4x + ay = 8$$
$$-4x \qquad -4x$$
$$ay = -4x + 8$$
$$\frac{ay}{a} = \frac{-4x + 8}{a}$$

$$y = \frac{-4}{a}x + \frac{8}{a}$$

We need the same slopes, so set the slopes equal and solve for a.

$$-\frac{6}{5} = \frac{-4}{a}$$

$$-6a = -20$$

$$\frac{-6a}{-6} = \frac{-20}{-6}$$

$$a = \frac{10}{3}$$

3. A

$$y = 2x + 5$$
$$y = x^2 - x + 9$$

To find the number of solutions, we can solve each equation for y and then set them equal to each other.

The two equations are already solved for y, so we can just set them equal to each other.

$$2x + 5 = x^2 - x + 9$$

Since there is an x^2, we have a quadratic equation. We should solve to get one side of the equation equal to zero, so we can factor or use the quadratic formula.

No Solution & Infinite Solutions Explanations

$2x + 5 = x^2 - x + 9$

$\underline{-2x \qquad\qquad -2x}$

$5 = x^2 - 3x + 9$

$5 = x^2 - 3x + 9$

$\underline{-5 \qquad\qquad -5}$

$0 = x^2 - 3x + 4$

This doesn't factor, so we should use the quadratic formula.

$a = 1, \ b = -3, \ c = 4$

$x = \dfrac{-b \pm \sqrt{b^2 - 4ac}}{2a}$

$x = \dfrac{-(-3) \pm \sqrt{(-3)^2 - 4(1)(4)}}{2(1)}$

$x = \dfrac{3 \pm \sqrt{9 - 16}}{2}$

$x = \dfrac{3 \pm \sqrt{-7}}{2}$

$\sqrt{-7}$ is imaginary,

so we have no real roots

4. C

$y = -2x + 1$

$y = x^2 + 3x - 2$

To find the number of solutions, we can solve each equation for y and then set them equal to each other.

The two equations are already solved for y, so we can just set them equal to each other.

$-2x + 1 = x^2 + 3x - 2$

Since there is an x^2, we have a quadratic equation. We should solve to get one side of the equation equal to zero, so we can factor or use the quadratic formula.

$-2x + 1 = x^2 + 3x - 2$

$\underline{+2x \qquad\qquad +2x}$

$1 = x^2 + 5x - 2$

$\underline{-1 \qquad\qquad -1}$

$0 = x^2 + 5x - 3$

This doesn't factor, so we should use the quadratic formula.

$a = 1, \ b = 5, \ c = -3$

$x = \dfrac{-b \pm \sqrt{b^2 - 4ac}}{2a}$

No Solution & Infinite Solutions Explanations

$$x = \frac{-5 \pm \sqrt{5^2 - 4(1)(-3)}}{2(1)}$$

$$x = \frac{-5 \pm \sqrt{25 + 12}}{2}$$

$$x = \frac{-5 \pm \sqrt{37}}{2}$$

we have 2 real solutions

$$\frac{-5 + \sqrt{37}}{2} \text{ and } \frac{-5 - \sqrt{37}}{2}$$

5. B

$y = 3x - 7$

$y = x^2 - 3x + 2$

To find the number of solutions, we can solve each equation for y and then set them equal to each other.

The two equations are already solved for y, so we can just set them equal to each other.

$$3x - 7 = x^2 - 3x + 2$$

Since there is an x^2, we have a quadratic equation. We should solve to get one side of the equation equal to zero, so we can factor or use the quadratic formula.

$$\begin{aligned} 3x - 7 &= x^2 - 3x + 2 \\ -3x & -3x \\ \hline -7 &= x^2 - 6x + 2 \\ +7 & +7 \\ \hline 0 &= x^2 - 6x + 9 \end{aligned}$$

We can factor this.

$$0 = x^2 - 6x + 9$$
$$0 = (x - 3)(x - 3)$$

We have a repeated factor of $(x - 3)$, so we end up with one solution $x = 3$.

The question asked for the number of solutions, so the answer is 1.

6. A

$3x = x^2 + t$

The equation above is a quadratic equation. It will have no real solutions if we get a negative number under the radical (the discriminant is negative) when we use the quadratic formula.

$$x = \frac{-b \pm \sqrt{b^2 - 4ac}}{2a}$$

$$b^2 - 4ac < 0$$

No Solution & Infinite Solutions Explanations

We have to get one side of the equation equal to zero first, so we can identify the values of a, b, and c.

$$3x = x^2 + t$$
$$-3x \qquad -3x$$
$$0 = x^2 - 3x + t$$

$a = 1$, $b = -3$, $c = t$

$$b^2 - 4ac < 0$$
$$(-3)^2 - 4(1)(t) < 0$$
$$9 - 4t < 0$$
$$+4t \quad +4t$$
$$9 < 4t$$
$$\frac{9}{4} < \frac{4t}{4}$$
$$2.25 < t$$

t could be any number greater than 2.25, so from the answers 3 is the answer.

No Solution & Infinite Solutions 2

1. A

$2x + 5y = 8$

$4x = ay + 16$

The two equations above are linear equations. We will end up with infinite solutions if the two equations are the exact same equations.

To better compare them, let's solve for y in both of them.

First equation:
$$2x + 5y = 8$$
$$-2x \qquad -2x$$
$$5y = -2x + 8$$
$$\frac{5y}{5} = \frac{-2x + 8}{5}$$
$$y = \frac{-2}{5}x + \frac{8}{5}$$

Second Equation:
$$4x = ay + 16$$
$$-16 \qquad -16$$
$$4x - 16 = ay$$

No Solution & Infinite Solutions Explanations

$$\frac{4x-16}{a} = \frac{ay}{a}$$

$$\frac{4}{a}x - \frac{16}{a} = y$$

The two equations above are linear equations. We will end up with no solution if the two equations are parallel: have the same slope and different y-intercepts.

To better compare them, let's solve for y in both of them.

The slopes of the two linear functions must be equal and the y-intercepts must be the same also.

First Equation

$$\frac{2y}{2} = \frac{3x-7}{2}$$

$$y = \frac{3}{2}x - \frac{7}{2}$$

Solve for the value of a that makes them equal.

$$\frac{-2}{5} = \frac{4}{a}$$

$$-2a = 20$$

$$\frac{-2a}{-2} = \frac{20}{-2}$$

$$a = -10$$

Second Equation

$$\frac{5y}{5} = \frac{ax+6}{5}$$

$$y = \frac{a}{5}x + \frac{6}{5}$$

The same can be done with the y-intercepts.

$$\frac{8}{5} = \frac{-16}{a}$$

$$8a = -80$$

$$a = -10$$

We need the same slopes, so set the slopes equal and solve for a.

$$\frac{3}{2} = \frac{a}{5}$$

2. D

$2y = 3x - 7$

$5y = ax + 6$

$$15 = 2a$$

No Solution & Infinite Solutions Explanations

$$\frac{15}{2} = \frac{2a}{2}$$

$$\frac{15}{2} = a$$

3. B

$y = -2x + 3$

$y = x^2 + 6x + 19$

To find the number of solutions, we can solve each equation for y and then set them equal to each other.

The two equations are already solved for y, so we can just set them equal to each other.

$$-2x + 3 = x^2 + 6x + 19$$

Since there is an x^2, we have a quadratic equation. We should solve to get one side of the equation equal to zero, so we can factor or use the quadratic formula.

$$\begin{aligned}-2x + 3 &= x^2 + 6x + 19\\ +2x & \quad\quad\quad +2x\end{aligned}$$

$$3 = x^2 + 8x + 19$$

$$\begin{aligned}3 &= x^2 + 8x + 19\\ -3 & \quad\quad\quad\quad -3\end{aligned}$$

$$0 = x^2 + 8x + 16$$

We can factor this.

$$x^2 + 8x + 16 = 0$$
$$(x+4)(x+4) = 0$$

We have a repeated factor of $(x + 4)$, so we end up with one solution $x = -4$.

The question asked for the number of solutions, so the answer is 1.

4. C

$y + 3 = 4x$

$y = x^2 + x - 1$

To find the number of solutions, we can solve each equation for y and then set them equal to each other.

The second equation is already solved for y, so we have to solve for y in the first equation.

$$\begin{aligned}y + 3 &= 4x\\ -3 & \quad -3\end{aligned}$$

$$y = 4x - 3$$

Now, we can set the two equations equal to each other.

$$x^2 + x - 1 = 4x - 3$$

Since there is an x^2, we have a quadratic equation. We should solve to get one side of the equation equal to zero, so we can factor or use the quadratic formula.

No Solution & Infinite Solutions Explanations

Since there is an x^2, we have a quadratic equation. We should solve to get one side of the equation equal to zero, so we can factor or use the quadratic formula.

$$x^2 + x - 1 = 4x - 3$$
$$\underline{-4x \qquad -4x}$$
$$x^2 - 3x - 1 = -3$$

$$x^2 - 3x - 1 = -3$$
$$\underline{\quad +3 \qquad +3}$$
$$x^2 - 3x + 2 = 0$$

We can factor this.

$$x^2 - 3x + 2 = 0$$
$$(x-2)(x-1) = 0$$

$$x - 2 = 0 \qquad x - 1 = 0$$
$$x = 2 \qquad x = 1$$

2 solutions

5. A

$y = -4x + 7$

$y = x^2 - 2x + 10$

To find the number of solutions, we can solve each equation for y and then set them equal to each other.

The two equations are already solved for y, so we can just set them equal to each other.

$$x^2 - 2x + 10 = -4x + 7$$

$$x^2 - 2x + 10 = -4x + 7$$
$$\underline{+4x \qquad\qquad +4x}$$
$$x^2 + 2x + 10 = 7$$

$$x^2 + 2x + 10 = 7$$
$$\underline{\qquad -7 \quad -7}$$
$$x^2 + 2x + 3 = 0$$

This doesn't factor, so we should use the quadratic formula.

$$a = 1, b = 2, c = 3$$

$$x = \frac{-b \pm \sqrt{b^2 - 4ac}}{2a}$$

$$x = \frac{-2 \pm \sqrt{2^2 - 4(1)(3)}}{2(1)}$$

$$x = \frac{-2 \pm \sqrt{4 - 12}}{2}$$

$$x = \frac{-2 \pm \sqrt{-8}}{2}$$

No Solution & Infinite Solutions Explanations

$\sqrt{-8}$ is imaginary, so we have no real roots

6. A

$-6x - t = x^2$

The equation above is a quadratic equation. It will have no real solutions if we get a negative number under the radical (the discriminant is negative) when we use the quadratic formula.

$$x = \frac{-b \pm \sqrt{b^2 - 4ac}}{2a}$$

$$b^2 - 4ac < 0$$

We have to get one side of the equation equal to zero first, so we can identify the values of a, b, and c.

$$-6x - t = x^2$$
$$+6x \qquad\qquad +6x$$

$$-t = x^2 + 6x$$
$$+t \qquad\qquad +t$$

$$0 = x^2 + 6x + t$$

$$a = 1, \; b = 6, \; c = t$$

$$b^2 - 4ac < 0$$
$$6^2 - 4(1)(t) < 0$$
$$36 - 4t < 0$$
$$+4t \quad +4t$$

$$36 < 4t$$

$$\frac{36}{4} < \frac{4t}{4}$$

$$9 < t$$

t could be any number greater than 9, so from the answers 10 is the answer.

Percent: Practice 1

1. 75 % of 36 is the same as 20% of what number?
   A) 7.2
   B) 9.6
   C) 135
   D) 180

2. Billy bought a shirt at a store that gave a discount of 30% off the original price. The total amount paid was d dollars, including 8% sales tax added to the discounted price. Which of the following represents the original price in terms of d?

   A) $(1.08)(.70)(d)$
   B) $\dfrac{d}{(.70)(1.08)}$
   C) $(.08)(.30)d$
   D) $\dfrac{d}{(.08)(.30)}$

3. At a factory, one new machine produces 35% more widgets than the older machine. If the new machine produces 162 widgets in one hour, how many widgets does the old machine produce in an hour?
   A) 42
   B) 57
   C) 105
   D) 120

4. At a high school, 16% of the students are seniors, 20% of the students are juniors, 29% of the students are sophomores, and the rest are freshmen. If there are 400 seniors, how many freshmen are there?
   A) 380
   B) 760
   C) 875
   D) 1,200

Percent: Practice 1

5. An item normally costs d dollars. It is on sale for 24% off, and a customer has a coupon for an additional 20% off the discounted price. What is the final sale price of the item, in terms of d?
    A) $0.532d$
    B) $0.48d$
    C) $0.44d$
    D) $0.56d$

6. A jacket is on sale for $104 after a 20% discount. What was the original price of the jacket?
    A) $81
    B) $125
    C) $130
    D) $185

7. The sum of two numbers is 33. One number is 20% more than the other number. What is the smaller number?
    A) 6.6
    B) 7
    C) 13.2
    D) 15

8. Mariya bought x movie tickets for $14.95 each. If tax is an additional 8.5%, which of the following represents the total cost of the x movie tickets, in terms of x?
    A) $14.95x + (0.085)(14.95)$
    B) $(0.085)(14.95x)$
    C) $(0.915)(14.95x)$
    D) $(1.085)(14.95x)$

Percent: Practice 2

1. 40% of 18 is the same as 30% of what number?
    A) 32
    B) 24
    C) 11.25
    D) 5.4

2. Shawna bought a dress at a store that gave a discount of 40% off the original price. The total amount paid was d dollars, including 6% sales tax added to the discounted price. Which of the following represents the original price in terms of d?

    A) $(1.06)(.60)(d)$
    B) $(.06)(.40)d$
    C) $\dfrac{d}{(.06)(.40)}$
    D) $\dfrac{d}{(.60)(1.06)}$

3. In an office, one new printer prints 40% more papers than the older printer. If the new printer prints 252 pages in one hour, how many pages does the old printer print in an hour?
    A) 353
    B) 180
    C) 150
    D) 100

4. At a middle school, 30% of the students are 6th graders, 38% of the students are 7th graders, and the rest are 8th graders. If there are 133 7th graders, how many 8th graders are there?
    A) 43
    B) 112
    C) 128
    D) 217

Percent: Practice 2

5. An item normally costs d dollars. It is on sale for 30% off, and a customer has a coupon for an additional 15% off the discounted price. What is the final sale price of the item, in terms of d?
    A) $0.45d$
    B) $0.55d$
    C) $0.595d$
    D) $0.675d$

6. A laptop is on sale for $770 after a 30% discount. What was the original price of the jacket?
    A) $800
    B) $1,000
    C) $1,100
    D) $2,567

7. The sum of two numbers is 20.16. One number is 40% more than the other number. What is the smaller number?
    A) 6.05
    B) 8.06
    C) 8.4
    D) 12.1

8. Salvatore bought x kid's meals for $8.95 each. If tax is an additional 7%, which of the following represents the total cost of the x movie tickets, in terms of x?
    A) $0.07(8.95x)$
    B) $1.07(8.95x)$
    C) $0.93(8.95x)$
    D) $8.95x + 0.07(8.95)$

Percent Explanations

Percent 1

1. C

75% of 36 is the same as 20% of what number

$.75(36) = .20x$

$27 = .20x$

$\dfrac{27}{.20} = \dfrac{.20x}{.20}$

$135 = x$

2. B

paid = d
original = x

30% off, so $.70x$
additional 8% tax, so times 1.08

$1.08(.70x) = d$

Solve for x

$\dfrac{1.08(.70x)}{(1.08)(.70)} = \dfrac{d}{(1.08)(.70)}$

$x = \dfrac{d}{(1.08)(.70)}$

3. D

New machine does 35% more than old machine

New = 1.35 OLD

$162 = 1.35x$

$\dfrac{162}{1.35} = \dfrac{1.35x}{1.35}$

$120 = x$

4. C

Senior 16%
Junior 20%
Soph. 29%
―――
65%

100% − 65% = 35%

Freshmen are 35% of students

Percent Explanations

Use the information about the seniors to find the total number of students.

__Seniors__

$$\frac{\%}{100} = \frac{PART}{WHOLE}$$

$$\frac{16}{100} = \frac{400}{x}$$

$$16x = 40000$$

$$x = 2500$$

There are 2,500 students total in the school.

Now, find the number of freshmen.

__FRESHMEN__

$$\frac{\%}{100} = \frac{PART}{WHOLE}$$

$$\frac{35}{100} = \frac{x}{2500}$$

$$87500 = 100x$$

$$875 = x$$

5. A

24% off → .76d

20% off additional, so

0.80(.76d)

6. C

0.608d

original Price = x

20% off, so 80%

.80x = sale price

.80x = 104

$$\frac{.80x}{.80} = \frac{104}{.80}$$

x = 130

7. D

First # = x

2nd # is 20% more = 1.20x

The sum of the two numbers is 33

x + 1.2x = 33

Percent Explanations

$2.2x = 33$

$\dfrac{2.2x}{2.2} = \dfrac{33}{2.2}$

$x = 15$

8. D

Movie tickets are $14.95 each and there are x movie tickets, so the cost of movie tickets is

$$\$14.95x$$

There is an additional 8.5% tax, so the cost will be 108.5% of the cost before tax.

$$(1.085)(14.95x)$$

Percent 2

1. B

40% of 18 is the same as 30% of what number

$.4(18) = .30x$

$7.2 = .30x$

$24 = x$

2. D

paid = d
original = x

40% discount, so $.60x$
additional 6% tax,
so times 1.06

$1.06(.60x) = d$

Solve for x

$\dfrac{1.06(.60x)}{(1.06)(.60)} = \dfrac{d}{(1.06)(.60)}$

$x = \dfrac{d}{(1.06)(.60)}$

3. B

New printer does 40% more than old machine

New = 1.40 OLD

New = $1.40x$

$252 = 1.40x$

$180 = x$

Percent Explanations

4. B

6th   30%
7th   38%

       68%

100% − 68% = 32%

8th graders are 32% of students

Use the information about 7th graders to find the total number of students

7th

$$\frac{\%}{100} = \frac{PART}{WHOLE}$$

$$\frac{38}{100} = \frac{133}{x}$$

$38x = 13300$

$$\frac{38x}{38} = \frac{13300}{38}$$

$x = 350$
↑
total students

8th

$$\frac{\%}{100} = \frac{PART}{WHOLE}$$

$$\frac{32}{100} = \frac{x}{350}$$

$11200 = 100x$

$112 = x$

5. C

30% off, so pay 70%

.70 d

Additional 15% off, so 85%

$.85(.70d) = .595d$

6. C

original = x

30% off, so pay 70%

.70x = SALE PRICE

.70x = 770

Percent Explanations

$$\frac{.70x}{.70} = \frac{770}{.70}$$

$$x = 1,100$$

7. C

one # = x
2nd # is 40% more = $1.4x$

The sum of two numbers is 20.16

$$x + 1.4x = 20.16$$

$$2.4x = 20.16$$

$$\frac{2.4x}{2.4} = \frac{20.16}{2.4}$$

$$x = 8.4$$

8. B

Kid's meals are $8.95 each and there are x kid's meals, so the cost of kid's meals is

$$8.95x$$

There is an additional 7% tax, so the cost will be 107% of the cost before tax.

$$1.07(8.95x)$$

Exponential Growth & Decay: Practice 1

Question 1 and 2 refer to the following information.

Melanie opened a bank account that earns 3 percent interest compounded annually. Her initial deposit was $200, and she uses the expression $200(x)^t$ to find the value of the account after t years.

1. What is the value of x in the expression?

2. Melanie's friend Elena found an account that earns 3.5 percent interest compounded annually. Elena made an initial deposit of $200 into this account at the same time Melanie made an initial deposit of $200 into her account. After 10 years, how much more money will Elena's initial deposit have earned than Melanie's initial deposit? (Round your answer to the nearest dollar)

3. Of the following four types of saving account plans, which option would yield exponential growth of the money in the account?
   A) Each successive year, 5% of the initial savings is added to the value of the account.
   B) Each successive year, 5.5% of the initial savings and $300 is added to the value of the account.
   C) Each successive year, 2% of the current value is added to the value of the account.
   D) Each successive year, $150 is added to the value of the account.

4. In planning maintenance for a city's infrastructure, a civil engineer estimates that, starting from the present, the population of the city will decrease by 15 percent every 20 years. If the present population of the city is 100,000, which of the following expression represents the engineer's estimate of the population of the city t years from now?
   A) $100{,}000(0.15)^{20t}$
   B) $100{,}000(0.15)^{\frac{t}{20}}$
   C) $100{,}000(0.85)^{20t}$
   D) $100{,}000(0.85)^{\frac{t}{20}}$

Exponential Growth & Decay: Practice 1

5. The function f is defined by $f(x) = 3^x + 1$. Which of the following is the graph of $y = -f(x)$ in the xy-plane?

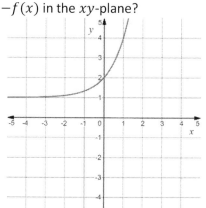

A)

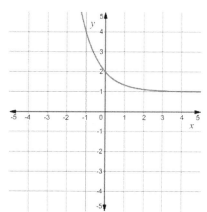

B)

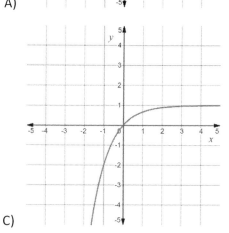

C)

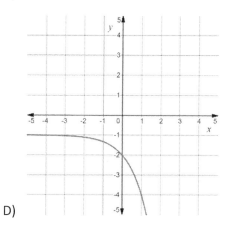

D)

6. Thomas deposited x dollars in his investment account on January 1, 2015. The amount of money in the account doubled each year until Thomas had 800 dollars in his investment account on January 1, 2019. What is the value of x?

7. Lydia has owned a tank of fish since 2017. The population of fish has grown at an average rate of 1 percent per year. There were approximately 20 fish in 2021. Which of the following functions represents the population of fish, P, t years since 2021?
   A) $P(t) = 20(1.01)^t$
   B) $P(t) = 20(1.1)^t$
   C) $P(t) = 1.1t + 20$
   D) $P(t) = 1.01t + 20$

Exponential Growth & Decay: Practice 1

8. During an experiment, Amanda added bacteria into a sealed container. The formula $P(t) = 50(1.02)^t$ above shows the relationship between the population, P, of the bacteria as a function of t, the number of hours that have passed since the bacteria was put into the container.

   By what percent should we expect the bacteria's population to increase between the start of hour 5 and the start of hour 6?

   A) 2%
   B) 20%
   C) 50%
   D) 120%

x	$f(x)$
0	3
1	6
2	12
3	24

9. Based on the table above, which description best describes function, f?
   A) The function has a linear relationship since it increases at a constant rate of 3.
   B) The function has a linear relationship since it changes by a factor of 2 for each increase of x.
   C) The function has an exponential relationship since it increases at a constant rate of 3.
   D) The function has an exponential relationship since it changes by a factor of 2 for each increase of x.

Exponential Growth & Decay: Practice 1

10. Samuel opened a saving account that earns 3 percent interest compounded annually. He initially deposited $100. Which of the following graphs could represent the value of his account t years after the initial deposit?

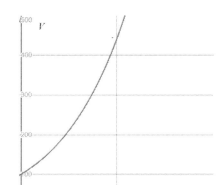
A)

B)

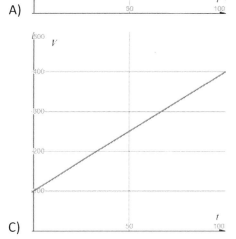
C)

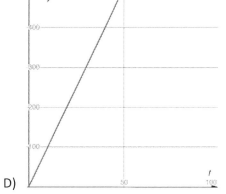
D)

Exponential Growth & Decay: Practice 2

Question 1 and 2 refer to the following information.

Jack opened a bank account that earns 2 percent interest compounded annually. Her initial deposit was $150, and she uses the expression $150(x)^t$ to find the value of the account after t years.

1. What is the value of x in the expression?

2. Jack's friend Alvin found an account that earns 1 percent interest compounded annually. Alvin made an initial deposit of $200 into this account at the same time Jack made an initial deposit of $150 into her account. After 10 years, how much more money will Alvin's initial deposit have earned than Jack's initial deposit? (Round your answer to the nearest dollar.)

3. Of the following four types of saving account plans, which option would yield exponential growth of the money in the account?
   A) Each successive year, 3% of the current value is added to the value of the account.
   B) Each successive year, $200 is added to the value of the account.
   C) Each successive year, 2% of the initial savings is added to the value of the account.
   D) Each successive year, 2.5% of the initial savings and $150 is added to the value of the account.

4. In planning maintenance for a city's infrastructure, a civil engineer estimates that, starting from the present, the population of the city will increase by 20 percent every 20 years. If the present population of the city is 500,000, which of the following expression represents the engineer's estimate of the population of the city t years from now?
   A) $500{,}000(1.20)^{20t}$
   B) $500{,}000(1.20)^{\frac{t}{20}}$
   C) $500{,}000(0.20)^{20t}$
   D) $500{,}000(0.20)^{\frac{t}{20}}$

Exponential Growth & Decay: Practice 2

5. The function f is defined by the equation $f(x) = 2^x$ above. Which of the following is the graph of $y = -f(x)$ in the xy-plane?

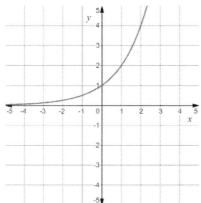
A)

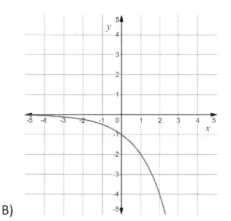
B)

C)

D)

6. Jessica deposited x dollars in his investment account on January 1, 2015. The amount of money in the account doubled each year until Thomas had 640 dollars in his investment account on January 1, 2020. What is the value of x?

7. The world's population has grown at an average rate of 1.9 percent per year since 1945. There were approximately 6 billion people in the world in 1999. Which of the following functions represents the world's population P, in billions of people, t years since 1999?
(1 billion = 1,000,000,000)
A) $P(t) = 1.019t + 6$
B) $P(t) = 1.19t + 6$
C) $P(t) = 6(1.019)^t$
D) $P(t) = 6(1.19)^t$

8. The formula $P(t) = 260(2.7)^t$ shows the relationship between the population, P, of a certain mushroom species on a one-acre plot of land as a function of t, the number of weeks that have passed since the mushrooms were first introduced on the plot.

By what percent should we expect the mushroom population to increase between the start of week 6 and week 7?

A) 70%
B) 170%
C) 270%
D) 540%

x	$f(x)$
0	1
1	4
2	7
3	10

9. Based on the table above, which description best describes function, f?
    A) The function has a linear relationship since it increases at a constant rate of 3.
    B) The function has a linear relationship since it changes by a factor of 3 for each increase of x.
    C) The function has an exponential relationship since it increases at a constant rate of 3.
    D) The function has an exponential relationship since it changes by a factor of 3 for each increase of x.

Exponential Growth & Decay: Practice 2

10. Samuel opened a saving account that earns 5 percent interest compounded annually. He initially deposited $120. Which of the following graph could represent the value of his account t years after the initial deposit?

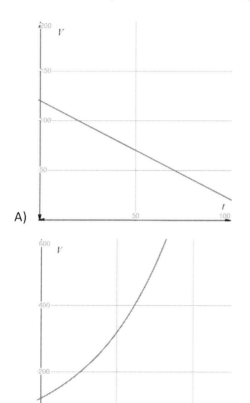

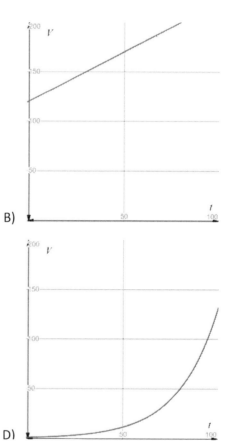

Exponential Growth & Decay Explanations

Exponential Growth & Decay 1

1. 1.03

   3% increase means 103% of original

   103% = 1.03

2. 13

   Melanie: $200(1.03)^{10} = 268.78$

   Elena: $200(1.035)^{10} = 282.12$

   $282.12 - 268.78 = 13.34$

   Round to 13

3. C

   A is linear because it grows by a constant amount (5% of the initial value) each year.

   B is linear because it grows by a constant amount (5.5% of the initial plus $300) each year.

   C is exponential because it grows by 2% of the current value. Each year there is a higher current value, so 2% of the current year's value is always greater than the previous year's value.

   D is linear because it grows by a constant amount ($150) each year.

4. D

   Decrease by 15%, so you're left with 85%.

   It decreases by 15% every 20 years, so you should divide the total number of years by 20 to see how many times it decreases by 15%.

5. D

   Plug in some simple values for x, such as 0 and 1.

   $y = 3^x + 1$

   $y = 3^0 + 1 = 1 + 1 = 2; \; (0, 2)$

   $y = 3^1 + 1 = 3 + 1 = 4; \; (1, 4)$

   Negating the function negates the y-values, so we end up with the following coordinates:

   $(0, -2)$ and $(1, -4)$

   Only choice D has those points.

6. 50

   work backwards

Year	Value
2019	800
2018	400
2017	200
2016	100
2015	50

7. A

   Exponential growth

   Increase of 1% is 101%

   101% = 1.01

   Note: D is linear growth

8. A

   $1.02 = 102\%$

   102% means 2% growth

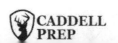

Exponential Growth & Decay Explanations

9. D

x	$f(x)$
0	3
1	6
2	12
3	24

×2
×2
×2

10. A

Initially deposited $100, so y-intercept is 100.

Grows exponentially since it earns 3%, so it should be curved up (not linear).

Exponential Growth & Decay 2

1. 1.02

2% growth is 102%
102% = 1.02

2. 38

JACK   ALVIN
$150(1.02)^{10}$ $200(1.01)^{10}$
182.85   220.93

220.93 − 182.85
38.08
round to 38

3. A

A is exponential because it grows by 3% of the current value. Each year there is a higher current value, so 3% of the current year's value is always greater than the previous year's value.

B is linear because it increases by a constant amount ($200) each year.

C is linear because it increases by a constant amount (2% of the initial amount) each year.

D is linear because it increases by a constant amount (2.5% of the initial amount plus $150) each year.

4. B

Increase by 20%, so will be 120% or a multiple of 1.20.

It increases by 20% every 20 years, so you should divide the total number of years by 20 to see how many times it increases by 20%.

5. B

Plug in some simple values for x, such as 0 and 1.

$y = 2^x$

$y = 2^0 = 1$; $(0, 1)$

$y = 2^1 = 2$; $(1, 2)$

Negating the function negates the y-values, so we end up with the following coordinates:

$(0, -1)$ and $(1, -2)$

Only choice B has those points.

Exponential Growth & Decay Explanations

6. 20

work backwards

2020 640
2019 320
2018 160
2017 80
2016 40
2015 20

7. C

Exponential growth

1.9% increase is 101.9%

101.9% = 1.019

Note: A is linear

8. B

2.7 = 270%

270% is 170% increase

9. A

x	f(x)
0	1
1	4
2	7
3	10

+3, +3, +3

10. D

Initially deposited $120, so y-intercept is 120.

Grows exponentially since it earns 5%, so it should be curved up (not linear).

Exponents: Practice 1

1. If $3x - 2y = 16$, what is the value of $\frac{27^x}{9^y}$?
   A) 2^3
   B) 3^{16}
   C) 9^2
   D) The value cannot be determined from the information given.

2. Which of the following is equal to $a^{\frac{5}{3}}$, for all values of a?
   A) $\sqrt{a^{\frac{1}{3}}}$
   B) $\sqrt{a^3}$
   C) $\sqrt[5]{a^3}$
   D) $\sqrt[3]{a^5}$

3. Which of the following is equal to $16^{\frac{2}{3}}$?
   A) 4
   B) $\sqrt[3]{16}$
   C) $\sqrt[3]{4}$
   D) $4\sqrt[3]{4}$

4. If $a^{\frac{b}{2}} = 81$ for positive integers a and b, what is one possible value of b?

5. The expression $\dfrac{x^{-4}y^{\frac{1}{3}}}{x^{\frac{1}{2}}y^{-2}}$, where $x > 1$ and $y > 1$, is equivalent to which of the following?
   A) $\dfrac{y^2\sqrt[3]{y}}{x^4\sqrt{x}}$
   B) $\dfrac{\sqrt[3]{y^2}}{\sqrt{x}}$
   C) $\dfrac{y^2\sqrt[3]{y}}{\sqrt[4]{x}}$
   D) $\dfrac{\sqrt[3]{y}}{\sqrt{x}}$

Exponents: Practice 1

6. If $a^{-\frac{1}{3}} = x$, where $a > 0$, what is a in terms of x?
   A) $\sqrt[3]{x}$
   B) $-\sqrt[3]{x}$
   C) $\frac{1}{x^3}$
   D) $-\frac{1}{x^3}$

7. If $x - 2y = 15$, what is the value of $\frac{3^x}{9^y}$?
   A) 3^2
   B) 3^{15}
   C) 9^2
   D) The value cannot be determined from the information given.

8. Which of the following is equal to $a^{\frac{3}{4}}$, for all values of a?
   A) $\sqrt{a^{\frac{1}{4}}}$
   B) $\sqrt[3]{a}$
   C) $\sqrt[4]{a}$
   D) $\sqrt[4]{a^3}$

9. Which of the following is equivalent to $2^{\frac{2}{3}}$?
   A) $\sqrt[3]{4}$
   B) $\sqrt[2]{8}$
   C) $\sqrt[2]{2}$
   D) $\sqrt[3]{2}$

10. If $a^{\frac{b}{8}} = 36$ for positive integers a and b, what is one possible value of b?

Exponents: Practice 1

11. The expression $\dfrac{x^2 y^{-\frac{1}{2}}}{x^{-\frac{1}{3}} y^1}$, where $x > 1$ and $y > 1$, is equivalent to which of the following?

   A) $\dfrac{\sqrt{y}}{\sqrt{x}}$

   B) $\dfrac{\sqrt[3]{x^2}}{y\sqrt{y}}$

   C) $\dfrac{x^2 \sqrt[3]{x}}{y\sqrt{y}}$

   D) $-\dfrac{\sqrt[3]{x^2}}{y\sqrt{y}}$

12. If $a^{-\frac{2}{3}} = x$, where $a > 0$, what is a in terms of x?

   A) $\sqrt[3]{x^2}$

   B) $\dfrac{1}{x^3}$

   C) $\sqrt{\dfrac{1}{x^3}}$

   D) $-\sqrt{x}$

Exponents: Practice 2

1. If $3x - y = 10$, what is the value of $\dfrac{125^x}{5^y}$?

   A) 5^{10}
   B) 25^2
   C) 125^1
   D) The value cannot be determined from the information given.

2. Which of the following is equal to $a^{\frac{3}{2}}$, for all values of a?

   A) $\sqrt{a^2}$
   B) $\sqrt{a^3}$
   C) $\sqrt[3]{a^2}$
   D) $\sqrt{a^3}$

3. Which of the following is equal to $12^{\frac{3}{4}}$?

   A) $\sqrt[3]{12}$
   B) $\sqrt[4]{12}$
   C) $\sqrt[4]{12^3}$
   D) $\sqrt[3]{12^4}$

4. If $a^{\frac{b}{3}} = 27$ for positive integers a and b, what is one possible value of b?

5. The expression $\dfrac{x^{-4} y^{\frac{1}{3}}}{x^{\frac{1}{2}} y^{-2}}$, where $x > 1$ and $y > 1$, is equivalent to which of the following?

   A) $\dfrac{y^2 \sqrt[3]{y}}{x^4 \sqrt{x}}$
   B) $\dfrac{\sqrt[4]{y^2}}{\sqrt{x}}$
   C) $\dfrac{y^2 \sqrt[4]{y}}{\sqrt[3]{x}}$
   D) $\dfrac{\sqrt[4]{y}}{\sqrt{x^3}}$

Exponents: Practice 2

6. If $a^{-\frac{1}{6}} = x$, where $a > 0$, what is a in terms of x?
    A) $\frac{1}{x^6}$
    B) $-\frac{1}{x^6}$
    C) $\sqrt[6]{x}$
    D) $-\sqrt[6]{x}$

7. If $2x - 3y = 20$, what is the value of $\frac{4^x}{8^y}$?
    A) 2
    B) 2^3
    C) 2^{20}
    D) The value cannot be determined from the information given.

8. Which of the following is equal to $a^{-\frac{1}{2}}$, for all values of a?
    A) $\sqrt{a^{\frac{1}{2}}}$
    B) $\sqrt[2]{a}$
    C) $-a$
    D) $\frac{1}{\sqrt{a}}$

9. Which of the following is equivalent to $25^{\frac{3}{4}}$?
    A) $\sqrt{5}$
    B) $5\sqrt{5}$
    C) $\sqrt[3]{5}$
    D) $\sqrt[4]{5}$

10. If $a^{\frac{b}{3}} = 64$ for positive integers a and b, what is one possible value of b?

Exponents: Practice 2

11. The expression $\frac{x^2 y^{-2}}{x^{-3} y^3}$, where $x > 1$ and $y > 1$, is equivalent to which of the following?

    A) $\frac{\sqrt{x}}{\sqrt{y}}$

    B) $\frac{\sqrt{y}}{\sqrt{x}}$

    C) $\frac{y^5}{x^5}$

    D) $\frac{x^5}{y^5}$

12. If $a^{-\frac{3}{4}} = x$, where $a > 0$, what is a in terms of x?

    A) $\sqrt{\frac{1}{x^3}}$

    B) $\sqrt[3]{\frac{1}{x^4}}$

    C) $\sqrt[3]{x^4}$

    D) $\sqrt[4]{x^4}$

Exponents Explanations

Exponents 1

1. B

$$\frac{27^x}{9^y} = \frac{(3^3)^x}{(3^2)^y} = \frac{3^{3x}}{2^{2y}}$$

$$3^{3x-2y} = 3^{16}$$

2. D

$a^{\frac{5}{3}}$ ← power, ← root

$\sqrt[3]{a^5}$

3. D

Answers are written in base 4, so change to base 4

$$16^{\frac{2}{3}} = (4^2)^{2/3} = 4^{4/3} = 4^{1\frac{1}{3}}$$

$$4^{1\frac{1}{3}} = 4^{1+\frac{1}{3}} = 4^1 \cdot 4^{1/3} = 4\sqrt[3]{4}$$

4. 2 or 4 or 8

$a^{\frac{b}{2}} = 81$

If $a = 81$, $\sqrt{81^1} = 81$

$\frac{b}{2} = 1$, $b = 2$

If $a = 9$, $\sqrt{9^2} = 81$

$\frac{b}{2} = 2$, $b = 4$

If $a = 3$, $\sqrt{3^4} = 81$

$\frac{b}{2} = 4$, $b = 8$

5. A

A negative exponent means to move the term to the numerator if it is in the denominator or move it to the denominator if it is in the numerator.

A power of 1/3 means cube root and 1/2 means square root.

6. C

$a^{-\frac{1}{3}} = x$

$\left(a^{-1/3}\right)^{-3} = (x)^{-3}$

$a = x^{-3}$

$a = \frac{1}{x^3}$

7. B

$$\frac{3^x}{9^y} = \frac{3^x}{(3^2)^y} = \frac{3^x}{3^{2y}} = 3^{x-2y}$$

$$3^{x-2y} = 3^{15}$$

Exponents Explanations

8. D

$a^{\frac{3}{4}}$ ← power, root

$\sqrt[4]{a^3}$

9. A

$2^{\frac{2}{3}}$ ← power, root

$\sqrt[3]{2^2}$

$\sqrt[3]{4}$

10. 8 or 16

$a^{\frac{b}{8}} = 36$

If $a = 36$, $\sqrt[b/8]{36^1} = 36$

$\frac{b}{8} = 1$, $b = 8$

If $a = 6$, $\sqrt[b/8]{6^2} = 36$

$\frac{b}{8} = 2$, $b = 16$

11. C

A negative exponent means to move the term to the numerator if it is in the denominator or move it to the denominator if it is in the numerator.

A power of 1/3 means cube root and 1/2 means square root.

12. C

$a^{-\frac{2}{3}} = x$

$\left(a^{-\frac{2}{3}}\right)^{-\frac{3}{2}} = (x)^{-\frac{3}{2}}$

$a = x^{-\frac{3}{2}}$

$a = \frac{1}{x^{3/2}}$

$a = \frac{1}{\sqrt{x^3}}$

Exponents 2

1. A

$\frac{125^x \cdot (5^3)^x}{5^y} = \frac{5^{3x}}{5^y} = 5^{3x-y}$

$5^{3x-y} = 5^{10}$

2. D

$a^{\frac{3}{2}}$ ← power, root

$\sqrt{a^3}$

Exponents Explanations

3. C

$12^{\frac{3}{4}}$ ← power, root

$\sqrt[4]{12^3}$

4. 3 or 9

If $a = 27$, $\sqrt[1]{27} = 27$

$\frac{b}{3} = 1$, $b = 3$

If $a = 3$, $\sqrt[3]{3^3} = 27$

$\frac{b}{3} = 3$, $b = 9$

5. A

A negative exponent means to move the term to the numerator if it is in the denominator or move it to the denominator if it is in the numerator.

A power of 1/3 means cube root and 1/2 means square root.

6. A

$a^{-\frac{1}{6}} = x$

$\left(a^{-\frac{1}{6}}\right)^{-6} = (x)^{-6}$

$a = x^{-6}$

$a = \frac{1}{x^6}$

7. C

$\frac{4^x}{8^y} = \frac{(2^2)^x}{(2^3)^y} = \frac{2^{2x}}{2^{3y}} = 2^{2x-3y}$

$2^{2x-3y} = 2^{20}$

8. D

$a^{-\frac{1}{2}} = \frac{1}{a^{\frac{1}{2}}} = \frac{1}{\sqrt{a}}$

9. B

$25^{3/4} = (5^2)^{3/4} = 5^{6/4}$

$5^{6/4} = 5^{3/2} = 5^{1\frac{1}{2}}$

$5^{1\frac{1}{2}} = 5^{1+\frac{1}{2}} = 5 \cdot 5^{\frac{1}{2}}$

$= 5\sqrt{5}$

10. 3 or 6 or 9 or 18

If $a = 64$, $\sqrt[1]{64} = 64$

$\frac{b}{3} = 1$, $b = 3$

Exponents Explanations

If $a = 8$, $\sqrt{8^2} = 64$

$\frac{b}{3} = 2$, $b = 6$

If $a = 4$, $\sqrt{4^3} = 64$

$\frac{b}{3} = 3$, $b = 9$

If $a = 2$, $\sqrt{a^6} = 64$

$\frac{b}{3} = 6$, $b = 18$

$a = \dfrac{1}{x^{4/3}}$

$a = \dfrac{1}{\sqrt[3]{x^4}}$

$a = \dfrac{1}{x^{5/2}}$ ← power / root

$a = \dfrac{1}{\sqrt{x^5}} = \sqrt{\dfrac{1}{x^5}}$

11. D

A negative exponent means to move the term to the numerator if it is in the denominator or move it to the denominator if it is in the numerator.

$\left(\dfrac{x^2 \, y^{-2}}{x^{-3} \, y^3}\right) = \dfrac{x^2 x^3}{y^2 y^3} = \dfrac{x^5}{y^5}$

12. B

$a^{-\frac{3}{4}} = x$

$\left(a^{-\frac{3}{4}}\right)^{-\frac{4}{3}} = (x)^{-\frac{4}{3}}$

$a = x^{-4/3}$

Imaginary Numbers: Practice 1

1. For $i = \sqrt{-1}$, what is the sum of $(8 + 4i)$ and $(7 - 6i)$?

A) $1 + 10i$

B) $15 + 2i$

C) $15 - 2i$

D) $1 - 10i$

2. What is the sum of complex numbers $11 + 4i$ and $4 + 2i$, where $i = \sqrt{-1}$?

A) $13 - 2i$

B) $15 + 6i$

C) $21i$

D) 15

3. Which of the following complex numbers is equal to $(10 - 11i) - (4 - 6i)$, where $i = \sqrt{-1}$?

A) $6 - 5i$

B) $14 + 17i$

C) $14 - 17i$

D) $6 + 5i$

4. What is the product of $6 + 9i$ and $3 + 3i$, where $i = \sqrt{-1}$?

A) 18

B) $18 + 27i$

C) $-9 - 9i$

D) $-9 + 45i$

Imaginary Numbers: Practice 1

5. For $i = \sqrt{-1}$, what is $(-12 - 5i) + (7 + 6i)$?

A) $5 + i$

B) $-5 + i$

C) -5

D) $19i$

6. If you simplify and write in $a + bi$ form, what is the value of b in the expression below?

$$\frac{1 + 2i}{2 - 3i}$$

7. If you simplify $(6 + 8i)(4 + 4i)$ and write in $a + bi$ form, what is the value of b?

8. Simplify and write in $a + bi$ form. What is the value of a in the expression below?

$$\frac{3 + 4i}{6 - 2i}$$

9. Simplify $(4 - 6i)(7 - 3i)$ and write in $a + bi$ form, what is the value of a?

10. Simplify and write in $a + bi$ form, what is the value of b in the expression below?

$$\frac{5 + 2i}{4 - 2i}$$

Imaginary Numbers: Practice 2

1. For $i = \sqrt{-1}$, what is the sum of $(9 + 6i)$ and $(5 - 4i)$?

A) $14i$

B) $14 - 2i$

C) $14 + 2i$

D) $14 - 10i$

2. What is the sum of complex numbers $6 + 8i$ and $2 + 6i$, where $i = \sqrt{-1}$?

A) $22i$

B) $4 + 2i$

C) $8 + 14i$

D) 8

3. Which of the following complex numbers is equal to $(9 - 6i) - (4 - 10i)$, where $i = \sqrt{-1}$?

A) $5 - 4i$

B) $5 + 4i$

C) $5 - 16i$

D) $13 - 6i$

4. What is the product of $3 + 4i$ and $5 + 7i$, where $i = \sqrt{-1}$

A) $-13 + 41i$

B) $-13 - 41i$

C) $15 + 15i$

D) $-15 - 15i$

Imaginary Numbers: Practice 2

5. For $i = \sqrt{-1}$, what is $(-13 + 2i) + (1 - 4i)$?

A) $20i$

B) $12 + 2i$

C) $-14 + 2i$

D) $-12 - 2i$

6. Simplify and write in $a + bi$ form. What is the value of b?

$$\frac{3 + 6i}{2 + 2i}$$

7. Simplify $(8 + 5i)(3 - 5i)$ and write in $a + bi$ form. What is the value of a?

8. Simplify and write in $a + bi$ form.

$$\frac{8 + 3i}{5 + 3i}$$

A) $\frac{64}{5} + i$

B) $\frac{49}{34} - \frac{9}{34}i$

C) $\frac{64}{5} - i$

D) $\frac{49}{34} + \frac{9}{34}i$

9. Simplify $(6 - 3i)(10 + 4i)$ and write in $a + bi$ form. What is the value of a?

10. Simplify the expression below and write in $a + bi$ form. What is the value of a?

$$\frac{4 + 6i}{5 - 3i}$$

Imaginary Numbers Explanations

Imaginary Numbers 1

1. C

$(8+4i)+(7-6i)$

$8+4i+7-6i$

combine like terms

$8+7+4i-6i$

$15-2i$

2. B

$(11+4i)+(4+2i)$

$11+4i+4+2i$

combine like terms

$11+4+4i+2i$

$15+6i$

3. A

$(10-11i)-(4-6i)$

$10-11i-4+6i$

Combine like terms

$10-4-11i+6i$

$6-5i$

4. D

$(6+9i)(3+3i)$

$18+18i+27i+27i^2$

$18+45i+27i^2$

$\ast\ i^2=-1$

$18+45i+27(-1)$

$18+45i-27$

$-9+45i$

5. B

$(-12-5i)+(7+6i)$

$-12-5i+7+6i$

combine like terms

$-12+7-5i+6i$

$-5+i$

Imaginary Numbers Explanations

6. 7/13

To simplify, multiply the numerator and denominator by the conjugate of the denominator.

The conjugate of the denominator is the same term as the denominator with the operation switched from addition to subtraction or subtraction to addition.

$$\frac{1+2i}{2-3i} \cdot \frac{(2+3i)}{(2+3i)}$$

$$\frac{2+3i+4i+6i^2}{4+6i-6i-9i^2}$$

$$\frac{2+7i+6(-1)}{4-9(-1)}$$

$$\frac{2+7i-6}{4+9}$$

$$\frac{-4+7i}{13}$$

$$\frac{-4}{13} + \frac{7}{13}i$$

$$a + bi$$

7. 56

$$(6+8i)(4+4i)$$

$$24+24i+32i+32i^2$$

$$24+56i+32(-1)$$

$$24+56i-32$$

$$-8+56i$$

$$a + bi$$

8. 1/4

To simplify, multiply the numerator and denominator by the conjugate of the denominator.

The conjugate of the denominator is the same term as the denominator with the operation switched from addition to subtraction or subtraction to addition.

$$\frac{3+4i}{6-2i} \cdot \frac{(6+2i)}{(6+2i)}$$

Imaginary Numbers Explanations

$$\frac{18 + 6i + 24i + 8i^2}{36 + 12i - 12i - 4i^2}$$

$$\frac{18 + 30i + 8(-1)}{36 - 4(-1)}$$

$$\frac{18 + 30i - 8}{36 + 4}$$

$$\frac{10 + 30i}{40}$$

$$\frac{10}{40} + \frac{30}{40}i$$

$$\frac{1}{4} + \frac{3}{4}i$$

↑
$a + bi$

9. 10

$(4 - 6i)(7 - 3i)$

$28 - 12i - 42i + 18i^2$

$28 - 54i + 18(-1)$

$28 - 54i - 18$

$10 - 54i$
↑
$a + bi$

10. 9/10

To simplify, multiply the numerator and denominator by the conjugate of the denominator.

The conjugate of the denominator is the same term as the denominator with the operation switched from addition to subtraction or subtraction to addition.

$$\frac{5+2i}{4-2i} \cdot \frac{(4+2i)}{(4+2i)}$$

$$\frac{20 + 10i + 8i + 4i^2}{16 + 8i - 8i - 4}$$

$$\frac{20 + 18i + 4(-1)}{16 - 4(-1)}$$

Imaginary Numbers Explanations

$$\frac{20+18i-4}{16+4}$$

$$\frac{16+18i}{20}$$

$$\frac{16}{20}+\frac{18}{20}i$$

$$\frac{4}{5}+\frac{9}{10}i$$

↑

$a + bi$

Imaginary Numbers 2

1. C

$(9+6i)+(5-4i)$

$9+6i+5-4i$

Combine like terms

$9+5+6i-4i$

$14+2i$

2. C

$(6+8i)+(2+6i)$

$6+8i+2+6i$

Combine like terms

$6+2+8i+6i$

$8+14i$

3. B

$(9-6i)-(4-10i)$

$9-6i-4+10i$

Combine like terms

$9-4-6i+10i$

$5+4i$

4. A

$(3+4i)(5+7i)$

$15+21i+20i+28i^2$

$15+41i+28(-1)$

Imaginary Numbers Explanations

$15 + 41i - 28$
$-13 + 41i$

5. D

$(-13 + 2i) + (1 - 4i)$
$-13 + 2i + 1 - 4i$
combine like terms
$-13 + 1 + 2i - 4i$
$-12 - 2i$

6. 3/4

To simplify, multiply the numerator and denominator by the conjugate of the denominator.

The conjugate of the denominator is the same term as the denominator with the operation switched from addition to subtraction or subtraction to addition.

$$\frac{3+6i}{2+2i} \cdot \frac{(2-2i)}{(2-2i)}$$

$$\frac{6 - 6i + 12i - 12i^2}{4 - 4i + 4i - 4i^2}$$

$$\frac{6 + 6i - 12(-1)}{4 - 4(-1)}$$

$$\frac{6 + 6i + 12}{4 + 4}$$

$$\frac{18 + 6i}{8}$$

$$\frac{18}{8} + \frac{6}{8}i$$

$$\frac{9}{4} + \frac{3}{4}i$$

$$\underset{\uparrow}{\frac{9}{4} + \frac{3}{4}i}$$
$a + bi$

7. 49

$(8 + 5i)(3 - 5i)$

$24 - 40i + 15i - 25i^2$

Imaginary Numbers Explanations

$24 - 25i - 25(-1)$

$24 - 25i + 25$

$49 - 25i$
↑
$a + bi$

8. B

To simplify, multiply the numerator and denominator by the conjugate of the denominator.

The conjugate of the denominator is the same term as the denominator with the operation switched from addition to subtraction or subtraction to addition.

$$\frac{8+3i}{5+3i} \cdot \frac{(5-3i)}{(5-3i)}$$

$$\frac{40 - 24i + 15i - 9i^2}{25 - 15i + 15i - 9i^2}$$

$$\frac{40 - 9i - 9(-1)}{25 - 9(-1)}$$

$$\frac{40 - 9i + 9}{25 + 9}$$

$$\frac{49 - 9i}{34}$$

$$\frac{49}{34} - \frac{9}{34}i$$

9. 72

$(6 - 3i)(10 + 4i)$

$60 + 24i - 30i - 12i^2$

$60 - 6i - 12(-1)$

$60 - 6i + 12$

$72 - 6i$
↑
$a + bi$

10. 1/17

$$\frac{4+6i}{5-3i} \cdot \frac{(5+3i)}{(5+3i)}$$

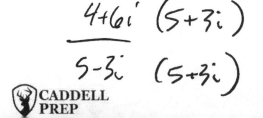

Imaginary Numbers Explanations

$$\frac{20 + 12i + 30i + 18i^2}{25 + 15i - 15i - 9i^2}$$

$$\frac{20 + 42i + 18(-1)}{25 - 9(-1)}$$

$$\frac{20 + 42i - 18}{25 + 9}$$

$$\frac{2 + 42i}{34}$$

$$\frac{2}{34} + \frac{42}{34}i$$

$$\frac{1}{17} + \frac{21}{17}i$$

$$\uparrow$$
$$a + bi$$

Circles: Practice 1

1. Which of the following is an equation of a circle in the xy-plane with center (1,2) and a radius with endpoint (2, 9).

   A) $(x-1)^2 + (y-2)^2 = 50$

   B) $(x-1)^2 + (y+2)^2 = 25\sqrt{2}$

   C) $(x+1)^2 + (y+2)^2 = 50$

   D) $(x+1)^2 + (y-2)^2 = 25\sqrt{2}$

2. In a circle with center O, central angle AOB has a measure of $\frac{5\pi}{3}$ radians. The area of the sector formed by central angle AOB is what fraction area of the circle?

3.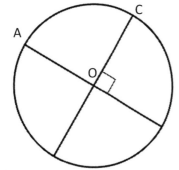

   The circle above with center O has a circumference of 48. What is the length of the minor arc $\overset{\frown}{AC}$?

   A) 12
   B) 16
   C) 36
   D) 48

Circles: Practice 1

4. $x^2 - 22x + y^2 - 12y = -148$

   The equation above defines a circle in the xy-plane. What are the coordinates of the center of the circle?

   A) (11,6)
   B) (5,3)
   C) (-11,-6)
   D) (-5,-3)

5. Points A and B lie on a circle with radius 3, and arc $\widehat{AB}$ has length $\frac{\pi}{3}$. What fraction of the circumference of the circle is the length of arc $\widehat{AB}$?

6. In the xy-plane, the graph of
   $x^2 - 6x + y^2 - 8y = 11$ is a circle. What is the radius of the circle?

   A) 5
   B) 6
   C) 25
   D) 36

7. The number of radians in a 210-degree angle can be written as $a\pi$, where a is a constant. What is the value of a?

8. A circle in the xy-plane has equation $(x - 4)^2 + (y - 3)^2 = 9$. Which of the following does NOT on the circle?

   A) (5, 6)
   B) (1, 3)
   C) (7, 3)
   D) (4, 0)

Circles: Practice 1

9.

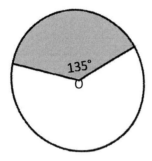

Point O is the center of the circle above. What fraction of the area of the circle is the area of the shaded region?

10. $(x-6)^2 + (y+5)^2 = 25$

In the xy-plane, the graph of the equation above is a circle. Point M is on the circle and has coordinates (6, 0). If $\overline{MR}$ is a diameter of the circle, what are the coordinates of point R?

A) (1,-5)
B) (6,-10)
C) (11,-5)
D) (6,-5)

11.

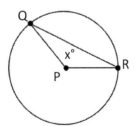

Note: Figure not drawn to scale.

In the circle above, Point P is the center and the length of arc $\overarc{QR}$ is $\frac{4}{5}$ of the circumference of the circle. What is the value of x?

Circles: Practice 1

12.

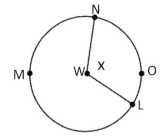

The circle above has center W, the length of the arc $\widehat{LON}$ is 5π, and x= 100°. What is the length of arc $\widehat{LMN}$?

    A) 13π
    B) 15π
    C) 21π
    D) 16π

13.

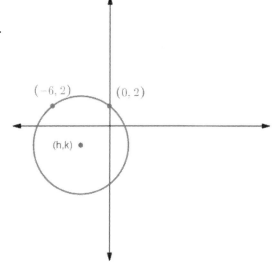

In the xy=plane above, the circle has center (h,k) and radius of 5. What is the value of k?

    A. -4
    B. -3
    C. -2
    D. -1

Circles: Practice 1

14. A circle in the xy-plane has center (4,-8) and radius 10. Which of the following is an equation of the circle?

A) $(x + 4)^2 + (y - 8)^2 = 100$
B) $(x + 4)^2 + (y - 4)^2 = 50$
C) $(x - 4)^2 + (y + 8)^2 = 100$
D) $(x + 4)^2 + (y - 4)^2 = 50$

Circles: Practice 2

1. Which of the following is an equation of a circle in the xy-plane with center (-3,3) and a radius with endpoint (4, 6)

A) $(x + 3)^2 + (y - 3)^2 = 52$

B) $(x - 3)^2 + (y + 3)^2 = 58$

C) $(x + 3)^2 + (y - 3)^2 = 58$

D) $(x - 3)^2 + (y + 3)^2 = 52$

2. In a circle with center O, central angle AOB has a measure of $\frac{7\pi}{5}$ radians. The area of the sector formed by central angle AOB is what fraction area of the circle?

3.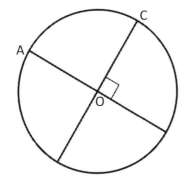

The circle above with center O has a circumference of 72. What is the length of the major arc AC?

A) 32
B) 54
C) 68
D) 72

Circles: Practice 2

4. $x^2 - 22x + y^2 + 16y = -121$

   The equation above defines a circle in the xy-plane. What are the coordinates of the center of the circle?

   A) (-11,8)
   B) (5,-4)
   C) (11,-8)
   D) (-5,4)

5. Points A and B lie on a circle with radius 4, and arc $\widehat{AB}$ has length $\frac{6\pi}{5}$. What fraction of the circumference of the circle is the length of arc $\widehat{AB}$?

6. In the xy-plane, the graph of $x^2 - 22x + y^2 + 4y = 44$ is a circle. What is the radius of the circle?

   A) 2
   B) 11
   C) 13
   D) 15

7. The number of radians in a 135-degree angle can be written as $a\pi$, where a is a constant. What is the value of a?

Circles: Practice 2

8. A circle in the xy-plane has equation $(x-2)^2 + (y+1)^2 = 16$. Which of the following does NOT lie on the circle?

   A) (6,-1)
   B) (2,-5)
   C) (-2,-1)
   D) (2,4)

9.

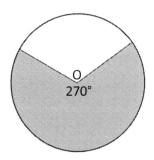

Point O is the center of the circle above. What fraction of the area of the circle is the area of the shaded region?

10. $(x-3)^2 + (y-2)^2 = 49$

   In the xy-plane, the graph of the equation above is a circle. Point M is on the circle and has coordinates (-4, 2). If $\overline{MR}$ is a diameter of the circle, what are the coordinates of point R?

   A) (3,9)
   B) (3,-5)
   C) (10,2)
   D) (3,3)

Circles: Practice 2

11.

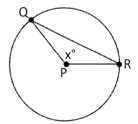

Note: Figure not drawn to scale.

In the circle above, Point P is the center and the length of arc $\widehat{QR}$ is $\frac{3}{8}$ of the circumference of the circle. What is the value of x?

12.

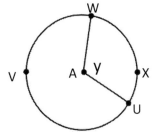

The circle above has center A, the length of the arc $\widehat{UXW}$ is 3π, and y= 60°. What is the length of arc $\widehat{UVW}$?

    A) 10π
    B) 6π
    C) 22π
    D) 15π

13.

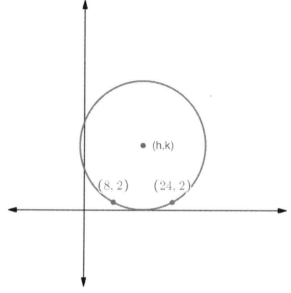

In the xy=plane above, the circle has center (h,k) and radius of 17. What is the value of k?

14. A circle in the xy-plane has center (-3,7) and radius 8. Which of the following is an equation of the circle?

A) $(x-3)^2 + (y-7)^2 = 32$
B) $(x+3)^2 + (y-7)^2 = 64$
C) $(x-3)^2 + (y+7)^2 = 32$
D) $(x-3)^2 + (y+7)^2 = 64$

Circles Explanations

Circles 1

1. A

   Equation of a circle is

   $(x-h)^2 + (y-k)^2 = r^2$

   So if the center is (1, 2), then $h = 1$ and $k = 2$

   We need to find the radius, so we should use the distance formula with the center (1,2) and a point on the circle (2,9)

   $d = \sqrt{(x_2-x_1)^2 + (y_2-y_1)^2}$

   $d = \sqrt{(2-1)^2 + (9-2)^2}$

   $d = \sqrt{(1)^2 + (7)^2}$

   $d = \sqrt{50}$

   $r = \sqrt{50}$

   $r^2 = 50$

   $(x-1)^2 + (y-2)^2 = 50$

2. 5/6

   $\dfrac{\theta}{2\pi} = \dfrac{\text{sector}}{\text{total A}}$

   $\dfrac{\frac{5\pi}{3}}{2\pi} = \dfrac{5\pi}{3} \div 2\pi$

   $\dfrac{\pi}{3} \cdot \dfrac{1}{2\pi}$

   $\dfrac{5\pi}{3} \cdot \dfrac{1}{2\pi} = \dfrac{5}{6}$

3. 12

   $\dfrac{x}{360} = \dfrac{L}{C}$

   $\dfrac{90}{360} = \dfrac{L}{48}$

   $\dfrac{1}{4} = \dfrac{L}{48}$

   $\dfrac{48}{4} = \dfrac{4L}{4}$

   $12 = L$

Circles Explanations

4. A

To find the center, we need to get the equation into the following form.

$$(x-h)^2 + (y-k)^2 = r^2$$

We will need to complete the square twice.

$$x^2 - 22x + y^2 - 12y = -148$$

Complete the square for the x terms and for the y terms.

$$\left(\frac{b}{2}\right)^2 \qquad \left(\frac{b}{2}\right)^2$$

$$\left(\frac{-22}{2}\right)^2 \qquad \left(\frac{-12}{2}\right)^2$$

$$121 \qquad 36$$

$$x^2 - 22x + y^2 - 12y = -148$$
$$+121 \qquad +36 \qquad +121$$
$$\qquad\qquad\qquad +36$$

$$x^2 - 22x + 121 + y^2 - 12y + 36 = 9$$

$$(x-11)^2 + (y-6)^2 = 9$$

$$\text{center} = (11, 6)$$

5. 1/36

$$\frac{L}{C}$$

$$L = \pi/3$$

$$C = 2\pi r$$
$$C = 2\pi (6)$$
$$C = 12\pi$$

$$\frac{L}{C} = \frac{\pi/3}{12\pi}$$

$$\frac{\pi}{3} \div 12\pi$$

$$\frac{\pi}{3} \cdot \frac{1}{12\pi}$$

$$\frac{\pi}{3} \cdot \frac{1}{12\pi} = \frac{1}{36}$$

6. B

To find the radius, we need to get the equation into the following form.

$$(x-h)^2 + (y-k)^2 = r^2$$

We will need to complete the square twice.

$$x^2 - 6x + y^2 - 8y = 11$$

Circles Explanations

Complete the square for the x terms and for the y terms.

$$\left(\frac{b}{2}\right)^2 \qquad \left(\frac{b}{2}\right)^2$$

$$\left(\frac{-6}{2}\right)^2 \qquad \left(\frac{-8}{2}\right)^2$$

$$9 \qquad 16$$

$$x^2 - 6x \quad + y^2 - 8y \quad = 11$$
$$+9 +16 \quad +9$$
$$ +16$$

$$x^2 - 6x + 9 + y^2 - 8y + 16 = 36$$
$$ \uparrow$$
$$ r^2$$

$$r^2 = 36$$
$$r = 6$$

7. 7/6

$$360° = 2\pi$$

set up a proportion

$$\frac{360}{2\pi} = \frac{210}{x}$$

$$360 x = 420\pi$$

$$\frac{360x}{360} = \frac{420\pi}{360}$$

$$x = \frac{420\pi}{360\pi}$$

$$x = \frac{42}{36}\pi = \frac{7}{6}\pi$$

$$a\pi$$

$$a = 7/6$$

8. A

Given $(x-4)^2 + (y-3)^2 = 9$, the center of the circle is (4,3) and the radius is 3. Make a sketch.

Start with the center and make points 3 units above, below, left and right of the center.

Circles Explanations

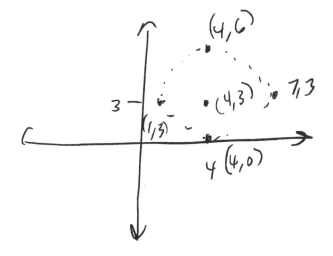

Make a sketch starting with the center and adding points 5 above, below, left and right of the center.

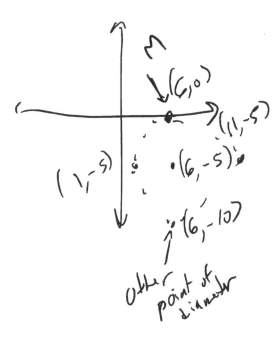

9. 3/8

$$\frac{x}{360} = \frac{s}{A}$$

$$\frac{135}{360}$$

reduce

$$\frac{135}{360} = \frac{3}{8}$$

10. B

Given the equation $(x-6)^2 + (y+5)^2 = 25$

the center of the circle is (6,-5) and the radius is 5.

11. 288

If the arc is $\frac{4}{5}$ of the circle, then the interior angle is $\frac{4}{5}$ of 360.

$$\frac{4(360)}{5}$$

$$\frac{4(360)}{5} = 288$$

Circles Explanations

12. A

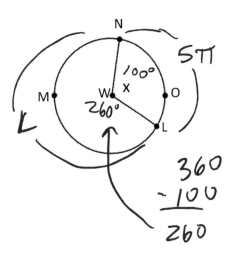

The intercepted arcs are proportionate to the inscribed angles.

$$\frac{100°}{5\pi} = \frac{260°}{L}$$

$$100L = 1300\pi$$

$$\frac{100L}{100} = \frac{1300\pi}{100}$$

$$L = 13\pi$$

13. C

The two points are at the same height, y-value of 2, so the center of the circle will have an x-coordinate that is right in the middle.

See the diagram below.

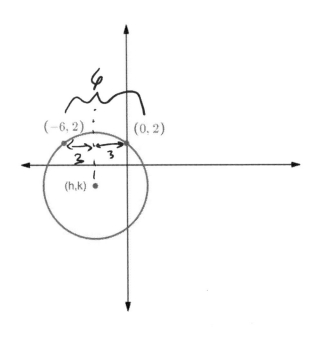

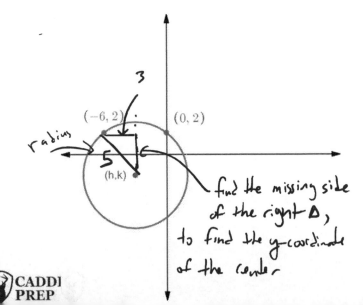

find the missing side of the right △, to find the y-coordinate of the center

Circles Explanations

$3^2 + x^2 = 5^2$

$9 + x^2 = 25$

$x^2 = 16$

$x = 4$

$k = -2$

14. C

Center $(4, -8)$
       h k

radius = 10

$(x-h)^2 + (y-k)^2 = r^2$

$(x-4)^2 + (y--8)^2 = 10^2$

$(x-4)^2 + (y+8)^2 = 100$

Circles 2

1. C

Equation of a circle is

$(x-h)^2 + (y-k)^2 = r^2$

So if the center is (-3, 3), then $h = -3$ and $k = 3$

We need to find the radius, so we should use the distance formula with the center (-3,3) and a point on the circle (4,6)

$d = \sqrt{(x_2-x_1)^2 + (y_2-y_1)^2}$

$d = \sqrt{(4--3)^2 + (6-3)^2}$

$d = \sqrt{(7)^2 + (3)^2}$

$d = \sqrt{58}$

$r = \sqrt{58}$

$r^2 = 58$

$(x-1)^2 + (y-2)^2 = 50$

2. 7/10

$\dfrac{\theta}{2\pi} = \dfrac{Sector}{Total\ Area}$

$\dfrac{7\pi/5}{2\pi} = \dfrac{7\pi}{5} \div 2\pi$

$\dfrac{7\pi}{5} \cdot \dfrac{1}{2\pi}$

$\dfrac{7\pi}{5} \cdot \dfrac{1}{2\pi} = \dfrac{7}{10}$

Circles Explanations

3. 18

$$\frac{x}{360} = \frac{L}{C}$$

$$\frac{90}{360} = \frac{L}{72}$$

$$\frac{1}{4} = \frac{L}{72}$$

$$\frac{72}{4} = \frac{4L}{4}$$

$$18 = L$$

4. C

To find the center, we need to get the equation into the following form.

$$(x - h)^2 + (y - k)^2 = r^2$$

We will need to complete the square twice.

$$x^2 - 22x + y^2 + 16y = -121$$

Complete the square for the x terms and for the y terms.

$$\left(\frac{b}{2}\right)^2 \qquad \left(\frac{b}{2}\right)^2$$

$$\left(\frac{-22}{2}\right)^2 \qquad \left(\frac{16}{2}\right)^2$$

$$121 \qquad 64$$

$$x^2 - 22x \quad + y^2 + 16y = -121$$
$$+121 \qquad\qquad +64 \quad\; \substack{+121 \\ +64}$$

$$x^2 - 22x + 121 + y^2 + 16y + 64 = 64$$

$$(x - 11)^2 + (y + 8)^2 = 64$$

$$\text{center} = (11, -8)$$

5. 3/20

$$\frac{L}{C}$$

$$L = 6\pi/5$$

$$C = 2\pi r$$

$$C = 2\pi(4)$$

Circles Explanations

$C = 8\pi$

$$\frac{L}{C} = \frac{6\pi/5}{8\pi}$$

$$\frac{6\pi/5}{8\pi} = \frac{6\pi}{5} \cdot \frac{1}{8\pi}$$

$$\frac{\cancel{6\pi}^{3}}{5} \cdot \frac{1}{\cancel{8\pi}_{4}} = \frac{3}{20}$$

6. C

To find the radius, we need to get the equation into the following form.

$$(x - h)^2 + (y - k)^2 = r^2$$

We will need to complete the square twice.

$x^2 - 22x + y^2 + 4y = 44$

Complete the square for the x terms and for the y terms.

$\left(\frac{b}{2}\right)^2 \qquad \left(\frac{b}{2}\right)^2$

$\left(\frac{-22}{2}\right)^2 \qquad \left(\frac{4}{2}\right)^2$

$121 \qquad 4$

$$x^2 - 22x + y^2 + 4y = 44$$
$$+121 \qquad +4 \; +121 \; +4$$

$x^2 - 22x + 121 + y^2 + 4y + 4 = 169$

$r^2 = 169 \qquad r^2$

$r = 13$

7. 3/4

$360° = 2\pi$

set up a proportion

$$\frac{360}{2\pi} = \frac{135}{x}$$

$360x = 270\pi$

$$\frac{360x}{360} = \frac{270\pi}{360}$$

$$x = \frac{270}{360}\pi$$

Circles Explanations

$$x = \frac{27}{36}\pi = \frac{3}{4}\pi$$

$$a\pi$$

$$a = 3/4$$

9. 3/4

$$\frac{x}{360} = \frac{s}{A}$$

$$\frac{270}{360}$$

reduce

$$\frac{270}{360} = \frac{27}{36} = \frac{3}{4}$$

8. D

Given $(x-2)^2 + (y+1)^2 = 16$, the center of the circle is (2-1) and the radius is 4. Make a sketch.

Start with the center and make points 4 units above, below, left and right of the center.

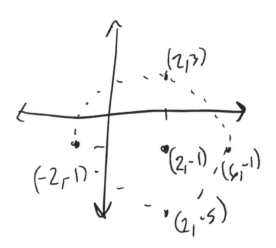

10. C

Given the equation $(x-3)^2 + (y-2)^2 = 49$

the center of the circle is (3,2) and the radius is 7.

Circles Explanations

Make a sketch starting with the center and adding points 7 above, below, left and right of the center.

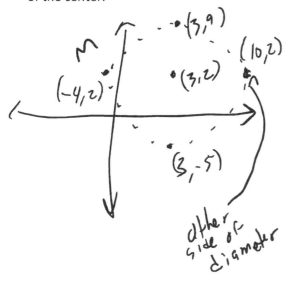

11. 135

If the arc is 3/8 of the circle, then the interior angle is $\frac{3}{8}$ of 360.

$$\frac{3(360)}{8}$$

$$\frac{3(\cancel{360}^{45})}{\cancel{8}^{1}} = 135$$

12. D

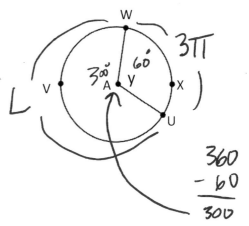

$$\begin{array}{r} 360 \\ -60 \\ \hline 300 \end{array}$$

The intercepted arcs are proportionate to the inscribed angles.

$$\frac{60°}{3\pi} = \frac{300°}{L}$$

$$60L = 900\pi$$

$$\frac{\cancel{60}L}{\cancel{60}} = \frac{900\pi}{60}$$

$$L = 15\pi$$

13. 17

The two points are at the same height, y-value of 2, so the center of the circle will have an x-coordinate that is right in the middle.

Circles Explanations

See the diagram below.

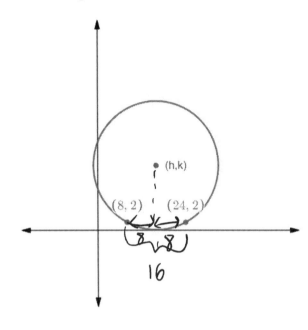

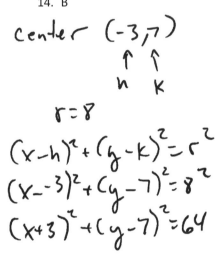

$8^2 + x^2 = 17^2$
$64 + x^2 = 289$
$x^2 = 225$
$x = 15$

$y = 2 + 15 = 17$
$y = 2$

14. B

center $(-3, 7)$
         ↑   ↑
         h   k

$r = 8$

$(x-h)^2 + (y-k)^2 = r^2$
$(x--3)^2 + (y-7)^2 = 8^2$
$(x+3)^2 + (y-7)^2 = 64$

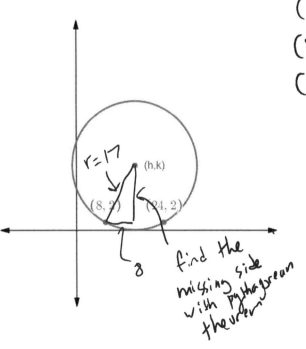

find the missing side with pythagorean theorem

$a^2 + b^2 = c^2$

Angles, Polygons & 3-D Shapes: Practice 1

1.

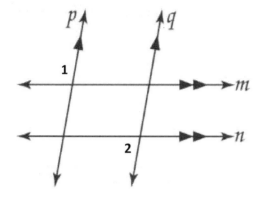

Note: Figure not drawn to scale.

In the figure above, lines m and n are parallel and lines p and q are parallel. If the measure of ∠1 is 62°, what is the measure of ∠2?

A) 138°

B) 118°

C) 28°

D) 62°

Angles, Polygons & 3-D Shapes: Practice 1

2.

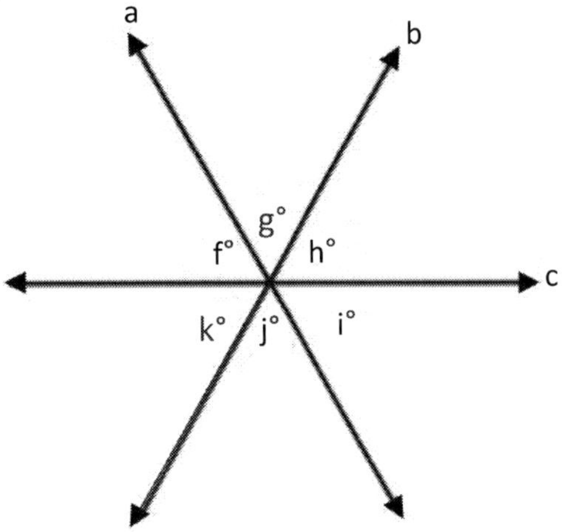

Note: Figure not drawn to scale.

In the figure above, lines a, b, and c intersect at a point. If $g + h = i + j$, which of the following must be true?

    I. i = f
    II. f = k
    III. j = h

A) I and II only

B) I and III only

C) II and III only

D) I, II and III only

Angles, Polygons & 3-D Shapes: Practice 1

3.

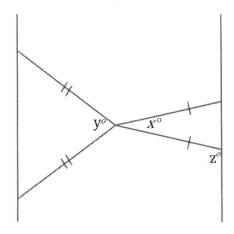

Note: Figure not drawn to scale.

Two isosceles triangles are shown above. If $230 - x = 3y$ and $y = 70$, what is the value of z?

4. Intersecting lines c, f, and m are shown below.

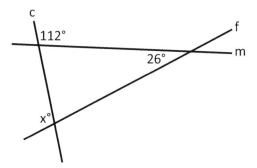

Note: Figure not drawn to scale.

What is the value of x?

Angles, Polygons & 3-D Shapes: Practice 1

5.

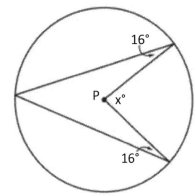

Note: Figure not drawn to scale.

Point P is the center of the circle in the figure above. What is the value of x?

6.

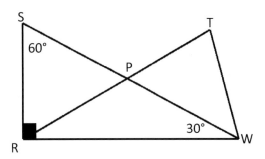

Note: Figure not drawn to scale.

In the figure above, $\overline{RT}$ and $\overline{SW}$ intersect at point P, RP = PW. What is the measure, in degrees of ∠SPR? (Disregard the degree symbol when gridding your answer.)

Angles, Polygons & 3-D Shapes: Practice 1

7.

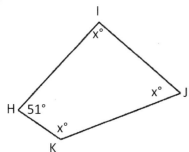

Note: Figure not drawn to scale.

In the figure above, what is the value of x?

A) 43

B) 103

C) 73

D) 163

8.

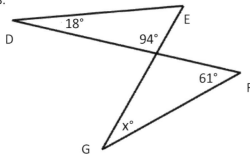

Note: Figure not drawn to scale.

In the figure above, what is the value of x?

A) 25

B) 94

C) 68

D) 89

9.

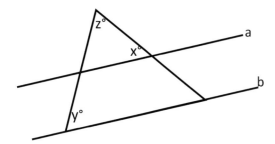

Note: Figure not drawn to scale.

In the figure above, lines *a* and *b* are parallel $y = 95°$, and $z = 53°$. What is the value of x?

A) 52

B) 42

C) 32

D) 62

10.

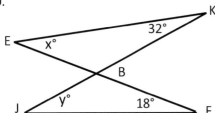

Note: Figure not drawn to scale.

In the figure above, $\overline{EF}$ intersects $\overline{JK}$ at B. If $x = 65°$, what is the value of y?

A) 56

B) 83

C) 79

D) 67

11.

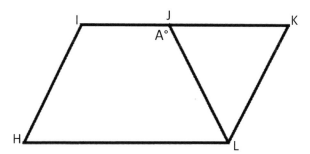

In quadrilateral HIKL above $\overline{IK} || \overline{HL}$ and $\overline{JK} = \overline{JL} = \overline{LK}$. What is the value of A?

A) 110

B) 180

C) 120

D) 140

12.

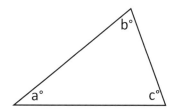

Note: Figure not drawn to scale.

In the triangle above, a = 56. What is the value of b + c?

A) 96

B) 150

C) 124

D) 88

Angles, Polygons & 3-D Shapes: Practice 1

13.

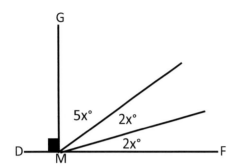

Note: Figure not drawn to scale.

In the figure above, point M lies on $\overline{EF}$. What is the value of 2x?

A) 80

B) 20

C) 40

D) 60

14.

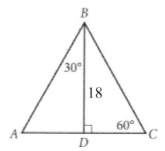

Note: Figure not drawn to scale.

In △ABC above, what is the length of $\overline{AD}$?

A) 4

B) 6

C) $6\sqrt{2}$

D) $6\sqrt{3}$

15.

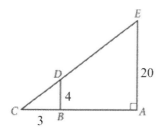

Note: Figure not drawn to scale.

In the figure above. $\overline{BD}$ is parallel to $\overline{AE}$. What is the length of $\overline{CE}$?

Angles, Polygons & 3-D Shapes: Practice 1

16.

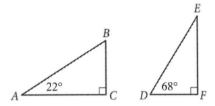

Note: Figure not drawn to scale.

Triangles ABC and DEF are shown above. Which of the following is equal to ratio $\frac{BC}{AB}$?

A) $\frac{DE}{DF}$

B) $\frac{DF}{DE}$

C) $\frac{DF}{EF}$

D) $\frac{EF}{DE}$

17.

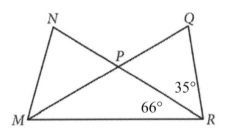

Note: Figure not drawn to scale.

In the figure above, $\overline{MQ}$ and $\overline{NR}$ intersect at point P, NP = QP and MP = PR. What is the measure, in degrees, of ∠QMR?

Angles, Polygons & 3-D Shapes: Practice 1

18.

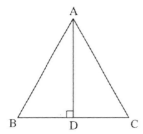

In the figure above, $\overline{AD}$ is a perpendicular bisector of $\overline{BC}$. $\overline{BA} = \overline{AC}$. ∠BAC = 34°. What is the measure of angle ∠B ?

19.

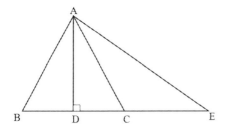

$\overline{AD}$ bisects $\overline{BC}$. $\overline{CE}$ is twice the length of $\overline{DC}$. $\overline{AB}$ = 10, $\overline{BD}$ = 6. What is the length of $\overline{AE}$?

A) 14

B) $4\sqrt{13}$

C) $2\sqrt{97}$

D) 19

Angles, Polygons & 3-D Shapes: Practice 1

20. The volume of a cone is 12π cubic inches. If the height is 4 inches, what is the diameter of the base of the cone in inches?

A) 2

B) 3

C) 4

D) 6

Angles, Polygons & 3-D Shapes: Practice 2

1.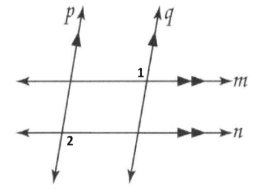

In the figure above, lines m and n are parallel and lines p and q are parallel. If the measure of
∠ 1 is 46°, what is the measure of ∠2?
A)154°
B)66°
C)46°
D)86°

Angles, Polygons & 3-D Shapes: Practice 2

2.

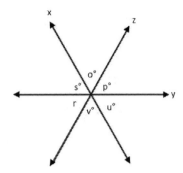

In the figure above, lines x, y, and z intersect at a point. If s + r = v + u, which of the following must be true?

    I. v = p
    II. o = p
    III. v = r

A) I and II only
B) I and III only
C) II and III only
D) I, II and III only

3.

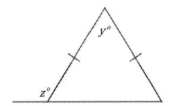

Note: Figure not drawn to scale.

An isosceles triangle is shown above. If $160 - 2x = 2y$ and $x = 16$, what is the value of z?

Angles, Polygons & 3-D Shapes: Practice 2

4. Intersecting lines u, v, and w are shown below.

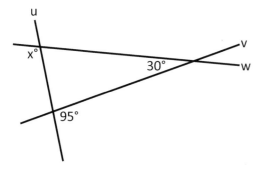

What is the value of x?

5.

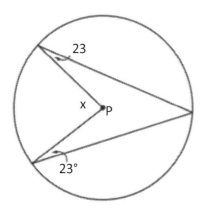

Point P is the center of the circle in the figure above. What is the value of x?

Angles, Polygons & 3-D Shapes: Practice 2

6.

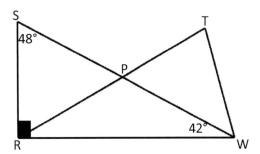

In the figure above, $\overline{RT}$ and $\overline{SW}$ intersect at point P, RP = PW. What is the measure, in degrees of ∠TPW? (Disregard the degree symbol when gridding your answer.)

7.

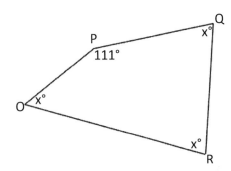

In the figure above, what is the value of x?

A) 83
B) 142
C) 21
D) 54

8.

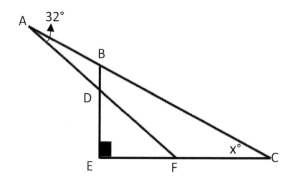

In the figure above where △DEF is a right isosceles triangle, what is the value of x?

A) 103
B) 45
C) 13
D) 77

9.

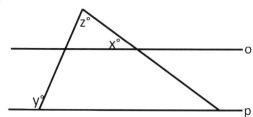

In the figure above, lines *a* and *b* are parallel y = 110, and z = 95. What is the value of x?

A) 55
B) 15
C) 100
D) 35

Angles, Polygons & 3-D Shapes: Practice 2

10.

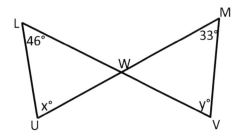

Note: Figure not drawn to scale.

In the figure above, $\overline{LV}$ intersects $\overline{UM}$ at W. If x = 85°, what is the value of y?

A) 49
B) 98
C) 103
D) 66

11.

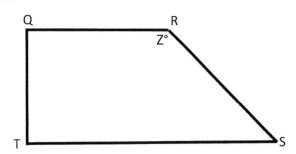

In quadrilateral TQRS above $\overline{QR} || \overline{TS}$ and $\overline{RS} = \sqrt{2}\ \overline{QT}$. What is the measure of angle Z?

A) 135
B) 150
C) 120
D) 225

Angles, Polygons & 3-D Shapes: Practice 2

12.

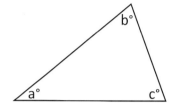

Note: Figure not drawn to scale.

In the triangle above, b = 93. What is the value of a + c?

A) 76
B) 87
C) 102
D) 93

13.

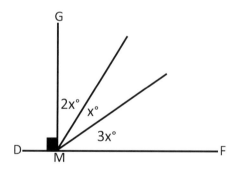

In the figure above, point M lies on $\overline{EF}$. What is the value of 3x?

A) 45
B) 15
C) 65
D) 70

14.

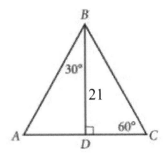

Note: Figure not drawn to scale.

In △ABC above, what is the length of $\overline{AD}$?

A) 5
B) 7
C) $7\sqrt{2}$
D) $7\sqrt{3}$

15.

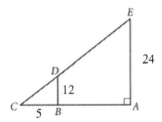

Note: Figure not drawn to scale.

In the figure above. $\overline{BD}$ is parallel to $\overline{AE}$. What is the length of $\overline{CE}$?

Angles, Polygons & 3-D Shapes: Practice 2

16.

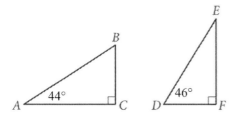

Note: Figure not drawn to scale.

Triangles ABC and DEF are shown above. Which of the following is equal to ratio $\frac{BC}{AC}$?

A) $\frac{AB}{DF}$

B) $\frac{AB}{DE}$

C) $\frac{DE}{AB}$

D) $\frac{DF}{EF}$

17.

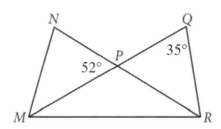

Note: Figure not drawn to scale.

In the figure above, $\overline{MQ}$ and $\overline{NR}$ intersect at point P, NP = QP and MP = PR. What is the measure, in degrees, of ∠QMR?

Angles, Polygons & 3-D Shapes: Practice 2

18.

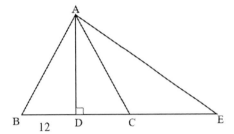

Note: Figure not drawn to scale.

$\overline{AD}$ bisects $\overline{BC}$. $\overline{CE}$ is twice the length of $\overline{DC}$. $\overline{AB} = 20$ and $\overline{BD} = 12$. What is the length of $\overline{AE}$?

A) 28
B) $8\sqrt{13}$
C) $4\sqrt{97}$
D) 38

19. A sphere has a volume of 36π cubic centimeters. What is the diameter of the sphere in centimeters?

A) 3
B) 6
C) 9
D) 12

20. A conical vessel filled with water has a radius of 2 ft and a height of 6 ft. If all of the water is transferred from the conical vessel to an empty cylindrical vessel that is standing upright with a radius of 3 ft and a height of 5 ft, what will the height of the water in the cylindrical vessel be?

Angles, Polygons & 3-D Shapes Explanations

Angles, Polygons & 3-D Shapes 1

1. B

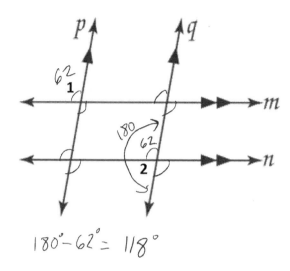

$180° - 62° = 118°$

2. A

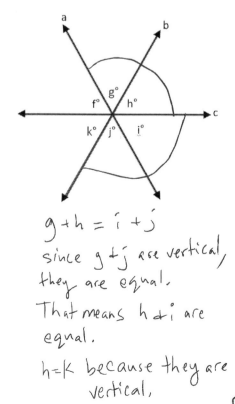

$g + h = i + j$
since $g + j$ are vertical,
they are equal.
That means h & i are equal.
$h = k$ because they are vertical,

$i = f$ because they are vertical
That means $h = i = k = f$

3. 100

$230 - x = 210$
$x = 20$

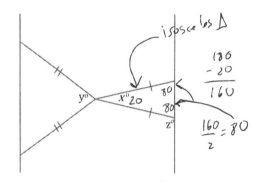

isosceles △

180
$- 20$
$\overline{160}$

$\dfrac{160}{2} = 80$

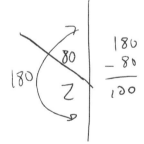

180
$- 80$
$\overline{100}$

Angles, Polygons & 3-D Shapes Explanations

4. 94

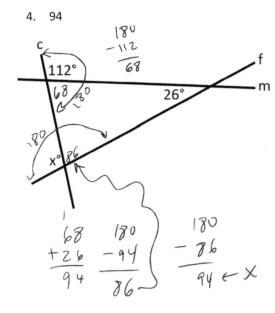

5. 64

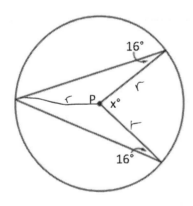

For this question, you should ask yourself, "Why is this figure drawn in a circle?"

The circle is used to show that certain lengths are equal: the radii

By adding the line, we can see three radii that make two isosceles triangles.

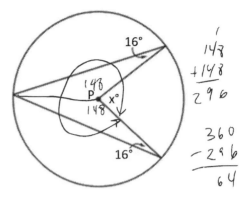

6. 60

RP=PW, so triangle RPW is an isosceles triangle. The base angles are both 30 degrees.

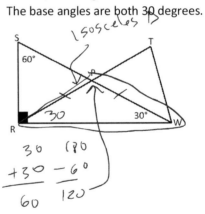

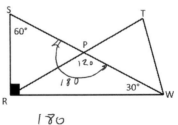

7. B

The angles of a quadrilateral add up to 360.

Angles, Polygons & 3-D Shapes Explanations

$x + x + x + 51 = 360$
$3x + 51 = 360$
$3x = 309$
$x = 103$

8. 25

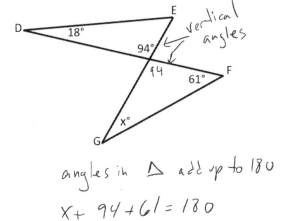

angles in △ add up to 180
$x + 94 + 61 = 180$
$x = 25$

9. C

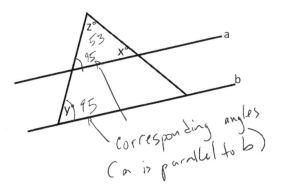

corresponding angles
(a is parallel to b)

$53 + 95 + x = 180$
$x = 32$

10. C

$\begin{array}{r} 65 \\ +32 \\ \hline 97 \end{array} \quad \begin{array}{r} 180 \\ -97 \\ \hline 83 \end{array}$

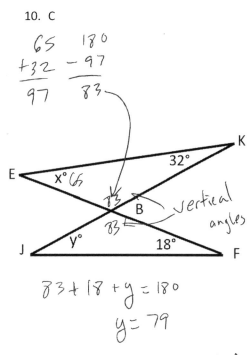

$83 + 18 + y = 180$
$y = 79$

11. 120

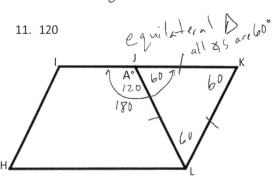

12. C

$a + b + c = 180$
$a = 56$

$\begin{array}{r} 56 + b + c = 180 \\ -56 \quad\quad\quad -56 \\ \hline b + c = 124 \end{array}$

Angles, Polygons & 3-D Shapes Explanations

13. C

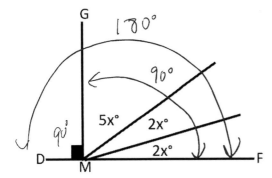

$5x + 2x + 2x = 90$
$9x = 90$
$x = 10$

$2x = 2(10) = 20$

Compare to 30-60-90 triangle on reference sheet

14. D

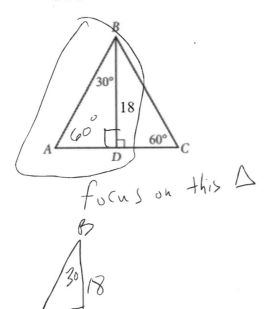

focus on this △

18 is opposite 60° and $x\sqrt{3}$ is opposite 60°, so $18 = x\sqrt{3}$
solve for x

$$\frac{18}{\sqrt{3}} = \frac{x\sqrt{3}}{\sqrt{3}}$$

$$\frac{18}{\sqrt{3}} = x$$

rationalize

$$\frac{18}{\sqrt{3}} \cdot \frac{\sqrt{3}}{\sqrt{3}} = \frac{18\sqrt{3}}{3} = 6\sqrt{3}$$

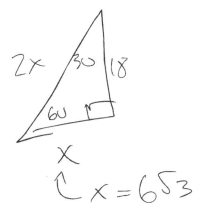

$x = 6\sqrt{3}$

15. 25

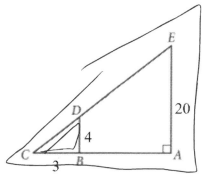

$\triangle CBD$ is similar to $\triangle CAE$, so the side lengths are proportionate

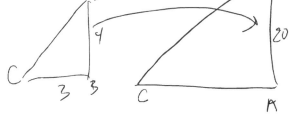

The ratio is $4:20$ or $1:5$.

Angles, Polygons & 3-D Shapes Explanations

To find the length of CE, we need the length of CD

Use pythagorean theorem

$a^2 + b^2 = c^2$
$3^2 + 4^2 = c^2$
$25 = c^2$
$5 = c$

$CD = 5$
CE is 5 times as long, so $CE = 25$

16. B

Find the missing angles, using the fact that the interior angles of a triangle add up to $180°$

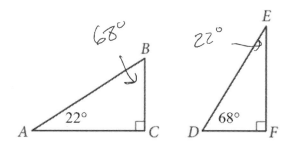

The two triangles have the same angles, so they are similar (the side lengths are proportionate)

Angles, Polygons & 3-D Shapes Explanations

This is an isosceles triangle, so the two angles across from the congruent sides have the same measure.

∠QMR IS 66°

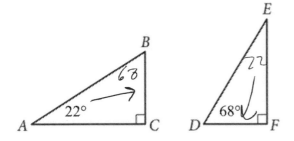

BC matches up with DF since they are both opposite the 22° angle, and AB match up with DE since they are both opposite the right angle.

$$\frac{BC}{AB} = \frac{DF}{DE}$$

18. 73

$\overline{BA} = \overline{AC}$, so triangle ABC is an isosceles triangle.

∠BAC = 34°

17. 66

NP = QP and MP = PR

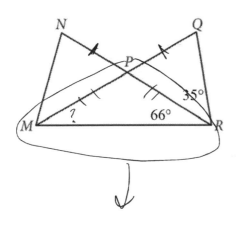

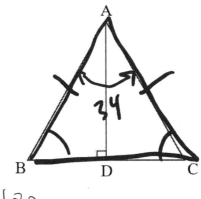

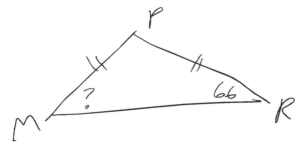

19. C

$\overline{AD}$ bisects $\overline{BC}$. This means $\overline{BD}$ and $\overline{DC}$ are both 6.

$\overline{CE}$ is twice the length of $\overline{DC}$, so $\overline{CE}$ is 12

Angles, Polygons & 3-D Shapes Explanations

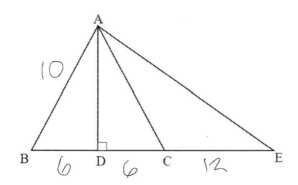

To find $\overline{AE}$, we could use Pythagorean theorem in right triangle ADE, but we don't know the length of $\overline{AD}$.

Therefore, we must use Pythagorean theorem in right triangle ADB to first find the length of $\overline{AD}$.

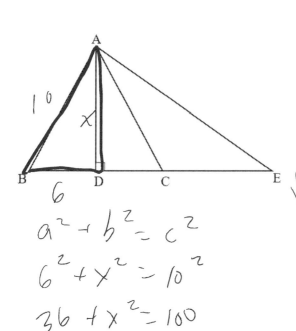

$a^2 + b^2 = c^2$
$6^2 + x^2 = 10^2$
$36 + x^2 = 100$
$x^2 = 64$
$x = 8$

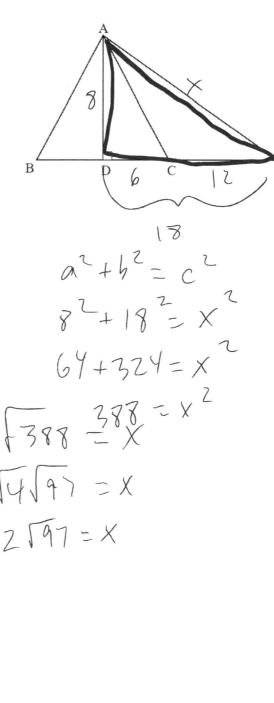

$a^2 + b^2 = c^2$
$8^2 + 18^2 = x^2$
$64 + 324 = x^2$
$\sqrt{388} = \sqrt{x^2}$
$\sqrt{4}\sqrt{97} = x$
$2\sqrt{97} = x$

20. D

$$V = \frac{1}{3}\pi r^2 h$$

$$12\pi = \frac{1}{3}\pi r^2(4)$$

$$(3)12\pi = 3\left(\frac{1}{3}\right)\pi r^2(4)$$

$$36\pi = \pi r^2(4)$$

$$\frac{36\pi}{\pi} = \frac{\pi r^2(4)}{\pi}$$

$$36 = r^2(4)$$

$$\frac{36}{4} = \frac{r^2(4)}{4}$$

$$9 = r^2$$

$$3 = r$$

diameter = $2r = 6$

Angles, Polygons & 3-D Shapes 2

1. C

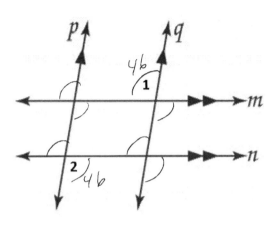

2. D

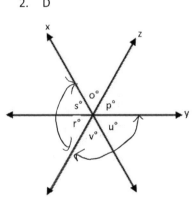

$s = u$ vertical angles

$s + r = v + u$

so $r = v$

$o = v$ vertical angles

$r = p$ vertical angles

$r = v = o = p$

Angles, Polygons & 3-D Shapes Explanations

3. 122

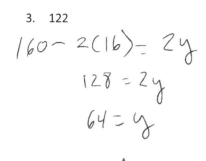

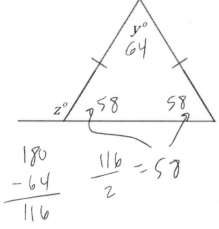

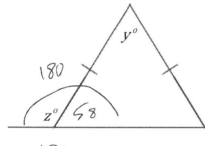

4. 115

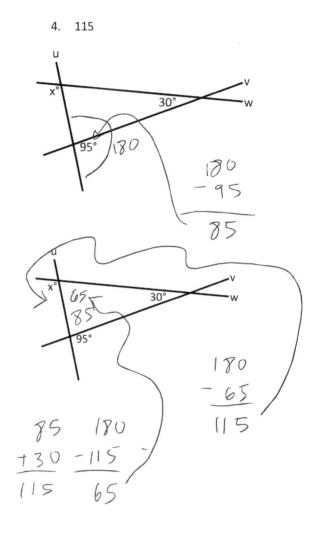

5. 92

For this question, you should ask yourself, "Why is this figure drawn in a circle?"

The circle is used to show that certain lengths are equal: the radii

By adding the line, we can see three radii that make two isosceles triangles.

Angles, Polygons & 3-D Shapes Explanations

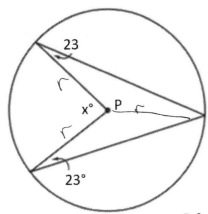

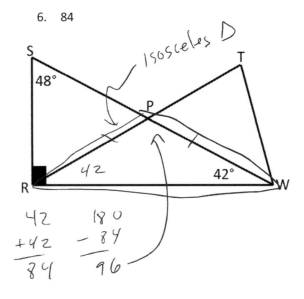

6. 84

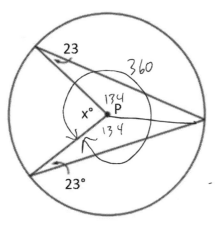

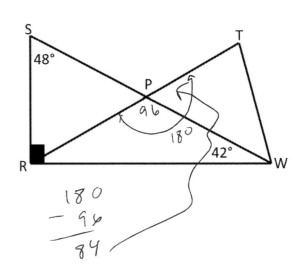

7. A

The angles of a quadrilateral add up to 360.

$$x + x + x + 111 = 360$$
$$3x + 111 = 360$$
$$3x = 249$$
$$x = 83$$

Angles, Polygons & 3-D Shapes Explanations

8. 13

$32 + 135 + x = 18$
$x = 13$

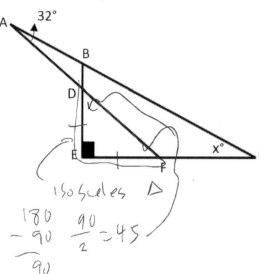

isosceles △

180
−90
―――
 90

$\dfrac{90}{2} = 45$

9. B

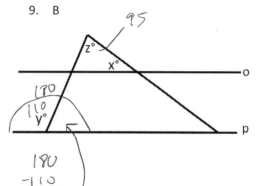

180
−110
―――
 70

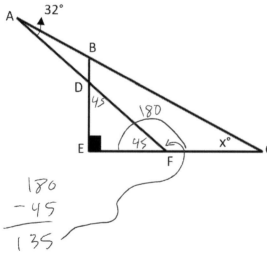

180
−45
―――
135

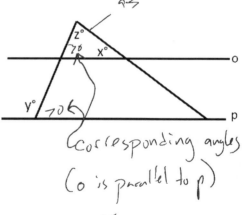

corresponding angles
(o is parallel to p)

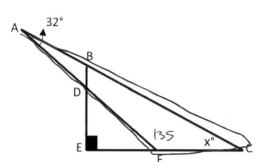

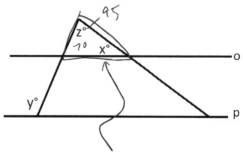

$70 + 95 + x = 180$
$x = 15$

Angles, Polygons & 3-D Shapes Explanations

10. B

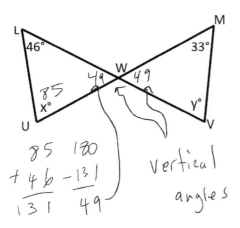

$$\begin{array}{cc} 85 & 180 \\ +46 & -131 \\ \hline 131 & 49 \end{array}$$

Vertical angles

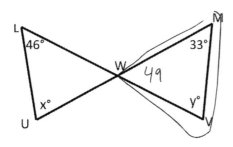

$$33 + 49 + y = 180$$
$$y = 98$$

11. A

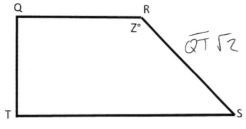

This brings to mind a special triangle from the reference table.

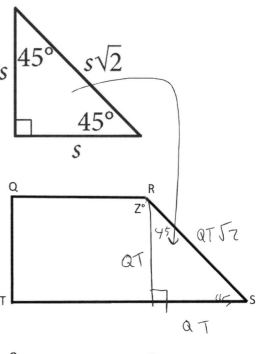

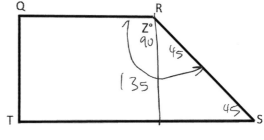

12. B

$$a + b + c = 180$$
$$a + 93 + c = 180$$
$$ -93 -93$$
$$a + c = 87$$

Angles, Polygons & 3-D Shapes Explanations

13.

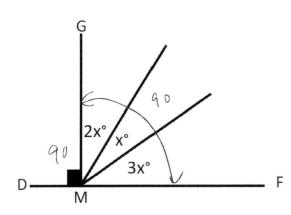

$2x + x + 3x = 90$
$6x = 90$
$x = 15$

$3x = 3(15) = 45$

14.

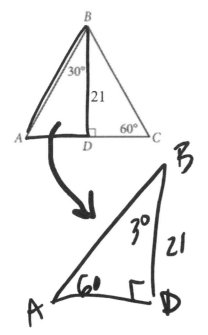

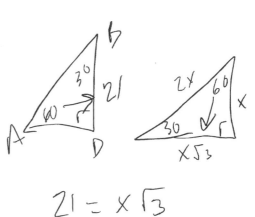

$21 = x\sqrt{3}$

solve for x

$\dfrac{21}{\sqrt{3}} = \dfrac{x\sqrt{3}}{\sqrt{3}}$

$x = \dfrac{21}{\sqrt{3}}$

rationalize

$\dfrac{21}{\sqrt{3}} \cdot \dfrac{\sqrt{3}}{\sqrt{3}} = \dfrac{21\sqrt{3}}{3} = 7\sqrt{3}$

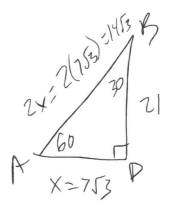

$2x = 2(7\sqrt{3}) = 14\sqrt{3}$

$x = 7\sqrt{3}$

Angles, Polygons & 3-D Shapes Explanations

15. 26

Triangle CBD is similar to triangle CAE

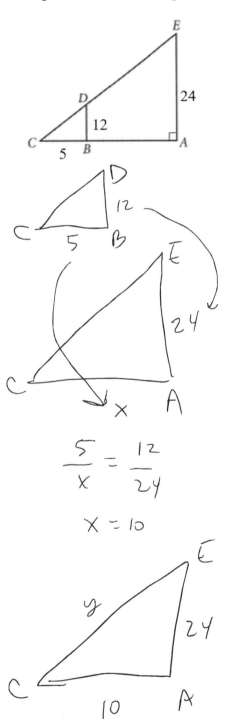

$$a^2 + b^2 = c^2$$
$$10^2 + 24^2 = y^2$$
$$100 + 576 = y^2$$
$$676 = y^2$$
$$26 = y$$

16. D

Find the missing angles, using the fact that the interior angles of a triangle add up to $180°$

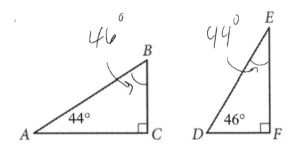

The two triangles have the same angles, so they are similar (the side lengths are proportionate)

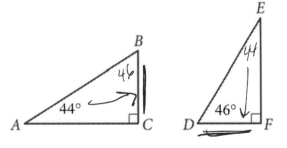

BC matches up with DF since they are both opposite the $24°$ angle, and AC match up with EF since they are both opposite the $46°$ angle.

Angles, Polygons & 3-D Shapes Explanations

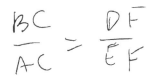

17. 26

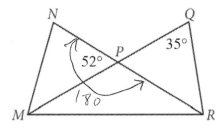

180
− 52
128

Triangle MPR is an isosceles triangle

180
−128
52

26
2)52

18. C

$\overline{AD}$ bisects $\overline{BC}$, so $\overline{BD}$ and $\overline{DC}$ are both 12.

$\overline{CE}$ is twice the length of $\overline{DC}$, so since $\overline{DC}$ = 20 then $\overline{CE}$ = 24.

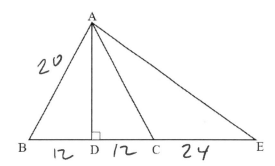

To find $\overline{AE}$, we could use Pythagorean theorem in right triangle ADE, but we don't know the length of $\overline{AD}$.

Therefore, we must use Pythagorean theorem in right triangle ADB to first find the length of $\overline{AD}$.

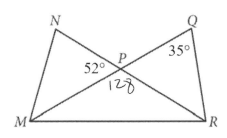

NP = QP and MP = PR

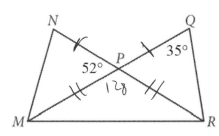

Angles, Polygons & 3-D Shapes Explanations

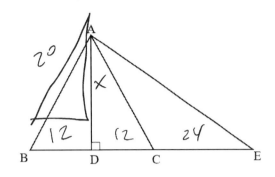

$$a^2 + b^2 = c^2$$
$$16^2 + 36^2 = x^2$$
$$256 + 1296 = x^2$$
$$1552 = x^2$$
$$\sqrt{16}\sqrt{97} = x^2$$
$$4\sqrt{97} = x$$

$$a^2 + b^2 = c^2$$
$$x^2 + 12^2 = 20^2$$
$$x^2 + 144 = 400$$
$$x^2 = 256$$
$$x = 16$$

19. B

$$V = \frac{4}{3}\pi r^3$$

$$36\pi = \frac{4}{3}\pi r^3$$

$$\frac{36\pi}{\pi} = \frac{\frac{4}{3}\pi r^3}{\pi}$$

$$36 = \frac{4}{3} r^3$$

$$\left(\frac{3}{4}\right) 36 = \frac{4}{3} r^3 \left(\frac{3}{4}\right)$$

$$27 = r^3$$

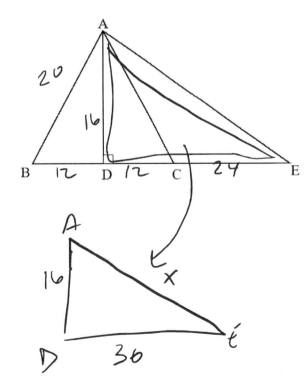

Angles, Polygons & 3-D Shapes Explanations

$3 = r$
diameter $= 2r = 6$

20.8/9

cone:

$V = \frac{1}{3}\pi r^2 h$

$V = \frac{1}{3}\pi (2)^2 (6)$

$V = 8\pi$

$8\pi = \pi (3)^2 h$

$\dfrac{8\pi}{\pi} = \dfrac{\pi \cdot 9 h}{\pi}$

$8 = 9h$

$\dfrac{8}{9} = \dfrac{9h}{9}$

$\dfrac{8}{9} = h$

Cylinder

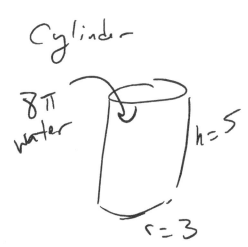

8π might not be enough to fill the entire cylinder, so the height might be less than 5 ft. We have to solve for the height.

$V = \pi r^2 h$

Trigonometry: Practice 1

1) In a right triangle, one angle measures x°, where $\cos x° = \frac{1}{3}$. What is $\sin(90° - x°)$?

2) In triangle DEF, the measure of ∠E is 90°. DE = 18, and EF = 24. Triangle ABC is similar to triangle DEF, where vertices A, B, and C correspond to vertices D, E, and F, respectively, and each side of triangle ABC is $\frac{1}{2}$ the length of the corresponding side of triangle DEF. What is the value of tan A?
   A) $\frac{3}{4}$
   B) $\frac{4}{5}$
   C) $\frac{4}{3}$
   D) $\frac{5}{4}$

3) If $\sin(B°) = \cos(C°)$. If $B = 3k - 23$ and $C = 2k - 12$, what is the angle measure of B?
   A) 25°
   B) 52°
   C) 38°
   D) 90°

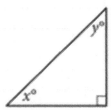

4) In the triangle above, the sine of y° is 0.8. What is the sine of x°?
   A) 0.6
   B) 0.2
   C) 0.48
   D) 1.25

Trigonometry: Practice 1

5) The number of radians in a 540-degree angle can be written as $a\pi$, where a is a constant. What is the value of a?

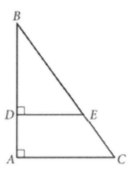

6) In the figure above, $\tan B = \frac{3}{4}$. If AC = 12 and EC = 5, what is the length of BD?
   A) 16
   B) 15
   C) 9
   D) 12

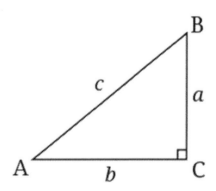

7) In triangle ABC, point D (not shown) lies on line AB. What is the value of $\cos(\angle BCD) - \sin(\angle DCA)$?

Trigonometry: Practice 1

8) Triangle ABC has right angle B. If $\tan A = \frac{3}{4}$, what is the value of cos C?
   A) $\frac{3}{5}$
   B) $\frac{4}{5}$
   C) $\frac{4}{3}$
   D) $\frac{3}{4}$

9) If $\cos x° = a$, which of the following must be true for all values of x?
   A) $\sin x° = a$
   B) $\cos (90° - x°) = a$
   C) $\sin (90° - x°) = a$
   D) $\cos (x^2)° = a^2$

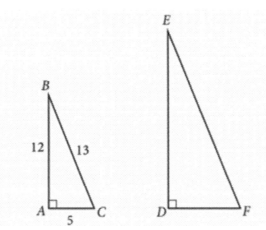

10) In the figure above, triangle ABC is similar to triangle DEF. What is the value of sin(F)?
    A) $\frac{5}{13}$
    B) $\frac{12}{13}$
    C) $\frac{12}{5}$
    D) $\frac{13}{5}$

Trigonometry: Practice 2

1) In a right triangle, one angle measures x°, where $\sin x° = \frac{2}{5}$. What is $\cos(90° - x°)$?

2) In triangle ABC, the measure of ∠B is 90°. ∠A = 60°, and ∠C = 30°. Triangle DEF is similar to triangle ABC, where vertices D, E, and F correspond to vertices A, B, and C, respectively, and each side of triangle DEF is 2 times the length of the corresponding side of triangle ABC. What is the value of cos F?
   A) $\frac{\sqrt{3}}{2}$
   B) $\frac{1}{2}$
   C) $\sqrt{3}$
   D) 2

3) If $\sin(a°) = \cos(b°)$. If $a = 6k + 5$ and $b = 3k + 4$, what is the value of k?
   A) 59
   B) 31
   C) 9
   D) 10.5

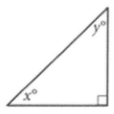

4) In the triangle above, the sine of y° is 0.8. What is cosine of x°?
   A) 0.6
   B) 0.8
   C) 0.48
   D) 1.25

Trigonometry: Practice 2

5) The number of radians in a 360-degree angle can be written as $a\pi$, where a is a constant. What is the value of a?

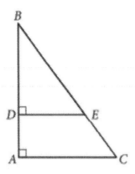

6) In the figure above, $\sin B = \frac{3}{5}$. If AC = 9 and DA = 3, what is the length of DE?
   A) 7
   B) 9
   C) 6.75
   D) 11.25

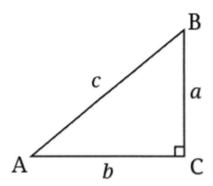

7) In triangle ABC, point D (not shown) lies on line AB. If the cosine of $\angle BCD$ is $\frac{5}{13}$, what is the sine of $\angle DCA$?

Trigonometry: Practice 2

8) Triangle ABC has right angle B. If $\sin A = \frac{3}{5}$, what is the value of cos C?
   A) $\frac{3}{5}$
   B) $\frac{4}{5}$
   C) $\frac{4}{3}$
   D) $\frac{3}{4}$

9) If $\sin x° = b$, which of the following must be true for all values of x, in which $x < 90$?
   A) $\sin a° = b$
   B) $\sin (90° - x°) = a$
   C) $\cos (90° - x°) = a$
   D) $\cos (x)° = a$

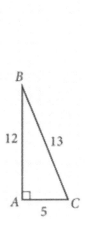
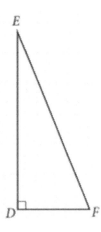

10) In the figure above, triangle ABC is similar to triangle DEF. What is the value of tan(E)?
    A) $\frac{5}{13}$
    B) $\frac{5}{12}$
    C) $\frac{12}{5}$
    D) $\frac{13}{5}$

Trigonometry Explanations

Trigonometry 1

1. 1/3

sine of an angle is equal to cosine of the complement

2. C

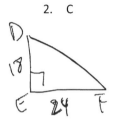 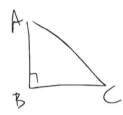

$$\tan A = \tan D = \frac{opp}{adj} = \frac{24}{18} = \frac{4}{3}$$

3. B

If $\sin B = \cos C$,

$B + C = 90$

$3k - 23 + 2k - 12 = 90$

$5k - 35 = 90$

$5k = 125$

$k = 25$

$B = 3k - 23 = 3(25) - 23$

$B = 52$

4. A

$$\sin y = 0.8 = \frac{8}{10} \leftarrow opp \atop \leftarrow hyp$$

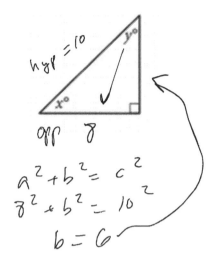

$a^2 + b^2 = c^2$
$8^2 + b^2 = 10^2$
$b = 6$

$$\sin x = \frac{opp}{hyp} = \frac{6}{10} = .6$$

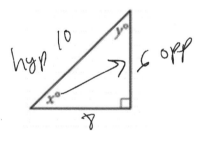

5. 3

$\pi = 180°$

$$\frac{\pi}{180} = \frac{x}{540}$$

$540\pi = 180x$

$$\frac{540\pi}{180} = \frac{180x}{180}$$

$3\pi = x$

$\subset 9\pi$

Trigonometry Explanations

$a = 3$

6. D

$\tan B = \dfrac{3}{4} = \dfrac{opp}{adj}$

The ratio is 3 to 4, but it doesn't necessarily mean that the lengths are 3 and 4. We should label the sides $3x$ and $4x$.

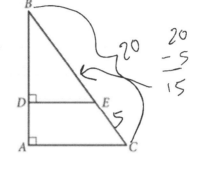

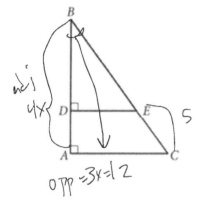

$opp = 3x = 12$

$3x = 12$
$x = 4$

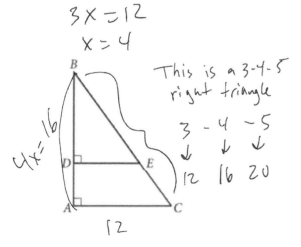

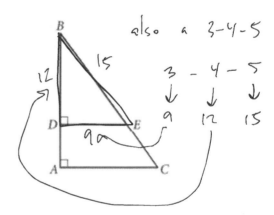

7. O

Draw point D on side AB

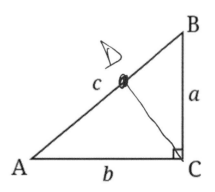

$\angle BCD$ and $\angle ACD$ are complementary, so $\sin(\angle DCA) = \cos(\angle BCD)$.

Trigonometry Explanations

Trigonometry 2

1. 2/5

sine of an angle is equal to cosine of the complement

2. A

30-60-90 triangle

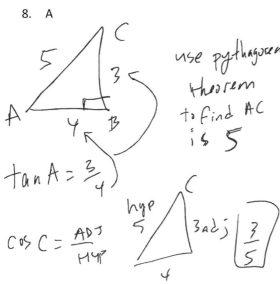

$\angle F = \angle C$, so to find $\cos F$, find $\cos C$

$\cos C = \dfrac{adj}{hyp} = \dfrac{x\sqrt{3}}{2x} = \dfrac{\sqrt{3}}{2}$

3. C

If $\sin a = \cos b$,

$a + b = 90$

$6k + 5 + 3k + 4 = 90$

$9k + 9 = 90$

$9k = 81$

$k = 9$

4. B

sine of an angle is equal to cosine of the complement

From the diagram, we can see that x and y are complementary, so $\sin(y) = \cos(x)$

$\sin(\angle DCA) - \cos(\angle BCD) = 0$

8. A

use pythagorean theorem to find AC is 5

$\tan A = \dfrac{3}{4}$

$\cos C = \dfrac{ADJ}{HYP}$

9. C

sine of an angle is equal to cosine of the complement

10. B

Angle F is the same measure as angle C, so find $\sin(C)$

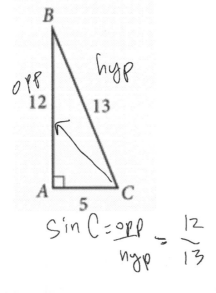

$\sin C = \dfrac{opp}{hyp} = \dfrac{12}{13}$

Trigonometry Explanations

5. 2

$\pi = 180°$

$$\frac{\pi}{180} = \frac{x}{360}$$

$360\pi = 180x$

$$\frac{360\pi}{180} = \frac{180x}{180}$$

$2\pi = x$

$a\pi \quad a = 2$

6. C

$\sin B = \frac{3}{5}$

The ratio is 3 to 5, but it doesn't necessarily mean that the lengths are 3 and 5. We should label the sides $3x$ and $5x$.

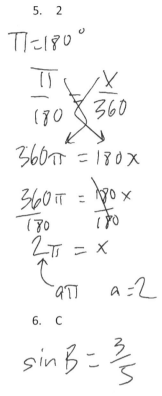

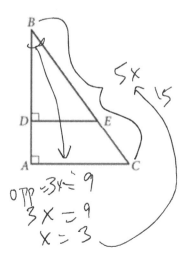

opp $= 3x = 9$
$3x = 9$
$x = 3$

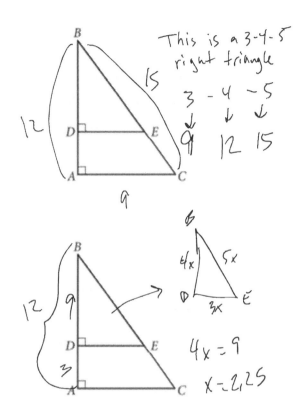

This is a 3-4-5 right triangle

3 - 4 - 5
↓   ↓   ↓
9 12 15

$4x = 9$
$x = 2.25$

$DE = 3x = 3(2.25) = 6.75$

7. 5/13

Draw point D on side AB

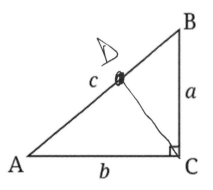

∠BCD and ∠ACD are complementary,
So $\sin(\angle DCA) = \cos(\angle BCD)$.

Trigonometry Explanations

$\sin(\angle DCA) = 5/13$

8. A

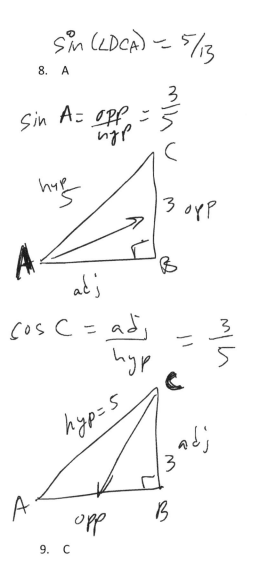

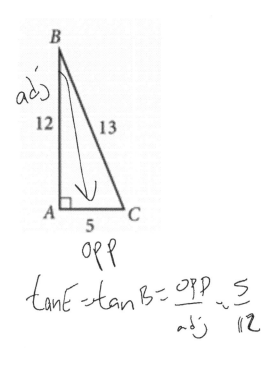

9. C

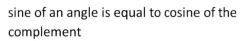

sine of an angle is equal to cosine of the complement

10. B

Angle E is the same measure as angle B, so find $\tan(B)$

Simplifying Rational Expressions: Practice 1

1) What is the sum of $\dfrac{3a}{4a-4}$ and $\dfrac{5a}{3a}$?

   A) $\dfrac{16a-7}{6(a-1)}$

   B) $\dfrac{12a+3}{20(a-1)}$

   C) $\dfrac{29a-17}{12(a-1)}$

   D) $\dfrac{29a-20}{12(a-1)}$

2) Which of the following is equivalent to $\dfrac{5x}{2x} + \dfrac{x-1}{2x^2-10x}$?

   A) $\dfrac{6x^2-29x-1}{2x(x-5)}$

   B) $3 - 2x^2 + 10x$

   C) $\dfrac{5x^2-24x-1}{2x(x-5)}$

   D) $\dfrac{6x-1}{2x(-4+x)}$

3) What is the sum of $\dfrac{x-6}{9x-18}$ and $\dfrac{6}{3}$?

   A) $\dfrac{x-3}{3(3x-4)}$

   B) $\dfrac{19x-42}{9(x-2)}$

   C) $\dfrac{11x-28}{18(x-2)}$

   D) $\dfrac{11x-30}{18(x-2)}$

4) Which of the following is equivalent to $\dfrac{3}{5b-5} - \dfrac{3}{2b+6}$?

   A) $\dfrac{-21-37b-10b^2}{15(b+1)}$

   B) $\dfrac{3}{10(b+1)}$

   C) $\dfrac{1+b}{3b-1}$

   D) $\dfrac{-9b+3}{10(b+3)(b+1)}$

Simplifying Rational Expressions: Practice 1

5) Which of the following is equivalent to the expression below?

$$\dfrac{\dfrac{1}{4}+\dfrac{2}{m-4}}{16}$$

A) $\dfrac{4+m}{16m-64}$

B) $\dfrac{m+4}{64m-256}$

C) $\dfrac{4m-16}{4+m}$

D) $\dfrac{m-2}{16}$

6) Which of the following is equivalent to the expression below?

$$\dfrac{2}{\dfrac{1}{2}-\dfrac{x}{4}}$$

A) $\dfrac{6x^2}{x^3-12}$

B) $\dfrac{36+x^3}{3x}$

C) $\dfrac{9x^2}{x^2-81}$

D) $\dfrac{8}{2-x}$

7) Which of the following is equivalent to the expression below?

$$\dfrac{\dfrac{x+4}{9}+\dfrac{x+4}{3}}{\dfrac{3x+12}{y}}$$

A) $\dfrac{9x+36}{yx^2+8yx+16y+3y^2}$

B) $\dfrac{y^2}{30x+120}$

C) $\dfrac{y-1}{3x+12}$

D) $\dfrac{4y}{27}$

Simplifying Rational Expressions: Practice 1

8) Which of the following is equivalent to the expression below?

$$\dfrac{\dfrac{y+4}{x^2}+\dfrac{1}{y}}{\dfrac{y}{x}}$$

A) $\dfrac{y+4+xy}{y^3+4y^2}$

B) $\dfrac{y^4+xy+4x}{y^4+4y^3}$

C) $\dfrac{y^2+8y+16}{y^2+4y+x^3}$

D) $\dfrac{y^2+4y+x^2}{xy^2}$

Simplifying Rational Expressions: Practice 2

1) What is the sum of $\frac{4}{3}$ and $\frac{n-4}{15n-15}$?
   A) $\frac{7n-8}{5(n-1)}$
   B) $\frac{5n+32}{6(n-5)}$
   C) $\frac{3n+4}{3(n-5)}$
   D) $\frac{n+4}{-n-10}$

2) Which of the following is equivalent to $\frac{6a}{a-5} + \frac{2}{a+2}$?
   A) $\frac{6a^2+14a-10}{(a-5)(a+2)}$
   B) $\frac{6a+2}{a-5}$
   C) $\frac{6a+3}{(a-3)}$
   D) $\frac{12a+2}{(a-5)(a+2)}$

3) What is the sum of $\frac{x+6}{x+4}$ and $\frac{2}{x+2}$?
   A) $\frac{2x+12}{(x+4)(x+2)}$
   B) $\frac{8x+20+x^2}{2(x+4)}$
   C) $\frac{2x+10}{(x+4)}$
   D) $\frac{x^2+10x+20}{(x+4)(x+2)}$

4) Which of the following is equivalent to $\frac{4}{x+6} - \frac{6}{x+3}$?
   A) $\frac{-1-x}{3(2-x)}$
   B) $\frac{x-3}{x-1}$
   C) $\frac{4x+20}{9(x-1)}$
   D) $\frac{-2x-24}{(x+6)(x+3)}$

Simplifying Rational Expressions: Practice 2

5) Which of the following is equivalent to the expression below?

$$\dfrac{9}{\dfrac{1}{3}+\dfrac{x}{16}}$$

A) $\dfrac{9+4x^2}{9}$

B) $\dfrac{432}{16+3x}$

C) $\dfrac{4x}{9x^2-64}$

D) $\dfrac{3x}{36-4x}$

6) Which of the following is equivalent to the expression below?

$$\dfrac{\dfrac{5}{2}}{\dfrac{4}{x}-\dfrac{1}{5}}$$

A) $\dfrac{25x+2}{10x}$

B) $\dfrac{25x}{40-2x}$

C) $\dfrac{40+5x^2}{16x}$

D) $\dfrac{5x^3}{4-x}$

7) Which of the following is equivalent to the expression below?

$$\dfrac{\dfrac{y}{5x}}{\dfrac{y}{x}-\dfrac{5}{y}}$$

A) $\dfrac{y^2}{5y^2-25x}$

B) $\dfrac{5x^2y-125}{y^2}$

C) $\dfrac{x^2y^2}{y-x^2}$

D) $\dfrac{25x^2}{y^3+5x^2}$

Simplifying Rational Expressions: Practice 2

8) Which of the following is equivalent to the expression below?

$$\dfrac{x-3}{\dfrac{25}{x-3}+\dfrac{y+3}{x-3}}$$

A) $\dfrac{25xy-75y75x-225}{y^2+6y-116}$

B) $\dfrac{x^2-6x+9}{28+y}$

C) $\dfrac{28-x}{y^2+6y+9}$

D) $\dfrac{x^2-6x+9}{25x-30+5y^2+30y}$

Simplifying Rational Expressions Explanations

Simplifying Rational Expressions 1

1. **D**

Sum of $\frac{3a}{4a-4}$ and $\frac{5a}{3a}$

$$\frac{3a}{4a-4} + \frac{5a}{3a}$$

Least common denominator is $(4a-4)(3a)$

$$\frac{3a(3a)}{4a-4(3a)} + \frac{5a(4a-4)}{3a(4a-4)}$$

$$\frac{9a^2}{(4a-4)(3a)} + \frac{20a^2-20a}{(3a)(4a-4)}$$

$$\frac{29a^2-20a}{3a(4a-4)}$$

$$\frac{a(29a-20)}{3a(4a-4)}$$

$$\frac{a(29a-20)}{3a(4a-4)}$$

$$\frac{29a-20}{12a-12}$$

$$\frac{29a-20}{12(a-1)}$$

2. **C**

$$\frac{5x}{2x} + \frac{x-1}{2x^2-10x}$$

Factor the denominators to find the least common denominator.

$$\frac{5x}{2x} + \frac{x-1}{2x(x-5)}$$

Least common denominator is $2x(x-5)$.

$$\frac{5x(x-5)}{2x(x-5)} + \frac{x-1}{2x(x-5)}$$

$$\frac{5x^2-25x}{2x(x-5)} + \frac{x-1}{2x(x-5)}$$

$$\frac{5x^2-24x-1}{2x(x-5)}$$

3. **B**

Sum of $\frac{x-6}{9x-18}$ and $\frac{6}{3}$

$$\frac{x-6}{9x-18} + \frac{6}{3}$$

Factor the denominators to find the least common denominator.

$$\frac{x-6}{9(x-2)} + \frac{6}{3}$$

Simplifying Rational Expressions Explanations

Least common denominator is $9(x-2)$.

$$\frac{x-6}{9(x-2)} + \frac{6}{3} \cdot \frac{(3)(x-2)}{(3)(x-2)}$$

$$\frac{x-6}{9(x-2)} + \frac{18(x-2)}{9(x-2)}$$

$$\frac{x-6}{9(x-2)} + \frac{18x-36}{9(x-2)}$$

$$\frac{19x-42}{9(x-2)}$$

4. D

$$\frac{3}{5b+5} - \frac{3}{2b+6}$$

Factor the denominators to find the least common denominator.

$$\frac{3}{5(b+1)} - \frac{3}{2(b+3)}$$

Least common denominator is $10(b+1)(b+3)$.

$$\frac{3\,(2)(b+3)}{5(b+1)(2)(b+3)} - \frac{3\,(5)(b+1)}{2(b+3)(5)(b+1)}$$

$$\frac{6(b+3)}{10(b+1)(b+3)} - \frac{15(b+1)}{10(b+1)(b+3)}$$

$$\frac{6b+18}{10(b+1)(b+3)} - \frac{15b+15}{10(b+1)(b+3)}$$

$$\frac{6b+18-15b-15}{10(b+1)(b+3)}$$

$$\frac{-9b+3}{10(b+1)(b+3)}$$

5. B

$$\frac{\frac{1}{4}+\frac{2}{m-4}}{16}$$

$$\frac{\frac{1}{4}+\frac{2}{m-4}}{\frac{16}{1}}$$

Least common denominator of the three denominators is $4(m-4)$. Multiply all terms by $4(m-4)$.

$$\frac{\frac{1}{4}(4)(m-4) + \frac{2}{m-4}(4)(m-4)}{\frac{16}{1}(4)(m-4)}$$

$$\frac{m-4 + 2(4)}{16(4)(m-4)}$$

$$\frac{m-4+8}{64(m-4)}$$

Simplifying Rational Expressions Explanations

$$\frac{m+4}{64(m-4)}$$

$$\frac{m+4}{64m+256}$$

6. D

$$\frac{2}{\frac{1}{2} - \frac{x}{4}}$$

$$\frac{\frac{2}{1}}{\frac{1}{2} - \frac{x}{4}}$$

Least common denominator is 4. Multiply all terms by 4.

$$\frac{\frac{2}{1}(4)}{\frac{1}{2}(4) - \frac{x}{4}(4)}$$

$$\frac{\frac{2(4)}{1}}{\frac{1(4)}{2}^2 - \frac{x(4)}{4}}$$

$$\frac{8}{2-x}$$

7. D

$$\frac{\frac{x+4}{9} + \frac{x+4}{3}}{\frac{3x+12}{y}}$$

Least common denominator is $9y$. Multiply each term by $9y$.

$$\frac{\frac{x+4}{9}(9y) + \frac{x+4}{3}(9y)}{\frac{3x+12}{y}(9y)}$$

$$\frac{\frac{x+4}{9}(9y) + \frac{x+4}{3}(9y)^3}{\frac{3x+12}{y}(9y)}$$

$$\frac{(x+4)y + (x+4)(3y)}{(3x+12)9}$$

$$\frac{xy + 4y + 3xy + 12y}{9(3x+12)}$$

Simplifying Rational Expressions Explanations

$$\frac{4xy + 16y}{9(3x+12)}$$

Factor as much as possible, so we can reduce.

$$\frac{4y(x+4)}{9(3)(x+4)}$$

$$\frac{4y(x+4)}{27(x+4)}$$

$$\frac{4y}{27}$$

8. D

$$\frac{\frac{y+4}{x^2} + \frac{1}{y}}{\frac{y}{x}}$$

Least common denominator is x^2y. Multiply each term by x^2y.

$$\frac{\frac{y+4}{x^2}(x^2y) + \frac{1}{y}(x^2y)}{\frac{y}{x}(x^2y)}$$

$$\frac{(y+4)(y) + x^2}{y(xy)}$$

$$\frac{y^2 + 4y + x^2}{xy^2}$$

Simplifying Rational Expressions 2

1. A

Sum of $\frac{4}{3}$ and $\frac{n-4}{15n-15}$

$$\frac{4}{3} + \frac{n-4}{15n-15}$$

Factor the denominators.

$$\frac{4}{3} + \frac{n-4}{15(n-1)}$$

Least common denominator is $15(n-3)$.

$$\frac{4(5)(n-1)}{3(5)(n-1)} + \frac{n-4}{15(n-1)}$$

$$\frac{20(n-1)}{15(n-1)} + \frac{n-4}{15(n-1)}$$

$$\frac{20n - 20}{15(n-1)} + \frac{n-4}{15(n-1)}$$

Simplifying Rational Expressions Explanations

$$\frac{21n - 24}{15(n-1)}$$

Factor and reduce.

$$\frac{3(7n-8)}{15(n-1)}$$

$$\frac{\cancel{3}(7n-8)}{\cancel{15}(n-1)}$$

$$\frac{7n-8}{5(n-1)}$$

2. A

$$\frac{6a}{a-5} + \frac{2}{a+2}$$

Least common denominator is $(a-5)(a+2)$.

$$\frac{6a}{a-5} \cdot \frac{(a+2)}{(a+2)} + \frac{2}{a+2} \cdot \frac{(a-5)}{(a-5)}$$

$$\frac{6a(a+2)}{(a-5)(a+2)} + \frac{2(a-5)}{(a-5)(a+2)}$$

$$\frac{6a^2 + 12a}{(a-5)(a+2)} + \frac{2a-10}{(a-5)(a+2)}$$

$$\frac{6a^2 + 14a - 10}{(a-5)(a+2)}$$

3. D

Sum of $\frac{x+6}{x+4}$ and $\frac{2}{x+2}$

Least common denominator is $(x+4)(x+2)$.

$$\frac{x+6}{x+4} \cdot \frac{(x+2)}{(x+2)} + \frac{2}{x+2} \cdot \frac{(x+4)}{(x+4)}$$

$$\frac{x^2 + 2x + 6x + 12}{(x+4)(x+2)} + \frac{2x+8}{(x+4)(x+2)}$$

$$\frac{x^2 + 10x + 20}{(x+4)(x+2)}$$

4. D

$$\frac{4}{x+6} + \frac{6}{x+3}$$

Least common denominator is $(x+6)(x+3)$.

$$\frac{4}{x+6} \cdot \frac{(x+3)}{(x+3)} - \frac{6}{x+3} \cdot \frac{(x+6)}{(x+6)}$$

$$\frac{4x+12}{(x+6)(x+3)} - \frac{6x+36}{(x+6)(x+3)}$$

Simplifying Rational Expressions Explanations

$$\frac{4x+12-6x-36}{(x+6)(x+3)}$$

$$\frac{-2x-24}{(x+6)(x+3)}$$

$$\frac{\frac{9(48)}{1}}{\frac{1(48)}{3}16+\frac{x(48)}{16}^3}$$

$$\frac{432}{16+3x}$$

6. B

$$\frac{\frac{5}{2}}{\frac{4}{x}-\frac{1}{5}}$$

Least common denominator is $10x$. Multiply each term by $10x$.

5. B

$$\frac{9}{\frac{1}{3}+\frac{x}{16}}$$

$$\frac{\frac{9}{1}}{\frac{1}{3}+\frac{x}{16}}$$

Least common denominator is 48. Multiply each term by 48.

$$\frac{\frac{9(48)}{1}}{\frac{1(48)}{3}+\frac{x(48)}{16}}$$

$$\frac{\frac{5}{2}(10x)}{\frac{4}{x}(10x)-\frac{1}{5}(10x)}$$

$$\frac{\frac{5}{2}(10x)^5}{\frac{4}{x}(10x)-\frac{1}{5}(10x)^2}$$

Simplifying Rational Expressions Explanations

$$\frac{25x}{40-2x}$$

7. A

$$\frac{\frac{y}{5x}}{\frac{y}{x}-\frac{5}{y}}$$

Least common denominator is $5xy$. Multiply each term by $5xy$.

$$\frac{\frac{y}{5x}(5xy)}{\frac{y}{x}(5xy)-\frac{5}{y}(5xy)}$$

$$\frac{\frac{y\cancel{(5xy)}}{\cancel{5x}}}{\frac{y\cancel{(5xy)}}{\cancel{x}}-\frac{5\cancel{(5xy)}}{\cancel{y}}}$$

$$\frac{y^2}{5y^2-25x}$$

8. B

$$\frac{x-3}{\frac{25}{x-3}+\frac{y+3}{x-3}}$$

$$\frac{\frac{x-3}{1}}{\frac{25}{x-3}+\frac{y+3}{x-3}}$$

Least common denominator is $x-3$. Multiply each term by $x-3$.

$$\frac{\frac{x-3}{1}(x-3)}{\frac{25}{x-3}(x-3)+\frac{y+3}{x-3}(x-3)}$$

$$\frac{\frac{x-3}{1}(x-3)}{\frac{25\cancel{(x-3)}}{\cancel{x-3}}+\frac{y+3\cancel{(x-3)}}{\cancel{x-3}}}$$

$$\frac{x^2-6x+9}{25+y+3}$$

$$\frac{x^2-6x+9}{y+28}$$

Equating Coefficients: Practice 1

1. $(3x^2 - 4x - 2) - (2x^2 - 7x - 9)$

If the expression above is rewritten in the form $ax^2 + bx + c$, where a, b and c are constants, what is the value of b?

2. $(4{,}659 + 150x^2) + (30x^2 - 210)$

If the expression above is rewritten in the form $ax^2 + b$, where a and b are constants, what is the value of b?

3. $(10x + 12)(5x + 4)$

If the expression above is rewritten in the form $ax^2 + bx + c$, where a, b and c are constants, what is the value of b?

4. $(5x^2 - 6x - 9) - 3(6x^2 + 5x + 11)$

If the expression above is rewritten in the form $ax^2 + bx + c$, where a, b and c are constants, what is the value of $b - c$?

5. $(1{,}953 + 295x^2) - 15(5x^2 - 12)$

If the expression above is rewritten in the form $ax^2 + b$, where a and b are constants, what is the value of $b - a$?

Equating Coefficients: Practice 1

6. $3(15x + 10)(-6x + 2)$

If the expression above is rewritten in the form $ax^2 + bx + c$, where a, b and c are constants, what is the value of $c - b$?

7. $2(-4x^3 - 3x - 14) - (-9 + 3x + 8x^3)$

If the expression above is rewritten in the form $ax^3 + bx + c$, where a, b and c are constants, what is the value of $a - c$?

8. $(-140 + 27x^2) - 12(4x^2 + 9)$

If the expression above is rewritten in the form $ax^2 + b$, where a and b are constants, what is the value of $a - b$?

9. $(4x^2 - 4)(13x^2 - 8)$

If the expression above is rewritten in the form $ax^4 + bx^2 + c$, where a, b and c are constants, what is the value of $a + c$?

10. $(-12x^2 + 8x + 4) - (13x^2 + 2x - 14)$

If the expression above is rewritten in the form $ax^2 + bx + c$, where a, b and c are constants, what is the value of b?

Equating Coefficients: Practice 2

1. $(-6x^2 - 2x + 4) - (12x^2 - 9x + 3)$

If the expression above is rewritten in the form $ax^2 + bx + c$, where a, b and c are constants, what is the value of b?

2. $(-101 + 60x^2) - (-70x^2 - 120)$

If the expression above is rewritten in the form $ax^2 + b$, where a and b are constants, what is the
value of b?

3. $(13x + 7)(6x + 12)$

If the expression above is rewritten in the form $ax^2 + bx + c$, where a, b and c are constants, what is the value of b?

4. $(6x^2 - 12x - 2) - 5(-3x^2 - 8x + 3)$

If the expression above is rewritten in the form $ax^2 + bx + c$, where a, b and c are constants, what is the value of $b + c$?

5. $(-486 + 100x^2) - 25(5x^2 - 2)$

If the expression above is rewritten in the form $ax^2 + b$, where a and b are constants, what is the
value of $a - b$?

Equating Coefficients: Practice 2

6. $4(13x + 6)(8x - 9)$

If the expression above is rewritten in the form $ax^2 + bx + c$, where a, b and c are constants, what is the value of $a + b$?

7. $5(-11x^3 + 14x + 10) + (-2 + 9x - 7x^3)$

If the expression above is rewritten in the form $ax^3 + bx + c$, where a, b and c are constants, what is the value of $a + b$?

8. $(807 + 22x^2) - 14(-2x^2 - 6)$

If the expression above is rewritten in the form $ax^2 + b$, where a and b are constants, what is the
value of $b + a$?

9. $(-9x^2 + 9)(3x^2 - 10)$

If the expression above is rewritten in the form $ax^4 + bx^2 + c$, where a, b and c are constants, what is the value of $b + c$?

10. $(13x^2 + 3x + 9) - (10x^2 + 11x - 10)$

If the expression above is rewritten in the form $ax^2 + bx + c$, where a, b and c are constants, what is the value of $a + b + c$?

Equating Coefficients 1

1. 3

$(3x^2-4x-2)-(2x^2-7x-9) = ax^2+bx+c$
$3x^2-4x-2-2x^2+7x+9 = ax^2+bx+c$
$x^2+3x+7 = ax^2+bx+c$

2. 4449

$(4659+150x^2)+(30x^2-210) = ax^2+b$
$180x^2+4449 = ax^2+b$

3. 100

$(10x+12)(5x+4) = ax^2+bx+c$
$50x^2+40x+60x+48 = ax^2+bx+c$
$50x^2+100x+48 = ax^2+bx+c$

4. 21

$(5x^2-6x-9)-3(6x^2+5x+11) = ax^2+bx+c$
$5x^2-6x-9-18x^2-15x-33 = ax^2+bx+c$
$-13x^2-21x-42 = ax^2+bx+c$

$b-c$
$(-21)-(-42) = 21$

Equating Coefficients Explanations

5. 1913

$(1953+295x^2)-15(5x^2-12) = ax^2+b$
$220x^2+2133 = ax^2+b$

$b-a = 2133-220 = 1913$

6. 150

$3(15x+10)(-6x+2) = ax^2+bx+c$
$(45x+30)(-6x+2) = ax^2+bx+c$
$-270x^2+90x-180x+60 = ax^2+bx+c$
$-270x^2-90x+60 = ax^2+bx+c$

$c-b$
$60--90 = 150$

7. 3

$2(-4x^3-3x-14)-(-9+3x+8x^3)$
$-8x^3-6x-28+9-3x-8x^3$
$-16x^3-9x-19 = ax^3+bx+c$

$a-c$
$-16--19 = 3$

8. 227

$(-140+27x^2)-12(4x^2+9)$
$-140+27x^2-48x^2-108$

Equating Coefficients Explanations

$-21x^2 - 248 = ax^2 + b$

$a - b$
$-21 - ^-248 = 227$

9. 84

$(4x^2-4)(13x^2-8) = ax^4 + bx^2 + c$

$52x^4 - 32x^2 - 52x^2 + 32 = ax^4 + bx^2 + c$

$52x^4 - 84x^2 + 32 = ax^4 + bx^2 + c$

$a + c$
$52 + 32 = 84$

10. 6

$(-12x^2 + 8x + 4) - (13x^2 + 2x - 14)$
$-12x^2 + 8x + 4 - 13x^2 - 2x + 14$
$-25x^2 + 6x + 28 = ax^2 + bx + c$

Equating Coefficients 2

1. 7

$(-6x^2 - 2x + 4) - (12x^2 - 9x + 3)$
$-6x^2 - 2x + 4 - 12x^2 + 9x - 3$
$-21x^2 + 7x + 1 = ax^2 + bx + c$

2. 19

$(-101 + 60x^2) - (-70x^2 - 120)$
$-101 + 60x^2 + 70x^2 + 120$
$130x^2 + 19 = ax^2 + b$

3. 198

$(13x + 7)(6x + 12) = ax^2 + bx + c$
$78x^2 + 156x + 42x + 84$
$78x^2 + 198x + 84 = ax^2 + bx + c$

4. 11

$(6x^2 - 12x - 2) - 5(-3x^2 - 8x + 3)$
$6x^2 - 12x - 2 + 15x^2 + 40x - 15$
$21x^2 + 28x - 17 = ax^2 + bx + c$

$b + c$
$28 + ^-17 = 11$

5. 411

$(-486 + 100x^2) - 25(5x^2 - 2) = ax^2 + b$
$-486 + 100x^2 - 125x^2 + 50 = ax^2 + b$
$-25x^2 - 436 = ax^2 + b$

$a - b$
$-25 - ^-436 = 411$

6. 140

$4(13x + 6)(8x - 9)$
$(52x + 24)(8x - 9)$
$416x^2 - 468x + 192x - 216$

Equating Coefficients Explanations

$$416x^2 - 276x - 216 = ax^2 + bx + c$$

$a + b$
$416 + {}^-276 = 140$

7. 17
$$5(-11x^3 + 14x + 10) + (-2 + 9x - 7x^3)$$
$$-55x^3 + 70x + 50 - 2 + 9x - 7x^3$$
$$-62x^3 + 79x + 48 = ax^2 + bx + c$$

$a + b = -62 + 79 = 17$

8. 941
$$(807 + 22x^2) - 14(-2x^2 - 6)$$
$$807 + 22x^2 + 28x^2 + 84$$
$$50x^2 + 891 = ax^2 + b$$

$b + a$
$891 + 50 = 941$

9. 27
$$(-9x^2 + 9)(3x^2 - 10) = ax^4 + bx^2 + c$$
$$-27x^4 + 90x^2 + 27x^2 - 90$$
$$-27x^4 + 117x^2 - 90 = ax^4 + bx^2 + c$$

$b + c$
$117 + {}^-90 = 27$

10. 14
$$(13x^2 + 3x + 9) - (10x^2 + 11x - 10)$$
$$13x^2 + 3x + 9 - 10x^2 - 11x + 10$$
$$3x^2 - 8x + 19 = ax^2 + bx + c$$

$a + b + c$
$3 + {}^-8 + 19 = 14$

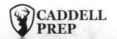

Dividing Polynomials: Practice 1

1. For a polynomial $f(x)$, the value of $f(-2)$ is -1. Which of the following must be true about $f(x)$?
   - A) $x + 1$ is not a factor of $f(x)$
   - B) $x - 1$ is not a factor of $f(x)$
   - C) $x + 2$ is not a factor of $f(x)$
   - D) $x - 2$ is not a factor of $f(x)$

2. The equation $\frac{6x^2+10x-28}{ax+6} = 3x - 4 - \frac{4}{ax+6}$ is true for all values of $x \neq -\frac{6}{a}$, where a is a constant. What is the value of a?
   - A) 6
   - B) 4
   - C) 3
   - D) 2

3. Which of the following is equivalent to $\frac{27x^3+9x^2-3x+20}{3x-2}$?
   - A) $9x^2 + 9x + 5 + \frac{30}{3x-2}$
   - B) $9x^2 + 9x + 5$
   - C) $9x^2 + 9x + \frac{30}{3x-2}$
   - D) $9x^2 + 9x + \frac{35}{3x-2}$

4. If $2x^2 - 11x + 29$ is divided by $2x + 3$, what is the value of the remainder?
   - A) 45
   - B) 50
   - C) 21
   - D) 29

5. The function f is defined by a polynomial. Some values of x and $f(x)$ are shown in the table below. Which of the following must be factor of $f(x)$?

x	$f(x)$
0	-8
2	0
6	16
8	24

   - A) $x - 2$
   - B) x
   - C) $x + 6$
   - D) $x - 8$

Dividing Polynomials: Practice 1

6. Which of the following is equivalent to $\frac{x^2+8x+15}{x^2+3x-10}$?

   A) $\frac{x+3}{x+5}$

   B) $\frac{x+3}{x-2}$

   C) $\frac{x+5}{x+3}$

   D) $\frac{x-5}{x+3}$

7. Which of the following is equivalent to $\frac{x^2+x-12}{x^2+5x+4}$?

   A) $\frac{x-6}{x+3}$

   B) $\frac{x-3}{x+1}$

   C) $\frac{x+3}{x-4}$

   D) $\frac{x-3}{x+4}$

Dividing Polynomials: Practice 2

1. For a polynomial $f(x)$, the value of $f(-5)$ is 0. Which of the following must be true about $f(x)$?
   A) $x + 3$ is a factor of $f(x)$
   B) $x + 3$ is not a factor of $f(x)$
   C) $x + 5$ is a factor of $f(x)$
   D) $x + 5$ is not a factor of $f(x)$

2. The equation $\dfrac{8x^2-12x-48}{ax-6} = 4x + 6 - \dfrac{12}{ax-6}$ is true for all values of $x \neq \dfrac{6}{a}$, where a is a constant. What is the value of a?
   A) 5
   B) 4
   C) 3
   D) 2

3. Which of the following is equivalent to $\dfrac{36x^3+18x^2-4x+20}{2x-3}$?
   A) $18x^2 + 36x + 52 + \dfrac{176}{2x-3}$
   B) $18x^2 + 36x + 52$
   C) $18x^2 + 36x + \dfrac{176}{3x-2}$
   D) $18x^2 + 36x + 52 - \dfrac{136}{2x-3}$

4. If $4x^2 - 88x + 484$ is divided by $2x + 5$, what is the value of the remainder?
   A) -239
   B) 239
   C) -729
   D) 729

5. The function f is defined by a polynomial. Some values of x and $f(x)$ are shown in the table below. Which of the following must be factor of $f(x)$?

x	$f(x)$
-1	15
0	8
1	3
2	0

   A) $x - 8$
   B) $x + 8$
   C) $x - 2$
   D) $x + 2$

Dividing Polynomials: Practice 2

6. Which of the following is equivalent to $\frac{x^2-5x+4}{x^2-x-1}$?

   A) $\frac{x-1}{x+3}$

   B) $\frac{x+3}{x-2}$

   C) $\frac{x+5}{x+1}$

   D) $\frac{x-5}{x-3}$

7. Which of the following is equivalent to $\frac{x^2+8x+7}{x^2-4x-5}$?

   A) $\frac{x-7}{x+5}$

   B) $\frac{x+8}{x+1}$

   C) $\frac{x+7}{x+1}$

   D) $\frac{x+7}{x-5}$

Dividing Polynomials 1

1. D

If $f(a) = 0$, then $(x - a)$ is a factor.

If $f(a) = b$ and $b \neq 0$, then $(x - a)$ is not a factor and $f(x)$ divided by $(x - a)$ gives a remainder of b.

Since $f(-2) \neq 0$, then $(x + 2)$, is not a factor.

2. D

When dividing polynomials, it is important to look at the first terms.

$$\frac{6x^2 + 10x - 28}{ax + 6} = 3x - 4 - \frac{4}{ax + 6}$$

In this case $6x^2$ divided by ax gives us $3x$, so a must be 2.

3. A

$$\frac{27x^3 + 9x^2 - 3x + 20}{3x - 2}$$

Let's do long division

$$\begin{array}{r}
9x^2 + 9x + 5 \\
3x-2 \overline{) 27x^3 + 9x^2 - 3x + 20} \\
-(27x^3 - 18x^2) \downarrow \\
\overline{ 27x^2 - 3x} \\
-(27x^2 - 18x) \downarrow \\
\overline{ 15x + 20} \\
-(15x - 10) \\
\overline{ \text{remainder} \longrightarrow 30}
\end{array}$$

$$9x^2 + 9x + 5 + \frac{30}{3x-2}$$

Dividing Polynomials Explanations

4. B

Let's do long division

$$\begin{array}{r}
x - 7 \\
2x+3 \overline{) 2x^2 - 11x + 29} \\
-(2x^2 + 3x) \downarrow \\
\overline{ -14x + 29} \\
-(-14x - 21) \\
\overline{ \text{remainder} \longrightarrow 50}
\end{array}$$

5. A

We can find the factor of a polynomial by finding which x-value makes the function equal to 0.

Since the function is zero when $x = 2$, then the factor is $(x - 2)$.

6. B

$$\frac{x^2 + 8x + 15}{x^2 + 3x - 10}$$

Since the answer choices don't have remainders, we are given a clue that we should factor the expressions and reduce.

Numerator:

$x^2 + 8x + 15$ (Add, Multiply)

$(x+5)(x+3)$

Dividing Polynomials Explanations

Denominator:

$x^2 + 3x - 10$ (Add, Multiply)

$(x+5)(x-2)$

The expression becomes:

$$\frac{(x+5)(x+3)}{(x+5)(x-2)}$$

Reduce

$$\frac{\cancel{(x+5)}(x+3)}{\cancel{(x+5)}(x-2)}$$

$$\frac{x+3}{x-2}$$

7. B

$$\frac{x^2 + x - 12}{x^2 + 5x + 4}$$

Since the answer choices don't have remainders, we are given a clue that we should factor the expressions and reduce.

Numerator:

$x^2 + x - 12$ (add to 1, multiply)

$(x+4)(x-3)$

Denominator:

$x^2 + 5x + 4$ (add, multiply)

$(x+1)(x+4)$

The expression becomes:

$$\frac{(x+4)(x-3)}{(x+1)(x+4)}$$

Reduce

$$\frac{\cancel{(x+4)}(x-3)}{(x+1)\cancel{(x+4)}}$$

$$\frac{x-3}{x+1}$$

Dividing Polynomials 2

1. C

If $f(a) = 0$, then $(x - a)$ is a factor.

If $f(a) = b$ and $b \neq 0$, then $(x - a)$ is not a factor and $f(x)$ divided by $(x - a)$ gives a remainder of b.

Since $f(-5) = 0$, $(x + 5)$ is a factor.

Dividing Polynomials Explanations

2. D

When dividing polynomials, it is important to look at the first terms.

$$\frac{8x^2 - 12x - 48}{ax - 6} = 4x + 6 - \frac{12}{ax - 6}$$

In this case $8x^2$ divided by ax gives us $4x$, so a must be 2.

3. A

$$\frac{36x^3 + 18x^2 - 4x + 20}{2x - 3}$$

Let's do long division

$$\begin{array}{r}
18x^2 + 36x + 52 \\
2x-3 \overline{\smash{\big)}\, 36x^3 + 18x^2 - 4x + 20} \\
-(36x^3 - 54x^2) \\
\hline
72x^2 - 4x \\
-(72x^2 - 108x) \\
\hline
104x + 20 \\
-(104x - 156) \\
\hline
\text{remainder} \longrightarrow 176
\end{array}$$

$$18x^2 + 36x + 52 + \frac{176}{2x-3}$$

4. D

Let's do long division

$$\begin{array}{r}
2x - 49 \\
2x+5 \overline{\smash{\big)}\, 4x^2 - 88x + 484} \\
-(4x^2 + 10x) \\
\hline
-98x + 484 \\
-(-98x - 245) \\
\hline
\text{remainder} \longrightarrow 729
\end{array}$$

5. C

We can find the factor of a polynomial by finding which x-value makes the function equal to 0.

Since the function is zero when $x = 2$, then the factor is $(x - 2)$.

6. A

$$\frac{x^2 - 5x + 4}{x^2 - x - 12}$$

Since the answer choices don't have remainders, we are given a clue that we should factor the expressions and reduce.

Numerator:

$x^2 - 5x + 4$ (add, multiply)

$(x-4)(x-1)$

Dividing Polynomials Explanations

Denominator:

$x^2 - x - 12$ ← add to -1, multiply

$(x-4)(x+3)$

The expression becomes

$$\frac{(x-4)(x-1)}{(x-4)(x+3)}$$

Reduce

$$\frac{\cancel{(x-4)}(x-1)}{\cancel{(x-4)}(x+3)}$$

$$\frac{x-1}{x+3}$$

7. C

$$\frac{x^2 + 8x + 7}{x^2 - 4x - 5}$$

Since the answer choices don't have remainders, we are given a clue that we should factor the expressions and reduce.

Numerator:

$x^2 + 8x + 7$ ← add, multiply

$(x+7)(x+1)$

Denominator:

$x^2 - 4x - 5$ ← add, multiply

$(x-5)(x+1)$

The expression becomes

$$\frac{(x+7)(x+1)}{(x-5)(x+1)}$$

Reduce

$$\frac{(x+8)\cancel{(x+1)}}{(x-5)\cancel{(x+1)}}$$

$$\frac{x+8}{x-5}$$

Transforming Functions: Practice 1

1) The maximum value of $f(x)$ is 5. What is the maximum value of $f(x-3)$?
   A) 2
   B) 3
   C) 5
   D) 8

2) The maximum value of $f(x)$ is 13. What is the maximum value of $f(x) - 4$?
   A) -4
   B) 9
   C) 13
   D) 17

3)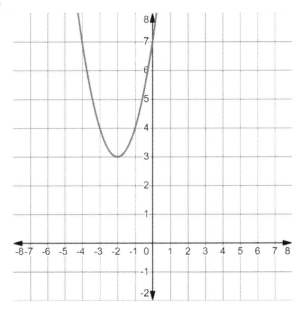

The graph of $f(x)$ is shown above. What will the minimum value of $f(x+2) - 4$ be?

   A) -4
   B) -1
   C) 3
   D) 7

Transforming Functions: Practice 1

4) The maximum value of $h(x)$ occurs when $x = 9$. What value of x will $g(x)$ be at a maximum if $g(x) = h(x - 3) + 1$?
   A) 6
   B) 8
   C) 9
   D) 12

5)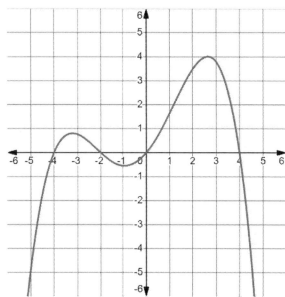

The graph of $f(x)$ is shown above. What will the maximum value of $f(x + 2) - 4$ be?

   A) 0
   B) 2
   C) 4.5
   D) 6

6) The minimum value of the function $f(x)$ is 5 and occurs when x is 3. The function $g(x)$ is $f(x - 2) + 3$. What are the coordinates of the minimum of $g(x)$?
   A) (1, 8)
   B) (4, 3)
   C) (1, 2)
   D) (5, 8)

Transforming Functions: Practice 2

1) The maximum value of $f(x)$ is 7. What is the maximum value of $f(x+2)$?
   A) 5
   B) 7
   C) 9
   D) 14

2) The minimum value of $f(x)$ is 3. What is the maximum value of $f(x)+2$?
   A) 2
   B) 3
   C) 5
   D) Unable to determine

3)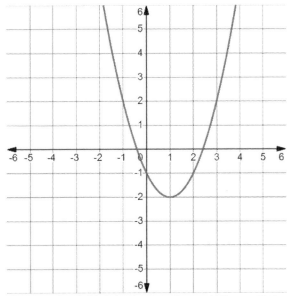

The graph of $f(x)$ is shown above. What will the minimum value of $f(x+3)+2$ be?
   A) -2
   B) 0
   C) 2
   D) 4

Transforming Functions: Practice 2

4) The maximum value of $f(x)$ occurs when $x = 2$. What value of x will $g(x)$ be at a maximum if $g(x) = f(x + 1) - 6$?
   A) -4
   B) 1
   C) 3
   D) 8

5)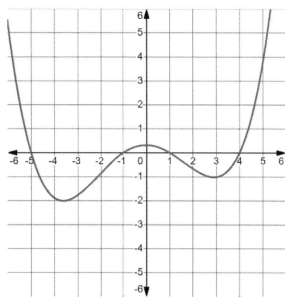

The graph of $h(x)$ is shown above. What will the minimum value of $h(x - 3) - 1$ be?

   A) -1
   B) -3
   C) -5
   D) -6

6) The maximum value of the function occurs at the coordinates (-3, 7). The function $g(x)$ is a transformation of $f(x)$. If $g(x) = f(x - 5) - 3$, what are the coordinates of the maximum value of $g(x)$?
   A) (2, 4)
   B) (-8, 10)
   C) (2, 10)
   D) (-8, 4)

Transforming Functions Explanations

Transforming Functions 1

1. C

The maximum value of $f(x)$ is 5.

$f(x-3)$ is a transformation of the function 3 units to the right.

The value of a function refers to the y-value.

Since the function does not move up or down, the maximum value remains 5.

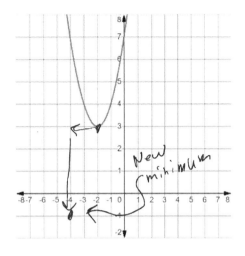

2. B

The maximum value of $f(x)$ is 13.

$f(x) - 4$ is a transformation of the function down 4 units.

The value of a function refers to the y-value.

Since the function moves down 4 units, the maximum value also moves down 4 units (decreases by 4).

The maximum value of $f(x) - 4$ is 9.

3. B

$f(x+2) - 4$ is a transformation of the function $f(x)$ left 2 units and down 4 units.

The value of a function refers to the y-value.

4. D

The maximum value of $h(x)$ occurs when $x = 9$.

$g(x)$ is $h(x-3) + 1$, which means $g(x)$ is a transformation of $h(x)$.

$h(x-3) + 1$ is a transformation of the function $h(x)$ right 3 units and up 1 unit.

If the maximum value occurs when x is 9, then the maximum value of $g(x)$ occurs when x is 12 because the function moved 3 units to the right.

5. A

$f(x+2) - 4$ is a transformation of the function $f(x)$ left 2 units and down 4 units.

The value of a function refers to the y-value.

Transforming Functions Explanations

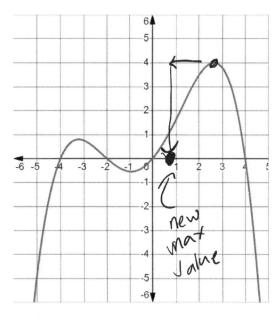

6. D

The minimum value of the function $f(x)$ is 5 and occurs when x is 3.

This means the coordinates of the minimum value are (3, 5).

$g(x)$ is $f(x-2)+3$, which means g(x) is a transformation of $f(x)$.

$f(x-2)+3$ is a transformation of the function $f(x)$ right 2 units and up 3 units.

Therefore, each x-value will increase by 2, and each y-value will increase by 3.

The coordinates of the minimum value are (5, 8).

Transforming Functions 2

1. B

The maximum value of $f(x)$ is 7.

$f(x+2)$ is a transformation of the function 2 units to the left.

The value of a function refers to the y-value.

Since the function does not move up or down, the maximum value remains 7.

2. G

The maximum value of $f(x)$ is 3.

$f(x)+2$ is a transformation of the function up 2 units.

The value of a function refers to the y-value.

Since the function moves up 2 units, the maximum value also moves down 2 units (increases by 2).

The maximum value of $f(x)+2$ is 5.

3. B

$f(x+3)+2$ is a transformation of the function $f(x)$ left 3 units and up 2 units.

The value of a function refers to the y-value.

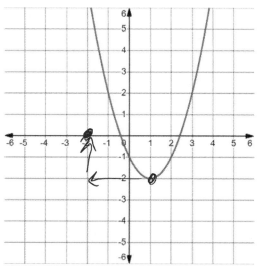

Transforming Functions Explanations

4. B

The maximum value of $h(x)$ occurs when $x = 9$.

$g(x)$ is $f(x + 1) - 6$, which means $g(x)$ is a transformation of $f(x)$.

$f(x + 1) - 6$ is a transformation of the function $f(x)$ left 1 unit and down 6 units.

If the maximum value occurs when x is 2, then the maximum value of $g(x)$ occurs when x is 1 because the function moved 1 unit to the left.

$g(x)$ is $f(x - 5) - 3$, which means g(x) is a transformation of $f(x)$.

$f(x - 5) - 3$ is a transformation of the function $f(x)$ right 5 units and down 3 units.

Therefore, each x-value will increase by 5, and each y-value will decrease by 3.

The coordinates of the minimum value are (2, 4).

5. B

$h(x - 3) - 1$ is a transformation of the function $h(x)$ right 3 units and down 1 unit.

The value of a function refers to the y-value.

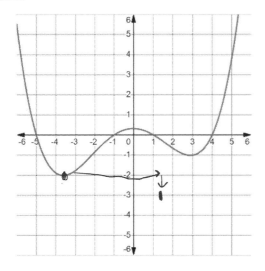

6. A

The minimum value of the function $f(x)$ occurs at the coordinates (-3, 7).

Solving for a Variable in Terms of Another: Practice 1

$$m = \frac{(\frac{r}{1500})(1+\frac{r}{1500})^N}{(1+\frac{r}{1500})^N - 1} P$$

1. The formula above gives the monthly payment m needed to pay off a loan of P dollars at r percent annual interest over N months. Which of the following gives P in terms of m, r, and N?

   A) $P = \frac{(\frac{r}{1500})(1+\frac{r}{1500})^N}{(1+\frac{r}{1500})^N - 1} m$

   B) $P = \frac{(1+\frac{r}{1500})^N - 1}{(\frac{r}{1500})(1+\frac{r}{1500})^N} m$

   C) $P = \left(\frac{r}{1500}\right) m$

   D) $P = \left(\frac{1500}{r}\right) m$

$$a = 2{,}352 + 1.15t$$

The speed of a sound wave in air depends on the air temperature. The formula above shows the relationship between a, the speed of a sound wave, in feet per second, and t, the air temperature, in degrees Fahrenheit (°F).

2. Which of the following expresses the air temperature in terms of the speed of a sound wave?

   A) $t = \frac{a - 2{,}352}{1.15}$

   B) $t = \frac{a + 2{,}352}{1.15}$

   C) $t = \frac{2{,}352 - a}{1.15}$

   D) $t = \frac{1.15}{a + 2{,}352}$

Solving for a Variable in Terms of Another: Practice 1

$$h = -20t^2 + vt + k$$

3. The equation above gives the height h, in feet, of a ball t seconds after it is thrown straight up with an initial speed of v feet per second from a height of k feet. Which of the following gives v in terms of h, t, and k?
   A) $v = h + k - 20t$
   B) $v = \dfrac{h-k+20}{t}$
   C) $v = \dfrac{h+k}{t} - 20t$
   D) $v = \dfrac{h-k}{t} + 20t$

4. The density d of an object is found by dividing the mass m of the object by its volume V. Which of the following gives the volume V in terms of d and m?
   A) $V = dm$
   B) $V = \dfrac{d}{m}$
   C) $V = \dfrac{m}{d}$
   D) $V = m + d$

5. A bricklayer uses the formula $n = 10lh$ to estimate the number of bricks, n, needed to build a wall that is l feet long and h feet high. Which of the following correctly expresses l in terms of n and h?
   A) $l = \dfrac{10}{nh}$
   B) $l = \dfrac{h}{10n}$
   C) $l = \dfrac{n}{10h}$
   D) $l = \dfrac{n}{10+h}$

6. When designing a stairway, an architect can use the riser-tread formula $24 \leq 2h + d \leq 25$, where h is the riser height, in inches, and d is the tread depth, in inches. For any given stairway, the riser heights are the same and the treat depths are the same for all steps in that stairway.

   Which of the following expresses the riser height in terms of the tread depth?
   A) $12 - d \leq h \leq 12.5 - d$
   B) $\dfrac{24-d}{2} \leq h \leq \dfrac{25-d}{2}$
   C) $24 - \dfrac{d}{2} \leq h \leq 25 - \dfrac{d}{2}$
   D) $48 - d \leq h \leq 50 - d$

Solving for a Variable in Terms of Another: Practice 1

Questions 7 & 8 reference the following information.

$$\text{Mosteller's formula: } A = \frac{\sqrt{hw}}{3600}$$

$$\text{Current's formula: } A = \frac{6+w}{1200}$$

The formulas above are used in medicine to estimate the body surface area A, in square meters, of infants and children whose weight w is measured in kilograms and whose height h is measured in centimeters.

7. Based on Current's formula, what is w in terms of A?
   A) $w = 1200A - 6$
   B) $w = 1200A + 6$
   C) $w = 1200(A - 6)$
   D) $w = 1200(A + 6)$

8. If Mosteller's and Current's formulas give the same estimate for A, which of the following expressions is equivalent to $\sqrt{hw}$?
   A) $\frac{3(6+w)}{\sqrt{w}}$
   B) $\frac{6+w}{4,320,000w}$
   C) $3(6+w)$
   D) $\frac{(6+w)^2}{9}$

9. The formula below is often used by project managers to compute E, the estimated time to complete a job, where O is the shortest completion time, P is the longest completion time, and M is the most likely completion time.

$$E = \frac{2O + 4M + 3P}{5}$$

Which of the following correctly gives P in terms of E, O, and M?
   A) $P = 5E - 2O - 4M$
   B) $P = -5E + 2O + 4M$
   C) $P = \frac{5E + 2O + 4M}{3}$
   D) $P = \frac{5E - 2O - 4M}{3}$

Solving for a Variable in Terms of Another: Practice 1

10. If $\frac{5a}{b} = \frac{1}{5}$, what is the value of $\frac{b}{a}$?
    A) $\frac{1}{25}$
    B) $\frac{1}{10}$
    C) 10
    D) 25

11. The volume of a cylinder is given by the formula $V = \pi r^2 h$, where r is the radius of the cylinder. Which of the following gives the radius of the cylinder in terms of the volume of the cylinder?
    A) $\sqrt{\frac{\pi h}{V}}$
    B) $\sqrt{\frac{V}{\pi h}}$
    C) $\frac{\pi h}{V}$
    D) $\frac{V}{\pi h}$

Solving for a Variable in Terms of Another: Practice 2

$$m = \frac{(\frac{r}{2000})(2+\frac{r}{2000})^N}{(2+\frac{r}{2000})^N - 2} P$$

1. The formula above gives the monthly payment m needed to pay off a loan of P dollars at r percent annual interest over N months. Which of the following gives P in terms of m, r, and N?

   A) $P = \frac{(\frac{r}{2000})(2+\frac{r}{2000})^N}{(2+\frac{r}{2000})^N - 2} m$

   B) $P = \frac{(2+\frac{r}{2000})^N - 2}{(\frac{r}{2000})(2+\frac{r}{2000})^N} m$

   C) $P = \left(\frac{r}{2000}\right) m$

   D) $P = \left(\frac{2000}{r}\right) m$

$$a = \sqrt{3500 + 12t}$$

2. The speed of a sound wave in air depends on the air temperature. The formula above shows the relationship between a, the speed of a sound wave, in feet per second, and t, the air temperature, in degrees Fahrenheit (°F).
   Which of the following expresses the air temperature in terms of the speed of a sound wave?

   A) $t = \frac{a - 3500}{12}$

   B) $t = \frac{a + 3500}{12}$

   C) $t = \frac{a^2 - 3500}{12}$

   D) $t = \frac{a^2 + 3500}{12}$

Solving for a Variable in Terms of Another: Practice 2

$$h = -30t^2 + vt + k$$

3. The equation above gives the height h, in feet, of a ball t seconds after it is thrown straight up with an initial speed of v feet per second from a height of k feet. Which of the following gives k in terms of h, t, and v?
   A) $k = h + 30t^2 - vt$
   B) $k = h + 30t^2 + vt$
   C) $k = \sqrt{h + 30t} - vt$
   D) $k = \dfrac{h-v}{t} + 30t$

4. The temperature of an object in Kelvin, K, is calculated by adding 273 to the temperature of the object in Celsius $°C$. Which of the following gives $°C$ in terms of K?
   A) $°C = 273K$
   B) $°C = \dfrac{K}{273}$
   C) $°C = K + 273$
   D) $°C = K - 273$

5. The formula to calculate gravitational force, F_g, is $F_g = \dfrac{Gm_1m_2}{r^2}$, where G is the gravitational constant, m_1 is mass of object one, m_2 is mass of object 2 and r is the distance from the center of m_1 to the center of m_2. Which of the following correctly expresses m_2 in terms of F_g, m_1, G, and r?
   A) $\dfrac{F_g G m_1}{r^2}$
   B) $\sqrt{\dfrac{F_g r}{m_1}}$
   C) $\dfrac{F_g r^2}{G m_1}$
   D) $F_g - \dfrac{G m_1}{r^2}$

Solving for a Variable in Terms of Another: Practice 2

6. A chef used the following formula to determine the number of eggs needed for her weekly order, $E = 6c + 3m + 4$, where E is the number of dozens of eggs, c is the number of cakes, and m is the number of dozens of muffins that will be baked that week. Which of the following expresses m in terms of E and c? Which of the following expresses the tread depth in terms of the riser heights?

   A) $\frac{E-6c}{3} - 4$
   B) $E - 2c - 4$
   C) $\frac{E-6c-4}{3}$
   D) $\frac{E}{3} - 6c - 4$

Questions 7 & 8 reference the following information.

$$\text{Gravitational force between two masses: } F_g = \frac{Gm_1m_2}{r^2}$$

$$\text{Gravitational force on Earth: } F_g = m_1 g$$

The formulas above are used in physics to calculate the gravitational force between two masses. The top formula is used to calculate the gravitational force between any two masses. The bottom formula is used to calculate the gravitational force between a mass and Earth.

7. Based on the formular for calculating the gravitational force between two masses, what is r^2 in terms of F_g, G, m_1 and m_2?

   A) $\frac{Gm_1m_2}{F_g}$
   B) $\sqrt{\frac{Gm_1m_2}{F_g}}$
   C) $F_g Gm_1m_2$
   D) $\frac{F_g}{Gm_1m_2}$

Solving for a Variable in Terms of Another: Practice 2

8. If the two formulas give the same estimate for F_g, which of the following expressions is equivalent to g?

   A) $Gm_1^2 m_2 r^2$
   B) $\dfrac{Gm_2}{r^2}$
   C) $\dfrac{Gm_2}{m_1 r^2}$
   D) $\dfrac{r^2}{Gm_1 m_2}$

9. The formula below is often used by project managers to compute E, the estimated time to complete a job, where O is the shortest completion time, P is the longest completion time, and M is the most likely completion time.

$$E = \frac{3O + 3M + 6P}{3}$$

   Which of the following correctly gives O in terms of E, P, and M?

   A) $O = E - M - 2P$
   B) $O = 3E - 3M - 6P$
   C) $O = \dfrac{E + M + 2P}{3}$
   D) $O = \dfrac{E - M - 2P}{3}$

10. If $\dfrac{4a}{b} = \dfrac{1}{9}$, what is the value of a?

    A) $\dfrac{36}{b}$
    B) $\dfrac{b}{36}$
    C) $\dfrac{1}{36}$
    D) 36

Solving for a Variable in Terms of Another: Practice 2

11. The volume of a cone is given by the formula $V = \frac{1}{3}\pi r^2 h$, where r is the radius of the cone. Which of the following gives the radius of the cone in terms of the volume of the cone?

A) $\sqrt{\dfrac{\pi h}{V}}$

B) $\sqrt{\dfrac{V}{\pi h}}$

C) $\sqrt{\dfrac{\pi h}{3V}}$

D) $\sqrt{\dfrac{3V}{\pi h}}$

Solving for a Variable in Terms of Another Explanations

Solving for a Variable in Terms of Another 1

1. B

$$m = \frac{\left(\frac{r}{1500}\right)\left(1+\frac{r}{1500}\right)}{\left(1+\frac{r}{1500}\right)^N - 1} P$$

multiply by reciprocal

$$\frac{\left(1+\frac{r}{1500}\right)^N - 1}{\left(\frac{r}{1500}\right)\left(1+\frac{r}{1500}\right)} m = P$$

2. A

$$a = 2352 + 1.15t$$
$$-2352 \quad -2352$$
$$a - 2352 = 1.15t$$

$$\frac{a-2352}{1.15} = \frac{1.15t}{1.15}$$

$$\frac{a-2352}{1.15} = t$$

3. D

$$h = -20t^2 + vt + k$$
$$+20t^2 \quad +20t^2$$

$$h + 20t^2 = vt + k$$
$$\quad -k \quad\quad -k$$

$$h + 20t^2 - k = vt$$

$$\frac{h + 20t^2 - k}{t} = \frac{vt}{t}$$

$$\frac{h}{t} + 20t - \frac{k}{t} = v$$

$$\frac{h-k}{t} + 20t = v$$

4. C

$$d = \frac{m}{v}$$

$$(v)d = \frac{m(v)}{v}$$

$$dv = m$$

$$\frac{dv}{d} = \frac{m}{d}$$

$$v = \frac{m}{d}$$

Solving for a Variable in Terms of Another Explanations

5. C

$$n = 10\ell h$$

$$\frac{n}{10h} = \frac{10\ell h}{10h}$$

$$\frac{n}{10h} = \ell$$

6. B

$$24 \leq 2h + d \leq 25$$
$$ -d -d -d$$

$$24 - d \leq 2h \leq 25 - d$$

$$\frac{24-d}{2} \leq \frac{2h}{2} \leq \frac{25-d}{2}$$

$$\frac{24-d}{2} \leq h \leq \frac{25-d}{2}$$

7. A

$$A = \frac{6+w}{1200}$$

$$(1200)A = \frac{6+w}{1200}(1200)$$

$$1200A = 6 + w$$
$$ -6 -6$$

$$1200A - 6 = w$$

8. C

$$\frac{\sqrt{hw}}{3600} = \frac{6+w}{1200}$$

$$(3600)\frac{\sqrt{hw}}{3600} = \frac{6+w}{1200}(3600)$$

$$\sqrt{hw} = (6+w)(3)$$

9. A

$$E = \frac{20 + 4M + 3P}{5}$$

$$(5)E = \frac{20 + 4M + 3P}{5}(5)$$

$$5E = 20 + 4M + 3P$$
$$-20 - 4M -20 - 4M$$

$$5E - 20 - 4M = 3P$$

$$\frac{5E - 20 - 4M}{3} = \frac{3P}{3}$$

$$\frac{5E - 20 - 4M}{3} = P$$

10. D

$$\frac{5a}{b} = \frac{1}{5}$$

Flip both sides

$$\frac{b}{5a} = \frac{5}{1}$$

Solving for a Variable in Terms of Another Explanations

(8) $\dfrac{b}{5a} = \dfrac{5(5)}{1}$

$\dfrac{b}{a} = 25$

11. D

$V = \pi r^2 h$

$\dfrac{V}{\pi h} = \dfrac{\pi r^2 h}{\pi h}$

$\dfrac{V}{\pi h} = r^2$

$\sqrt{\dfrac{V}{\pi h}} = \sqrt{r^2}$

$\sqrt{\dfrac{V}{\pi h}} = r$

Solving for a Variable in Terms of Another 2

1. B

$M = \dfrac{\left(\frac{r}{2000}\right)\left(2+\frac{r}{2000}\right)^N}{\left(2+\frac{r}{2000}\right)^N - 2} P$

multiply by reciprocal

$\dfrac{\left(2+\frac{r}{2000}\right)^N - 2}{\left(\frac{r}{2000}\right)\left(2+\frac{r}{2000}\right)^N} M = P$

2. C

$a = \sqrt{3500 + 12t}$

$a^2 = \sqrt{3500 + 12t}^2$

$a^2 = 3500 + 12t$

$-3500 \quad -3500$

$a^2 - 3500 = 12t$

$\dfrac{a^2 - 3500}{12} = \dfrac{12t}{12}$

$\dfrac{a^2 - 3500}{12} = t$

3. A

$h = -30t^2 + vt + k$

$+30t^2 - vt \quad +30t^2 - vt$

$h + 30t^2 - vt = k$

4. D

$K = C + 273$

$-273 \quad -273$

$K - 273 = C$

5. C

$F_g = \dfrac{G m_1 m_2}{r^2}$

Solving for a Variable in Terms of Another Explanations

$$(r^2)F_g = \frac{Gm_1m_2}{r^2}(r^2)$$

$$F_g r^2 = Gm_1m_2$$

$$\frac{F_g r^2}{Gm_1} = \frac{\cancel{G}\cancel{m_1}m_2}{\cancel{G}\cancel{m_1}}$$

$$\frac{F_g r^2}{Gm_1} = m_2$$

6. B

$$E = \cancel{6c} + 3m \cancel{+4}$$
$$-6c - 4 \quad -\cancel{6c} \quad -\cancel{4}$$

$$E - 6c - 4 = 3m$$

$$\frac{E - 6c - 4}{3} = \frac{\cancel{3}m}{\cancel{3}}$$

7. A

$$(r^2)F_g = \frac{Gm_1m_2}{r^2}(r^2)$$

$$F_g r^2 = Gm_1m_2$$

$$\frac{\cancel{F_g}r^2}{\cancel{F_g}} = \frac{Gm_1m_2}{F_g}$$

$$r^2 = \frac{Gm_1m_2}{F_g}$$

8. A

$$m_1 g = \frac{Gm_1m_2}{r^2}$$

$$\frac{\cancel{m_1} g}{\cancel{m_1}} = \frac{Gm_1m_2}{r^2} / m_1$$

$$g = \frac{G\cancel{m_1}m_2}{\cancel{m_1}r^2}$$

$$g = \frac{Gm_2}{r^2}$$

9. A

$$(3)E = \frac{30 + 3M + 6P}{3}(3)$$

$$3E = 30 + 3M + 6P$$
$$-3M - 6P \quad -3M - 6P$$

$$3E - 3M - 6P = 30$$

$$\frac{3E - 3M - 6P}{3} = \frac{30}{3}$$

$$E - M - 2P = 0$$

10. B

$$\frac{4a}{b} = \frac{1}{9}$$

$$(b)\frac{4a}{b} = \frac{1}{9}(b)$$

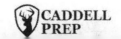

Solving for a Variable in Terms of Another Explanations

$$4a = \frac{b}{9}$$

$$\frac{4a}{4} = \frac{\frac{b}{9}}{4}$$

$$a = \frac{b}{36}$$

11. D

$$V = \tfrac{1}{3}\pi r^2 h$$

$$(3)V = \tfrac{1}{3}\pi r^2 h \,(3)$$

$$3V = \pi r^2 h$$

$$\frac{3V}{\pi h} = \frac{\pi r^2 h}{\pi h}$$

$$\frac{3V}{\pi h} = r^2$$

$$\sqrt{\frac{3V}{\pi h}} = r$$

Absolute Value: Practice 1

1) Which of the following expressions can be negative for some real value of x?
    A) $|2x - 3| + 1$
    B) $|3 - 4x| + 2$
    C) $|-2x + 3| + 1$
    D) $|2x + 20| - 2$

2) What is the value of $-2|x - 3| + 4$ if $x = -2$?
    A) -6
    B) -2
    C) 2
    D) 14

3) What is the value of $|-3x + 4| - 2$ if $x = 4$?
    A) 18
    B) 14
    C) 10
    D) 6

4) Which of the following is a possible solution to the equation below?
    $|3x - 5| = 7$
    A) $\frac{2}{3}$
    B) 2
    C) 4
    D) $\frac{35}{3}$

Absolute Value: Practice 1

5) Which of the following is a possible solution to the equation below?

$|-4x + 3| - 5 = -4$

A) -2
B) 1
C) 2
D) 6

6) Which of the following is the solution to the inequality below?
$|x - 3| \leq 4$
A) $-3 \leq x \leq 7$
B) $-3 \leq x \leq 1$
C) $-1 \leq x \leq 7$
D) $-1 \leq x \leq 8$

7) A research group estimates that there are 5,000 fish in a certain lake. The actual number of fish may be 500 more or less than the estimate. Which of the following expressions represents the possible number of fish, f, in the lake?
A) $|5,000 + 500| \leq f$
B) $|f + 500| \geq 5,000$
C) $|5,000 - f| \leq 500$
D) $500 \leq |f - 5,000|$

Absolute Value: Practice 2

1) Which of the following expressions can never be negative for any real value of x?
   A) $|3x + 4| - 1$
   B) $|-100x + 2| + 1$
   C) $|5x - 12| - 3$
   D) $|4x - 4| - 2$

2) What is the value of $|5 - x| + 7$ if $x = 3$?
   A) -1
   B) 7
   C) 9
   D) 19

3) What is the value of $3 - |4x + 2|$ if $x = -7$?
   A) -27
   B) -23
   C) 29
   D) 33

4) Which of the following is a possible solution to the equation below?

   $|-2x - 1| = 7$

   A) -5
   B) -2
   C) 3
   D) 4

Absolute Value: Practice 2

5) Which of the following is a possible solution to the equation below?

$|5x + 3| - 7 = 10$

A) -4
B) -3
C) 1
D) 12

6) Which of the following is the solution to the inequality below?
$|x - 5| \leq 3$
A) $-2 \leq x \leq 8$
B) $-8 \leq x \leq 2$
C) $-4 \leq x \leq 16$
D) $2 \leq x \leq 8$

7) A sports stadium is estimated to sell 30,000 hot dogs on a Saturday. The actual number of hot dogs sold may be 2,000 more or less than the estimate. Which of the following expressions represents the possible number of hot dogs sold, d, on a Saturday?
A) $|d + 2,000| \geq 30,000$
B) $2,000 \leq |d - 30,000|$
C) $|30,000 + 2,000| \leq d$
D) $|30,000 - d| \leq 2,000$

Absolute Value Explanations

Absolute Value 1

1. C

The absolute value of any real expression will be positive. In order to be negative, you must subtract from the positive number.

Choice D is the only choice that has subtraction at the end.

    A) $|2x - 3| + 1$ is a positive number +1
    B) $|3 - 4x| + 2$ is a positive number +2
    C) $|-2x + 3| + 1$ is a positive number +1
    D) $|2x + 20| - 2$ is a positive number -2, so this could be negative

2. A

Value of $-2|x - 3| + 4$ if $x = -2$

$$-2|(-2) - 3| + 4$$

Treat the absolute value bars like parenthesis and simply everything inside them before making is positive

$$-2|-5| + 4$$
$$-2(5) + 4$$
$$-10 + 4$$
$$-6$$

3. D

Value of $|-3x + 4| - 2$ if $x = 4$

$$|-3(4) + 4| - 2$$

Treat the absolute value bars like parenthesis and simply everything inside them before making is positive

$$|-12 + 4| - 2$$
$$|-8| - 2$$
$$8 - 2$$
$$6$$

4. C

You can substitute the answers in for x and see which one works, or you can solve.

$$|3x - 5| = 7$$

$$3x - 5 = 7 \qquad 3x - 5 = -7$$
$$+5 \quad +5 \qquad +5 \quad +5$$
$$3x = 12 \qquad 3x = -2$$
$$\frac{3x}{3} = \frac{12}{3} \qquad \frac{3x}{3} = \frac{-2}{3}$$
$$x = 4 \qquad x = -2/3$$

Absolute Value Explanations

5. B

You can substitute the answers in for x and see which one works, or you can solve.

$|-4x+3|-5=-4$
$+5 +5$

$|-4x+3| = 1$

$-4x+3 = 1 \qquad -4x+3 = -1$
$-3-3 \qquad -3-3$

$-4x = -2 \qquad -4x = -4$
$\dfrac{-4x}{-4} = \dfrac{-2}{-4} \qquad \dfrac{-4x}{-4} = \dfrac{-4}{-4}$

$x = \dfrac{1}{2} \qquad x = 1$

6. C

$|x-3| \le 4$

flip negate

$x - 3 \le 4 \qquad x - 3 \ge -4$
$+3 +3 \qquad +3 +3$
$x \le 7 \qquad\quad x \ge -1$

$-1 \le x \le 7$

7. C

The difference between the estimate (5,000) and the actual number, f, must be less than 500.

$|5,000 - d| \le 500$

difference

Absolute Value 2

1. B

The absolute value of any real expression will be positive. In order to be negative, you must subtract from the positive number.

Choice B is the only choice that has addition at the end, so it can never be negative

A) $|3x + 4| - 1$ is a positive number - 1
B) $|-100x + 2| + 1$ is a positive number +1
C) $|5x - 12| - 3$ is a positive number -3
D) $|4x - 4| - 2$ is a positive number - 2

Absolute Value Explanations

2. C

Value of $|5 - x| + 7$ if $x = 3$

$|5-3|+7$

Treat the absolute value bars like parenthesis and simply everything inside them before making is positive

$|5-3| + 7$
$|2| + 7$
$2 + 7$
9

3. B

Value of $3 - |4x + 2|$ if $x = -7$

$3-|4(-7)+2|$

Treat the absolute value bars like parenthesis and simply everything inside them before making is positive

$3-|-28+2|$
$3-|-26|$
$3-26$
-23

4. C

You can substitute the answers in for x and see which one works, or you can solve.

$|-2x-1| = 7$

$-2x-1=7 \qquad -2x-1=-7$
$\quad +1 +1 \qquad\qquad +1\ +1$
$-2x = 8 \qquad\quad -2x = -6$
$\dfrac{-2x}{-2} = \dfrac{8}{-2} \qquad \dfrac{-2x}{-2} = \dfrac{-6}{-2}$
$x = -4 \qquad\qquad x = 3$

5. A

You can substitute the answers in for x and see which one works, or you can solve.

$|5x+3|-7 = 10$
$\qquad\quad +7\ +7$
$|5x+3| = 17$

$5x+3=17 \qquad 5x+3=-17$

Absolute Value Explanations

$$5x+3=17 \qquad 5x+3=-17$$
$$\underline{-3 \ -3} \qquad \underline{-3 \quad -3}$$
$$5x=14 \qquad 5x=-20$$
$$\frac{5x}{5}=\frac{14}{5} \qquad \frac{5x}{5}=\frac{-20}{5}$$
$$x=\frac{14}{5} \qquad x=-4$$

7. D

The difference between the estimate (30,000) and the actual number, d, must be less than 500.

$$|30{,}000-d| \le 500$$

difference

6. D

$$|x-5| \le 3$$

flip   negate

$$x-5 \le 3 \qquad x-5 \ge -3$$
$$\underline{+5 \ +5} \qquad \underline{+5 \ +5}$$
$$x \le 8 \qquad x \ge 2$$

$$2 \le x \le 8$$

Free Goodwill

People who help others (with zero expectation) experience <u>higher levels of fulfillment, live longer, and make more money</u>.

I'd like to create the opportunity to deliver this value to you during your studying experience.

If you have found this book valuable so far, please take a brief moment right now to leave an honest review of the book and its contents. It will cost you $0, take less than 60 seconds, and earn you some free goodwill.

Your review will help other students reach their goals, just like this book is helping you reach yours.

To easily review this book, scan here:

Scan here & leave an honest review. Thanks! Glyn

Made in the USA
Middletown, DE
28 February 2023

25458919R00429